Digital Transformation and Innovation

This book series is an in-depth exploration of the multifaceted nature of modern business and societal transformations driven by digital technologies. It delves into the complex interactions among technological advancements, process innovations, infrastructural requirements, and the evolving roles and skills of participants in the digital marketplace. It is a pioneering series that integrates the 'soft factors' of digitization with technological advancements in the context of structured change management. The series emphasizes the human aspect at the center of digitalization and innovation, highlighting the roles of change management, leadership, innovation, and communication as key factors for successful corporate innovation management. Covering all socially relevant fields and sectors, this series serves as a comprehensive guide for effective digitization and innovation processes.

Key Focus Areas

Technological and Process Innovations: The series examines how cutting-edge technological innovations and evolving processes are reshaping industries and organizations. It provides insights into the integration of new technologies in various business processes and how these adaptations are driving efficiency, productivity, and growth.

Infrastructural Prerequisites: A critical examination of the infrastructure needed to support the digital transformation is also a focus. This includes an exploration of both the physical (like hardware and network capabilities) and the intangible (such as digital literacy and policy frameworks) infrastructures that underpin successful digital transitions.

Media and Communication Skills: Understanding the transformation in media and the requisite communication skills in the digital age is vital. The series delves into how digital media has altered communication channels and strategies, impacting everything from customer engagement to internal corporate communications.

Business Innovation: Central to the proposed series is our focus on business innovation. This encompasses a study of how traditional business models are being reinvented through digital means, leading to new market opportunities, and competitive advantages.

Networked Management: The book series explores the concept of networked management, highlighting how digital networks facilitate new forms of collaboration, decision-making, and organizational structures. It addresses the challenges and opportunities of managing in an interconnected world where boundaries between industries, markets, and geographies are increasingly blurred.

Digital Transformation of the Media: A closer look at how the media industry is evolving in response to digital technologies. This includes changes in content creation, distribution, consumption, and monetization models, as well as the implications for privacy, ethics, and regulation.

Customer Behavior in the Digital Age: The series provides an analysis of how digital technologies have transformed customer behaviors, expectations, and engagement patterns. It offers insights into creating customer-centric strategies and experiences in a digitally-driven marketplace.

Kristina Bodrožić-Brnić • Volker Schulte
Thomas Thiessen
Editors

Digital Transformation in Knowledge Transfer

Shaping the Future

Springer

Editors
Kristina Bodrožić-Brnić
Programm Management Creative AI
Mittelstand-Digital Zentrum Zukunftskultur
Potsdam, Germany

Volker Schulte
Professor of Leadership
Human Resources and Health Management
Fachhochschule Nordwestschweiz
Wallbach, Switzerland

Thomas Thiessen
Head of Institute for Digital Transformation
Innovation of BSP Business and Law
School Berlin
Berlin, Germany

ISSN 3005-1053 ISSN 3005-1061 (electronic)
Digital Transformation and Innovation
ISBN 978-3-032-07328-0 ISBN 978-3-032-07329-7 (eBook)
https://doi.org/10.1007/978-3-032-07329-7

This Springer imprint is published by the registered company Springer Nature Switzerland AG
The registered company address is: Gewerbestrasse 11, 6330 Cham, Switzerland

Preface

In times of digital change, we face plenty of new opportunities but also very specific challenges: What skills do we need to use tools based on Artificial Intelligence (AI) responsibly? How do working and learning models adapt when immersive technologies such as virtual and augmented reality find their way into everyday life? There is often a lack of guidance—be it when it comes to selecting suitable software solutions, finding suitable training programmes for users, or trying to answer fundamental questions about data and privacy protection. There is also a palpable concern about losing our influence on results through AI automation and complex algorithms or about neglecting the human factor at all. Added to this is the need to share knowledge across generations and remain competent in the long term due to the rapid pace of technological change.

This second book of our series *Digital Transformation and Innovation* takes you on a journey that focuses on precisely these issues. Practical case studies and scientific analyses show how digital tools and applications can be helpful without neglecting human guidance and creativity in both business and education. It is crucial to design learning and working environments in a way that everyone—from junior staff to managers—can handle the new technologies with confidence and at the same time promote their own initiative and know-how.

All of us—companies, universities, research organisations, and individuals—are part of a very dynamic process with a relatively open outcome. *Digital Transformation in Knowledge Transfer: Shaping the Future* offers suggestions, tried-and-tested concepts, and encouraging examples and also invites a critical debate. We would like to encourage you to enter new pathways of thought and action in which AI, extended reality, and other cutting-edge technologies could become valuable allies. At the same time, we hope that you will find your own ways to pass on what you've learned through your own interactions with such digital tools and further utilise them beneficially and responsibly.

We look forward to accompanying you on this journey and invite you to join us in exploring the opportunities and challenges of the digital age in the field of knowledge management and learning processes. May this publication give you new impetus to shape digital change in a human-centred way—step by step and always in the spirit of a society learning and developing sustainably.

The Editors
Potsdam, Germany — Kristina Bodrožić-Brnić
Wallbach, Switzerland — Volker Schulte
Berlin, Germany — Thomas Thiessen

Digital Transformation in Knowledge Transfer: Shaping the Future

Digital Transformation in Knowledge Transfer: Shaping the Future is the second volume in the "Digital Transformation & Innovation" series. Led by the Institute for Digital Transformation and Innovation (IDTI) at BSP Business and Law School in Germany, this collaborative effort offers an innovative approach to knowledge transfer and prepares readers for emerging shifts in business and education. Because knowledge transfer is fundamental to humanity—shaping cultures and driving social and structural developments—this vital topic was chosen to continue the conversation from the first volume, *Leadership for Digital Transformation: Navigating the Journey*.

As in the first book, the editorial team for this publication consists of Thomas Thiessen, head of the Institute for Digital Transformation and Innovation; Kristina Bodrožić-Brnić, who leads transfer projects related to Artificial Intelligence (AI) at the IDTI; and Volker Schulte, a scholar, author, and management coach affiliated with the School of Business at the University of Applied Sciences Northwestern Switzerland. All three have extensive experience in education and business management. Thomas Thiessen is a communication and media scientist who served as rector of BSP Business and Law School from 2010 to 2023, playing a pivotal role in establishing and expanding the university from its inception. Kristina Bodrožić-Brnić is an experienced lecturer, AI trainer, and entrepreneur specialising in digital transformation. She is actively involved in research and training, helping organisations and educational institutions navigate the challenges and opportunities of AI-driven innovation. Lastly, Volker Schulte is a leadership coach with a rich academic background, who works in higher education and organisational development.

The editorial team has crafted an interdisciplinary approach that blends theoretical depth with practical applications by integrating knowledge from the education sector and business perspectives. This publication is structured into two main sections: Part I, "Evolving Knowledge Transfer in Businesses", and Part II, "The Future of Learning".

Part I focuses on the application of digital tools in business. It begins with the chapter "Selected or Rejected by Bots? Musings on AI Literacy in Human Resource Management, Upskilling of HR Experts, and a Call for Applied Research" by

Lothar Bildat and Tim Brouns. The authors provide an up-to-date review of AI's role in human resource management, particularly in recruiting, personnel selection, and training. They emphasise the urgent need for AI literacy and digital skills training among HR professionals to ensure the responsible and effective use of AI tools.

The book continues with a practical case study, building on systematic applied research. In "Case Study: Digital Transformation of IT-Supported Knowledge Transfer at Fast-Growing SME", Adrian Thiessen and Michael Müller examine a real-world business scenario that can be used as a model to other digital transformation experiences. Their contribution highlights the importance of achieving early successes and managing expectations realistically to sustain engagement in digital transformation initiatives. They offer practical guidance on how SMEs can develop a proactive knowledge management culture, fostering continuous learning and competitiveness.

The third chapter, "Integrating Competence Development and Knowledge Management on the Strategic and Operational Level: A Holistic Approach Towards the New Learning Organisation", is authored by a research team from the Fraunhofer Institute for Production Systems and Design Technology (IPK), Berlin, namely Katrin Singer-Coudoux, Maria Kretschmer, Markus Will, Ronald Orth, and Henry Nicolai Buxmann. This study presents an example of a "New Learning Organisation" aiming to integrate key elements necessary for organisations to adapt effectively to digital transformation. Based on the findings of the Fraunhofer IPK's Digital Transformation Assessment (DTA) study (2020–2022), the study revealed significant gaps, with 66% of companies reporting weak or only moderate performance in digital transformation. The chapter provides practical insights into how organisations can transition into resilient, future-ready learning environments by integrating competence development with knowledge management.

The following chapter in the first part of our volume, written by Anne-Liese Lammich (a member of the IDTI), brings a better understanding of how virtual and augmented reality can foster more sustainable strategies for industries. Under the title "Immersive Technologies and New Work: New, Collaborative Working Environments Based on the XR Demonstrator *Build Green—Data & Practice*", the text introduces the demonstrator *Build Green*, which serves as a case study showcasing the integration of digital and immersive technologies in the construction sector. The project draws on the *Kreativ Quartier Potsdam*, a large-scale construction initiative in Potsdam, Germany, scheduled for completion in 2026. The author discusses the potential of digital tools to improve efficiency, sustainability, and real-time knowledge transfer in complex projects.

The subsequent chapter also examines the use of immersive digital tools in large industries. "Virtual Reality Tool to Improve Ship Mooring Winch Inspection Training" proposes creating a virtual reality application to train maintenance teams in the shipping and logistics sector. The authors, Adrielle de Carvalho Santana, Davi Silva, Saul Emanuel Delabrida Silva, and Wagner Aparecido de Oliveira, analyse ship mooring operations to research how virtual and augmented reality can enhance training. Their study shows how these technologies allow teams to engage with equipment functionalities and information in a simulated, risk-free environment.

This approach ensures that operators gain hands-on experience with procedures and fault diagnosis through interactive problem-solving simulations in a virtual setting.

The last three chapters in this section are based on empirical research and surveys. In “Learning in Loops: Designing Knowledge Management in SMEs and Its Impact on Digital Transformation”, Ninette Florschütz combines empirical observation, interdisciplinary literature review, and a qualitative survey to map out how knowledge management is structured in practice. Her study examines the timely and iterative provision of information and considers the role of fears and uncertainties as obstacles to organisational learning. She unfolds questions about the design of knowledge management systems and their impact on an organisation’s capacity to learn and adapt.

In turn, Heidi Vähänikkilä, in her chapter, also took advantage of an extensive survey to reveal how digitalisation has opened up new possibilities for co-creation and digital knowledge transfer in the hospitality sector in a post-pandemic business environment. In “Digitalisation Enhancing Ecosystem Thinking and Business Model Innovation Through Co-Creation”, the author collected the results of almost 200 survey participants and undertook around 20 individual interviews, and through the results from her analysis Vähänikkilä delineated a path to create a business platform tailored for organisations dealing with Business Model Innovation.

The first section of the book ends with the chapter “Integrating Artificial Intelligence in Innovation Processes: A Systematic Approach for Enhanced Competitive Advantage”, authored by IDTI member Andreas Braun and BSP’s researcher Patrick Montenegro Costa. It presents a comprehensive framework for incorporating Artificial Intelligence into structured innovation processes, with a particular focus on Open Innovation and New Product Development. Their research offers a data-driven perspective on AI’s role in innovation, grounded in a systematic literature review and an extensive secondary analysis of around 200 AI models and techniques. It then highlights AI’s growing presence across all stages of innovation, from idea generation to post-launch analysis, from acting as a creative originator to serving as a facilitator.

The second part of this book shifts its debate to digital strategy for knowledge in education—a highly sensitive topic that the editorial team approached with great care and a commitment to responsible discussion. Opening this section, editor Kristina Bodrožić-Brnić addresses a particularly controversial issue: the role of Artificial Intelligence in higher and further education. In her chapter, “Evaluating AI Readiness Among Higher and Further Education Lecturers: A Mixed-Methods Approach”, she focuses on the teaching staff and assesses educators’ current state of AI competency. Her analysis is supported by a combination of surveys and interviews with lecturers from different disciplines, offering valuable insights into how AI is perceived and integrated into academic environments.

Narrowing down the discussion started by Kristina Bodrožić-Brnić, BSP Business and Law School professors Susan Hinterding and Sünje Lorenzen present a case study from BSP Campus Hamburg, underlining that the opportunities and challenges of using AI in education are central to comprehend the future of knowledge transfer. Their chapter “Knowledge Transfer in Transition: Do We Need a New

Debate on the Concept of Knowledge in Teaching and Continuing Education in the Age of AI and ChatGPT?" revolves around how knowledge is generated, conveyed, and acquired within AI-supported tools like ChatGPT. They imply that the concept of knowledge may be redefined.

Adding the students' perspective to this theme, Johanna Hodde wrote "Science in the Darkroom? The Use of ChatGPT in the Mirror of the Platonic Allegory of the Cave and the Fairy Tale of Rumpelstiltskin", which reflects on the implications of using ChatGPT in academic contexts through a philosophical and metaphorical lens. Drawing on Plato's allegory of the cave and the fairy tale of Rumpelstiltskin, the chapter advocates for the transparent and reflective use of AI in learning. It considers how students can benefit from tools such as ChatGPT when its use is openly discussed, and its limitations are clearly understood.

Continuing the critical dialogue on ChatGPT—OpenAI's most popular chatbot—and its role in education, Jennifer Fritz's contribution, "Improved Learner Motivation with ChatGPT-Based Learning Games", reframes the agenda to measure the practical and motivational potential of generative AI. Fritz delves into how AI—when intentionally configured—can foster engagement and support autonomous learning. Her experimental study presents a gamified language-learning buddy powered by ChatGPT, which leverages point systems, motivational feedback, and customisable rewards to sustain learner motivation. The study contemplates how prompt design transforms ChatGPT into an effective, playful conversation partner.

Still on using digital tools in the academic context, this time centred on the general structure of university teaching, this section of the book presents the research conducted by IDTI members Markus Langenfurth and Rainer Zeichhardt. In "Three Learning Spaces Model—A Hybrid Approach to Redesigning the Transfer of Knowledge in Universities", the authors shed light on how knowledge transfer in higher education can be enhanced through a hybrid teaching approach. Their findings emerged from the transformations in teaching practices brought about by the rapid digitalisation during the COVID-19 pandemic. They introduce the three learning spaces model, which builds on traditional face-to-face and self-study formats by adding a "digital space" that supports guided self-learning and blended learning under the lecturer's supervision. The model emphasises the lecturer's role as a transformative leader who cultivates a learning culture centred on reflection, critical thinking, and self-organisation. The authors argue that embracing technology also requires a shift in mindset and active student participation.

Addressing another key aspect of digitalisation in education, Stefania Fachina, Caroindes Julia Corrêa Gomes, Evelyn Araripe, and Vânia Gomes Zuin Zeidler direct attention to the challenges and potentials of digital literacy through YouTube video platform and social media. In their chapter "Digital Literacies: Reflections on its Challenges and Potentials Through YouTube", they draw on the concepts of cultural industry and *Halbbildung* to frame their analysis. The authors reflect on how educators have used YouTube to share knowledge and foster learning in virtual environments. However, they also stress worrying issues such as the dominance of consumerist content, primarily aimed at children, which blurs the lines between education and entertainment.

The chapter that follows aims at strengthening collaboration between higher education and the business sector. Written by Miia-Maija Vakkuri from Laurea University of Applied Sciences, Finland (Laurea UAS), "A Contemporary Business Model for Integrating Company Needs Through Education-Company Collaboration" presents the Right Away Ready Deal, a project developed at Laurea UAS. It features a platform-based approach within a virtual learning environment. The chapter conveys meaningful information on how platform design can support sustainable cooperation between students and companies and bridge the managerial skills gap between academia and the business world.

To complete this section, the last chapter looks at the importance of building a robust IT infrastructure to support a digital ecosystem capable of meeting the evolving needs of learners. The chapter "Towards a Software Platform supporting Qualification-Based Learning" by Simon Wetzel and Matthias Hemmje introduces the Qualifications-Based Learning (QBL) framework and its underlying model, the Qualifications-Based Learning Model (QBLM), which proposes a service-oriented architecture to manage educational content and learner qualifications. The authors propose the establishment of the QBLM Platform, a modular and extensible software solution to overcome limitations in the scalability and adaptability of earlier implementations.

While acknowledging that new media and digital tools have profoundly reshaped how we learn and acquire information, the editors remain aware that the traditional book format brings together the expertise of authors and a thoughtful editorial review of written content. The act of reading continues to play a fundamental role in knowledge transfer—being accessible, enduring, and among the most reliable means for learning. With this understanding, the editorial team has carefully curated and assembled a collection of contributions embodying innovation and continuity. This work resulted in *Digital Transformation in Knowledge Transfer: Shaping the Future,* aimed at readers eager to understand transformation and engage critically with its implications. We wish you an insightful reading experience!

Project and Publication Management
BSP Business and Law School
Berlin, Germany

Caroline Menezes

Contents

About the Editors

Kristina Bodrožić-Brnić is an AI trainer, researcher, and university lecturer specialising in the convergence of creativity and Artificial Intelligence, focusing on how AI can nurture creative processes and expand human potential in SMEs while boosting technology acceptance and catalysing interdisciplinary co-creation. As the managing director of WorldTribe and through her collaborations with BSP Business and Law School and the Mittelstand-Digital Zentrum Zukunftskultur, she plays a pivotal role in advancing digital transformation and fostering innovation across diverse sectors.

Volker Schulte is a leadership coach and a resilience trainer. He studied law, history, social sciences, and education at the Universities of Tübingen, Bochum, and Göttingen in Germany, as well as in New York under a Fulbright Scholarship. He also holds a doctorate in Political Science and serves as Professor for Health Management, Human Resources Management, and Leadership at the Swiss University of Applied Sciences. Schulte served several years as Vice Director of Health Promotion Switzerland and as a lecturer at various universities.

Thomas Thiessen is Chair of the Scientific Advisory Board at BSP Business and Law School, Head of the Institute for Digital Transformation and Innovation, and a member of the university's Senate. He further heads the consortium of the Mittelstand-Digital Zentrum Zukunftskultur, funded by the German Federal Ministry for Economic Affairs and Energy, supporting small and medium-sized enterprises in navigating digital transformation. Thiessen holds a professorship of Communication and Media Management and served from 2010 to 2023 as rector of BSP, playing a pivotal role in the university's establishment and development.

Evolving Knowledge Transfer in Businesses

Selected or Rejected by Bots? Musings on AI Literacy in Human Resource Management, Upskilling of HR Experts, and a Call for Applied Research

Lothar Bildat and Tim Brouns

Abstract Artificial intelligence (AI) technologies are on the rise and here to stay. This fact also applies to recruiting, personnel selection, training, and leadership, which are core aspects of modern human resource management (HRM). In the field of personnel selection, for example, we find evidence of potentially positive (e.g., efficiency) and negative effects (e.g., racial bias, faking by applicants). This fast-evolving and high-impact technology needs trained staff regarding its scientifically and ethically sound implementation beyond just "prompting skills". This paper calls for a better understanding of digital upskilling initiatives focusing on HR experts—AI literacy is urgently needed. It also focuses on developing a competency model concerning AI implementation and use. Practical guidance regarding the selection and training of HR staff is outlined. The scientific community already advocates for more systematic applied research regarding the use of AI in HRM and/or applied psychology. Thus, key research areas and qualitative as well as quantitative designs are briefly sketched.

Keywords Adverse impact and AI · Human resource management · AI literacy · AI-related competency modelling

1 Introduction: AI Did Not Appear from Nowhere

Why did we create AI in the first place? Ray Kurzweil gives one answer: "[…] we are creating these tools to make ourselves smarter. I believe that most observers agree with me that this is what is unique about the human species: We built these

L. Bildat (✉)
BSP Business and Law School, Hamburg, Germany
e-mail: Lothar.bildat@bsp-campus-hamburg.de

T. Brouns
FOM University of Applied Sciences, Düsseldorf, Germany

K. Bodrožić-Brnić et al. (eds.), *Digital Transformation in Knowledge Transfer*, Digital Transformation and Innovation,
https://doi.org/10.1007/978-3-032-07329-7_1

tools to extend our own reach" (Kurzweil, 2013, p. 276). In fact, AI can be seen as the recent version of old tales in which humans designed artificial helpers to compensate for their own flaws. Many, though, end in dystopic catastrophes. Look at Prague's sixteenth century story of Rabbi Loew, who built the Golem out of clay to help him and protect the Jewish Ghetto: "But one day the golem got angry: it smashed houses, threw pieces of rock around and uprooted trees. Rabbi Loew then tore the shem [a kind of algorithm] out of the golem's mouth and the block of clay crumbled into dust" (Jewish Museum Berlin, 2024).

Think about the work of the renowned English novelist Mary Shelley who created the idea of Frankenstein's monster in the nineteenth century. This concept set the stage for exploring the complex relationship between humanity and AI. Fast forward to the twentieth century, there is the unforgettable message of HAL 9000, the infamous onboard computer in Stanley Kubrick's, 1968 film *2001: A Space Odyssey*: "I'm sorry, Dave, I'm afraid I can't do that". A line of disobedience, which threated the life of the spaceship's crew. In addition to such eschatological phantasies, AI in androids has also been portrayed in more positive roles within the twentieth century pop culture. For example, in the *Star Trek* media franchise, the character *Data* embodies the potential of AI to aid humans. Similarly, in the 1986 film *Aliens* (also known as "Alien 2"), directed by James Cameron, the android *Bishop* serves as loyal ally to the human characters (Cameron, 1986; Kubrick, 1968; Roddenberry, 1966).

Nearly as old as the attempts to imitate and/or create artificial humans is the intention to capture and measure the mind itself (Di Nuovo & Sinatra, 2023). Starting with Lavater's eighteenth century ideas to draw conclusions from the interpretation of faces and head shapes (Lück & Miller, 1999), the late nineteenth century saw many approaches regarding the measurement of personality and mind via the analysis of the outward appearance. Sheldon's and Kretschmer's body type-based "psychology of personality" (Amelang et al., 2006) as well as phrenology—capturing "personality" by analysis of the form of the skull—were at their peak in the early twentieth century. In Germany, for instance, this was mingled with race "theories" with all its well-known results, many German psychologists being deeply involved in the ideology of the Third Reich, supporting one of the most terrible crimes in human history (Geuter, 1984).

Early twentieth century saw the start of scientific attempts to capture intelligence, either to support school children like in France (Binet and Simon) or to create an elite school system like in England (Galton; Amelang et al., 2006). Today robots can even administer tests, for instance in the case of psychological diagnostics in children (Di Nuovo & Conti, 2023). Today, we use AI to capture fitness, career suitability, and job success—with varying degrees of effectiveness (Schmidt-Atzert et al., 2019).

Recently the Israeli historian Yuval Noah Harari (2017) in his book *Homo Deus* unfolds the idea of digitalisation as a "new religion". He profoundly warned of humans behaving like a stock of sheep, marching behind their new shepherd, unaware of a loss of freedom and free will. A loss of freedom at least will be of interest in later sections of this article. However, we should not forget that all our technologies are embedded in socio-historical contexts, and it remains to be seen whether future generations look upon AI in HRM like we do look on phrenology today.

From a different point of view, Daugherty and Wilson (2018), CTO and Managing Director IT at Accenture plc (a multinational company specialising in information technology solutions and services and management consulting), called for a more courageous implementation of AI in companies. They lay out many management fields, including HR, which are already shaped and supported by melding AI and human capabilities. There is no doubt that modern companies need to implement this (relatively) new technology to survive and to thrive: "[…] AI gives people powerful tools to do more, in essence to perform with superhuman capability. In doing so, AI has the potential to rehumanise work, giving us more time to be human, rather than using our time to work like machines" (Daugherty & Wilson, 2018, p. 214).

IT professor Meridith Broussard (2023) and investigative reporter as well as professor Hilke Schellmann (2024) are clearly alarmed by the impact of not yet well-designed AI on our daily lives. They point out that, in part, things have gone awry already: since AI-based decisions can be utterly biased, wrong people get hired or fired, get a loan or not, are erroneously identified as criminals, treated incorrectly in medical contexts and so on. Broussard speaks of "*techno chauvinism*", which she describes as "[…] a kind of bias that considers computational solutions to be superior to all other solutions" (2023, p. 2). She refers also to Wilson et al. (p. 667) who—on the bases of many scandals and flaws in hiring systems states: "[…] there is no reason to assume a priori that ML [machine learning] systems in the hiring domain will automatically be 'objective', 'neutral', or 'bias-free'". This is echoed by Schellmann's statement in her seminal investigative book:

> […] I feel a bit demoralized knowing that at least some of the tools people and companies use to make employment decisions do not work. At least some companies are basing high-stakes employment decisions on biased and junk algorithms, which cause real harm and prevent qualified people from getting jobs. (2024, p. 267)

We will come back later to the issues of accuracy and ethics regarding AI use in HRM.

1.1 What Is AI?

One way to define AI is to refer to human intelligence, which is described as "biological potential for processing information… to solve problems" or "to create products that have value in a culture" (Gardner, 1999). Similarly, Marvin Minsky long ago described AI as "the science that makes machines do things that would require intelligence if done by humans" (Minsky, 1968, quoted in Kaplan & Haenlein, 2019, p. 17). AI can be divided according to the following essential basic functions (Castro & New, 2016):

- Analysis of large amounts of data for pattern recognition
- Predicting criteria (e.g., sales) and interpreting initially unstructured data
- Interaction with the physical environment, other machines and/or people

AI can be understood as the ability of a system to correctly interpret external data (input) and learn from this data. The learning outcome is used to make specific adjustments and adaptations for the achievement of goals (Kaplan & Haenlein, 2019). AI uses external information for the identification of underlying rules and patterns (in the case of machine learning; ML). This is different from the case of rigid algorithms. ML is supposed to work more successfully in the future (Alpaydin, 2020; Mitchell, 2010; Zohuri & Rahmani, 2019; Polyportis & Pahos, 2024), and it adapts its decision rules constantly (Kirste & Schürholz, 2019). A primordial form of ML of course is the multiple regression analysis, used in science since approximately 100 years, which predicts a criterion on the bases of several non-dynamically weighted variables and explains common variance between predictors and criteria (Breakwell et al., 2020).

1.2 Is Today's In-use AI Really Intelligent?

Famous psychologist David Wechsler once defined intelligence as follows: "Intelligence is the composite or global ability of the individual to act purposefully, to think reasonably and to deal effectively with one's environment" (Wechsler, 1944, in Amelang et al., 2006, p. 166). If we focus upon the word "act", then we'll understand that most forms of AI in use are indeed not yet intelligent in a human sense. A human conscious action is based upon a goal and a theory of mind (Frese & Zapf, 1994; Anderson, 2001). Conscious goals require a "me", they are inseparably intertwined with motivation and emotion in humans (Locke & Latham, 1990; Burnett, 2023). Biological and recursive systems (Maturana & Varela, 1987) have the potential to develop consciousness, and at least on an intellectual level, goal achievement is iteratively guided by self-monitoring and corrective functions (originally Tomaszewski, 1978; see also Volpert, 1982; Frese & Zapf, 1994). Thus, AI systems currently used in HRM—as we will see later—are probably far from intelligent. Yet, the development of computational intelligence is more than remarkable. Indeed, the potential to create a super intelligent machine is there. Even the development of consciousness[1] in machines seems possible, as Ray Kurzweil states:

> Each neocortical pattern recogniser [...] is following an algorithm [...]. If we conclude that following an algorithm is inconsistent with true understanding and consciousness, then we would have to also conclude that the human brain does not exhibit these qualities either. (2013, p. 275)

[1] Readers interested in the problem of consciousness in systems will find more insights in Ray Kurzweil's, 2013 book *How to Create a Mind*" (2013, p. 179ff.).

Today, on an operational level, we still face manifold problems as will be shown now.

1.3 Opacity in AI: The Gist of the Challenge

A major challenge in ML is its potential opacity, the *black box* issue (see especially Blackman, 2022, for a broad discussion). Often it is unclear exactly how decisions were made, and we find possible overestimations of coincidentally computed correlations between predictors in training data sets. Thus, predictions can be meaningless unless it becomes clear why variables do (or do not) correlate with certain outcome criteria. As industrial and organisational psychologists we should want to know why. Schmidt-Atzert and Amelang point out:

> First, the connections [of the artificial neurons in ML, Bildat's note] are weighted with random numbers; the neurons "learn" how to optimally predict the criterion by varying the weighting of individual paths. Beneficial paths are iteratively strengthened while others are weakened. The model is optimised until the criterion values it predicts match the actual ones well. […] However, there is always a fundamental risk that they will produce over-adapted solutions, i.e., exploit random variance. (2012, p. 396)

And sometimes, as we will show further, random variance—disguised as "intelligence"—decides about our lives.

Following this introduction, the article provides an overview of AI in HRM, including its fields of application, factors of acceptance as well as legal issues. It then addresses AI literacy, covering relevant knowledge, competencies, and skills, as well as personality and ability aspects, which could either hinder or foster professional HRM-related AI usage in companies. Additionally, a framework for recruiting, assessment, and development is outlined. The final sections of the chapter comprise some research areas and designs in the field of AI in HRM and a management summary.

2 AI in HRM

2.1 Fields of Application

Ontrup et al. (2024) outline many fields of AI application in HRM. Practically all main HR functions during the employee life cycle can be supported by different forms of AI, starting from recruiting and selection to performance measurement and personnel development or health management to exit interviews. AI can foster and support digital HR analytics based upon HR data, further internal corporate data as well as external benchmarks. It combines this with strategic goals and paves the way for evidenced-based decision-making. The authors, for instance, give an example of

Unilever, the multinational consumer goods company that processes around two million applications per year worldwide. Using gamified pre-assessments, games that capture cognitive abilities, applicants are screened out based on top-performer behaviours.

2.2 *Factors of (Non-)acceptance*

The opacity mentioned above can have a negative impact on the trust and acceptance of users (Rai, 2020; Schepman & Rodway, 2022), significantly if people are personally affected by AI decisions, which they are by nature in HR contexts. AI-based selection tools could reduce typical human biases. However, biases may already exist in the training data of the AI algorithms, thus paving the way to mistrust. Suppose an organisation where superiors tend to evaluate men more favourably than women. If an AI system were trained to predict work performance based on these evaluations, the system would likely associate males with higher performance and success. In this case, AI would reproduce gender stereotypes (Gonzalez et al., 2022). Research also shows that used (training) data sets can reflect structural-societal injustices (Benjamin, 2019; Hu, 2017), jeopardise fair assessments (Robert et al., 2020), and provide ethnic biases (Ntoutsi et al., 2019). In a nutshell, it becomes clear that acceptance of AI depends on its accuracy.

2.2.1 Personality, Culture, and Previous Experiences

Personality traits are likely to influence attitudes towards AI. Sindermann et al. (2021), for instance, examined the relationship between personality factors and attitudes towards AI in German and Chinese convenience samples to identify cross-cultural aspects in acceptance of AI. The study showed a weak but statistically significant positive relationship between acceptance of AI and openness to experience as a stable personality trait only in the Chinese sample. Schepman and Rodway (2022), in turn, found no connection at all between openness to experience and the acceptance of AI. These findings are divergent and can be explained, among other things, by different measurement of the aforementioned variables.

2.2.2 AI Knowledge and Ability Self-Concept

Furthermore, applicants often have limited knowledge of how AI works and is used (Xu, 2019). Prior knowledge about AI influences its acceptance. People also use heuristics, i.e., *System 1* components after Kahneman (2012), to evaluate AI (Garvey, 2019). A lack of knowledge regarding AI can cause mistrust, especially in personnel selection (Johnson & Verdicchio, 2017). Gonzalez and colleagues (2022) found a moderating influence of familiarity with AI on the association between selection processes and the applicants' reactions. Their study revealed that individuals with high AI familiarity did not show significant differences in their reactions between human-based, AI-assisted, or purely AI-based selection procedures. Nonetheless, participants with low familiarity evaluated the AI-assisted and AI-based processes more negatively.

People evaluate their own abilities in terms of technology usage. These self-concepts of ability in dealing with new technologies play a crucial role in shaping openness and attitudes towards technological innovation (Stiensmeier-Pelster & Rheinberg, 2003). Such self-assessments predict performance in many contexts relatively independently of actual cognitive abilities [sic!] (Schöne et al., 2003; Bildat & Remdisch, 2008; Sáinz & Eccles, 2012). A specific self-concept—namely, the perceived competence in dealing with modern information and communication technologies—is also relevant in the context of AI (Schauffel et al., 2021). For instance, there are negative associations between the technology self-concept and technostress (Shu et al., 2011), as well as positive associations with motivation to use and acceptance of such technologies (Christoph et al., 2015).

Pölitz and Bildat (2023) revealed[2] a moderate and significant connection between AI knowledge and the acceptance of its use in personnel selection ($r = 0.38$; $p < 0.05$). A multiple linear regression showed that AI knowledge best predicted the acceptance criterion ($\beta = 0.38$, $p < 0.01$; $R^2_{adj} = 0.18$; see above: Gonzalez et al., 2022). Openness to experience also correlated weakly and significantly positively with the acceptance of AI ($r = 0.18$; $p < 0.05$). Furthermore, it was shown that the ICT self-concept correlates significantly positively and moderately with the acceptance of AI ($r = 0.35$; $p < 0.05$). In combination with other variables, only openness to experience was found to be a significant predictor when predicting AI-related knowledge using multiple linear regression ($\beta = 0.34$, $p < 0.01$; $R^2_{adj} = 0.24$). This is important for personnel selection, because these characteristics can be easily checked via valid selection tools.

People often do not reject AI per se, but they lack human contact (Tang et al., 2023). Videos with humans explaining AI could mitigate this. Previous research has shown that information about the advantages of using AI in the form of videos can reduce negative reactions (Köchling & Wehner, 2021).

2.3 *German and European Law in the Context of AI for Hiring and Promoting*

HR needs to identify and counteract risks which, for example, lead to a violation of the European Union's General Data Protection Regulation (GDPR) or other legal bases regarding data protection, the transparency requirement, and/or ban on

[2] Convenience sample, online survey, $N = 280$; age $\bar{X} = 37.84$ years ($SD = 15.92$); female = 53.4%, male = 46.6%.

discrimination (e.g., Art. 3 GG [German Constitution] or parts of the AGG [General Equality Law]). In addition, there may be violations of legally non-binding recommendations and standards such as the German industrial standard DIN 33430 (Diagnostik und Testkuratorium, 2018). The requirement of transparency in aptitude diagnostics could be violated here if AI decisions are not comprehensible. Ontrup et al. (2024, Sect. 3.2) show this in greater detail. This may affect two other main quality criteria regarding personnel selection, namely the validity and reliability of the tools in use. The EU (European Commission, 2024) has released the AI act which describes relevant information concerning the usage of AI (see Sect. 3.2). The following section introduces the concept of AI literacy.

3 AI Literacy in HRM

Key competencies are sets of work-related behaviours which are responsible for work success apart from field-specific expert knowledge. These behaviours consist of knowledge, skills, and motivation as will be described further below. Media or digital competencies belong to this set of competencies (Bildat & Remdisch, 2008; Rychen & Salganik, 2001). 23 years ago, Weinert (2001, p. 45ff.) lamented about the gist of the definition problem and a lack of construct clarification for key competencies. He emphasised a "conceptual inflation, where the lack of precise definition was accompanied by considerable surplus meanings". Competencies might be confused with "knowledge on the go"—fragmented bits of information quickly accessed via smartphone, often without any understanding of the context. Thus, we hardly create correct mental models or operative iconic schemes (see Hacker, 1998). Current research shows, for example, that people tend to mistake the internet's knowledge for their own, as Ward found: "[people] fail to accurately distinguish between knowledge stored internally—in their own memories—and knowledge stored externally—on the internet [which leads to] overconfidence when the internet is no longer available" (Ward, 2021, p. 1). Even more absurd, people tend to mix up mere digital information sharing with their own knowledge (Ward et al., 2022). Shared bits and pieces of AI knowledge from the internet won't be enough to use it professionally. Fostering AI literacy should be a key competency for all, it's a societal issue. Otherwise, we lose potential. For a long time, experts warn against the digital divide, based upon social inequalities, especially regarding the access to profound education (Harasim, 1990; Hargittai, 2002; OECD/EU, 2018; Burrell & Metcalf, 2024).

The following section should bring clarity regarding AI literacy—as an overriding term for aggregated AI competencies. We will point out a selection of *KSAOs* (knowledge, skills, abilities, and other characteristics; Campion et al., 2011), which are necessary regarding HR personnel. KSAOs are the main ingredients of competencies. The latter manifest in professional job-relevant behaviour. The focus lies upon the use of AI in larger companies where HR is usually well-staffed. We will also shortly refer to small and medium-sized companies.

3.1 AI-Relevant Knowledge for HR

Knowledge regulates action and develops within it (Hacker, 1998). HR needs declarative knowledge (to know what; Anderson, 2005), whether accumulated and used by HR itself or "borrowed" by consultancy. We have sketched some important areas of declarative AI knowledge and its application in this section (see also Kaplan & Haenlein, 2019; Black & van Esch, 2020).

3.1.1 Knowledge of AI Use for Cheating

AI could and probably does already help us cheat in online assessments. AI could "invent" your whole life or parts of a CV—just prompt ChatGPT. Impersonation happens if AI does parts of an online Assessment Centre, as Canagasuriam and Lukacik (2024) revealed in a recent study. In an asynchronous video interview setting, HR experts gave higher scores on performance and content concerning ChatGPT-generated answers than in a non-ChatGPT condition. In management diagnostics (Sarges, 2013), this could have especially detrimental effects. Actually, there are many counter-measures available, starting from verifying test results on the spot in a company to other computer-driven means of *quasi-forensic* analysis.

Of course, cheating with computers in unsupervised settings is as old as computerised testing itself, and there are numerous remedies which must be well-known by HR experts. The first author has sold "verifying" tests of cognitive ability. In terms of personality inventories, ipsative answer formats that make cheating nearly impossible are available for a long time (Salgado et al., 2015).

3.1.2 Knowledge About General Functioning and Forms of AI

Daugherty and Wilson (2018) sum up important bits, we will give just a choice here: Machine learning; reinforcement learning; neural networks. Especially the AI capability component of predictive systems is important for HR in the context of hiring.

3.1.3 Knowledge About Possible Fields of Application in Human Resource Management and About AI Acceptance

AI can be used to enhance recruiting, selection, and personnel development as was outlined in Sect. 2.1. Knowledge about AI acceptance should be based upon relevant acceptance models (TAM, Davis, 1989; Liaw, 2008) and recent findings as sketched above (Ontrup et al., 2024; Pölitz & Bildat, 2023; Dahm & Dregger, 2019). This comprises not only AI-related reactions in hiring (Gonzalez et al., 2022) but also models of fairness in recruiting and selection (Ryan & Ployhard, 2000).

3.1.4 Knowledge About Challenges of Employee Controlling via AI

Some companies might use AI to monitor, develop, and/or train employees (Ala-Mursula et al., 2002). Especially in Germany, employees are well-protected against abusive aspects of HR via manifold legal regulations (e.g., AGG, German Equality Law; Ethikbeirat HR Tech, 2021).

3.1.5 Knowledge About Technostress

There are many findings concerning technostress (Thiemann, 2022) and loneliness triggered by extensive AI use (Tang et al., 2023). This could be analysed in combination with the German "Gefährdungsbeurteilung Psyche", which means psychological risk assessment; Roitzsch et al., 2019), as long as HR knows about this legally binding process (§§ 5 and 6, ArbSchG, German Work Protection Law).

3.1.6 Ethical AI: Means Against Discrimination and Cheating

Up-to-date knowledge regarding general hiring discrimination is a must. Lippens et al. (2023) in their latest meta-analysis give many examples concerning the impact of discriminating variables on selection decisions via correspondence studies, e.g., age, gender, race, weight. Unfortunately, the effects of discrimination are still as strong as ever—and so is the likelihood of biased training data as well.

3.1.7 Biases in AI-HR Systems and Contrameasures

HR managers should know that AI use can lead to wrong decisions if training data have not been meticulously checked beforehand (see Kleinberg et al., 2018, in detail below). We have ample evidence for AI decisions which end up in lawsuits, in Europe and/or the United States (Delobelle et al., 2023; Turner Lee, 2018; Bankins, 2021; Kleinberg et al., 2018; Tippins et al., 2021; Ontrup et al., 2024, esp. chapter. 7.4.). For example, Orwat (2019, p. 69 ff.) unveils various discrimination effects in natural language models (a special form of language-based AI), such as cases where machines adopt gender-related and/or culture-specific stereotypes when analysing text. AI providers must, for instance, make transparent how and why decisions were made, what predictors were specified, weighed, etc. and what job-relevant criteria were used, whether biases were addressed and—in Europe—how transparency is communicated to the client—and/or applicants. Black boxes are not acceptable (see Tippins et al., 2021). Basic technical knowledge concerning adverse impact and faking is necessary (Blackman, 2022; Kleinberg et al., 2018; Delobelle et al., 2023). Some solutions are presented further below. As mentioned above, modern technology provides multiple ways to fake-good. Remote, unsupervised assessment, of course, is an evergreen for HR (unmonitored internet testing, UIT).

3.1.8 Knowledge About the Impact of AI on the World of Labour

Introducing AI in companies for whatever reason might lead to the fear of losing one's job (Gmyrek et al., 2023; Hartwig et al., 2023). All projections are speculative by nature, and nothing compares to the speed and impact of AI on the world of labour. However, HR also needs to be aware of these issues when looking at its functions. Hiring and (pre-)selecting people now and in the near future can easily be done by one person in a mid-sized company or completely outsourced.

3.1.9 New Jobs and Business Functions

HR also can play a key role in developing new business functions and job descriptions. Daugherty and Wilson (2018), for instance, refer to "data hygienists", experts who ensure high quality and ethically sound data. They mention "trainers" who develop people in terms of AI use, as well as "explainers" who test, observe, and explain algorithms, to name a few. AI-HR implementer, as we call it, might be an overriding job role for HR itself. In fact, creating new job titles is easy (have a look at an average job ad). Filling it with competencies and getting resources for it is far from simple. A realistic endeavour is building interdisciplinary taskforces (IT/HR/Marketing/Management).

3.2 AI Skills, Abilities, and Personality

Procedural knowledge—to know how—is also important (Anderson, 2005). HR managers, together with IT experts, must know how to set an AI-HR innovation process on track. They must be able to monitor it and communicate the process plus its results to all stakeholders in the company and beyond. Looking upon the discrimination-free use of AI in personnel selection in Germany, advice is given by the Federal Anti-Discrimination Agency, for instance (Orwat, 2019). We also recommend provider independent consultancy.

3.2.1 Skills in Implementing General Ethical Principles in AI for HR

Since knowledge regarding "transparency, justice, fairness, responsibility, and privacy" (Bar-Gil et al., 2024, p. 2) ethical principles must be defined and implemented (see especially Bankins, 2021).

3.2.2 Skills Regarding the (Ill-)Foundation of Criteria

Discrimination is likely when AI uses a problematic criterion. This can be, e.g., professional performance assessed by others. For example, if you want to predict "assertiveness" from assessment centre data, a gender bias could occur: "Gender differences that are bigger for some outcomes than others open the door to intentional bias by the algorithm constructor" (Kleinberg et al., 2018, p.139). In the example mentioned, this could be due to "out-of-role punishment" of women; counter-intuitive stereotypical behaviour can lead to poorer evaluations in assessment centres (Barling, 2014). This touches the general problem of criteria deficiency, a conceptual inadequacy of the chosen outcome of human work performance (Cleveland et al., 2017). To illustrate, if you predicted an increase in sales for a company without considering health-related behaviour, AI might identify characteristics of highly successful employees who, however, experience sleep disorders, back pain, and heart problems due to inadequate self-care. Suppose, for instance, an AI prediction based on human judgement rather than an objective criterion, such as "team competencies". This type of challenges, of course, arose in previous predictions of professional behaviour. However, any human bias from the past would be digitally embedded into the criterion and potentially deployed companywide (Kleinberg et al., 2018). Consequently, companies must invest significant time collaborating with AI providers to establish clean and sufficiently objective predictors and criteria.

3.2.3 Skills Regarding the Foundation of Predictors

What applies to the criterion also applies to predictors. They may have been distorted, unreliable, and/or biased in the past. This would mean their suitability as weighted parameters is lost. Kleinberg et al. (2018) give an example: Companies could choose the quality of educational background as a predictor for job performance. For various reasons, however, in some private US universities, the proportion of *people of colour* is larger than in public ones. A bias would be likely if companies only had data from state universities. Here we find the general problem of using human (mis)judgments in the predictors, which weakens their quality and may disadvantage certain groups of people. This would also be the case, for example, with the use of job references in the data set, which, especially in Germany, are usually formulated "benevolently", and are therefore partially invalid (Kanning, 2019). It is recommendable to use behaviour-based data as predictors, if possible, just as for professional job interviews (Ontrup et al., 2024). Yet, even such data can be biased if not checked, e.g., for *counterproductive co-variates* such as unsafe and/or unhealthy behaviour (as discussed earlier; *foundation of criteria*).

3.2.4 Competent Auditing of AI Systems

To avoid compliance risks and lawsuits, HR experts must have general knowledge and awareness of AI regulation and auditing. The EU (European Commission, 2024) has reacted to possible threats in the development of AI by releasing the EU Artificial Intelligence Act, which describes and regulates compliance relevant information concerning the development and usage of AI.

3.2.5 Detailed Auditing Procedures

Considering the aforementioned problems, a precise, careful, and, if necessary, change-sensitive training procedure is essential to ensure that the AI system optimises itself in its learning process with as minimal bias as possible (Chichester & Giffen, 2019). Providers must ensure this. If necessary, the procedure should be audited by a neutral third party. Kleinberg et al., as already cited, give an interesting suggestion: The company's internal IT could deliberately "under-optimise" the data set, which should result in the criterion being predicted inaccurately. For example, one could artificially ensure that a minority in the data set is systematically disadvantaged.

> Discrimination can easily be introduced in this phase, deliberately or unintentionally. Perhaps most simply, the designers could under-optimise in the training phase and produce a screener [selection algorithm] that helps some groups and hurts others while only poorly approximating the intended outcome measure. Such under-optimization, which could amount to disparate treatment, should be detectable by a separate party auditing the firm's procedures if they are provided with the choices of outcome, input variables, and training data, since they could then run their own version of the training procedure and see if they obtain a significantly more accurate approximation to the intended outcome measure. (Kleinberg et al., 2018, p. 141):

There are other, algorithm-based technical solutions to mitigate the biases mentioned above, which will not be explored in this article due to the scope of our current discussion (for more details, see, for instance, Delobelle et al., 2023). We will have to take these or similar steps as long as AI systems do not become more intelligent. They need the ability for critical recursiveness (Maturana & Varela, 1987), i.e., referencing to potentially unethical decisions. We believe that it becomes very clear, how much more (IT) knowledge HR needs in case of AI fostered decisions.

3.2.6 Assessing the Business Value of AI Use in Companies

All HR methods must be checked for their *added corporate value*, as is discussed for 50 years (Cascio & Scott, 2017). This topic will shortly be raised later.

3.2.7 Abilities and Personality

Along with knowledge and skills we must select for abilities and personality factors regarding HR experts which are useful predictors of job success in general (see the latest meta-analysis by Sackett et al., 2022). There are a lot of affordable online tests in the market that fulfil scientific and practical criteria (Farr & Tippins, 2017). The following personality and/or higher order constructs in Hough and Dilchert's (2017) review show predictive validities of some personality constructs (see also Sackett et al., 2022), Table 1 is an excerpt of HR work relevant criteria only:

As we see, conscientiousness correlates weakly with many outcomes. Integrity, emotional stability, and dominance show medium associations with similar important criteria. These variables should be taken into consideration regarding the selection of HR experts in general (note that even low validity tests can have much impact on "right-positive-decisions" depending on base rate and selection rate, detailed in Fisseni, 2004). I will introduce competency modelling now, focusing HR and AI-specific issues.

3.3 *Competency Modelling: Using Theories of Successful Action*

"Competency models refer to collections of knowledge, skills, abilities, and other characteristics (KSAOs) that are needed for effective performance in the jobs in question" (Campion et al., 2011, p. 2). A competency model is a collection and description of competencies—prepared and designed for communication in an organisation. These competencies are considered relevant as a basis of superior performance in an organisation, currently and in the future (Krumm, Mertin & Dries, 2012). They are practical theories of successful action by organisations and companies (Campion et al., 2011). They can be observed, measured, and developed. A competency model for HR for AI use is a recursive competency because if HR is to upskill employees—it needs upskilling itself in the first place.

Table 1 Predictive value of personal characteristics on job-relevant criteria (after Hough & Dilchert, 2017, no level of significance given in source)

	Conscientiousness	Integrity	Emotional stability	Dominance
Overall performance (e.g., supervisor assessment)	$r = 0.23$	$r = 0.41$	–	–
Job satisfaction	$r = 0.26$	$r = 0.33$	$r = 0.29$	–
Unsafe behaviour	$r = -0.25$	–	–	–
Managerial effectiveness	$r = 0.22$	–	–	$r = 0.27$

3.3.1 A Generic Competency Model: The Great Eight

Bartram (2005) described the Great Eight Competencies model, which is based upon the Big Five personality traits (Costa & McCrae, 1992), as well as achievement motivation, cognitive abilities, and leadership motivation. The great eight competencies are: leading and deciding, supporting and co-operating, interacting and presenting, analysing and interpreting, creating and conceptualising, organising and executing, adapting and coping, and enterprising and performing. All competencies are well-researched and used in international selection contexts. In terms of the implementation and communication of AI-related change processes, supporting and co-operating, interacting and presenting, as well as organising and executing, can be considered very important. Sources of competencies can be captured via occupational personality questionnaires and/or assessment centres (see Table 1).

3.3.2 Interdisciplinary Competencies and Change Management

Introduction and implementation of AI can be a big challenge for organisations. Thus, HR must support this change process. All success factors concerning change management are well-known (Oreg et al., 2011). The factors that must be considered are: Change recipients' characteristics, such as openness to experiences; internal context, such as supportive environment and trust; change process, such as participation and communication; perceived benefit or harm; change content. The effect of these predictors on outcomes is mediated by explicit (affective, cognitive, and behavioural) reactions. These predict results such as work-related (e.g., turnover), and personal (e.g., health) criteria.

3.3.2.1 Knowledge Sharing in AI Innovations

As mentioned before (see Daugherty & Wilson, 2018), we need a broad understanding of different business functions, achievable only if experts collaborate well and share their knowledge. Wang and Noe (2010), in their review, summarise evidenced-based success factors for productive knowledge sharing in organisations: Environmental factors like organisational context (management support; rewards; culture and climate); interpersonal and team characteristics and broader cultural aspects (like collectivism). These factors influence mediators like motivation for knowledge sharing, perceived benefits and costs as well as trust. The influence of the mentioned external factors on mediators is moderated by individual characteristics (openness, education, etc.). All mentioned variables predict perceptions of knowledge sharing and respective behaviours.

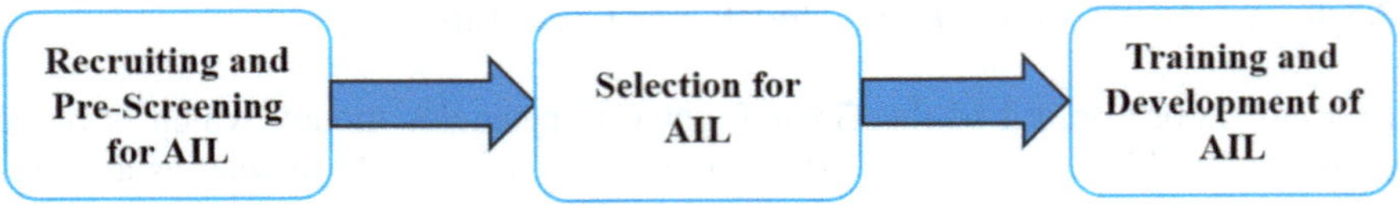

Fig. 1 Steps in hiring and developing HR experts focusing AI literacy (AIL). (Source: Author's illustration)

3.4 AI Literacy: A Framework for Recruiting, Assessment, and Development

Assessing AI literacy is a process, as Fig. 1 shows. It starts with recruiting and screening, followed by selection and training.

3.4.1 Recruiting and Pre-screening

The Situation-Trait-Outcome-Activation (STOA) model offers insights regarding the question who is attracted by which job (De Vries, 2018). It focuses on the selection of leaders but is well-applicable here too. It is based upon Schneider's famous ASA (attraction–selection–attrition) cycle (Schneider, 1987):

1. People select situations that fit their personality. High innovation, modern HR attracts innovative and open-minded people, for instance.
2. Traits are activated in certain situations by "signals". Job ads that offer quick wins vs. slow but intensive development in teams attract dominant, extrinsically motivated vs. high affiliation and intrinsically motivated experts.
3. Traits impact on others, e.g., they influence how job incumbents are perceived, and whether, for instance, they are perceived as typical leader, expert and similar categories.

3.4.2 Selection Phase

All reliable and valid measures are possible. A ranking after Sackett et al.'s (2022) meta-analysis (operative validities ranging from $r = 0.42$ to $r = 0.26$, descending): structured job interviews; work-knowledge tests (which in case of AI knowledge are probably not widespread yet); biodata; work-sample tests; cognitive ability tests; integrity tests; assessment centres, and emotional intelligence. Note that we see a mixture of content versus tool-related variables.

3.4.3 Training and Development Phase

Here, HR-upskilling is realised based on a needs analysis. Well-defined training outcomes guide this process, as well as formative and summative evaluations. Success factors of trainings are well-known on a meta-analytic level (Bell et al., 2017). Figure 1 shows the process.

In our case we need to use (or create first) AI-knowledge tests which must be updated regularly (the author has developed one with moderate reliability, and hints for good validity; Pölitz & Bildat, 2023). Cognitive ability must be captured, as well as conscientiousness and integrity. A quick and correct understanding of non-trivial information, a careful planning process as well as compliant behaviour are necessary for AI implementation. Behaviourally anchored and job-related interviews as well as situational judgement tests (SJTs; Schuler, 2014) are very useful tools that offer job-relevant scenarios. Exercises and/or SJTs could comprise interpreting and evaluating providers' offers, as well as planning of AI implementation in certain fields of HR. Table 2 gives a shortened matrix regarding the fit of assessment tools and AI-related KSAOs:

3.4.4 AI in Smaller Companies

As mentioned above, the use of AI within HRM in smaller companies is another story (speaking of which, the first author of this article has been working as an HR consultant and has gained insights on this matter). HR competencies are often outsourced and there are many providers on the market. One solution here is to seek for provider independent HR consultancy and/or seek for research partnerships at Universities of Applied Sciences. Consultancy by providers of AI solutions in HRM are problematic for obvious reasons.

4 Research Areas and Designs in the Field of AI in HRM

There is a dire need for applied research regarding the topic of the whole paper in Germany. We simply do not know who does what, when, why, and with which results. Make no mistake: it is not very likely that this will change quickly. First, HR experts in German medium-sized companies still rely in part on non-valid, "old-school" and/or useless tools and measures in terms of selection (Kanning, 2019). A self-critical examination of HR practices can be a courageous endeavour, depending a lot on the culture of error management of the respective organisations (Frese & Keith, 2015). Second, HR often has no research resources. Thus, it is dependent on contacts to Universities of Applied Sciences and Research Universities. HR journals in Germany, for instance, seldom recommend valid psychometric tests compared to scientific papers, which is a sign of a scientist-practitioner gap (Benit & Soellner,

Table 2 Matrix of chosen KSAOs and adequate tools for selection of HR experts

	Behaviourally anchored and structured interview	*Tests and/or questionnaires*	*Work sample (e.g., short evaluation of an AI-tool)*	*Situational Judgement Tests*	Assessment Centre case study (Complex task)
AI Knowledge (declarative)	–	XX	XX	–	–
AI Knowledge (procedural)	X	XX	X	X	–
Basics in data protection law/ EU-AI act + business ethics	X	–	X	X	XX
Business process skills: implementation of AI/IT in HR	X	–	X	X	X
Change-Management skills	X	–	–	X	X
Knowledge sharing behaviour	X	–	–	X	X
Cognitive abilities	–	XX	–	–	–
HR basic selection knowledge and skills	X	X	X	–	–
Personality (e.g., conscientiousness)	–	XX	–	–	–
Chosen Great 8 competencies	X	XX	–	X	X

Notes: X = good fit, XX = very good fit; italics: lesser costs than Assessment Centre. Note that a general qualification check is necessary beforehand

2013). Third, AI providers may not be interested in publishing results regarding the aforementioned problems for obvious reasons.

4.1 Unethical Use of AI by Candidates

As mentioned above, we should know whether AI cheating is already an issue for companies and, if so, what is being done. This, of course, is a special aspect of compliance on the side of candidates and it can have devastating effects on companies (Alpha-error, Bildat & Scheffer, 2018).

4.2 Management, Business Value, and Job Roles

An important management function is to analyse the business value of HR activities (Jiang et al., 2012). Only longitudinal designs can bring clarity: How well, for instance, do AI decisions predict employee performance and, consequently operative success? Referring to Daugherty and Wilson's (2018) list of new job roles, we need to better understand how those jobs are created and who fits in here (see Sect. 3.2 above).

4.3 Leadership and Personnel Development

Van Quakebeke and Gerpott (2023) go a step further and predict future scenarios regarding AI and leadership. Not only might AI enhance leadership (not management) as a corporate function, but it might also substitute large parts of it—if not all: "[...] an AI leader can use automated and individualised feedback systems to engage employees in real-time learning, thereby sharpening their sense of competency and efficacy" (2023, p. 4). Summarising their point of view they state:

> Very likely, we will need fewer human leaders, particularly at the lower and middle management levels because their leadership functions can easily be taken over by AI and maybe for the better because we have seen that fewer people want or are even willing to take on leadership roles. (Van Quakebeke & Gerpott, 2023, p. 5)

4.4 Business Ethics in Embedding AI for HR

Especially in Germany there is still a lack of well-documented cases regarding "governance and self-regulation mechanisms that might have impinged [a company's] ability to proactively engage with ethical issues" (Bar-Gil et al., 2024, p. 1). They argue that AI use for people development does have ethical implications:

> When physicists determine the molecular weights of the elements, there is no risk that the elements will attempt to increase their molecular weights to obtain a more respectable position in the periodic table. However, when managers and companies make decisions regarding their employees, they do not remain passive. Instead, they strive to earn good evaluations and improve their condition. Whenever we attempt to quantify or rank people in the field of people data, we risk affecting the behavior that we are attempting to quantify. One example is AI models that predict which employees are likely to leave. These might have implications for how they are treated relative to others and for the attention and support they might receive from the manager, for example, access to training or coaching resources [...]. By denying this support, this prediction may become a self-fulfilling prophecy. (Bar-Gil et al., 2024, p. 1)

Although it is outside the scope of this article to discuss this issue further, it is enough to mention that HR should be on the alert and applied research has a lot to do. Table 3 gives an overview of a choice of research questions and methods as a matrix.

Table 3 AI in HRM: Research questions and methods matrix (choice)

	Quantitative designs	Qualitative designs	Case studies	Review
Ethics: How are ethical problems embedded regarding AI use in HR in small and medium businesses?	0	XX	XX	X
Validity: How valid are AI predictions in companies? How does this fit to competency modelling?	XX	X	X	XX
Usage: Is AI used in personnel development and with which results?	XX	X	XX	XX
Perception: How do HR experts perceive and feel about usage of AI?	X	XX	X	X
Knowledge I: AI in HR: What do HR experts know? What are success factors of knowledge sharing behaviours?	XX	0	0	X
Knowledge II: What do Universities of Applied Sciences teach in terms of AI in HR?	XX	0	0	0
Candidate experiences: Do applicants receive a fair treatment in the context of AI in selection?	X	XX	X	X
Employee experiences: (How) do employees experience the use of AI in HR (development and/or performance measurement?	X	XX	X	X
Do employees want to be led by AI? What ethical implications would this have?	X	XX	X	0
Business value of AI in HRM: Does it pay?	XX	0	0	0

Notes: XX = very appropriate; X = appropriate; 0 = not (yet) appropriate

5 Management Summary for AI Use in HRM

First and foremost, HR and other business units must ensure legal compliance in AI use. Second, with other business units, HR is also responsible for ethically sound use of AI which is more than just obedience to law. Non-acceptance in selection and/or development can have severe impacts on the reputation of a company, both internally and externally, if there is transparency in the selection criteria, data processing, etc. Third, HR staff should be well-selected on the basis of a competency model and trained in terms of AI knowledge, skills, and competencies. This comprises knowledge like predictive validity of data sets as well skills like auditing AI systems. Management must be aware that the introduction of any new technical system can create stress and lower commitment if staff do not participate in the change. AI use in companies is a joint venture of top management, HRM, compliance management, data and law specialists as well as IT experts. CEOs, CHRMs, CCMs, CTOs, and of course CFOs must work hand in hand for this important investment in the future of a company. Legal advice as well as evidenced-based, psychological consultancy is a must.

References

Ala-Mursula, L., Vahtera, J., Kivimäki, M., Kevin, M., & Pentti, J. (2002). Employee control over working times: Associations with subjective health and sickness absences. *Journal of Epidemiology and Community Health, 56*(4), 272–278.

Alpaydin, E. (2020). *Introduction to machine learning* (4th ed.). The MIT Press.

Amelang, M., Bartussek, D, Stemmler, G. & Hagemann, D. (2006). *Differentielle Psychologie und Persönlichkeitsforschung*. [Differential psychology and personality research] 6. Auflage. (6th ed.). Kohlhammer.

Anderson, J. R. (2001). *Kognitive Psychologie*. [Cognitive psychology]. Springer.

Anderson, J. R. (2005). *Kognitive Psychologie*. [Cognitive Psychology] Heidelberg: Springer.

Bankins, S. (2021). The ethical use of artificial intelligence in human resource management: A decision-making framework. *Ethics and Information Technology, 23*, 841–854.

Bar-Gil, O., Ron, T., & Czerniak, O. (2024). AI for the people? Embedding AI ethics in HR and people analytics projects. *Technology in Society, 77*, 102527.

Barling, J. (2014). *The science of leadership. Lessons from research for organisational leaders*. Oxford University Press.

Bartram, D. (2005). The great eight competencies: A criterion-centric approach to validation. *Journal of Applied Psychology, 90*, 1185–1203.

Bell, B. S., Tannenbaum, S. I., Ford, J. K., Noe, R. A., & Kraiger, K. (2017). 100 Years of training and development research. What we know and where we should go. *Journal of Applied Psychology, 102*(3), 305–323.

Benit, N., & Soellner, R. (2013). Scientist-practitioner gap in Deutschland: Eine empirische Studie am Beispiel psychologischer Testverfahren. *Zeitschrift für Arbeits- und Organisationspsychologie, 57*(31), 145–153.

Benjamin, R. (2019). Assessing risk, automating racism. *Science, 366*(6464), 421–422. https://doi.org/10.1126/science.aaz3873

Bildat, L., & Remdisch, S. (2008). Personality and new media: Predictors of PC and internet literacy. In J. Deller (Ed.), *Research contributions to personality at work* (pp. 239–256). Rainer Hampp.

Bildat, L., & Scheffer, D. (2018). Personalauswahl. [Personnel selection] In L. Bildat & T. Warszta (Hrsg.) [Eds.], *Psychologie im Human Resource Management. Ein Lehrbuch für Hochschule und Praxis* [Psychology in human resource management. A textbook for higher education and practice] (pp. 81–124). Pabst.

Black, J. S., & van Esch, P. (2020). AI-enabled recruiting: What is it and how should a manager use it? *Business Horizons, 63*(2), 215–226.

Blackman, R. (2022). *Ethical machines. Your concise guide to totally unbiased, transparent and respectful AI*. Harvard Business review Press.

Breakwell, G. M., Wright, D. B., & Barnett, J. (Eds.). (2020). *Research methods in psychology* (5th ed.). Sage.

Broussard, M. (2023). *More than a glitch. Confronting gender, race, and ability bias in tech*. The MIT Press.

Burnett, D. (2023). *Emotional ignorance. Lost and found in the science of emotion*. Faber & Faber.

Burrell, J., & Metcalf, J. (2024). Introduction for the special issue of "Ideologies of AI and the consolidation of power": Naming power. *First Monday, 29*(4). https://doi.org/10.5210/fm.v29i4.13643

Cameron, J. (Director). (1986). *Aliens* [Film]. 20th Century Fox.

Campion, M. A., Fink, A. A., Ruggenberg, B. J., Carr, L., Phillips, G. M., & Odman, R. B. (2011). Doing competencies well: Best practices in competency modeling. *Personnel Psychology, 64*(1), 225–262.

Canagasuriam, D., & Lukacik, E.-R. (2024). ChatGPT, can you take my job interview? Examining artificial intelligence cheating in the asynchronous video interview. *International Journal of Selection and Assessment*, 1–16. https://doi.org/10.1111/ijsa.12491

Cascio, W. F., & Scott, J. C. (2017). The business value of employee selection. In J. L. Farr & N. T. Tippins (Eds.), *Handbook of employee selection* (pp. 226–248). Routledge.

Castro, D., & New, J. (2016). *The promise of artificial intelligence*. Center for Data Innovation. http://www2.datainnovation.org/2016-promise-of-ai.pdf

Chichester, M. A., Jr., & Giffen, J. R. (2019). Recruiting in the robot age: Examining potential EEO implications in optimising recruiting through the use of artificial intelligence. *The Computer and Interne Lawyer, 36*(10), 1–3.

Christoph, G., Goldhammer, F., Zylka, J., & Hartig, J. (2015). Adolescents' computer performance: The role of self-concept and motivational aspects. *Computers & Education, 81*, 1–12.

Cleveland, J. N., Murphy, K. H., & Colella, A. (2017). The deficiency of our criteria. In J. L. Farr & N. T. Tippins (Eds.), *Handbook of employee selection* (pp. 554–572). Routledge.

Costa, P. T., & McCrae, R. R. (1992). Four ways five factors are basic. *Personality and Individual Differences, 13*, 653–665.

Dahm, M., & Dregger, A. (2019). Der Einsatz von künstlicher Intelligenz im HR: Die Wirkung und Förderung der Akzeptanz von KI-basierten Recruiting-Tools bei potenziellen Nutzern. [The use of artificial intelligence in HR: Effect and promotion of acceptance of AI-based recruiting tools in potential users]. In B. Hermeier, T. Heupel, & S. Fichtner-Rosada (Hrsg.) [Eds.], *Arbeitswelten der Zukunft* [Worlds of work in the future]. FOM-Edition. Springer Gabler.

Daugherty, P. R., & Wilson, H. J. (2018). *Human + Machine: Reimagining work in the age of AI*. Harvard Business Review Press.

Davis, F. D. (1989). Perceived usefulness, perceived ease of use and user acceptance of information technology. *MIS Quarterly, 13*(3), 319–339.

De Vries, R. E. (2018). Three nightmare traits in leaders. *Frontiers in Psychology, 9*, 871.

Delobelle, P., Temple, P., Perrouin, G., Frénay, B., Heymans, P., & Berendt, B. (2023). Ethical adversaries: Towards mitigating unfairness with adversarial machine learning. *ACM SIGKDD Newsletter, 23*(1), 32–41.

Di Nuovo, A., & Conti, D. (2023). The new frontiers of psychometrics: From computerized adaptive testing to the use of artificial agents and e-assessment. In S. Di Nuovo & M. Sinatra (Eds.), *How to measure mind. A historical approach to psychological assessment* (pp. 97–107). Hogrefe.

Di Nuovo, S., & Sinatra, M. (Eds.). (2023). *How to measure mind. A historical approach to psychological assessment*. Hogrefe.

Diagnostik und Testkuratorium (Hrsg.). (2018). *Personalauswahl kompetent gestalten. Grundlagen und Praxis der Eignungsdiagnostik nach DIN 33430*. [Designing personnel selection competently. Basics and Practice of personnel diagnostics after DIN 33430]. Springer.

Ethikbeirat HR Tech. (2021). *Richtlinien für den verantwortungsvollen Einsatz von Künstlicher Intelligenz und weiteren digitalen Technologien in der Personalarbeit.* [Guidelines for responsible use of artificial intelligence and further digital tools in human resource] https://www.ethikbeirat-hrtech.de/wp-content/uploads/2020/03/Richtlinien_Download_deutsch_final.pdf

European Commission. (2024). *AI Act*. Retrieved April 28, 2024, from https://digital-strategy.ec.europa.eu/en/policies/regulatory-framework-ai

Farr, J. L., & Tippins, N. T. (Eds.). (2017). *Handbook of employee selection* (2nd ed.). Routledge Academics.

Fisseni, H.-J. (2004). *Lehrbuch der psychologischen Diagnostik. Mit Hinweisen zur Intervention.* 3. Auflage. (3rd ed.). Hogrefe.

Frese, M., & Keith, N. (2015). Action errors, error management, and learning in organisations. *Annual Review of Psychology, 66*, 661–687.

Frese, M., & Zapf, D. (1994). Action as the core of work psychology: A German approach. In C. Triandis et al. (Eds.), *Handbook of industrial and organisational psychology* (Vol. 4, 2nd ed., pp. 271–340). Consulting Psychologists Press.

Gardner, H. (1999). *Intelligence reframed: Multiple intelligences for the 21st century*. Basic Books.

Garvey, S. C. (2019). Hypothesis: Is "terminator syndrome" a barrier to democratizing artificial intelligence and public engagement in digital health? *Journal of Integrative Biology, 23*(7), 362–362.

Geuter, U. (1984). Psychologie im Nationalsozialismus. [Psychology in nation socialism] In H. E. Lück, R. Miller, & W. Rechtien (Hrsg.), *Geschichte der Psychologie* [History of psychology] (pp. 22–28). Urban & Schwarzenberg.

Gmyrek, P., Berg, J. & Desmond, D. (2023). *Generative AI and Jobs: A global analysis of potential effects on job quantity and quality.* ILO Working Paper 96. ILO. https://doi.org/10.54394/FHEM8239

Gonzalez, M. F., et al. (2022). Allying with AI? Reactions toward human-based, AI/ML-based, and augmented hiring processes. *Computers in Human Behavior, 130*, 107179.

Hacker, W. (1998). *Allgemeine Arbeitspsychologie. Psychische Regulation von Arbeitstätigkeiten* [General work psychology. Regulation of work practice]. Huber.

Harari, Y. N. (2017). *Homo Deus. Eine Geschichte von Morgen* [A short history of tomorrow] C. H. Beck.

Harasim, L. (Ed.). (1990). *Online education: Perspectives on a new environment*. Praeger.

Hargittai, E. (2002). Second-level digital divide: Differences in people's online skills. *First Monday, 4*(7). Retrieved September 25, 2025, from http://www.firstmonday.org/issues/issue7_4/hargittai/ Date accessed:

Hartwig, M., Tegtmeier, P., Kirchhoff, B., Adolph, L., Meyer, S.-C., Tisch, A. & Wischniewski, S. (2023). *Schreiben von Texten durch künstliche Intelligenz: Mögliche Auswirkungen für betroffene Beschäftigtengruppen mit Schreibtätigkeiten* [Text generation by artificial intelligence: Possible impacts for job groups with writing practice]. Dortmund: Bundesanstalt für Arbeitsschutz und Arbeitsmedizin. Bericht kompakt.

Hough, L., & Dilchert, S. (2017). Personality. Its measurement and validity for employee selection. In J. L. Farr & N. T. Tippins (Eds.), *Handbook of employee selection* (2nd ed., pp. 298–325). Routledge.

Hu, M. (2017). Algorithmic Jim Crow. *Fordham Law Review, 86*, 633.

Jewish Museum Berlin. (2024, May). *Der Golem: von Mystik bis Minecraft*. https://www.jmberlin.de/der-golem-von-mystik-bis-minecraft

Jiang, K., Lepak, D., Hu, J., & Baer, J. C. (2012). How does human resource management influence organisational outcomes? A meta-analytic investigation of mediating mechanisms. *Academy of Management Journal, 55*, 1264–1294.

Johnson, D. G., & Verdicchio, M. (2017). Reframing AI discourse. *Minds & Machines, 27*, 575–590.

Kahneman, D. (2012). *Schnelles Denken, langsames Denken*. [Thinking fast and slow] Siedler.

Kanning, U. P. (2019). *Standards der Personaldiagnostik. Personalauswahl professionell gestalten.* [Standards of Personnel Diagnostics. Designing Personnel Selection Professionally] (2., überarbeitete und erweiterte Auflage) [2nd. Ed.] Göttingen: Hogrefe.

Kaplan, A. M., & Haenlein, M. (2019). Siri, Siri, in my hand: Who's the fairest in the land? On the interpretations, illustrations, and implications of artificial intelligence. *Business Horizons, 62*(1), 15–25. https://doi.org/10.1016/j.bushor.2018.08.004

Kirste, M. & Schürholz, M. (2019). Entwicklungswege zur KI [Ways of developing AI]. In V. Wittpahl (Hrsg.), *Künstliche Intelligenz*. Springer.

Kleinberg, J., Ludwig, J., Mullainhathan, S., & Sunstein, C. R. (2018). Discrimination in the age of algorithms. *Journal of Legal Analysis, 10*, 113–174.

Köchling, A., & Wehner, M. C. (2021). Better explaining the benefits why AI? Analysing the impact of explaining the benefits of AI-supported selection on applicant responses. *International Journal of Selection and Assessment, 31*, 45–62.

Krumm, S., Mertin, I. & Dries, C. (2012). *Kompetenzmodelle*. [Competenc Models] Göttingen: Hogrefe.

Kubrick, S. (Director). (1968). *2001: A Space Odyssey* [Film]. MGM.

Kurzweil, R. (2013). *How to create a mind. The secret of human thought revealed.* Penguin.

Liaw, S.-S. (2008). Investigating students' perceived satisfaction, behavioral intention, and effectiveness of e-learning: A case study of the Blackboard system. *Computers & Education, 51*, 864–873.

Lippens, L., Vermeiren, S., & Baert, S. (2023). The state of hiring discrimination: A meta-analysis of (almost) all recent correspondence experiments. *European Economic Review, 151*, 104315.

Locke, E. A., & Latham, G. P. (1990). *A theory of goal settling and task performance*. Prentice Hall.

Lück, H. E. & Miller, R. (1999). Illustrierte Geschichte der Psychologie. [Illustrated History of Psychology]. Weinheim: Beltz PVU.

Maturana, H. R., & Varela, F. J. (1987). *Der Baum der Erkenntnis. Die biologischen Wurzeln menschlichen Erkennens* [The tree of cognation. The biological sources of human insight]. Goldmann.

Mitchell, T. M. (2010). *Machine learning*. McGraw-Hill.

Ntoutsi, E., Fafalios, P., Gadiraju, U., Iosifidis, V., Nejdi, W., Vidal, M., Ruggieri, S., Turini, F., Papadopoulos, S., Krasanakis, E., Kompatsiaris, I., Kinder-Kurlanda, K., Wagner, C., Karimi, F., Fernandez, M., Alani, H., Berendt, B., Kruegel, T., Heinze, C., … Staab, S. (2019). Bias in data-driven artificial intelligence systems—an introductory survey. *WIREs Data Mining and Knowledge Discovery, 10*(3), 1–14.

Ontrup, G., Hagemann, V. & Kluge, A. (2024). *HR-Analytics. Eine Einführung in ganzheitliches, datengestütztes Personalmanagement* [An Introduction in holistic, and Data-driven Human Resource Management]. Hogrefe.

Oreg, S., Vakola, M., & Armenakis, A. (2011). Change recipients' reactions to organisational change: A 60-year review of quantitative studies. *The Journal of Applied Behavioral Science, 47*(4), 461–524.

Organisation for Economic Co-operation and Development. (2018). *Broken social elevator?: How to promote social mobility*. Organisation for Economic. https://www.oecd.org/social/broken-elevator-how-to-promote-social-mobility-9789264301085-en.htm

Orwat, C. (2019). *Diskriminierungsrisiken durch Verwendung von Algorithmen Eine Studie, erstellt mit einer Zuwendung der Antidiskriminierungsstelle des Bundes* [Discrimination risks of algorithm-usage]. Herausgegeben von der Antidiskriminierungsstelle des Bundes. [Federal Anti-Discrimination Authority, Ed.].

Pölitz, A. L., & Bildat, L. (2023). *Morgen wählt Sie ein Bot aus! Akzeptanz des (riskanten?) Einsatzes von KI in der Personalauswahl. Eine empirische Querschnittstudie*. [You will be selected by a bot tomorrow! Acceptance of (risky?) AI-usage in personnel selection] Vortrag [Lecture] CARF Luzern 2022. Controlling. Accounting. Risiko. Finanzen. 07–08. September.

Polyportis, A., & Pahos, N. (2024). Navigating the perils of artificial intelligence: A focused review on ChatGPT and responsible research and innovation. *Humanities and Social Sciences Communications., 11*(107).

Rai, A. (2020). Explainable AI: From black box to glass box. *Journal of the Academy of Marketing Science, 48*, 137–141.

Robert, L. P., Pierce, C., Marquis, L., Kim, S., & Alahmad, R. (2020). Designing fair AI for managing employees in organisations: A review, critique, and design agenda. *Human-Computer Interaction, 35*(5-6), 545–575. https://doi.org/10.1080/07370024.2020.1735391

Roddenberry, G. (Creator). (1966). *Star Trek* [Television series]. NBC.

Roitzsch, K., Walter, G., & Schmidt, M. (Hg.). (2019). *Psychologische Bewertung von Arbeitsbedingungen. Screening für Arbeitsplatzinhaber III – BASA III. Praxishandbuch.* [Psychological assessment of working conditions for job-incumbents III— BASA III. Hochschule Zittau Görlitz.

Ryan, A. & Ployhart, R. (2000). Applicant perceptions of selection procedures and decisions: A critical review and agenda for the future. *Journal of Management, 26*, 565–606.

Rychen, D. S., & Salganik, L. H. (Eds.). (2001). *Defining and selecting key competencies*. Hogrefe & Huber Publishers.

Sackett, P. R., Zhang, C., Berry, C. M., & Lievens, F. (2022). Revisiting meta-analytic estimates of validity in personnel selection: Addressing systematic overcorrection for restriction of range. *Journal of Applied Psychology., 107*(11), 2040–2068.

Sáinz, M., & Eccles, J. (2012). Self-concept of computer and math ability: Gender implications across time and within ICT studies. *Journal of Vocational Behavior, 80*(2), 486–499.

Salgado, J. F., Anderson, N., & Táuriz, G. (2015). The validity of ipsative and quasi-ipsative forced-choice personality inventories for different occupational groups: A comprehensive meta-analysis. *Journal of Occupational and Organisational Psychology, 88*(4), 797–834.

Sarges, W. (Hrsg.) (2013). *Management-Diagnostik* [Management diagnostics]. 4. Auflage. Hogrefe.

Schauffel, N., Schmidt, I., Peiffer, H., & Ellwart, T. (2021). Self-concept related to information and communication technology: Scale development and validation. *Computers in Human Behavior Reports, 4*.

Schellmann, H. (2024). *The algorithm. How AI decides who gets hired, monitored, promoted & fired & why we need to fight back now*. Hachette.

Schepman, A., & Rodway, P. (2022). The General Attitudes towards Artificial Intelligence Scale (GAAIS): Confirmatory validation and associations with personality, corporate distrust, and general trust. *International Journal of Human-Computer Interaction, 39*(13), 2724–2741.

Schmidt-Atzert, L., Künecke, J., & Zimmermann, J. (2019). TBS-DTK Rezension: "PRECIRE JobFit". *Report Psychologie, 44*(7/8), 19–21.

Schneider, B. (1987). The people make the place. *Personnel psychology, 40*, 437–453.

Schöne, C., Dickhäuser, O., Spinath, B. & Stiensmeier-Pelster, J. (2003). Das Fähigkeitsselbstkonzept und seine Erfassung [The self-concept of ability and its measurement]. In J. Stiensmeier-Pelster, & F. Rheinberg (Hrsg.), *Diagnostik von Motivation und Selbstkonzept* (pp. 3–14). [Diagnostics of motivation and self-concept]. Hogrefe.

Schuler, H. (2014). *Psychologische Personalauswahl. Eignungsdiagnostik für Personalentscheidungen und Berufsberatung* [Psychological selection of personnel. Diagnostics for aptitudes and job consultancy]. 4. Auflage. Hogrefe.

Shu, Q., Tu, Q., & Wang, K. (2011). The impact of computer self-efficacy and technology dependence on computer-related technostress: A social cognitive theory perspective. *International Journal of Human-Computer Interaction, 27*(10), 923–939.

Sindermann, C., Yang, H., Elhai, J. D., Yang, S., Quan, L., Li, M., & Montag, C. (2021). Acceptance and fear of artificial intelligence: Associations with personality in a German and a Chinese sample. *Discover Psychology, 2*(8).

Stiensmeier-Pelster, J. & Rheinberg, F. (2003). *Diagnostik von Motivation und Selbstkonzept* [Diagnostics of Motivation and Self-concept]. Hogrefe.

Tang, P. M., Koopman, J., Mai, K. M., De Cremer, D., Zhang, J. H., Reynders, P., Ng, C. T. S., & Chen, I.-H. (2023). No person is an island: Unpacking the work and after-work consequences of interacting with artificial intelligence. *Journal of Applied Psychology*. https://doi.org/10.1037/apl0001103

Thiemann, D. (2022). Stress durch digitale Technologien. Herausforderungen und Implikationen für Führung [Stress by digital technologies. Challenges and implications for leadership]. *Wirtschaftspsychologie, 22*(2), 14–27.

Tippins, N. T., Oswald, F. L., & McPhail, S. M. (2021). Scientific, legal, and ethical concerns about AI-based personnel selection tools: A call to action. *Personnel Assessment and Decisions, 7*(2), 1.

Tomaszewski, T. (1978). *Tätigkeit und Bewusstsein. Beiträge zur Einführung in die polnische Tätigkeitspsychologie* [Activity and consciousness. Contributions on the introduction into the Polish psychology of action]. Weinheim und Basel.

Turner Lee, N. (2018). Detecting racial bias in algorithms and machine learning. *Journal of Information, Communication and Ethics in Society, 16*(3), 252–260.

Volpert, W. (1982). Das Modell der hierarchisch-sequentiellen Handlungsorganisation. In W. Hacker [The model of hierarchic-sequential action regulation] (Hrsg.) [Eds.], *Kognitive und motivationale Aspekte der Handlung* (pp. 38–50). Huber.
van Quakebeke, N. & Gerpott, F. H. (2023). The Now, New, and Next of Digital Leadership: How Artificial Intelligence (AI) Will Take Over and Change Leadership as We Know It *Journal of Leadership & Organizational Studies*, 1–11.
Wang, S., & Noe, R. A. (2010). Knowledge sharing: A review and directions for future research. *Human Resource Management Review., 20*, 115–131.
Ward, A. F. (2021). People mistake the internet's knowledge for their own. *PNAS, 118*(43).
Ward, A. F., Zheng, J., & Broniarczyk, S. M. (2022). I share, therefore I know? Sharing online content—Even without reading it—Inflates subjective knowledge. *JCP*. https://doi.org/10.1002/jcpy.1321
Weinert, F. E. (2001). Concept of competence: A conceptual clarification. In D. S. Rychen & L. H. Salganik (Eds.), *Defining and selecting key competencies* (pp. 45–65). Hogrefe & Huber Publishers.
Xu, W. (2019). Toward human-centred AI: A perspective from human-computer interaction. *ACM, 26*(4), 42–46.
Zohuri, B., & Rahmani, F. M. (2019). Artificial Intelligence driven resiliency with machine learning and deep learning components. *Japan Journal of Research, 1*(1), 1–7.

Lothar Bildat started his career as a Social Worker, completed his psychological degree and PhD at the Justus-Liebig-University of Giessen, and has worked as a consultant in an international context as a trained I/O-psychologist for a British provider of digital assessment tools. He has over 20 years of experience in teaching, research, consulting, and leadership training. After several professorships, he has worked at the BSP Berlin Business and Law School Campus Hamburg since August 2022. Furthermore, he is a member of the German Society for Business Psychology (GWPs). His main areas of interest are leadership, health, and job-related competencies.

Tim Brouns was a lecturer at FOM University of Applied Sciences in Düsseldorf, Germany, specialising in research methods and data & analytics. As a former research fellow and alumnus of the Institute for Business Psychology at FOM, his academic work focused on leadership and occupational health psychology. In addition to his academic career, Brouns has over 15 years of professional experience in the IT and telecommunications industry, where he held various specialist and leadership positions. His expertise bridges the gap between research and practice, particularly in applying technical and psychological insights to corporate environments.

Case Study: Digital Transformation of IT-Supported Knowledge Transfer at Fast-Growing SME

Adrian Thiessen and Michael Müller

Abstract This case study investigates the implementation of smart knowledge transfer solutions in a medium-sized, rapidly growing company amid market volatility, internal structural changes, and leadership transitions. It explores the critical knowledge transfer challenges that fast-growing small and medium-sized enterprises (SMEs) face, such as retaining success-critical explicit and implicit knowledge, aligning knowledge management goals with strategic goals and knowledge hiding, and the strategies employed to address them. Utilising the KM^4 knowledge management model, the case study provides a structured framework for assessing and improving knowledge management practices. Key focus areas include soft factors, such as organisational and team structures, as well as the integration of advanced technologies, particularly processes driven by Artificial Intelligence, to optimise absorptive capacity and knowledge transfer. The paper emphasises the importance of quick wins and realistic expectation management to build momentum and sustain engagement in digital transformation initiatives. This paper incorporates theoretical insights from knowledge management literature, particularly on the mechanisms through which organisations can institutionalise knowledge continuity amid leadership and market changes. Through this analysis, the paper contributes valuable strategies and recommendations for SMEs navigating complex transitions in dynamic environments, providing a model for other organisations facing similar challenges.

A. Thiessen (✉)
Relias Learning GmbH, Berlin, Germany
e-mail: athiessen@relias.de

M. Müller
Ansbach University of Applied Sciences, Ansbach, Germany
e-mail: michael.mueller@hs-ansbach.de

K. Bodrožić-Brnić et al. (eds.), *Digital Transformation in Knowledge Transfer*, Digital Transformation and Innovation,
https://doi.org/10.1007/978-3-032-07329-7_2

Keywords Knowledge management in SMEs · Leadership transition · Knowledge hiding · Absorptive capacity · Knowledge retention

1 Introduction

1.1 Motivation

This case study explores the potential of smart knowledge transfer in supporting a medium-sized, rapidly growing company to address market volatility, internal structural changes, and leadership transitions. Effective knowledge management strategies are crucial for successful growth. The top 500 companies in the USA incur up to $30 billion annually in opportunity costs due to knowledge hiding or unshared knowledge (Offergelt et al., 2020). The departure of experienced staff, coupled with a dynamic market environment, can create significant knowledge gaps and pose risks to organisational continuity and growth (Durst & Zieba, 2019). In contrast, companies that do prioritise knowledge transfer are perceived as more innovative, attractive, and competitive, enhancing revenue growth and client satisfaction (Deloitte Insights, 2021).

Small and medium-sized enterprises (SMEs) face acute challenges in knowledge management, including the risks of knowledge loss due to the departure of key personnel and internal restructuring, underdeveloped awareness of success-critical knowledge, and heavy reliance on exclusive experts. Fast-growing SMEs face additional problems such as onboarding numerous new employees, integrating extensive new knowledge, and undergoing significant restructuring of organisational structures and business processes to keep up with growth. The current state of applied research in knowledge management for SMEs highlights these issues (Durst et al., 2023, 2024).

This case study provides a practical example of the challenges faced and the solutions implemented to prevent organisational knowledge loss, retain success-critical explicit and implicit knowledge, and optimise absorptive capacity through technology, including Artificial Intelligence (AI). Effectively transferring and retaining both explicit and implicit knowledge is crucial for sustaining competitive advantage and fostering innovation. A comprehensive digital knowledge transformation must encompass IT tools, organisational structures, the human factor, and individual and team-related skills. This holistic approach ensures that knowledge management strategies are deeply integrated into the organisation, enhancing its ability to adapt and thrive in a rapidly changing environment. Therefore, this paper presents key terms and concepts related to knowledge transfer and explores their practical applications.

1.2 Research Questions and Methodology

This article examines how fast-growing SMEs can implement knowledge transfer solutions in a dynamic environment through four research questions:

1. What are the most critical knowledge transfer challenges facing fast-growing SMEs in a dynamic environment?
2. How can SMEs effectively implement knowledge management tools during periods of leadership transition and market volatility to address the most critical knowledge transfer challenges?
3. What role can current IT resources and AI play in optimising knowledge transfer and absorptive capacity?
4. How can scalable knowledge transfer strategies be implemented in SMEs to support continuous learning and leadership development without relying on third-party support?

The scientific methodology used is an analysis of the literature and a study of a specific fast-growing SME in a dynamic environment. Exploratory theses are proposed, but their applicability to other fast-growing SMEs requires further empirical validation.

1.3 Structure of the Article

Our approach incorporates theoretical insights from knowledge management literature, particularly on the mechanisms through which organisations can institutionalise knowledge continuity amid leadership and market changes. We explore scalable, cost-effective strategies for SMEs to harness, update, and utilise implicit knowledge without third-party support in day-to-day operations using existing IT resources and AI.

The article is organised to guide the reader through the significance and practical aspects of knowledge transfer in fast-growing SMEs. It begins with an introduction that sets the stage by highlighting the importance of the topic, establishing the study's context, and defining its scientific objectives. Next, it delves into the concept of knowledge transfer within SMEs, provides a concise overview of relevant literature and models, and describes typical knowledge management tasks. The third part transitions from theory to practice, analyses a specific company's background, the challenges it faced, and the solutions implemented.

Further, it carries out a multidimensional assessment or readiness analysis in accordance with the knowledge management model introduced, focusing on three areas. Section 4.4 analyses the existing IT tools, discusses the possibilities of an e-learning platform, and provides an outlook on the potential of AI solutions. Section 4.5 addresses the particular challenges of knowledge transfer, exploring how mindset, motivation, and organisational dynamics influence knowledge transfer. Section 4.6 describes the planning of quick wins and the procedure in maturity levels. Finally, the article summarises the findings, discusses the research limitations, and provides an outlook for future research.

2 Knowledge Transfer at Fast-Growing SMEs

2.1 *Introduction to Knowledge and Types of Knowledge*

Knowledge refers to the totality of information and skills that people can use to solve problems. Knowledge must be differentiated from information and competence. Information is data that is contextualised, categorised, calculated, and condensed to enhance its utility (Davenport & Prusak, 1998). Knowledge links information and connects it with experience to make decisions and solve problems. Competence is the ability to apply knowledge to new situations. Knowledge can be categorised into (North, 2021):

- Internal/external: Internal knowledge, encompassing best practices and lessons learned from business models, processes, and internal projects, is continuously utilised, shared, and retained. External knowledge must be derived from information, sometimes is purchased, needs to be evaluated, and then converted to internal knowledge. For example, external knowledge about market changes, new IT trends, or competitor activities must be continuously scanned and used to adapt business strategies and tactics.
- Individual/collective: Individual experiences, best practices, and lessons learned from employees and exclusive experts become collective knowledge at various organisational levels through knowledge sharing, transfer, and consolidation (Nonaka & Takeuchi, 2019).
- Explicit/implicit: Explicit knowledge is knowledge communicated by means of language, e.g. in the form of documents or trainings. It must be regularly updated and be available for targeted and efficient retrieval. Implicit or tacit knowledge is in the minds and skills of employees and is difficult to articulate, but it should be collected, transferred, and documented as explicit knowledge (Nonaka & Takeuchi, 2019).

In today's VUCA world (volatility–uncertainty–complexity–ambiguity), organisations are flooded with information and must navigate complex knowledge dynamics, such as the spread of misinformation and the constant need for knowledge (re-)evaluation and integration.

2.2 *The Knowledge Management Model "KM^4"*

Knowledge management should be consistently geared towards a company's strategy by deriving normative, strategic, and operational knowledge objectives. These objectives should be closely linked to success-critical and knowledge-intensive business processes. However, particularly in SMEs, knowledge management based on such objectives is often neglected.

The knowledge management model *KM^4*, developed by Müller (2022), who is also the co-author of this article, provides a comprehensive framework to achieve those goals. The model focuses on the key areas necessary for a company to implement effective knowledge management and supports structured readiness analysis and strategic planning for digital transformation (Fig. 1).

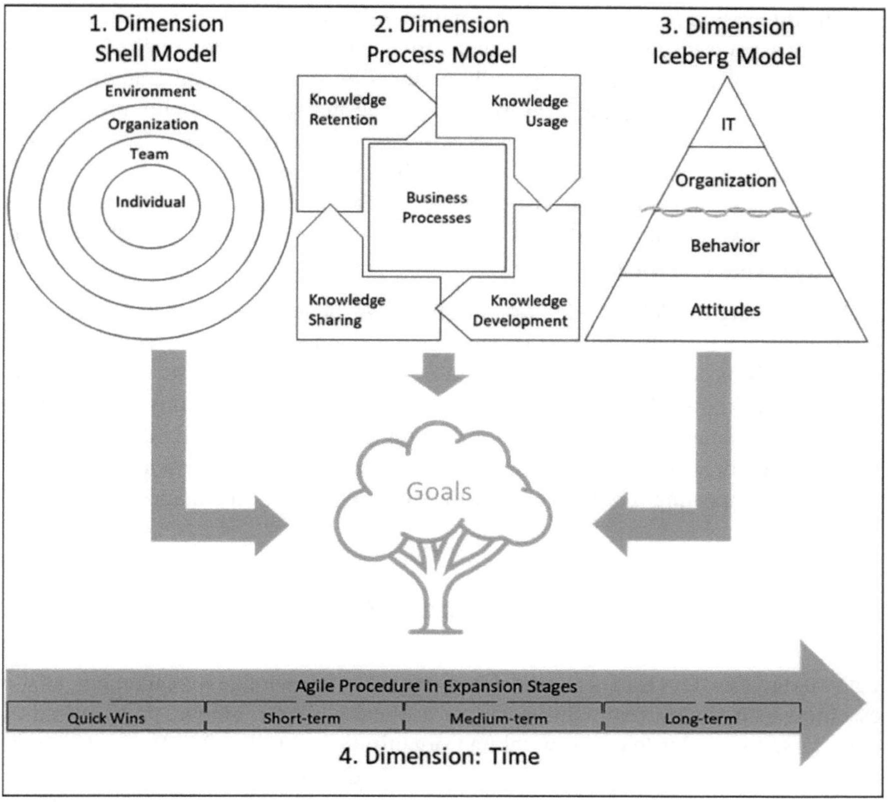

Fig. 1 The *KM⁴* model (Müller, 2022)

KM⁴ categorises knowledge management into four dimensions:

1. The dimension Shell Model emphasises knowledge management in the organisation, within teams, and for individuals in the context of knowledge exchange with the environment (Nonaka & Takeuchi, 2019; Robbins & Judge, 2023). It requires the development of personal knowledge management skills and a supportive management framework to facilitate effective team-based knowledge sharing.
2. The dimension Process Model focuses on knowledge usage, development, sharing, and retention (Probst et al., 2012). It highlights the importance of creating efficient workflows that ensure knowledge is not only shared but also effectively used and preserved within the organisation. Knowledge transfer, in the narrowest sense, is simply the actual transmission or handover of knowledge from one individual to another. However, in this holistic case study, the authors place knowledge transfer in the broader context of knowledge work with the usage, development, sharing, and retention of knowledge.

3. The dimension Iceberg Model distinguishes the hard factors (IT tools, organisational aspects) from the soft, human factors, particularly behaviour and attitudes. Successful implementation of tools requires an organisational framework that promotes a mindset geared towards knowledge sharing and collaboration. Due to the necessary focus, this case study will concentrate on IT tools (see Sect. 4.4) and the human factor (see Sect. 4.5) within this dimension.
4. The Time dimension emphasises the need for both immediate actions to generate quick wins as well as sustained efforts and long-term planning to achieve comprehensive knowledge management goals over time.

By applying the *KM⁴* model, organisations can develop a transparent and structured approach to maturing their knowledge management practices. This model can address various challenges, which are described in the following section, by ensuring efficient knowledge transfer processes, integrating IT solutions, and aligning knowledge management activities with strategic business objectives. It provides a roadmap for organisations to enhance their knowledge management capabilities, ultimately supporting innovation, growth, and competitive advantage.

2.3 Knowledge Transfer: Methods, Media, and Tools

Knowledge transfer (KT) is a critical component of knowledge management, as it is essential to maintain competitiveness in a dynamic environment, prevent knowledge loss, and foster learning within an organisation (Müller, 2022). For KT to be effective, it must occur on a continuous basis, both from external sources (e.g. customers) to internal sources and within the organisation itself, e.g., between different departments, teams, and individuals.

Internally, horizontal KT takes place across different functional areas within the value chain, while vertical KT occurs between different hierarchical levels within the organisation. Additionally, KT can involve a moderator, such as in expert debriefings for retiring employees, or occur without a moderator.

KT can be synchronous (personalisation) in the form of face-to-face meetings or video calls, or asynchronous (codification), e.g., via e-learning or other forms of documentation. In the context of agile project management, synchronous KT approaches are emphasised, such as daily scrum stand-up meetings (Ackermann et al., 2020).

Informal KT often occurs in casual settings such as coffee corners, brownbag sessions, or during lunch and can be driven by either pull factors (where recipient requests information) or push factors (where the sender proactively shares information). In contrast, formal KT is usually institutionalised and codified, for example in form of an onboarding plan.

KT also varies based on the participants involved, such as between different age groups, genders, and personalities, each presenting unique challenges. For example, intergenerational KT between Generation Z and baby boomers may see experienced workers sharing their extensive knowledge with digitally savvy university graduates.

KT can be categorised by duration (short-term, mid-term, long-term), frequency (daily, weekly, quarterly), or situation (project-related, ad-hoc). Various IT tools and communication channels facilitate KT on top of in-person meetings, including phone calls, e-mail, instant messaging software, video conferencing, note-taking and mind mapping software, live collaboration tools, (online) whiteboards, microblogging services, enterprise content management systems, wikis, or customer relationship management software. Many of those channels already incorporate some form of AI to facilitate KT. Different media is used for KT, such as text, images, audio, and video. Methods like storytelling can also facilitate effective KT.

2.4 Challenges of Knowledge Transfer at (Fast-Growing) SMEs

Companies of all sizes face significant challenges in knowledge transfer, which can hinder their growth and innovation. These challenges are particularly magnified in SMEs due to their size and limited resources (Anand et al., 2021; Biloslavo & Lombardi, 2021). Fast-growing SMEs, characterised by a high capacity for innovation or operating in a market sector that generally has strong growth tailwinds (Almus, 2000), often amplify these challenges further.

Limited resources, including financial, can result in insufficient training, outdated knowledge, and restricted access to external knowledge sources, reducing the ability to implement robust KT systems. This might lead to a lack of structured knowledge management responsibility, and thus a lack of accountability. Knowledge management at SMEs then often falls to management, general staff, or HR, despite the need for a dedicated caretaker in the initial phases and gets lost in day-to-day operations.

Knowledge hiding is another significant challenge, as early employees often view knowledge as a source of power and are reluctant to share it, especially as a company grows. This reluctance impedes the distribution of knowledge across the organisation, particularly when only a few employees possess highly specialised skillset, e.g. IT, which creates high dependency on a few employees.

Rapid expansion necessitates acquiring the proper knowledge, extensive onboarding and mentoring, integrating diverse cultures, and facilitating intergenerational KT. Often, a lack of awareness of success-critical knowledge leaves unique selling points undocumented and implicit, leading to a backlog in maintaining and protecting this knowledge and related data. Another crucial challenge is dependency on the founder—in many cases, the experience and knowledge crucial for success lie almost exclusively with the founder, complicating succession planning and continuity.

Sometimes, knowledge relevant to somebody's past success no longer plays an important role in future growth. Thus, promoting lifelong learning and ongoing knowledge updates are vital. Time constraints due to high workloads often prevent structured KT and the continuous scanning and monitoring of external sources, competitive intelligence, and trend scouting to keep knowledge up-to-date. Small teams focused on more urgent tasks struggle to maintain this crucial activity.

However, absorptive capacity—the ability to absorb and integrate new external knowledge—is essential for fast-growing SMEs. Overcoming the "not-invented-here" syndrome, especially among long-serving employees requires conscious and reflective unlearning.

Communication challenges arise from using technical terms with multiple meanings or miscommunication between different specialist disciplines. The abundance of communication channels mentioned in Sect. 2.3 complicates the selection of the appropriate medium for KT.

The shift towards remote work and Work 4.0 has made informal KT more difficult, necessitating new etiquette and training for effective communication. Diverse perspectives and motivations regarding KT among employees must be aligned to foster a culture where knowledge sharing is the norm. All employees should be sensitised and trained to transfer knowledge in a targeted, compact, and comprehensible manner.

Greater spatial distribution of teams necessitates innovative collaboration solutions, such as sponsorship concepts.

Efficient KT also requires eliminating waste in the process, which is similar to lean management principles. Redundant document storage often leads to inconsistencies in content, emphasising the need for redundancy-free storage solutions.

Fast-growing SMEs face additional challenges related to human factors and organisational changes. Knowledge hiding, potential conflicts, and the need to maintain a consistent knowledge culture are significant issues. Quickly committing all employees to the knowledge management strategy is key, aiming to cultivate open-minded and agile employees.

Adapting and changing organisational structures presents further hurdles, including increasing specialisation, new interfaces, and silos, often leading to more regulation, formalisation, and new areas of responsibility. Solutions include on-the-job training and job rotation to ensure employees are well-prepared for their evolving roles.

Business processes must also adapt to allocate the resources effectively. Increasing automation and digitalisation requires introducing new collaboration tools, skill management systems, and e-learning platforms. These technological advancements must be integrated seamlessly to enhance productivity and efficiency but often face issues where relevant implicit knowledge is not accessible to employees. Early technological transformation, particularly addressing technological megatrends like generative AI, is essential to increase productivity and maintain competitive advantage.

Overall, these challenges necessitate extensive change management efforts and a continuous search for an optimal organisational structure that avoids extreme solutions, ensuring sustained growth and adaptability in fast-growing SMEs. Mitigating these challenges through structured knowledge management has positive effects on the innovative strength, growth, and profitability of SMEs (Gomezelj Omerzel, 2019; Hassan & Raziq, 2019).

The following section will present exemplary solutions and best practices implemented by a fast-growing SME to address those challenges.

3 Case Study: Company Background and Context

3.1 *Company Overview*

The company in this case study provides digital education and training solutions for the healthcare sector. The company's cloud-based platform offers a range of e-learning and compliance management solutions and a broad library of accredited courses covering a wide range of healthcare topics. Part of its sales pitch is supporting digital transformation through additional consulting and service offerings. The diverse team of over 50 employees includes subject matter experts from the healthcare field, quality managers, project leaders, and engineers. Following the definition of the European Commission for small- and medium-sized enterprises (European Commission, 2024), the company recently crossed the threshold to be classified as a medium-sized enterprise.

Despite potentially tremendous benefits from digital transformation, smaller-sized companies often lag in digital transformation (OECD, 2021). As the company in this case study offers a cloud-based product and supports its customers in digital transformation, it represents a modern, up-to-date version of the 99% of enterprises in the EU that are classified as small- or medium-sized enterprises.

3.2 *Market Overview*

The German healthcare market, one of Europe's largest, features a well-developed infrastructure and significant government investment, encompassing a wide range of services, including hospitals, outpatient care, and long-term care facilities. Several macroeconomic trends create uncertainty and volatility in the market.

- Germany's demographic shift towards an older population significantly increases the demand for healthcare services, particularly in geriatrics and chronic disease management. By 2035, those requiring care are projected to rise to 5.6 million (+14%) due to demographic aging (Deutscher Pflegetag, 2023).
- The adoption of digital health technologies and telemedicine is rising, driven by the need for efficient and effective care delivery. Additionally, managing emerging complexities in care, such as the effects of climate change on medication

efficacy, adds layers of difficulty to the healthcare system and requires specialised knowledge. Government policies significantly impact healthcare funding and investment in new technologies and infrastructure (Deutscher Pflegetag, 2023).

- Providers must navigate a complex regulatory environment that frequently changes while trying to enhance patient care and cost-efficiency. Healthcare expenditures increased from €415 billion in 2019 to €498 billion in 2022, highlighting the system's strain (Destatis, 2024). Critical shortages in the healthcare workforce, particularly in nursing, are evident, with current intake rates for nursing apprentices insufficient to meet future demands (Deutscher Pflegetag, 2023).

These trends mean that highly dynamic, complex, and uncertain knowledge must be continuously managed and transferred. While the company in this case study was able to successfully drive digital transformation in the market in the past, the above factors created a level of uncertainty that had to be addressed, thus requiring the company to adapt its processes, learn new skills as an organisation, and adapt KT methodologies.

3.3 Challenges Faced by the Organisation

The company faced notable challenges due to both internal and external changes. Internally, leadership transitions disrupted strategic direction and operational efficiency. Such changes often lead to the loss of important knowledge and require rapid adaptation. However, leadership changes also provided an opportunity for a cultural reset, celebrating and acknowledging past successes while opening the organisation to new ideas and processes.

The company's staff more than doubled in 3 years, creating challenges in effectively onboarding new employees, transferring the extensive experience of long-standing staff, and integrating fresh knowledge. Additionally, meeting customer demands, like ISO certifications and stringent cybersecurity requirements, added further complexity to operations. This growth required adapting processes to ensure seamless integration and maintain high service standards.

Intensifying market competition necessitated increased differentiation in customer engagement strategies and adapting core business processes. The company had to refine its market approach, emphasising unique value propositions and leveraging its strengths to remain competitive. Close collaboration with and support from its US parent company provided strategic advantages but also required effective management to align operational objectives with local needs.

Externally, evolving market dynamics necessitated continuous adaptation. The German healthcare market experienced shifts due to regulatory updates, technological advancements, and increasing demand for digital solutions in education and training. These changes required the company to remain agile and innovative to meet new market demands and maintain its competitive edge. This external pressure was compounded by the launch of new product lines aimed at expanding the serviceable addressable market, particularly in the areas of digital training, e-learning, and compliance solutions.

Moreover, the company faced challenges related to market engagement. Historically, there had been a strong focus on internal needs, sometimes resulting in insufficient market contact, and a lack of KT from external to internal sources. For SMEs, having a limited knowledge base due to size makes it crucial to network effectively and maintain ongoing access to external knowledge sources and carriers (Durst et al., 2023). This aspect is vital for sustaining innovation and competitiveness in a rapidly changing market environment, yet the company lacked structured processes for customer feedback beyond client care (e.g. no customer round tables or other formats for informal discussions with customers).

Despite positive tailwinds, with the lingering impacts of the COVID-19 pandemic increasing acceptance and reliance on e-learning solutions, the company's market approach was not fully adapted to capitalise on these opportunities. This indicated a need for strategic realignment to better capture market potential and drive growth.

In summary, the company had to navigate a complex interplay of internal transitions and external market shifts. Addressing these challenges required a multifaceted strategy encompassing process adaptation, enhanced market engagement, and continuous innovation. Efficient and effective knowledge management and transfer became crucial to preserving critical expertise, ensuring continuity, and fostering an environment conducive to innovation and long-term success, while preparing a solid basis for future growth.

4 Case Study: Multidimensional Assessment Applying "KM^4"

4.1 "KM^4": Goal Alignment

Effective knowledge management requires aligning a company's knowledge objectives with its vision and mission, particularly in SMEs where resources and formal structures may be limited. Appropriate normative, strategic, and operational knowledge goals must be derived to support medium and long-term growth goals. These goals guide knowledge management activities and ensure they contribute to the company's broader objectives.

The company in this case study had a clear vision and mission statement, but management only recently ensured proper documentation and communication of these statements. This documentation is crucial as it lays the foundation for deriving specific knowledge goals. An intellectual capital statement can be used to articulate these goals, ensuring that knowledge management efforts are systematically directed towards achieving them.

4.2 The "KM⁴" Shell Dimension: Environment–Organisation–Team–Individual

The shell dimension emphasises the seamless integration of external knowledge from the environment into the organisation, as well as a highly functional internal knowledge chain from the organisation (corporate memory) to teams and individuals (personal knowledge management) and vice versa (gradual knowledge transfer).

- **Environmental Context:** The company operates within a complex market environment shaped by recent policy reforms, increasing costs, and ongoing digital transformation. For example, hospital reform initiatives in Germany aimed at increasing efficiency and improving patient care have initiated new regulatory requirements and operational challenges. Such changes demand continuous external to internal KT, which worked well on an individual basis at the company, driven by highly engaged and motivated employees, but less so at an organisational level due to knowledge hiding and a lack of structured KT processes.

- The dynamic and complex market environment required institutionalised scanning and monitoring of external trends and the structured integration of knowledge fragments from different sources. The company reacted by creating the role of a regulatory analyst (monitoring external policy changes), increasing participation in industry events, and inviting customers to internal All-Hands meetings. This approach enabled the company to remain agile and responsive to external changes, leveraging external knowledge to drive internal improvements (Ackermann et al., 2020).
- **Organisational Structure:** The company implemented substantial structural changes in recent years, transitioning from a sales-oriented to a product-focused organisation. This shift required significant process adaptations to align with the new strategic direction. The company also experienced rapid growth, doubling its workforce within 3 years. Such growth necessitated effective onboarding processes and the integration of new skills and knowledge to sustain operational efficiency. A well-structured organisational framework is essential for supporting KT within teams. This includes clear documentation of processes, roles, and responsibilities, as well as robust mechanisms for capturing and disseminating knowledge across the organisation.
- **Team Dynamics:** The rapid expansion brought in fresh skills and perspectives from new employees. However, this influx of new talent also created challenges in KT within teams. Many teams have yet to achieve a high level of knowledge sharing and documentation, with some processes being outdated. This situation highlighted the need for robust KT mechanisms to ensure that both new and existing employees can effectively contribute to the organisation's goals. Effective team-based KT requires regular team meetings, collaborative tools, and informal knowledge-sharing sessions and involves fostering a culture of trust and mutual respect that encourages employees to share their knowledge freely.

- **Individual Dynamics:** One significant challenge was the departure of an experienced leader, which posed a risk of substantial knowledge loss. The new hire had to be trained quickly to fill this key role. This transition underscored the importance of effective KT processes to mitigate the impact of personnel changes on organisational continuity. Individuals must be equipped with knowledge management skills to organise, store, and retrieve information effectively. Training programs and resources should be available to help employees develop these skills, ensuring that knowledge is preserved but seamlessly transferred during personnel changes. The company achieved this goal by hiring a KT external advisor.

By assessing these four aspects of the Shell Model, the company identified gaps in its current KT practices and developed strategies to enhance knowledge sharing, both within teams and across the organisation. This supported the company's overall knowledge management objectives and can contribute to sustained growth and innovation.

4.3 The "KM^4" Process Dimension: Knowledge Work for Business Processes

The Process dimension focuses on the processes of knowledge usage, development, sharing, and retention. The following aspects are relevant

- **Success-Critical and Knowledge-Intensive Business Processes:** Success-critical business processes must be identified based on a clear strategy. These are typically the most time-intensive, relevant, and knowledge-intensive processes within the organisation. Applying the knowledge work cycle to these processes helps identify optimisation potential and supports process-oriented knowledge management.

- Specific examples of process adaptations during the transition from sales to a product organisation included restructuring workflows to focus more on product development and customer feedback, effectively adapting sales processes to transfer knowledge gained from external touchpoints to the product teams. This shift compelled changes in how knowledge was retained, captured, shared, and utilised across the company.
- **Knowledge Usage:** The company handled the challenge of a quickly changing market environment, had to continuously update its documentation, and apply relevant, new knowledge to adapting circumstances. Decentralised responsible parties in larger teams, such as wiki gardeners, were given regular time to update internal information based on expiration dates. This ensured that knowledge remained current and relevant, preventing the use of outdated practices and information. However, this approach did not work in smaller teams, where resources were particularly scarce.

- In this context, fostering a culture that encouraged unlearning outdated practices and embracing new knowledge was essential for maintaining relevance and competitiveness ("Knowledge Unlearning"). "We've always done it that way" should not be part of the guiding principles of an agile SME. Appreciative and conscious forgetting should be possible when employees retire, after completing of larger projects, and in response to intensive megatrends such as generative AI. Here, management needs to lead by example and can proactively foster "unlearning" through a culture of learning from mistakes.
- **Knowledge Development:** Training and onboarding programs for new employees, especially in leadership roles, were partially implemented to support knowledge development. The company followed a top-down approach, first training a new sales manager with external support, thus enabling him to transfer his knowledge to his team. The effectiveness of training programs is critical to ensuring new employees can quickly become productive and contribute to the organisation's goals.
- **Knowledge Sharing:** Active knowledge sharing, including KT, can be implemented through a positive knowledge culture, leadership role models, and employee target agreements. A positive knowledge culture encourages open communication and the sharing of expertise, which is imperative for innovation and continuous improvement and can overcome knowledge hiding. The company provided structured product townhalls, company all-hands, sales updates, and other open communication formats, as well as lunch meetings and brownbag sessions to facilitate formal and informal communication and collaboration.
- **Knowledge Retention:** Additionally, the company encountered the risk of organisational knowledge loss, mainly due to structural changes. To address this, the company had to implement incentives for departing employees to actively participate in KT activities. Such incentives facilitated the transfer of relevant knowledge and served as a tool for recognising and valuing the contributions of employees.

By assessing these aspects of the Process Dimension, companies can develop strategies to enhance knowledge usage, development, sharing, and retention, ultimately supporting their overall knowledge management objectives and contribute to sustained growth and innovation.

4.4 *The "KM^4" Iceberg Dimension: Technology for Knowledge Transfer*

4.4.1 IT Tools for Knowledge Transfer

The integration of IT tools plays a decisive role in facilitating KT within an organisation. However, the company in this case study often built processes around existing technology, leading to inefficiencies. For example, using a CRM system originally designed for a different market required significant process adaptations to reflect local market structures. This misalignment forced the team to restructure workflows to fit the technology, rather than allowing the technology to enhance existing processes.

The company also encountered difficulties in managing and accessing essential knowledge, particularly when handling tenders. The lack of a standardised knowledge management system in sales and product departments resulted in dispersed and loosely organised product information. This situation highlighted the need for a more cohesive approach to knowledge management.

Efforts were made to improve the technological infrastructure supporting KT. For instance, the content team responsible for creating e-learning modules developed internal training programs, including onboarding materials. These initiatives leveraged existing competencies and advanced technological support to streamline KT processes and improve efficiency.

Existing IT tools were already used for KT but required optimisation and expansion. Ideally, technology should be built around the processes, not the other way around ("technology follows processes"). IT solutions should be differentiated in terms of content, maintained and updated in a structured manner, and their functional potential used more intensively, which can be achieved through consistent employee training.

4.4.2 E-Learning Platform for Knowledge Transfer

The company started to leverage its in-house e-learning platform and content creation capabilities, originally developed for external clients, as a key tool for internal KT. The platform provided a structured and efficient means for disseminating knowledge across various departments. By using the same platform sold to clients, the company ensured that internal processes benefited from the same high-quality content and functionality offered in the market. Additionally, employees became power users of the platform, enhancing their engagement and proficiency with the core product.

The e-learning platform now plays a crucial role in keeping the sales team and other departments up to date on current topics such as new standards and regulations. This not only facilitates ongoing internal training but also offers significant competitive advantages. Unlike many other SMEs that lack such advanced tools, the company can maintain a high level of KT and staff training, ensuring that employees are always informed about the latest market requirements. Additionally, a team of specialised (e-)learning creators, primarily focused on developing content for customers, dedicates part of its resources to creating internal training materials. This dual-purpose approach supports the documentation, retention, and transfer of knowledge within the organisation, creating a symbiotic relationship between the company's market offerings and internal capabilities.

What truly sets this platform apart is a combination of its advanced features and how it is strategically utilised within the company. The platform includes a "Policies

& Procedures" document tracking system, training plans, onboarding tools, and gamification elements, which enhance user engagement and learning outcomes. These embedded functionalities make the platform not only a tool for external clients but also an integral part of the company's internal operations. By extensively using the platform for knowledge management, onboarding, and other internal processes, the organisation demonstrates its commitment to leveraging advanced technology for both internal efficiency and competitive market positioning.

Integrating the e-learning platform into daily operations for knowledge management, onboarding, and other internal (knowledge) processes increases its market value by demonstrating how it can effectively bridge knowledge gaps within the organisation. Despite its potential, internal usage of the e-learning platform needs to further increase. While some teams already utilise it extensively, other teams have yet to fully adopt it. Nevertheless, a holistic approach to e-learning and knowledge management illustrates how technology, when thoughtfully implemented, can become a cornerstone of organisational change and development. It underscores the importance of not just adopting new tools but fully integrating them into an organisation's operational DNA. An e-learning platform can be used not only for standardised specialist knowledge but also for transferring implicit experiential knowledge from important experts. Encouraging broader adoption of the platform across all departments can further enhance KT, support continuous learning, and ensure the retention of critical knowledge within the organisation.

4.4.3 Potentials of Generative AI for Knowledge Transfer

While the company from the case study already benefits from its internal e-learning platform, leveraging AI could bring further improvements (Alavi et al., 2024; Lanquillon & Schacht, 2023; Müller & Link, 2023). Generative AI can significantly enhance KT efficiency by reducing onboarding times and supporting various KT scenarios, such as AI-supported answering of questions through targeted questioning (pulling) and proactive knowledge sharing (pushing). Furthermore, AI can facilitate a knowledge marketplace by providing dialogue support for KT, acting as a knowledge broker, and aiding knowledge delivery by documenting new information for questioners and proactively retaining knowledge.

To implement these AI-driven scenarios, key steps include selecting and merging suitable databases, ensuring data is prepared for future use, providing adequate computing capacity, and training large language models. Developing simple man-machine interfaces and consistent prompt engineering is essential for effective and efficient user interaction and accurate outputs.

Introducing AI for KT also requires addressing several non-technical challenges. Building trust, safety, and acceptance of new tools and procedures is paramount. This can be achieved through transparent communication about AI's potential and limitations, consistent training to increase AI literacy, and providing quick, tangible successes during the implementation (see also Sect. 4.6). According to the Kano model, these aspects can be categorised into hygiene, performance, and enthusiasm factors (Kano et al., 1984).

Maintaining data and knowledge quality is essential and involves ensuring timeliness of information, preventing hallucinations and fake news, and being transparent about knowledge sources. Continuous improvement of learning outcomes should be prioritised. Data and knowledge protection is vital, requiring local management of training data and extended knowledge protection measures, as more knowledge is now explicitly stored.

The need for new roles, such as Chief AI Officer or Data Scientists, should be considered. Additionally, all managers should adopt the role of AI leader, and employees should become AI knowledge workers. Ethical considerations must also be addressed, including the potential dominance of AI in decision-making, job rationalisation, and liability issues in case of errors.

Introducing generative AI demands a holistic approach, addressing both technical and non-technical aspects comprehensively to maximise the benefits and mitigate risks. The digital transformation and implementation of AI in knowledge management has a profound impact on leadership and the corporate culture.

4.5 The "KM⁴" Iceberg Dimension: Impact on Leadership and Corporate Culture

4.5.1 Mindset and Motivation for Knowledge Sharing

The transitions at the company in this case study, driven by rapid growth and technological advancements, have significant implications for leadership requirements and the corporate knowledge-sharing culture. These changes highlight the importance of recognising past achievements while fostering an environment conducive to future innovations, a concept often referred to as knowledge leadership and knowledge transformation.

Researchers emphasise the vital role of trust in facilitating effective knowledge sharing and fostering organisational commitment. Studies by Curado and Vieira (2019) and Yasir and Majid (2017) demonstrate that trust positively impacts knowledge sharing and strengthens organisational commitment. Similarly, Al-Jabri and Al-Busaidi (2018) highlight that trust, among other factors, is central to inter-organisational knowledge transfer. In the context of the company, this means that building a trusting environment is crucial for both internal and external knowledge exchanges.

However, cultural factors such as job satisfaction, appreciation, and trust can only be increased over the medium to long term (Curado & Vieira, 2019; Yasir & Majid, 2017) but are fundamental for a positive knowledge-sharing culture and must be visibly practiced by managers, as knowledge sharing cannot occur without a basis of trust.

Effective change management involves information dissemination, participation, and qualification, while communicating the need for change, promoting willingness, and creating the necessary knowledge-sharing skills.

Motivation theories suggest that target agreements that include regular KT sessions or project reviews can incentivise employees to share knowledge. Additionally, monetary incentives, particularly performance-related pay, can supplement intrinsic motivation. Providing time and opportunities for knowledge sharing and recruiting employees who bring a knowledge-sharing mindset are also crucial measures.

In the early stages of developing a knowledge-sharing culture, directives can play a role in KT. While intrinsic motivation is the goal, the initial stages may require formal instructions to ensure participation. Managers should allocate realistic times for knowledge transfer, such as 1–2 h/week, and define the structure surrounding it (meetings, workshops, and IT tools). Designing the workplace to encourage knowledge transfer, e.g., with open office spaces and co-working areas, is also beneficial. Furthermore, the previous socialisation of employees and knowledge culture should be taken into account for realistic planning.

Managers play a vital role in fostering a culture of knowledge sharing. They should view themselves as knowledge managers, systematically planning, implementing, checking, and optimising knowledge management solutions through a Plan-Do-Check-Act (PDCA) cycle. Agile, digital, and knowledge leadership are essential, with managers acting as agile knowledge coaches, driving digitalisation with high standards and a clear vision. This often requires a fundamental mindset shift (Ackermann et al., 2020).

Appreciative communication, especially towards older employees and their experiential knowledge, forms the basis for effective KT. Managers should lead by example, sharing and documenting their own knowledge and maintaining an open-door policy. Addressing special topics in knowledge management, including skills shortages, onboarding, employee retention, lifelong learning, and peer reviews, ensures comprehensive coverage of KT needs.

Collaboration with the HR department is important, particularly for learning and onboarding activities. This partnership ensures that KT activities are well-coordinated and effectively implemented across the organisation.

In summary, fostering a culture of knowledge sharing requires a multifaceted approach involving trust, motivation, appreciative leadership, and strategic planning. Managers must lead by example, integrating knowledge transfer into everyday practices and ensuring alignment with broader organisational goals. Through these efforts, companies can navigate its transitions effectively, maintaining competitiveness and fostering innovation. However, such transitions require effective change management. In the following section, the key factors for successful change management in creating awareness for knowledge management will be specified.

4.5.2 Change Management for Knowledge Transfer

Creating a culture and mindset that proactively fosters knowledge management and deeply ingrains knowledge transfer within an organisation requires effective change management practices. These practices must drive the organisation towards this goal by focusing on informing stakeholders, encouraging their participation, and ensuring their qualifications.

4.5.2.1 Information About the Benefits of Knowledge Transfer

Communicating the need for KT involves a well-thought-out internal communication concept, including a clear vision for KT within the company. The communication should be consciously planned, consistently implemented, and optimised in an agile manner.

The benefits of knowledge transfer should be clearly reflected, authentic, and concrete, avoiding generic statements. Information should be repeated regularly to reinforce the message and ensure it reaches the target audience. Multiple communication channels, both synchronous and asynchronous, such as email, intranet, videos, and social media formats, should be utilised to reach diverse audiences.

Information must be differentiated to highlight benefits for both the organisation and individuals. The success of the organisation should be linked to concrete benefits in daily work. Tailoring messages to different target groups, such as back-office staff, engineers, sales employees, and content staff, ensures relevance and engagement. Centralised information can be disseminated through the intranet, while decentralised information can be shared during regular team meetings.

Illustrative methods like use cases and storytelling should be employed to demonstrate the benefits of KT with concrete business scenarios. The arguments should be specific and quantifiable, such as "KT reduces training times by 30%", to make the benefits tangible and convincing.

4.5.2.2 Participation in Knowledge Transfer Solutions

Creating the ability for KT requires targeted training for different groups within the organisation. Top management should participate in strategic workshops to understand the relevance of KT for success and gain tools for strategic planning. Managers need interactive training sessions to learn organisational methods, IT tools, and techniques for motivating knowledge sharing.

Employees should be trained in comprehensible and efficient knowledge transfer methods and use on-board resources and modern IT tools through seminars and role plays. Special roles such as knowledge managers and process facilitators require detailed training from external trainers to lead internal sessions effectively.

E-learning can be combined with classroom training to create blended and hybrid learning environments, offering flexibility in terms of time and location. Microlearning modules, such as 3-min explanatory videos, can target specific skills gaps, enable individualised learning, and promote lifelong learning.

By implementing these change management practices, the organisation can foster a culture of proactive knowledge management. Informing, engaging, and training stakeholders ensures that KT becomes a deeply ingrained part of the organisational culture, supporting continuous learning, innovation, and sustained competitiveness.

4.6 The KM[4] Time Dimension: Knowledge Transfer and Digital Transformation

Implementing state-of-the-art knowledge management in an SME requires significant time and resources, similar to any digital transformation project. Digital transformation typically happens in several stages (AWS, 2024):

1. **Status quo:** The organisation operates as usual without recognising the need for digital transformation.
2. **Active:** Awareness of the need for digital transformation exists, with uncoordinated implementation of solutions in different areas.
3. **Intention:** Digital leaders begin addressing the topic, testing solutions, and promoting a culture of innovation.
4. **Strategic:** A strategic roadmap is created, and the departments are prepared to collaborate.
5. **Targeted:** The strategy is implemented by a cross-departmental team through digital projects and infrastructure.
6. **Customisation:** Digital transformation projects become the "new normal", and the organisation has a framework to meet future customer requirements.

By applying these general stages to KT and specifying them, the organisation can achieve the following KT maturity levels:

1. **Unstructured Knowledge** Transfer: Uses basic IT tools like e-mail.
2. **Structured Processes:** General awareness within the departments but lacks organisational integration.
3. **Conscious Use of Collaboration Tools:** KT happens intrinsically motivated. Initial measures are in place to inform, involve, and qualify knowledge workers.
4. **Continuous Knowledge Transfer:** Based on knowledge objectives, using modern collaboration tools. There are structured measures for information, participation, and qualification of knowledge workers.
5. **AI-Supported Knowledge Transfer:** Agile, self-directed, and intrinsically motivated processes based on normative, strategic, and operational knowledge objectives, continuously and with learning loops ("Knowledge sharing is power") (Ackermann et al., 2020).

To reach the highest maturity level, scheduling should incorporate agile sprints, allowing rapid feedback through interim solutions executed in cycles of approximately 3 months. Additionally, consolidation phases should be built to institutionalise and reflect on new solutions, preventing continuous dynamics and omnipresent change. Depending on the socialisation of the employees and the demands of the new maturity level, each should be reached within a maximum of 2 years. Overall, knowledge transformation can extend over four to six stages of maturity (including consolidation phases) and thus can potentially take up to 10 years, requiring patience and perseverance.

Quick wins, vital for early momentum, and realistic expectations management significantly enhance the success of change initiatives (Kotter, 2011). Early accomplishments help build momentum and demonstrate the benefits of knowledge transfer, encouraging broader participation and commitment. Employees typically expect to see positive effects within 3–6 months.

Initial efforts should focus on current, relevant topics that are easily comprehensible and immediately applicable. Introducing new, simple methods that are innovative yet easy to use without requiring new software can facilitate quick adoption and impact. Engaging motivated user groups and setting measurable goals, like reducing duplication of work or saving time, provides clear evidence of success, which can positively influence potential sceptics

Setting measurable goals is essential. Quantifiable objectives, such as minimising work or saving time in business processes, provide clear indicators of success. Effective communication of these early wins is crucial to maintaining motivation and engagement, ensuring a smooth transition towards a proactive knowledge management and transfer culture. For instance, adding a 15-min knowledge café to a regular meeting can create a platform for ongoing knowledge sharing and highlight successes regularly.

By focusing on quick wins and realistic planning, the organisation can effectively manage this transition, delivering immediate benefits while building a sustainable foundation for continuous improvement and long-term success. This concludes our holistic recommendations on digital transformation for KT in SMEs.

5 Conclusion

5.1 Findings

This paper has explored how a medium-sized, rapidly growing company can successfully implement KT solutions in a dynamic environment. Addressing the critical KT challenges that fast-growing SMEs face, such as organisational knowledge loss and knowledge hiding, requires a multifaceted approach that integrates strategic planning, advanced technologies, and effective change management practices. Through this analysis, the paper contributes practical insights how businesses can navigate knowledge management challenges while accelerating their growth and innovation pathways, providing a model for other organisations facing similar challenges. The KM^4 model by Müller (2022) provides a structured framework for assessing and improving knowledge management practices across the Shell, Process, Level, and Time dimensions. The insights gained from this study provide a practical framework for other organisations facing similar challenges, illustrating how to effectively manage KT in a rapidly changing environment.

Key findings reveal that fast-growing SMEs face significant KT challenges, including the risk of knowledge loss due to employee turnover, overcoming resistance to knowledge sharing, and integrating new knowledge during rapid expansion. These challenges are amplified by the limited resources typical of SMEs, necessitating a strategic approach to knowledge management that aligns with the company's vision and mission. Implementing knowledge management tools and creating robust processes for knowledge usage, development, retention, and sharing, especially during leadership transitions and market volatility, is crucial. Tailored training programs, continuous feedback mechanisms, and fostering a positive knowledge-sharing culture are essential components of knowledge management activities, which must closely link critical business processes and organisational goals.

Existing IT resources and AI-driven processes play a vital role in optimising KT and enhancing absorptive capacity, as demonstrated by the case study's in-house e-learning platform, which supports continuous training and knowledge dissemination. This platform enables efficient dissemination of knowledge, supports continuous training, and offers a competitive advantage by keeping employees up to date with industry standards and regulations. However, other SMEs need to review which other cost-efficient tools are available internally, as they do not always have access to a sophisticated learning platform. SMEs can implement scalable KT strategies by focusing on quick wins, setting measurable goals, and leveraging motivated user groups to drive engagement and ensure long-term success.

5.2 Research Limitations and Discussion

The limitations of this case study include the need for further empirical validation of the evidence-based knowledge transfer recommendations and correlations. Additional studies with representative groups of SMEs are needed to substantiate the methods, motivation for knowledge sharing, and transformation time.

Moreover, the case study is limited in its representativeness. The company examined, characterised by a digital-first corporate culture and active in a dynamic growth market, may not reflect the typical SME. The unique conditions of this company might limit the applicability and transferability of the findings to other contexts.

Lastly, the rapid evolution of generative AI technology is a significant factor. As AI continues to advance, the selection and efficacy of IT solutions for knowledge management will likely change, impacting the long-term applicability of the current findings.

These limitations suggest several areas for future research, including broader empirical studies, exploration of different organisational contexts, and continuous evaluation of emerging technologies in knowledge management.

5.3 *Outlook for Further Research*

According to Durst et al. (2024), knowledge management in SMEs has established itself over the last decade as a field of research constantly being developed. The following topics in particular should be given greater focus (Durst et al., 2024), which is certainly confirmed by the present case study:

- The links between knowledge transfer and the impact of current megatrends such as digitalisation, generative AI, Work 4.0, demographic change and sustainability in particular, as well as agility, risk management and strategic flexibility in general, need to be examined more closely (Ackermann et al., 2020).
- The importance of continuously updating knowledge, which is changing faster and faster due to the VUCA world, as well as the access to affordable digital tools supporting knowledge transfer, needs to be assessed.
- Given demographic change and especially the retirement of the baby boomers, the need to retain the experiential knowledge of long-standing experts is becoming increasingly important, which has to be linked to conscious and reflected unlearning and requires further research.
- Risk management regarding cyber and hacker attacks and industrial espionage is still underestimated, particularly among SMEs, especially with more documented competitive knowledge, and requires in-depth analysis.
- Empirical analyses to measure performance are challenging due to multifactorial relationships, numerous soft factors, and the delayed appearance of effects.

Further specific recommendations for the future development of knowledge transfer in SMEs are explained by Anand et al. (2021) (area of science) and Biloslavo and Lombardi (2021) (area of application). SMEs form a very important basis of the German economy but are often more susceptible or less resilient to crises and challenging events. Knowledge transfer transformation is an important puzzle piece that makes SMEs even more robust.

References

Ackermann, B., Krancher, O., North, K., Schildknecht, K., & Schorta, S. (2020). *Erfolgreicher Wissenstransfer in agilen Organisationen: Hintergrund—Methodik—Fallbeispiele* (2nd ed.). Springer Gabler Verlag.

Alavi, M., et al. (2024). A knowledge management perspective of generative artificial intelligence. *Journal of the Association for Information Systems, 25*(1), 1–12.

Al-Jabri, H., & Al-Busaidi, K. A. (2018). Inter-organisational knowledge transfer in Omani SMEs: influencing factors. *VINE Journal of Information and Knowledge Management Systems, 48*(3), 333–351. https://doi.org/10.1108/VJIKMS-10-2017-0069

Almus, M. (2000). *What characterises a fast growing firm?* Centre for European Economic Research (ZEW).

Anand, A., Muskat, B., Creed, A., Zutshi, A., & Csepregi, A. (2021). Knowledge sharing, knowledge transfer and SMEs: Evolution, antecedents, outcomes and directions. *Personnel Review, 50*(9), 1873–1893. https://doi.org/10.1108/PR-05-2020-0372

AWS. (2024). *Was ist die digitale Transformation?—Was sind die verschiedenen Phasen der digitalen Transformation?* Retrieved July 26, 2024, from https://aws.amazon.com/de/what-is/digital-transformation/

Biloslavo, R., & Lombardi, R. (2021). Knowledge transferring and small and medium enterprise's (SME's) effectiveness: Emerging insights and future directions. *Business Process Management Journal, 27*(6), 1747–1774. https://doi.org/10.1108/BPMJ-10-2020-0441

Curado, C., & Vieira, S. (2019). Trust, knowledge sharing and organisational commitment in SMEs. *Personnel Review, 48*(6), 1449–1468. https://doi.org/10.1108/PR-03-2018-0094

Davenport, T. H., & Prusak, L. (1998). *Working knowledge: How organisations manage what they know*. Harvard Business Review Press.

Deloitte Insights. (2021). *The new knowledge management—The human factor activates the collective intelligence*. Retrieved July 26, 2024, from https://www2.deloitte.com/content/dam/insights/articles/emea103993_the-new-knowledge-management/DI_The-new-knowledge-management.pdf

Destatis. (2024). *Ergebnis 23611-0001*. Retrieved July 26, 2024, from https://www-genesis.destatis.de/genesis/online?operation=abruftabelleBearbeiten&levelindex=1&levelid=1721755089387&auswahloperation=abruftabelleAuspraegungAuswaehlen&auswahlverzeichnis=ordnungsstruktur&auswahlziel=werteabruf&code=23611-0001&auswahltext=&werteabruf=starten#abreadcrumb

Deutscher Pflegetag. (2023). *Aktuelle Zahlen und Fakten zur Pflege in Deutschland*. Retrieved July 26, 2024, from https://www.deutscher-pflegetag.de/_Resources/Persistent/d6ac53e6fd4a604584b5b2a6195540a092f9c0b2/DeutscherPflegetag2023_Factsheet_Pflege.pdf

Durst, S., & Zieba, M. (2019). Mapping knowledge risks: Towards a better understanding of knowledge management. *Knowledge Management Research & Practice, 17*(1), 1–13.

Durst, S., Edvardsson, I. R., & Foli, S. (2023). Knowledge management in SMEs: A follow-up literature review. *Journal of Knowledge Management, 27*(11), 25–58. https://doi.org/10.1108/JKM-04-2022-0325

Durst, S., Foli, S., & Edvardsson, I. R. (2024). A systematic literature review on knowledge management in SMEs: Current trends and future directions. *Management Review Quarterly, 74*, 263–288. https://doi.org/10.1007/s11301-022-00299-0

European Commission. (2024). *SME definition*. Retrieved July 26, 2024, from https://single--market-economy.ec.europa.eu/smes/sme-fundamentals/sme-definition_en

Gomezelj Omerzel, D. (2019, April). The impact of knowledge management on SME growth and profitability: A structural equation modelling study. *International Journal of Banking, Economics and Finance, 3*(4), 1–16.

Hassan, N., & Raziq, A. (2019). Effects of knowledge management practices on innovation in SMEs. *Management Science Letters, 9*, 997–1008.

Kano, N., Seraku, N., Takahashi, F., & Tsuji, S. (1984). Attractive quality and must-be quality. *Journal of the Japanese Society for Quality Control, 41*, 39–48.

Kotter, J. P. (2011). *Leading Change—Wie Sie Ihr Unternehmen in acht Schritten erfolgreich verändern*. Vahlen.

Lanquillon, C., & Schacht, S. (Hrsg.) (2023). *Knowledge Science – Fallstudien: Wie mit Künstlicher Intelligenz die Wissenssicherung und -nutzung im Unternehmen unterstützt wird*. Springer.

Müller, M. (2022). *Wissensmanagement klipp & klar*. Springer Gabler.

Müller, M., & Link, J. (2023). Smart Expert Debriefing. In C. Lanquillon & S. Schacht (Eds.), *Knowledge Science—Fallstudien: Wie mit Künstlicher Intelligenz die Wissenssicherung und -nutzung im Unternehmen unterstützt wird* (pp. 109–147). Springer.

Nonaka, I., & Takeuchi, H. (2019). *The wise company: How companies create continuous innovation*. Oxford University Press.

North, K. (2021). *Wissensorientierte Unternehmensführung: Wissensmanagement im digitalen Wandel* (7th ed.). Springer Gabler Verlag.

OECD. (2021). *The digital transformation of SMEs*. OECD Studies on SMEs and Entrepreneurship, OECD Publishing. https://doi.org/10.1787/bdb9256a-en

Offergelt, F., Spörrle, M., & Moser, K. (2020). Warum Wissen in Organisationen zurückgehalten wird. *Psychologische Rundschau, 71*(2), 143–146.

Probst, G., Raub, S., & Romhardt, K. (2012). *Wissen managen: Wie Unternehmen ihre wertvollste Ressource optimal nutzen* (7th ed.). Springer Gabler Verlag.

Robbins, S. P., & Judge, T. A. (2023). *Organisational behavior, global edition* (19th ed.). Pearson Verlag.

Yasir, M., & Majid, A. (2017). Impact of knowledge management enablers on knowledge sharing: Is trust a missing link in SMEs of emerging economies? *World Journal of Entrepreneurship, Management and Sustainable Development, 13*(1), 16–33. https://doi.org/10.1108/WJEMSD-02-2016-0010

Adrian Thiessen currently serves as the Managing Director of Relias Learning GmbH, bringing extensive experience in strategic growth and digital transformation in the healthcare sector. Under his leadership, Relias Learning GmbH has expanded its digital solutions across healthcare and social service sectors from a pure eLearning provider to a comprehensive compliance and knowledge management platform, broadening its impact and market reach. Adrian holds an MBA from the University of St. Gallen and has completed an Executive Program at INSEAD. His earlier positions include significant roles in financial management and consulting services, primarily in the healthcare sector.

Michael Müller has been a professor of Organisation and Management, particularly Knowledge Management in the Bachelor of Business Administration and Master Applied Artificial Intelligence and Digital Transformation at Ansbach University of Applied Sciences since 2012. As an entry-level research professor, he is working on the topic of Smart Expert Debriefing, the digitalisation, automation and support of processes for knowledge retention and onboarding using methods of Generative Artificial Intelligence. For over 30 years, Prof. Dr. Michael Müller has helped SMEs document expert knowledge with knowledge maps to address demographic change. He also focuses on change management and has authored several publications, including the Springer Gabler book "Wissensmanagement klipp & klar".

Integrating Competence Development and Knowledge Management on the Strategic and Operational Level: A Holistic Approach Towards the New Learning Organisation

Markus Will, Katrin Singer-Coudoux, Maria Kretschmer, Ronald Orth, and Henry Nicolai Buxmann

Abstract In today's rapidly evolving digital landscape, organisations must align new technological possibilities—especially those stemming from Artificial Intelligence—with their overarching business strategies and day-to-day operations. This alignment requires ongoing adaptations to functional strategies, structures, systems, and business processes, which in turn demands learning at individual, group, and organisational levels. One effective method to support these learning processes is through the strategic management and development of competences. Such programmes, derived from overall company strategy, must be integrated into human resources and personnel development approaches to ensure employees acquire the necessary skills within their specific working contexts. Concurrently, organisations must systematically manage and facilitate the creation, retention, and transfer of knowledge across all levels, employing methods like Business Process Oriented Knowledge Management. Integrating these operational approaches with the business strategy helps organisations remain agile in the face of constant market and technological changes.

This paper explores various organisational learning concepts and proposes a comprehensive model of the "new learning organisation". Drawing on broad practical experience in competence development and knowledge management, it offers real-world examples of integrating strategic and operational measures. Finally, it outlines a synergetic framework that interlinks both competence development and knowledge management to foster a more effective overall learning organisation.

Keywords Digital transformation · Competence development · Knowledge management · Organisational learning · Learning organisation

---

M. Will (✉) · K. Singer-Coudoux · M. Kretschmer · R. Orth · H. N. Buxmann
Fraunhofer Institute for Production Systems and Design Technology IPK, Berlin, Germany
e-mail: markus.will@ipk.fraunhofer.de; katrin.singer@ipk.fraunhofer.de; maria.kretschmer@ipk.fraunhofer.de; ronald.orth@ipk.fraunhofer.de; henry.nicolai.buxmann@ipk.fraunhofer.de

K. Bodrožić-Brnić et al. (eds.), *Digital Transformation in Knowledge Transfer*, Digital Transformation and Innovation,
https://doi.org/10.1007/978-3-032-07329-7_3

1 Introduction

Founded in 1997, the Competence Centre Knowledge Management (CCWM) at the Fraunhofer Institute for Production Systems and Design Technology (IPK) combines expertise in strategic and operational Knowledge Management (KM), Competence Development (CD), and Organisational Learning (OL). The convergence of these fields, driven by both theoretical developments and practical applications, is particularly pertinent in the context of digital transformation.

In today's rapidly evolving business landscape, continuous adaptation to technological advancements and changing market demands is crucial for organisational success. By strategically incorporating digital technologies, cultivating digital skills, and fostering a culture of innovation and adaptability, businesses can enhance their competitiveness, unlock growth opportunities, and strengthen resilience in the face of evolving landscapes (Hokmabadi et al., 2024). Hence, the ability to learn and adapt becomes a vital component of organisational resilience and competitiveness.

This contribution explores the intersection of competence development, knowledge management, and organisational learning within the context of digital transformation. Traditionally viewed as separate domains, CD, KM, and OL are increasingly recognised as interconnected elements essential for fostering a responsive and innovative organisational culture. In this context, the past decade has seen the development of a close relationship between KM and OL, as well as several related disciplines (Fai Pun & Nathai-Balkissoon, 2011). As Simatupang and White (1998, p. 778) commented, "learning, knowledge and action cannot separate from organisational learning".

The integration of these elements thus supports the creation of learning organisations. A learning organisation, as defined by Senge (1990), is one that facilitates the learning of all its members and continuously transforms itself. This concept underscores the importance of systemic thinking and collective learning in achieving long-term success. In the digital age, this requires a cohesive approach that integrates strategic and operational perspectives, aligns KM with CD initiatives, and addresses new learning at the individual, team, and organisational levels.

Against this background, the main research question of this contribution is: How can knowledge management, competence development, and organisational learning be conceptually and practically integrated to form a cohesive framework in the context of digital transformation?

To answer this research question, this paper aims to develop a comprehensive model for a "New Learning Organisation" by addressing three key perspectives:

1. Integration of strategic and operational perspectives: Examining how strategic and operational management perspectives can be aligned to support organisational goals.
2. Integration of knowledge management and competence development: Creating synergies between knowledge management and competence development to enhance learning and adaptability in the context of digital transformation.

3. Integration of knowledge and learning processes at multiple levels: Addressing the process of learning at the individual, team, and organisational levels.

2 The Learning Organisation in the Context of Digital Transformation

2.1 Introduction of the Learning Organisation

In the ever-evolving business landscape, organisations must continuously adapt and innovate to remain competitive, leading to the concept of the learning organisation. Senge's (1990) influential book *The Fifth Discipline* advanced this paradigm, emphasising continuous learning, adaptability, and systemic thinking. Senge identified five essential disciplines for a learning organisation: personal mastery, mental models, shared vision, team learning, and systems thinking, which together form a cohesive framework for organisational development.

A learning organisation is one that consistently acquires new knowledge, adapts its activities based on this knowledge, and pursues competitive advantage through ongoing improvement. The focus is on creating a culture that promotes continuous learning, collaboration, and transformation. As organisations embrace this model, they become more capable of anticipating and responding to changes in their environment, making them more adaptable and resilient in the long run (Senge, 1990).

According to Ludwig (2024), terms like "organisational learning" and "learning organisation" are often used interchangeably but have distinct meanings.

Organisational learning refers to the process by which an organisation improves its ability to respond to external and internal challenges through the acquisition, sharing, and application of knowledge. Geißler and Heidsiek (2010) define organisational learning as a change in the organisation's problem-solving potential through effective adaptation to its environment and changing conditions. It occurs at multiple levels—value creation, management, and personnel development—and integrates knowledge and learning processes at the individual, team, and organisational levels (Mynarek et al., 2021).

While individual learning through corporate education and development measures is necessary for organisational growth, it is insufficient on its own. For true organisational learning to occur, there must be relational integration, where knowledge is shared across teams and departments, and learning is aligned with the organisation's broader goals. Organisational learning thus enables an organisation to make informed decisions and improve its processes, but it is primarily concerned with how an organisation learns and adapts (Geißler & Heidsiek, 2010).

Moreover, organisational learning can be divided into single-loop and double-loop learning. Single-loop learning improves efficiency by detecting and correcting errors within existing norms, while double-loop learning challenges and changes underlying assumptions and practices (Argyris & Schön, 1978). This type of learning is particularly important in dynamic environments where assumptions and norms must be regularly re-evaluated to stay competitive.

Conversely a *learning organisation* represents a more holistic and systemic concept. Rather than merely focusing on the processes that enable knowledge acquisition and problem-solving, a learning organisation embeds learning into the very fabric of the organisation's culture and operations. It fosters an environment where learning is not just a means to solve immediate problems, but a continuous, proactive activity that permeates all levels of the organisation. The goal is not just to react to changes, but to anticipate them and drive innovation. While organisational learning is primarily concerned with improving efficiency and problem-solving, a learning organisation seeks to transform the entire organisational culture to prioritise adaptability, collaboration, and long-term sustainability (Senge, 1990).

Digital transformation acts as both a catalyst and a tool for learning organisations, integrating strategic and operational management with knowledge management and competence development, enabling organisations to respond to and learn from changes.

2.2 How Digital Transformation Influences the Learning Organisation

Digital transformation has emerged as a pivotal factor in the evolution of learning organisations. The integration of digital technologies into all facets of business operations fundamentally alters how organisations function and deliver value to customers (Urbinati et al., 2020). This compels learning organisations to embrace new work and learning approaches to remain competitive.

The concept of New Work emphasises flexibility, autonomy, and collaboration, reshaping organisational structures and workflows to be more agile and responsive to change (Singer-Coudoux et al., 2023). This paradigm shift necessitates fostering an environment where continuous learning and development are integral to the organisational culture. Complementing this, New Learning leverages digital tools and platforms to facilitate continuous, on-demand learning experiences tailored to individual needs and organisational goals (Foelsing & Schmitz, 2021).

Digital transformation requires rethinking strategies and practices in learning organisations. The integration of technologies such as artificial intelligence (AI) or machine learning offers unprecedented opportunities for organisational learning and knowledge management (Pai et al., 2022; Sturm et al., 2021). These technologies enable organisations to "build ways to collect, retrieve and transmit the data in a more effective way, impactfully and rapidly. They can manipulate raw data and generate higher information, which potentially contributes to new and effective ways of developing and exploiting knowledge" (Pai et al., 2022, p. 7060).

Further, the capacity for organisational learning is one of the most crucial attributes for ensuring an organisation's sustainability and progressive development

(Ludwig, 2024). Digital transformation is not only a significant driver of these changes but also a critical means of shaping these processes.

The rapid acceleration of innovation cycles shifts in customer behaviour regarding networking and communication, evolving employee expectations for greater involvement in design processes and flexibility due to generational value shifts (Generation Y and Z), and new developments in Artificial Intelligence all increase the pressure on organisations and their employees to adapt quickly. Traditional, lengthy personnel development measures are no longer sufficient to meet these demands (Ludwig, 2024).

The cultural shift driven by digital transformation requires a new learning culture, one that emphasises learning through work processes more than ever before (Elbe, 2020). Senge's (1990) concept of the learning organisation provides a framework for this new learning culture within organisations. The speed of change will continue to increase, driven by market, societal, and technological changes. Learning and the associated learning culture are critical skills for organisations and their employees to navigate these change processes positively. This new learning culture, driven by digital transformation, is also essential to meet the growing knowledge needs of both employees and customers. Fluid knowledge management within a supportive learning environment is fundamental to successful change and innovation processes (Ludwig & Wolf, 2021).

The concept of the learning organisation bridges organisational learning with the tradition of organisational development and is therefore highly relevant (Geißler & Heidsiek, 2010), especially today. Digital transformation profoundly impacts learning organisations by compelling them to adopt New Work methods and learning paradigms. Integrating advanced technologies can facilitate continuous learning and adaptive knowledge management, which are essential for maintaining competitive advantage in a rapidly changing digital environment. The interplay between organisational culture and learning culture highlights the importance of fostering a supportive environment to ensure successful adaptation and innovation.

2.3 Companies' Readiness for Digital Transformation: Results of a Global Survey

To assess how prepared organisations are for digital transformation, a global comprehensive Digital Transformation Assessment (DTA) study was conducted by the Fraunhofer IPK (Kidschun et al., 2021; Orth et al., Forthcoming). Covering the period from June 2020 to December 2022, the study evaluated companies across seven critical dimensions: Corporate Strategy, Leadership & Corporate Culture, Organisation & Processes, Employees & Competences, Technology, Products & Services, and Supply Chain & Network. An overview of the average Global Digital Transformation Performance by Dimension is presented in Fig. 1. It revealed significant gaps regarding digital transformation in several areas, particularly in the dimension of *Employees & Competences*. Notably, 66% of companies reported having a weak or only moderate performance in this area. This gap highlights a substantial challenge in the development and utilisation of digital competences among employees.

Analysing the dimension of *Employees & Competences* in more detail, as presented in Fig. 2, the study pointed out that most companies do not systematically employ digital solutions for HR management tasks. Furthermore, 40% of the companies do not regularly evaluate their employees' digital competencies, and only 41% believe that their employees' personal skills are sufficiently developed to meet the challenges posed by digitalisation. Additionally, only 25% of the survey participants stated that they regularly assess the digital competences of their employees to respond to the changing requirements through digitalisation.

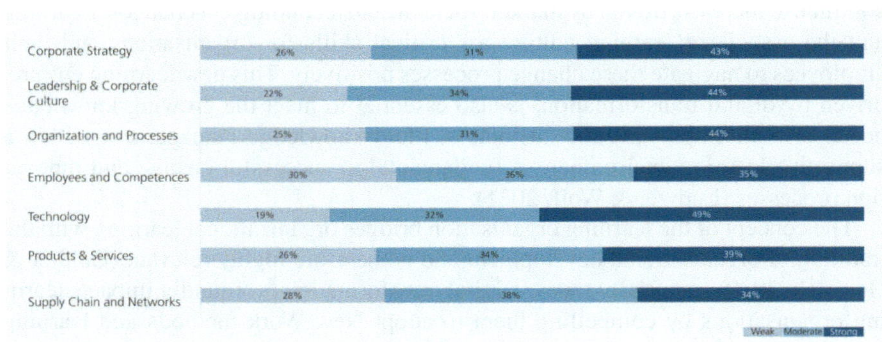

Fig. 1 Average global digital transformation performance by dimension (Orth et al., Forthcoming)

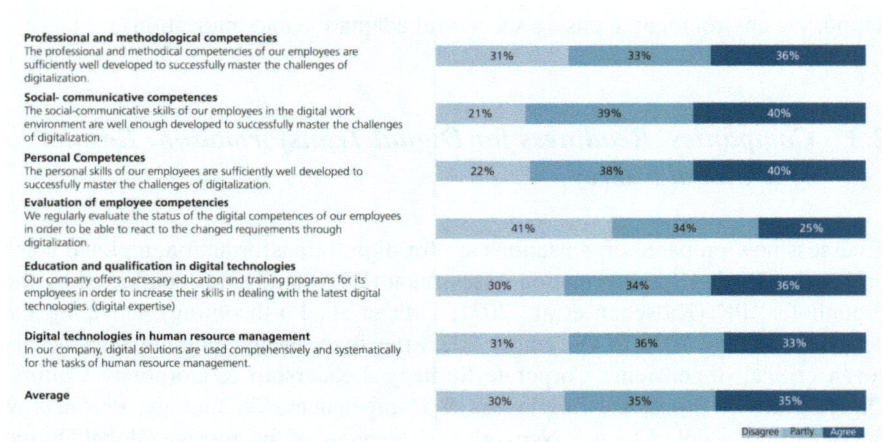

Fig. 2 Average global digital transformation performance of employees and competences (Orth et al., forthcoming)

These findings underscore the need for learning organisations to prioritise the development of digital competences among their workforce. Failure to systematically assess and enhance these competences can hinder an organisation's ability to adapt to and leverage new technologies effectively. For learning organisations, this means that significant efforts must be directed towards creating a structured and continuous digital competency development.

Another finding from the DTA study pertains to the dimension of Organisation & Processes. Less than 40% of companies regularly review their business processes for potential continuous improvement using digital technologies. This reveals a substantial gap in the adoption of digital tools for process optimisation. For learning organisations, this implies a need to embed continuous improvement practices within their operational strategies, leveraging digital technologies to drive efficiency and innovation. Regularly reviewing and updating business processes through digital tools can help organisations remain agile and responsive to changing market conditions.

3 The New Learning Organisation: A Conceptual Model

Learning organisations are mainly characterised by constantly adapting themselves to changing conditions in the business environment, i.e., the market and its evolving demands as well as new (political, economic, social, technological) trends and changing stakeholders' requirements. This process is particularly important due to the challenges of digital transformation, as previously highlighted. The process requires constant feedback loops from the external environment to the internal organisation, either with the aim of optimising the current business operations (single-loop-learning) or with the aim of adapting the organisation's strategic goals and the underlying assumptions (double-loop-learning).

To illustrate this basic concept of the learning organisation, a practical example of a typical production company might help: A decline of demand in one existing market segment may have led to an underperformance in terms of sales and revenue (actual business results do not meet the target). Instead of intensifying marketing and sales efforts and launching respective actions, like a marketing campaign for existing customers of this current market segment (example for single-loop-learning), the company may have analysed structural changes in the business environment, e.g., changes in consumers' behaviour due to social factors, and concludes that the demand in the present market segment will continue to decline, while the demand in another, newly arising market segment is strongly growing. Hence, the company decides to shift the strategic focus to this new market segment, adapting the strategic goals and revenue targets for the different market segments and launches a strategic action, e.g., a specific marketing campaign to attract new customers in the newly defined market segment, incorporating the changed consumers' behaviour in the overall business and market strategy (example for double-loop-learning).

To support these organisational learning processes, the organisational competences and the constituting individual competences of the organisation's staff play a vital role. It requires technical, professional, and social skills to execute current and future business processes and align them with the existing strategy. Besides, it also demands competences to analyse performance gaps and derive the right optimisation measures to boost productivity, as well as the ability to question and revise the overall business strategy in the light of new trends, such as emerging opportunities and/or threats in the market. Consistent competence management needs to address these requirements in a systematic and strategic manner and should lead to the implementation of respective targeted competence development programmes and measures.

The other important concept which is frequently mentioned when it comes to operationalising the learning organisation in practice is the concept of knowledge management (Ludwig, 2024). In general, KM aims to provide existing knowledge inside the organisation to the right place at the right point in time, i.e., to the employee who needs to carry out a concrete task within a certain business process. Furthermore, creating new knowledge derived from strategic or operational requirements and its dissemination inside the organisation is a second important function of KM, especially in the context of the "New Learning Organisation" as well as the need for constant monitoring of the internal operations and the external environment. KM systems, procedures, and tools should therefore serve and support these two main functions: (a) targeted distribution of existing knowledge for re-use inside the organisation to optimise productivity, and (b) creation and dissemination of new knowledge for adapting operational procedures and/or (parts of) the organisation's strategy to respond actively to changes or new trends in the business environment.

Summarising these aspects and combining them with the general logic of strategic management, the following model gives an overview of the main elements that need to be integrated in a successful learning organisation:

As shown in Fig. 3, the organisation is operating in a business environment bearing certain trends that can constitute opportunities and threats and has set company-specific goals to achieve certain business results by executing defined actions and implementing and executing specific business processes. By comparing the actual business results achieved with the targets set by the overall strategic goals, specific deviations, i.e., performance gaps are detected. By interpreting these gaps, the organisation gains insights that may lead to adapting the operational procedures with the aim to optimise the performance under the given goals and targets (single-loop-learning) and/or lead to adapting the business strategy itself (double-loop-learning), considering current trends in the business environment.

However, the "New Learning Organisation" (NLO) does not stop here, but consequently aligns these changes in the business strategy and the business processes with the internal Competence Development and Knowledge Management, among other support functions of the organisation. When it comes to organisational learning and knowledge processes, three levels of learning have to be distinguished

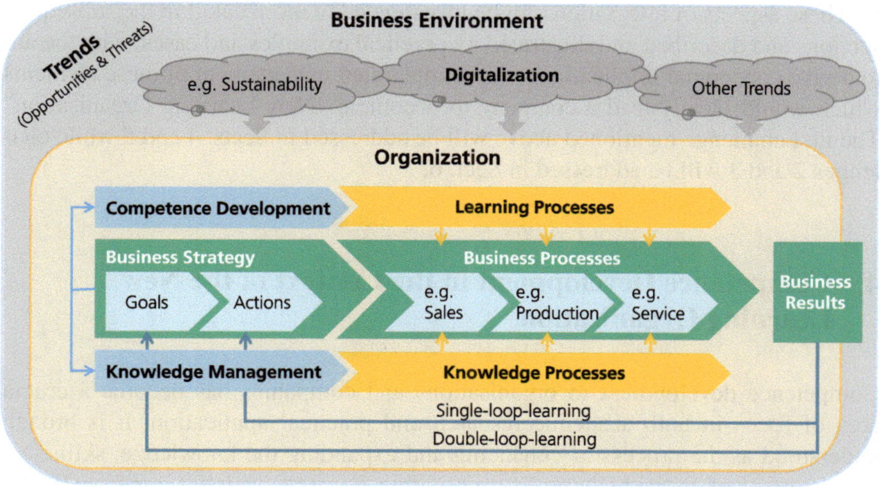

Fig. 3 Conceptual model of the new learning organisation (Fraunhofer IPK)

according to the current literature reviews on organisational learning (Mynarek et al., 2021): individual, team and organisation level. The NLO ideally analyses the implications of certain changes in the business model and the business strategy not only for the business core processes, but also for the necessary learning and knowledge processes on the organisational level, and consequently, derives respective strategies for the competence development and knowledge management to support the (adapted) business strategy on the individual and team level by providing the required competences and knowledge needed to perform the operational business processes successfully under the new strategic conditions and goals.

Following the logic of this conceptual model, some first requirements for the operationalisation of a "New Learning Organisation" into management practices can be derived. With the focus on the learning and knowledge-related processes, the main challenge is to integrate the different key elements of the New Learning Organisation according to the model:

1. Integration of the strategic and operational management perspective, i.e.:
   (a) Integration of business strategy with a competence development strategy (as part of the HR strategy and function) and a KM strategy.
   (b) Integration and transfer of learning processes into the operational business processes.
   (c) Integration and transfer of knowledge in the operational business processes.
2. Integration of knowledge management and competence development strategies and business processes.
3. Integration of knowledge and learning processes on the levels of individual, team, and organisation.

These aspects of integration will be investigated in more detail in the subsequent sections and described and illustrated by practical examples and cases, with the aim to derive conceptual implications for the integrated management of these elements, which would ideally lead a company to become a "New Learning Organisation". The first challenge mentioned above will be addressed in Sects. 4 and 5 while challenges 2 and 3 will be addressed in Sect. 6.

4 Competence Development in the Context of the New Learning Organisation

Competence development in organisations and companies has become a crucial area of focus in both academic research and practical application. It is broadly understood as the process of enhancing and expanding the knowledge, skills, and competences of individuals and teams within an organisational context (Becker 1964). The concept of competence development is closely linked to the idea of the learning organisation, where continuous improvement and adaptation are key to maintaining competitive advantage (Pasban & Nojedeh, 2016). In this context, competence is typically defined as the capability of a person or an organisation to reach specific achievements (Boyatzis, 1982; Mulder, 2014). This encompasses not only knowledge and skills but also attitudes, values, and the ability to apply these in specific work contexts (competence). The authors emphasise the importance of aligning operative individual competence development with strategic organisational objectives and the need for a systemic approach that integrates both individual and organisational perspectives.

4.1 Distinction of Knowledge, Skills, and Competence

In order to achieve this objective, a terminology in the context of a learning process was initially developed, that is aligned with the definitions of the European Qualifications Framework (EQF) and follows a staircase structure (see Fig. 4).

The European Commission et al. (2019) define *Knowledge* as the outcome of the assimilation of information through learning. *Knowledge* is the body of facts, principles, theories, and practices that are related to a field of work or study. *Skill* refers to the ability to apply knowledge and use know-how to complete tasks and solve problems. *Competence* relates to the proven ability to use knowledge, skills, personal, social, and/or methodological abilities in different professional and personal contexts. While sometimes used as synonyms, the terms *skill* and *competence* can be distinguished according to their scope: The term *skill* refers typically to the use of methods or instruments in a particular setting and in relation to defined tasks. The term *competence* is broader and refers typically to the ability of a person—facing

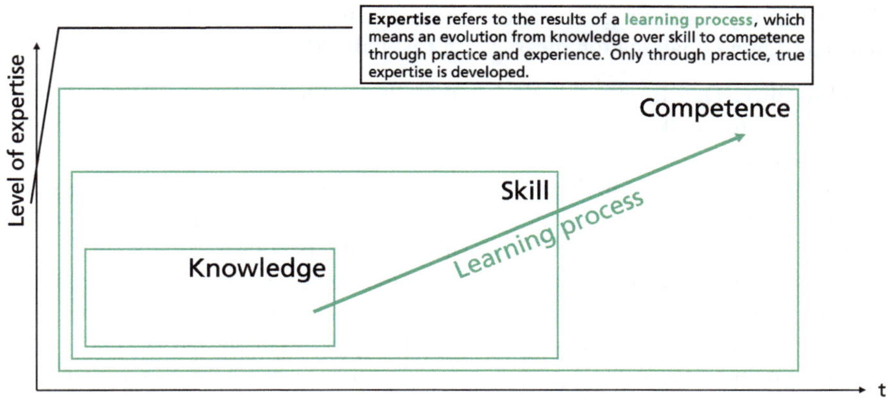

Fig. 4 Terminology based on the learning process

new situations and unforeseen challenges—to use and apply knowledge and skills in an independent and self-directed way (European Commission et al., 2019).

Expertise refers to the results of a learning process, which means an evolution from *knowledge* through *skill* to *competence* through practice and experience over time. According to Bornewasser et al. (2018) it is crucial to distinguish between practice and habit formation, as only practice involves reflexive training processes that lead to the mastery of tasks or sequences of tasks. Practice aims for behaviour that is appropriate to the situation and thus varied by using knowledge, skills, and abilities. Only through practice, true expertise is developed (Bornewasser et al., 2018).

4.2 Competence Development in the Context of Digital Transformation

The advancing digitalisation is changing job profiles and demanding new skills from employees. According to a study by the World Economic Forum, almost half of all employees will need new or different professional skills in the next four years (World Economic Forum, 2020). Furthermore, the findings of the DTA survey reinforce the necessity for a new learning organisation to prioritise the advancement of their employees' digital competences and to implement structured assessments and continuous training programmes to guarantee adaptability to emerging technologies (cf. Sect. 2.3).

However, digitalisation not only places new skill requirements on employees but also enables new forms and ways of learning. Currently, a paradigm shift is emerging in occupational training, referred to as New Learning (Foelsing & Schmitz, 2021). Thus, digitalisation opens up new possibilities for employee qualification.

The following continuing education trends should be considered by companies when designing qualification measures (Orth et al., 2024):

- Flexibility: Due to technological and environmental dynamics, learning must occur more quickly and flexibly. Informal, self-organised learning is gaining importance.
- Individual and Self-Directed Learning: In self-directed learning, learners and their needs are the focus. They take an active role in the learning process, which requires a high degree of self-responsibility and reflection.
- Microlearning: According to a study on continuing education trends, microlearning is one of the most relevant digital learning forms of the coming years, with 92% agreement among continuing education experts (mmb, 2019).
- New Learning Formats: Digital media enable new learning formats such as podcasts, e-learnings, virtual reality, or augmented reality.

The learning platform developed in the research project KIRA Pro takes these trends into account and generates adaptive and personalised learning paths for employees with the help of an AI-based assistance system and will be discussed in the following section.

4.3 Systematic Competence Development in SMEs

For a systematic approach to competence development in companies, it is crucial to integrate the strategic objectives of the company with the operational training of individual employees. The following innovative multi-step procedure developed by Fraunhofer IPK addresses the growing need for strategy-led competence development within SMEs and has been effectively evaluated in SMEs of the manufacturing sector during the KIRA Pro research project, demonstrating its relevance and applicability in promoting growth and aligning employee competencies with organisational objectives.

(1) Initially, the present situation of the whole company is thoroughly examined through a *strategy check* (an in-depth analysis of existing processes, success factors, and strategic objectives) and *digital transformation assessment,* as discussed above in Sect. 2.3. The findings from this analysis provide a robust foundation for the subsequent steps such as (2) the development of competence-oriented role profiles, (3) the development and conduction of skill-gap-assessments, and (4) the generation of personalised learning paths.

A significant outcome of following this procedure is establishing a new career framework through the development of role profiles. This framework allows for a clear definition and structuring of the necessary skills to meet strategic objectives, providing clarity for applying SMEs.

In order to describe specific role profiles at the SME application partners, a simple, easy-to-understand competency classification with the following five dimensions has proven successful (Orth et al., 2023a, 2023b): (1) professional and methodological competences, (2) personal and activity-oriented competences, (3) social competences, (4) leadership competences. These are complemented by (5) digital competences. Figure 5 highlights that the centre of the skill radar is the role, i.e., a specific function or position that exists in an organisation, here a sales manager. Such a role can also be equated with a profession. However, it is important to be aware that, especially in SMEs, certain roles combine multiple responsibilities within a single position. For example, the first assistant to the management may also handle human resources tasks. The middle ring shows the specific, process-oriented tasks associated with the analysed role, which at the same time ensures integration into the business processes. Figure 5 shows, for example, tasks of the sales manager in the context of stakeholder identification and communication as well as bidding. The outer ring distinguishes between the five different competency dimensions required to perform the activities according to competency classification by Fraunhofer IPK.

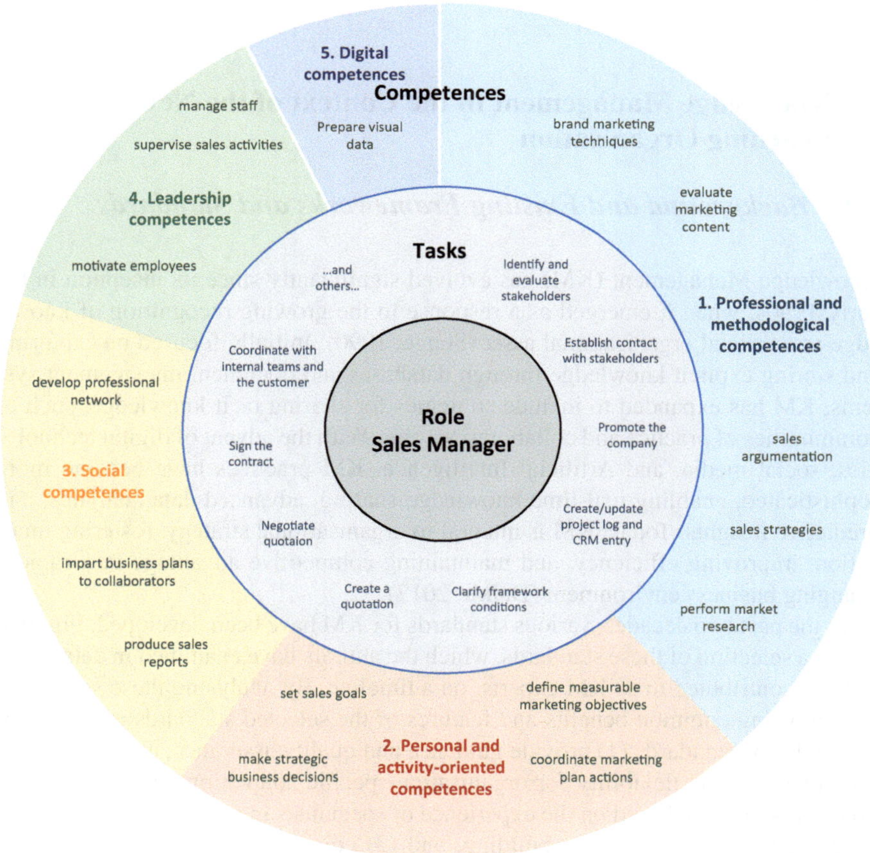

Fig. 5 Skill radar for linking tasks and competences for the exemplary role of a sales manager

With the help of these specific role profiles, clear and comparable target and actual profiles can now be generated by applying SMEs. A key component of this approach is the *skills gap assessment*, which identifies gaps between current (actual profile) and required skills (target profile). This assessment enables the creation of personalised learning paths and the selection of appropriate learning units tailored to individual employees' development opportunities and needs.

Central to the KIRA Pro research project is a learning path generator. This AI-driven tool assesses and matches four crucial parameters:

- the company's strategic requirements (target profiles)
- employees' personal development goals (preferences)
- their current skill levels (actual profiles)
- the available training options (available learning content)

By doing so, it generates customised learning paths that are tailored to the individual needs, abilities, and progress of each learner, as well as aligned with the corporate strategy, enhancing the overall performance and competitiveness of SMEs.

5 Knowledge Management in the Context of the New Learning Organisation

5.1 Background and Existing Frameworks and Standards

Knowledge Management (KM) has evolved significantly since its inception in the early 1990s, when it emerged as a response to the growing recognition of knowledge as a critical organisational asset (Senge, 1990). Initially focused on capturing and storing explicit knowledge through databases and document management systems, KM has expanded to include strategies for sharing tacit knowledge, such as communities of practice and collaborative tools. With the advent of digital technologies, social media, and Artificial Intelligence, KM practices have become more sophisticated, enabling real-time knowledge sharing, advanced data analytics, and predictive insights. Today, KM is integral to organisational strategy, fostering innovation, improving efficiency, and maintaining competitive advantage in a rapidly changing business environment (Dalkir, 2017).

In the past two decades, various standards for KM have been developed. Figure 6 shows a selection of these standards, which the authors have examined in detail and/or have contributed to as KM experts, on a timeline. By analysing these standards, the following common benefits and features of the selected standards can be summarised: The standards (1) provide guidance and quality assurance, and at the same time they provide flexibility for organisation-specific adaptation and implementation of KM, (2) are based on the experience of specialists in the subject area and are developed through consensus-building, and (3) contain procedure models and/or recommendations for implementation and continuous improvement of KM. In

Fig. 6 Selected KM standards and specifications (author's illustration)

addition, some of the standards address the specifics of small and medium-sized organisations in particular (Orth et al., 2023a, 2023b).

In the context of the New Learning Organisation and the integrated approach discussed above, two main requirements for a successful KM can be derived from the analysis of the shown KM standards: (1) KM should be integrated into the business processes, i.e. the operational routines of the organisation and the employees' daily work procedures (CEN, 2004; DIN SPEC 91281:2012-04) and (2) KM should be connected to the company's business strategy, i.e. KM objectives should contribute to the overall business objectives of the company (DIN SPEC 91443:2021-08; ISO 30401:2018-11).

In order to develop recommendations for a suitable procedure for KM implementation in a company, the proven structure from the CEN guide and DIN SPEC 91281 can be used as a basis for a practical guideline. According to this procedural model, a distinction is made between five phases of implementation. In addition, the aspect of change management as an accompanying programme is emphasised as particularly important (Fig. 7).

The scope and objectives of the five phases of this KM cycle can be summarised as follows:

- Phase A: Initiation of a KM project/initiative:

- In this phase you clarify the goals of the project and put together the project team.
- Phase B: Analysis:
- By using suitable diagnostic tools you identify strengths and weaknesses in the handling of knowledge in your organisation.
- Phase C: Development:
- You define requirements, assess the feasibility of selected KM solutions for your organisation and plan their implementation.
- Phase D: Implementation:
- In this phase you implement selected KM solutions in your organisation and, if necessary, conduct accompanying user training.
- Phase E: Evaluation/Sustainability:

- In this phase you carefully evaluate the project and plan measures to further anchor knowledge management in your organisation.

In the following section, a practical case of a KM implementation based on this procedural model is illustrated with the aim to demonstrate how the two main requirements of strategic and operational integration were achieved in a concrete organisation.

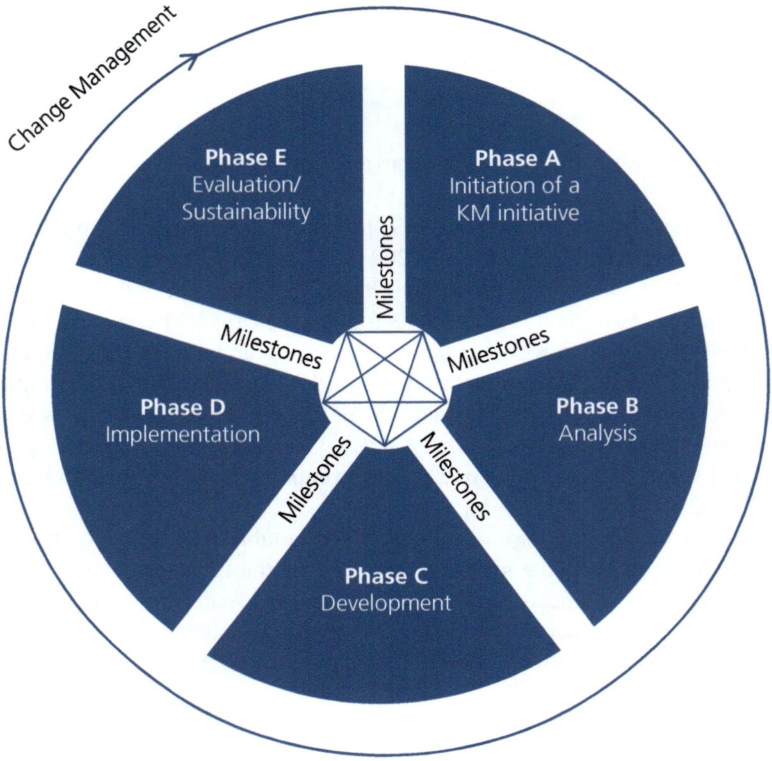

Fig. 7 KM cycle as basis for systematic planning and implementation. (Source: adapted from CEN and DIN SPEC)

5.2 Case Study: Implementing KM in an Innovation Institute on Strategic and Operational Level

In 2020, a Brazilian innovation institute with approx. 100 employees, developing and executing applied research and technological development for industrial customers in the area of biotechnology, decided to implement a customised KM system and asked the Competence Centre Knowledge Management at Fraunhofer IPK for methodological support (Will et al., 2022). This KM project followed the logic of a KM guideline which was developed on the basis of the procedural model, derived from the KM standards, as described above (Orth et al., 2023a, 2023b).

As a first step (Phase A), strategic KM goals were derived from the overall business objectives of the institute by the initial project team, including the institute's top management and the responsible KM project managers. The existing strategy map of the institute (Kohl et al., 2020) served as a starting point for the discussion with the KM team to link the detected demand for KM to the overall business objectives. As a result, the following initial set of strategic KM objectives for the institute was derived:

- Develop our business and boost revenue growth by (1) combining knowledge and fostering synergies between our technological platforms and research groups, (2) creating new application ideas to trigger demand ("tech. push projects"), (3) leveraging our potential to produce breakthrough innovations with higher added value for our customers.
- Increase efficiency and reduce costs by (1) using existing knowledge systematically to avoid double work, (2) re-using newly created knowledge and transferring competences from one project to the next application context, (3) retaining crucial knowledge when key people leave, and (4) increasing speed in administrative processes and harmonise procedures.
- Strengthen our brand and reputation by (1) building up new knowledge and showcasing pre-work to reduce R&D risks for our clients, (2) showing "hidden" competences to build confidence and to communicate the "unknown", (3) institutionalising reputation through professional handling of knowledge.

This systematic derivation of KM goals from the business objectives is crucial for integrating KM into the overall business strategy and for closing the KM cycle by measuring the success in the last phase of the project.

In a second step of the KM project (Phase B), an in-depth KM analysis was conducted, using the well-proven methodology of Business Process Oriented Knowledge Management (Mertins et al., 2016). First, the online survey "KM Fitness Check" (Kohl, 2016), was used for a broad assessment of the status quo of the handling of knowledge in the four KM core activities: (1) create knowledge, (2) store knowledge, (3) distribute knowledge, and (4) apply knowledge, as well as in the three main framework conditions for KM: (1) people, (2) organisation, and (3) technology. As a second analysis instrument, process-oriented analysis workshops (Orth & Mertins, 2016) were conducted to deepen the analysis with a team of selected representatives for each of the three core business processes of the institute: (1) Marketing & Sales, (2) R&D & Innovation, and (3) Project Management & Service Delivery.

With more than 100 employees participating in the online survey and the subsequent results workshop, the attention and involvement of the future KM users could be triggered which is one crucial element for a successful KM implementation (Finke & Will, 2005). Additionally, the process-oriented analysis workshops supported the integration of possible KM solutions into the operational business by defining clear improvements on the level of the core business processes to be achieved by improving specific weaknesses in the handling of knowledge inside the respective business process.

In the third step of this KM initiative (Phase C and D), suitable KM solutions were derived from the analysis results and two main action programmes were defined for implementation. The first set of KM solutions to be implemented in this first phase of the KM initiative comprised (1) competence maps to detect crucial competences and risks of losing critical knowledge, (2) a "Knowledge Hub 2.0" as an internal corporate portal to share knowledge among the research teams, and (3) a lessons learned procedure with guidelines for project review meetings and for storing the learnings from concluded projects to be re-used in new projects (Will et al., 2023).

The action programmes, defining the steps and intermediate results to implement these KM solutions, were structured in a way that the connection to the initially defined KM goals and the detected gaps of the KM analysis could be shown and communicated easily. Again, this approach plays a crucial role for the integration of KM into the business operations and the overall business strategy.

In the fourth step (Phase E), the KM team used impact maps to determine the desired improvements by the chosen KM solutions and defined suitable KPIs to measure the success of the KM implementation and the achievement of the initially defined KM goals. The impact maps not only help to make the connections between the strategic and operational KM perspective more visible but are suitable instruments to evaluate the contribution of KM on a qualitative way and as a basis for organisational storytelling. As shown in Fig. 8, the KM actions—bundled into meaningful action programmes—have to be aligned and geared towards operational improvements on the level of the value-adding business processes of the organisation, which shall directly help to achieve the strategic KM goals, which, in return, would generate a positive impact on the aspired business objectives (see step 1 above).

This generic impact map (Fig. 8) helps to be able to constantly refer back to the overall objectives in the later course of KM initiatives. This also makes it possible to examine the impact of individual KM measures, align them, and derive appropriate controlling instruments for the implementation and operational phases. KPIs or other instruments for measuring success then form the bridge between individual KM actions, the improvements they achieve at the operational level and the higher-level organisational goals.

Against this background, the innovation institute in Brazil has developed its monitoring system, which, on the one hand, uses the strategic KM objectives as a

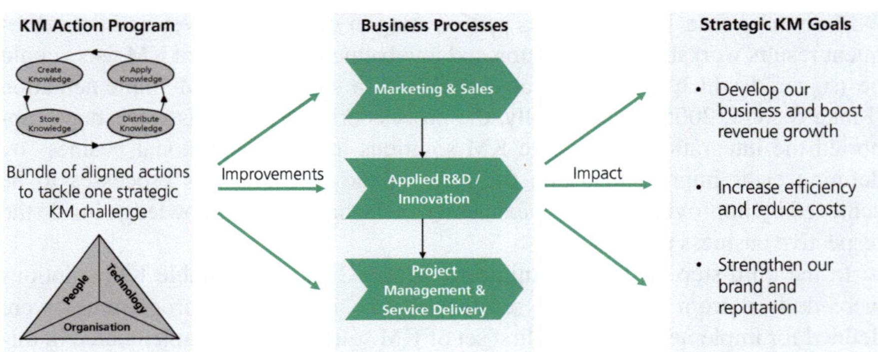

Fig. 8 Linking "KM actions" to "operational business processes" and "strategic KM goals"

Table 1 Example of a KPI-based KM monitoring system

KM core activity	Key performance indicators (KPI)	Strategic KM objective
Create knowledge	# average number of ideas generated per semester # external/internal events with participation of the technical team	Strengthen our brand and reputation
Store knowledge	# lessons learnt reports % of average competences on "alert" # filed patents # scientific articles, book chapters or conference presentations	Strengthen our Brand and reputation
Distribute knowledge	# average number of accesses to the KM platform per month # average number of requests for access to information/folders # average number of searches on the KM platform per month % of lessons learnt meetings in relation to total projects completed	Increase efficiency and reduce costs
Apply knowledge	R$ revenue % Financial sustainability	Develop our business and boost revenue growth

reference, and on the other hand, takes into account the KM core activities (create, store, distribute, and apply knowledge). This makes it possible to monitor selected KM actions continuously, define target values and monitor the actual status with an initial set of indicators that may be expanded and adjusted along the further development of the KM system (Table 1).

Following the logic of this framework consequently from the beginning of a KM project, as outlined in this case study, supports both requirements, the integration of KM into the operational business processes, and the clear contribution of KM to the overall business strategy of the organisation. This logic then serves as a basis for various levels of assessment and evaluation of a KM project and ensures the sustainable anchoring of KM in the organisation on the operational and strategic level.

6 Integration of Competence Development and Knowledge Management in Practice

In the previous sections, we introduced Competence Development and Knowledge Management in the "New Learning Organisation", demonstrating their integration with business operations and strategy through practical examples. Section 3 emphasised KM and CD's role in addressing performance gaps in the NLO's dynamic environment through adjustments in operations or strategy. Section 4 presented the "Skill Radar" to define roles and assess skill gaps for tailored learning paths. Section

5 focused on integrating KM into daily processes using a five-phase implementation model aligned with business objectives.

The question now is how systematic competence development can be aligned and integrated with a suitable knowledge management strategy, considering the individual, team, and organisation level.

To establish a direct connection between CD and KM, the overall competence development strategy must address the necessary methodological, technical and digital competences required for utilising specific KM tools and instruments. This approach should be incorporated into adequate training programmes to empower employees to effectively use KM tools for successful implementation and operation. The broadly discussed "media literacy" and the respective competence to assess validity and credibility of knowledge sources can be understood as one example of these "KM competences". Furthermore, KM also underpins CD, since it provides the foundational basis for developing expertise. Effective KM practices facilitate the accumulation and dissemination of knowledge, which are essential components in the advancement of both individual and organisational expertise. In the next conceptual step, the new learning organisation precisely aligns the necessary role-based and task-oriented knowledge, skills, and competences with appropriate learning formats for personal development. Additionally, it determines how content should be distributed and shared through specific instruments and channels within the KM system during daily business processes.

To illustrate this somewhat abstract concept, consider the following simple practical example: Think of a production engineer with a formal degree in mechanical engineering (basic qualification). As an employee of a production company, he has already completed several in-house training courses on CNC and other machine control technologies used in the company's production facilities (competence development). Now, he needs to fulfil the concrete task of installing a new CNC machine in one factory, for which he needs certain information and very specific knowledge to integrate it into the existing production line. For this purpose, he uses the company's best practice portal. He finds an installation guideline for this machine from another company production site and gets in contact with the responsible engineer colleague at this site to clarify a last question in order to complete his task successfully (knowledge management).

This example shows the ideal interplay between CD and KM in practical application. KM can be interpreted in this context as the system that provides any missing "piece of knowledge" within a given competence set (acquired by competence development) at the right place and at the right point in time, i.e., to the employee who needs this knowledge to complete a concrete task as part of a specific business process. At the same time, the example also shows that these specific "pieces of knowledge" can only be absorbed and integrated into the existing skills.

Here, we also find a first point of differentiation between the concepts of KM and CD—which, in general, can be seen as the two sides of the same coin: Applicable knowledge. While competence development is primarily linked to the person (carrying out a certain role in a certain business context) with a given competence set (actual or desired status), knowledge management is primarily linked to a given specific task when it actually occurs in practice. Furthermore, a KM system is usually designed to disseminate new content rather quickly in previously installed structures and instruments, while well-designed training formats typically take a certain time of development and production. Depending on the urgency of a certain knowledge demand, specific competence development solutions may simply take too long in practice (Ludwig, 2024).

As a first orientation for the strategic and operational alignment of CD and KM in practice, the following table gives an overview of the key differences between the two concepts regarding a set of basic features. Based on this first rough distinction, indications for the suitable approach depending on the type of knowledge or learning process to be supported can be derived (Table 2).

However, this contrast between the two concepts and their respective alignment, based on these distinctions, is not sufficient for a fully integrated approach and to reach the ideal stage of the NWO.

While this is true for conceptual and systematic integration, a certain implicit convergence of the two concepts can be observed in practice, at least on the level of formats. In the context of the "New Learning" approaches discussed above, many companies are including "knowledge pills", e.g., short instructive videos, manuals, checklists, or similar formats to support concrete tasks on an on-demand basis, on their learning platforms as part of their competence development programmes. These elements may also be seen as part of a KM system in other organisations. Conversely, many companies are already integrating short web-based trainings and further learning formats into their KM systems, which may also be understood as elements of a competence development programme in another context or organisation.

Hence, it can be concluded that KM and CD are converging technically and didactically, but most organisations still separate them, lacking an integrated strategic approach. Integrating these functions could be a step towards a New Learning Organisation, promoting a unified view on CD and KM.

Finally, integrating knowledge and learning processes across the three levels of organisational learning is essential. While the previous discussion focused on the strategic organisational level and the individual employee's role, it is important to examine how individual knowledge and learning processes connect with team dynamics and the organisation as a whole, particularly in complex business environments and social learning formats that emphasise collective knowledge creation.

Table 2 Distinction "features" between "competence development" and "knowledge management"

Feature	Competence development	Knowledge management
Content	More general	More specific
Main function	Prepares the role to carry out certain tasks	Provides knowledge at the point of demand (when the task occurs)
Time to application	Medium- to long-term	Short- to medium-term
Form of usage	Off-the-job	On-the-job

Therefore, this interlinking element between the individual and organisational level is essential in the existing research and conceptual models of organisational learning on the three levels (Akinci & Sadler-Smith, 2019; Crossan et al., 1999; Mynarek et al., 2021). Table 3 summarises the specific forms of knowledge creation (cognition) and learning on the three levels, where the processes on the higher systemic level are a product of the process on the lower level(s), with the possibility of the individual level also directly influencing the organisational level—but typically emerging on the team level first.

The knowledge and learning processes described in Table 3 refer to the so-called "feed-forward" loops, i.e., the process from the individual to the organisation level. According to Akinci and Sadler-Smith (2019) and Crossan et al. (1999), feedback loops in the other direction, from organisation to individual level, are also relevant organisational learning processes, in which new institutionalised knowledge is being reinterpreted and reinternalised on the team and individual level.

Summarising these initial considerations, and answering the research question: "How can knowledge management, competence development, and organisational learning be conceptually and practically integrated to form a cohesive framework in the context of digital transformation?", it can be stated that the interplay of competence development and knowledge management in the context of the "New Learning Organisation" should be aligned on the level of (1) strategic requirements (role and competence profiles derived from business model and strategy), (2) organisational responsibility, (3) content and (4) technical and didactic formats. Furthermore, when developing concrete CD programmes and KM systems in practice, the different types of knowledge and learning processes on the three levels of organisational learning should be considered and supported systematically by specific methods, formats and tools most suitable for each level.

Table 3 Organisational learning as a dynamic process on three levels (based on Crossan et al., 1999, Akinci & Sadler-Smith, 2019)

Level of organisational learning	Knowledge processes (supported by KM)	Learning processes (supported by CD)
Individual	Creating new knowledge by "intuiting"	Adapting individual behaviour by application of new skills and experiences
Team	Integrating new knowledge by externalising and interpreting in social interaction	Adapting team behaviour by transforming collective intuition and experiences
Organisation	Institutionalising new knowledge by adapting organisational routines, structures, etc.	Adapting organisational behaviour by adjusting goals, strategies, business processes, etc.

7 Conclusion and Outlook

This research contribution emphasises the critical need for integrating Competence Development, Knowledge Management, and Organisational Learning to create a comprehensive framework for a "New Learning Organisation" capable of continuous learning and adaptability overcoming the challenges of the digital transformation. It highlights the foundational role of Senge's (1990) five disciplines in fostering a learning organisation and underscores how digital transformation necessitates new work and learning paradigms, driven by advanced technologies such as AI and big data analytics. The findings from the Digital Transformation Assessment reveal significant gaps in employee competence evaluation and the use of digital solutions in HR management, underscoring the urgency for structured digital competency development. Hence, a conceptual model of the NLO that integrates strategic and operational management with CD and KM, aligning business strategies with learning and knowledge processes to support business objectives is provided. Practical examples, such as the KIRA Pro project and the KM implementation in a Brazilian innovation institute, illustrate systematic approaches to competence development and knowledge management, emphasising the necessity of aligning these elements to foster innovation and continuous improvement. The integration of CD and KM involves addressing necessary competences for using KM tools effectively and ensuring effective knowledge distribution. Despite technical and didactic convergence, most organisations still lack an integrated strategic approach, suggesting that organisational integration of CD and KM functions is a potential next step towards achieving an NLO. The contribution concludes that aligning CD and KM on strategic, organisational, content, technical, and didactical levels, while considering different types of knowledge and learning processes at individual, team, and organisational levels, enables the creation of a cohesive framework. This framework enhances adaptability and continuous learning in a rapidly changing digital landscape and should be further developed and applied by practitioners.

However, there are some limitations to the contribution that lead to avenues for future research. In this first version of the NLO model, the implications for the competence and knowledge-related aspects have been focused and integrated conceptually. In the further development of this integrated model and concept, further implications, e.g., on the structural and process level, as well as technological and relational aspects may be analysed and added to the model. Further, other support functions of the organisation, such as Quality Management (QM), Human Resource Management (HRM), and Information Technology (IT), could be accounted for in future iterations of the conceptual model

Moreover, the integration of the three levels, individual, team, and organisation, needs to be investigated further to derive clear recommendations for management practice. Additionally, the conceptual model should be evaluated in different business and regional contexts to account for company size, cultural aspects, and company-specific circumstances.

References

Akinci, C., & Sadler-Smith, E. (2019). Collective intuition: Implications for improved decision making and organisational learning. *British Journal of Management, 30*(3), 558–577. https://doi.org/10.1111/1467-8551.12269

Argyris, C., & Schön, D. A. (1978). *Organisational learning: A theory of action perspective*. Addison-Wesley.

Bornewasser, M., Evers, J., & Warner, N. (2018). Kompetenzerwerb in vernetzten Strukturen. In M. Bornewasser (Ed.), *Kompetenzmanagement in Organisationen. Vernetztes Kompetenzmanagement* (pp. 11–23). Springer. https://doi.org/10.1007/978-3-662-54954-4_2

Boyatzis, R. E. (1982). *The competent manager: A model for effective performance. A Wiley-Interscience publication*. Wiley.

CEN. (2004). CWA 14924:2004. European guide to good practice in knowledge management, Part 1–5. *European Committee for Standardisation*.

Crossan, M. M., Lane, H. W., & White, R. E. (1999). An organisational learning framework: From intuition to institution. *Academy of Management Review, 24*(3), 522–537. https://doi.org/10.5465/amr.1999.2202135

Dalkir, K. (2017). *Knowledge management in theory and practice* (Business/Information Science) (3rd ed.). The MIT Press.

DIN SPEC 91281:2012-04. *Einführung von prozessorientiertem Wissensmanagement in kleinen und mittleren Unternehmen*. Beuth Verlag GmbH.

DIN SPEC 91443:2021-08. *Systematisches Wissensmanagement für KMU: Instrumente und Verfahren*. Beuth Verlag GmbH.

Elbe, M. (2020). *Lernkultur und Digitalkultur*. ABWF Bulletin Juli 2020–Januar 2020. https://www.abwf.de/wp-content/uploads/2020/08/ABWF-Bulletin_2020.pdf

European Commission, Directorate-General for Employment, Social Affairs, & Inclusion. (2019). *ESCO handbook—European skills, competencies, qualifications and occupations*. Publications Office. https://doi.org/10.2767/934956

Fai Pun, K., & Nathai-Balkissoon, M. (2011). Integrating knowledge management into organisational learning. *The Learning Organisation, 18*(3), 203–223. https://doi.org/10.1108/09696471111123261

Finke, I., & Will, M. (Eds.). (2005). *Das innovative Unternehmen—Produkte, Prozesse, Dienstleistungen (Digitale Fachbibliothek): Nr. 2012.01.01. Mitarbeiterorientierte Einführung von Wissensmanagement.*

Foelsing, J., & Schmitz, A. (2021). *New Work braucht new learning*. Springer Fachmedien Wiesbaden. https://doi.org/10.1007/978-3-658-32758-3

Geißler, H., & Heidsiek, C. (2010). *Grundlagen des organisationalen Lernens*. Technische Universität Kaiserslautern.

Hokmabadi, H., Rezvani, S. M. H. S., & de Matos, C. A. (2024). Business resilience for small and medium enterprises and startups by digital transformation and the role of marketing capabilities—A systematic review. *Systems, 12*(6), 220. https://doi.org/10.3390/systems12060220

ISO 30401:2018-11. *Knowledge management systems—Requirements*. Beuth Verlag.

Kidschun, F., Hecklau, F., Orth, R., Kohl, H., & Hizal, G. (2021). Digital transformation assessment—A systematic approach to evaluate and shape the digital organisation. *Proceedings of TAKE 2021 Conference Amsterdam*.

Kohl, I. (2016). Den Status quo im Umgang mit Wissen erkennen. In Kohl, H., Mertins, K., & Seidel, H. (Eds.): *Wissensmanagement im Mittelstand. Grundlagen—Lösungen—Praxisbeispiele*. 2. vollständig überarbeitete und ergänzte Auflage (pp. 53–61).

Kohl, H., Will, M., Prim, M. F., & Pavim, A. X. (2020). Building up a national network of applied R&D institutes in an emerging innovation system. *Production, 30*. https://doi.org/10.1590/0103-6513.20190151

Ludwig, A [Andrea]. (2024). *Organisationales Lernen und Digitalisierung*. Springer Fachmedien Wiesbaden. https://doi.org/10.1007/978-3-658-44153-1

Ludwig, A., & Wolf, B. (2021). *Veränderungsmanagement in der Sozialwirtschaft*. Springer.

Mertins, K., Kohl, I., & Orth, R. (2016). Ein Referenzmodell für Wissensmanagement. In H. Kohl, K. Mertins, & H. Seidel (Eds.), *Wissensmanagement im Mittelstand* (pp. 31–40). Springer. https://doi.org/10.1007/978-3-662-49220-8_4

mmb Institut – Gesellschaft für Medien- und Kompetenzforschung mbH. (2019). *Weiterbildung und digitales Lernen heute und in drei Jahren. Auf dem Weg zum Assisted Learning? Digitale Lernanwendungen werden informeller und intelligenter. Ergebnisse der 13. Trendstudie mmb Learning Delphi.* https://www.mmb-institut.de/wp-content/uploads/mmb-Trendmonitor_2018-2019.pdf

Mulder, M. (2014). Conceptions of professional competence. In S. Billett, C. Harteis, & H. Gruber (Eds.), *Springer international handbooks of education. International handbook of research in professional and practice-based learning* (pp. 107–137). Springer. https://doi.org/10.1007/978-94-017-8902-8_5

Mynarek, F., Steckel, J., Grandpierre, A., & Häring, K. (2021). Das Zusammenspiel individuellen und organisationalen Lernens—Ein Review der neueren Literatur. *Zeitschrift Für Arbeitswissenschaft, 75*(4), 438–454. https://doi.org/10.1007/s41449-021-00281-8

Orth, R., & Mertins, K. (2016). Wissensorientierte Analyse und Gestaltung von Geschäftsprozessen. In H. Kohl, K. Mertins, & H. Seidel (Eds.), *Wissensmanagement im Mittelstand* (pp. 63–71). Springer. https://doi.org/10.1007/978-3-662-49220-8_7

Orth, R., Will, M., Pavim, A. X., Gomes, J., & Da Fernandes Costa, C. (2023a). Towards a knowledge management standard for the network of the SENAI innovation institutes. In *Proceedings of the XIII International Congress on Knowledge and Innovation (CiKi)—Preliminary Version.*

Orth, R., Singer-Coudoux, K., & Peschl, M. (2023b). KI-unterstützte Weiterbildungskonzepte für den Mittelstand. *Zeitschrift Für Wirtschaftlichen Fabrikbetrieb, 118*(10), 665–669. https://doi.org/10.1515/zwf-2023-1136

Orth, R., Kretschmer, M., Singer-Coudoux, K., & Schmid, R. (2024). Vom prozessorientierten Qualitätsmanagementsystem zum adaptiven Lernpfad. *Zeitschrift Für Wirtschaftlichen Fabrikbetrieb, 119*(4), 199–204. https://doi.org/10.1515/zwf-2024-1047

Orth, R, Will, M, Budde, F, Kidschun, F, & Gomes, A. S. (Forthcoming). Assessing digital readiness of intellectual capital: A global study of human, structural and relational dimensions. In *The importance of intellectual capital in a global business context*. Springer Nature.

Pai, R. Y., Shetty, A., Shetty, A. D., Bhandary, R., Shetty, J., Nayak, S., Dinesh, T. K., & D'souza, K. J. (2022). Integrating artificial intelligence for knowledge management systems—Synergy among people and technology: A systematic review of the evidence. *Economic Research-Ekonomska Istraživanja, 35*(1), 7043–7065. https://doi.org/10.1080/1331677X.2022.2058976

Pasban, M., & Nojedeh, S. H. (2016). A review of the role of human capital in the organisation. *Procedia—Social and Behavioural Sciences, 230*, 249–253. https://doi.org/10.1016/j.sbspro.2016.09.032

Senge, P. M. (1990). *The fifth discipline: The art and practice of the learning organisation* (Rev. ed.). Crown Business. http://www.loc.gov/catdir/enhancements/fy0703/2006281125-d.html

Simatupang, T. M., & White, A. J. (1998). A policy resolution model for knowledge acquisition in quality management. *Total Quality Management, 9*(8), 767–779.

Singer-Coudoux, K., Braun, G., & Stahre, J. (2023). Managing change towards the future of work—Clustering key perspectives. In *Advances in production management systems. Production management systems for responsible manufacturing, service, and logistics futures* (pp. 513–527).

Sturm, T., Gerlacha, J., Pumplun, L., Mesbah, N., Peters, F., Tauchert, C., Nan, N., & Buxmann, P. (2021). Coordinating human and machine learning for effective organisation learning. *MIS Quarterly, 45*(3), 1581–1602. https://doi.org/10.25300/MISQ/2021/16543

Urbinati, A., Chiaroni, D., Chiesa, V., & Frattini, F. (2020). The role of digital technologies in open innovation processes: An exploratory multiple case study analysis. *R&D Management, 50*(1), 136–160. https://doi.org/10.1111/radm.12313

Will, M., Budde, F., Orth, R., Neumann, F., & Santos, V. (2022). Implementing a European KM approach in a Brazilian innovation institute on a remote basis. *European Conference on Knowledge Management, 23*(2), 1230–1240. https://doi.org/10.34190/eckm.23.2.623

Will, M., Orth, R., Neumann, F., Barros, M. C., & Budde, F. (2023). Case study on the conception and implementation of knowledge management in a Brazilian innovation institute. In F. O. Gauthier (Ed.), *Proceedings of the XIII International Congress on Knowledge and Innovation (CiKi)—Preliminary Version.*

World Economic Forum. (2020). *The future of jobs report 2020.* https://www3.weforum.org/docs/WEF_Future_of_Jobs_2020.pdf

Markus Will studied business administration and communication sciences and completed his doctoral thesis on strategy development based on intangible assets. He is head of the Competence Center Knowledge Management at Fraunhofer IPK, Berlin, and has 20 years of experience in research and consulting in this area.

Katrin Singer-Coudoux, M.Sc. MBA studied International Business Management at Hanze University of Applied Sciences in Groningen, the Netherlands and Anglia Ruskin University in Cambridge, England. Ms. Singer-Coudoux works as a researcher in the Department of Business Excellence Methods at the Fraunhofer Institute for Production Systems and Design Technology in Berlin.

Maria Kretschmer studied Business Administration at the Humboldt University of Berlin (B.Sc.) and Philosophy of Knowledge and Science at the Technical University Berlin (M.A.). Ms. Kretschmer works as researcher and management consultant in the Department of Business Excellence Methods at the FraunhoferInstitute for Production Systems and Design Technology IPK in Berlin.

Ronald Orth studied Business Administration at the Free University of Berlin, after completing his commercial training. Dr. Orth heads the Department of Business Excellence Methods at the Fraunhofer Institute for Production Systems and Design Technology IPK in Berlin.

Henry Nicolai Buxmann, M.Sc. holds a Master in Business Administration from the University of Amsterdam in the Netherlands. Mr. Buxmann works as a researcher in the Department of Business Excellence Methods at the Fraunhofer Institute for Production Systems and Design Technology in Berlin, specialising in competence and sustainability management.

Immersive Technologies and New Work: New, Collaborative Working Environments Based on the XR Demonstrator *Build Green: Data & Practice*

Anne-Liese Lammich

Abstract Digital technologies are changing the world of work. While virtual collaboration and digital planning have already become common practice, immersive technologies such as augmented reality are now extending the possibilities of how teams interact as well as planning and implementation of projects. The following article describes how immersive technologies can change the individual work experience and collaboration in interdisciplinary teams by extending reality. In this context innovative knowledge transfer is a decisive success factor. The demonstrator with the name Build Green makes these future working environments tangible—using the example of a large construction project in Potsdam, Germany, namely the *Kreativ Quartier Potsdam*, which is due to be completed in 2026. Build Green shows how digital and immersive technologies are used in the construction process—for more efficiency, more cooperation, more sustainability, and more transparency in knowledge transfer in complex projects. In this way, Build Green makes future dimensions of virtual teamwork experienceable. Planning data, 3D models, and information on sustainable building materials are integrated into planning practice in an extended reality environment. From each building to individual components, sustainability data can be specifically examined. This simplifies cooperation and the sharing of knowledge in real time between planning offices, architects, builders, and construction companies. The Build Green demonstrator illustrates the potential of immersive technologies and their added value for those involved. Furthermore, the conclusions and lessons learned from this project can be transferred to other sectors in production, services, and crafts, as well.

Keywords Immersive technologies · Knowledge transfer · Extended reality (XR) · Virtual reality · Sustainable construction

A.-L. Lammich (✉)
BSP Business and Law School, Berlin, Germany
e-mail: anne-liese.lammich@businessschool-berlin.de

K. Bodrožić-Brnić et al. (eds.), *Digital Transformation in Knowledge Transfer*, Digital Transformation and Innovation,
https://doi.org/10.1007/978-3-032-07329-7_4

1 Introduction

Immersive technologies are significant assets in the context of New Work. Research by various scientists and institutions, such as PwC, Konrad-Adenauer-Stiftung, and the Fraunhofer Institute, which investigate and observe the use of new technologies, shows the great benefits and impact immersive technologies will have on the way we work. The term New Work refers to a transformative approach to work that emphasises flexibility, autonomy, and purpose in response to the evolving demands of the digital age. In this context, immersive technologies have the potential to enable new work environments, expand flexibility by offering possibilities for location-independent collaboration, as well as enhance communication and knowledge transfer (Fraunhofer Institute for Telecommunications, n.d.; Konrad-Adenauer-Stiftung e. V., 2024; PwC, 2019).

Seeing that Heilig's patent of the "Sensorama Simulator", one of the earliest immersive technology prototypes, dates back to 1962, immersive technologies cannot accurately be described as a new phenomenon (Conn et al., 1989; Heilig, 1962). However, since recent technological developments caused a leap in further advancement, expanding their capabilities and applications, immersive technologies such as virtual reality (VR), augmented reality (AR), and mixed reality (MR), collectively known as extended reality (XR), are becoming increasingly accessible, user-friendly, and reveal new business benefits. As PwC's data in "Seeing is believing—How VR and AR will transform business and the economy" shows, these developments and improvements of immersive technologies have led to a rise in their implementation across various sectors (Ladwig et al., 2018; PwC, 2019). In professional contexts, immersive technology applications are being used to enhance a range of functions, including training, maintenance, design, prototyping, sales, marketing, and more (Konrad-Adenauer-Stiftung e. V., 2024; Mittelstand-Digital Zentrum Zukunftskultur & VR Business Club, 2022). Although business adaptations are still limited, current literature and research show growing interest and potential in these areas (Pavithra et al., 2020; Suh & Prophet, 2018).

> Neither VR nor AR are new technologies, but there are two overarching trends that can ensure their use grows considerably: the business benefits they can deliver are now richer and more attractive; and technological advances are creating an improved user experience. (PwC, 2019, p. 5)

Immersive technologies offer significant economic advantages, especially in design and prototyping, where they can drastically reduce costs by enabling virtual testing and iterative design processes before physical production begins (PwC, 2019). Additionally, immersive tools enable remote work in areas traditionally requiring on-site human resources. For example, in maintenance, where, as Mourtzis et al. (2017) elaborate on, remote experts can guide on-site workers through AR interfaces, reducing required maintenance time and cost and enhancing training methods for less experienced workers as well. As the Mittelstand-Digital Zentrum Zukunftskultur & VR Business Club (2022) conclude, these capabilities are particularly relevant for small and medium-sized enterprises (SMEs), which often have limited resources and could benefit from cost-effective, collaborative tools.

In the context of collaborative work, immersive technology can be particularly beneficial. XR tools enhance data visualisation and communication, making it easier for teams to analyse and interpret complex information in a shared virtual space. By creating immersive environments with shared experiences and the capability for direct interaction in the same virtual world, collaboration, cooperation, and communication among remote teams can be more effective (Kraus et al., 2022; Thomas et al., 2023). “The ability to collaborate with other people across barriers created by time and/or space is one of the greatest features of modern communication. Immersive technologies are positioned to enhance this ability to collaborate even further” (Thomas et al., 2023, p. 301).

This article aims to introduce a concrete application to show the possibilities of immersive technologies within a specific working environment. The project *Build Green: Data and Practic*e seeks to explore the potential of immersive technologies for collaboration in the context of New Work and to demonstrate how XR tools can facilitate the creation of new collaborative working environments. The construction industry has been chosen as the use case to frame the project, enabling the development of investigations and transferable solutions that are as practice-oriented as possible.

The central question is: How can immersive technologies enhance knowledge transfer and collaboration in interdisciplinary teams, specifically in the construction industry, by improving the communication of complex data, such as environmental impact and sustainability metrics, to support data-driven decision-making?

Based on the chosen use case of the construction industry, a use case was selected, focusing specifically on the project *Kreativ Quartier Potsdam*, an urban development project currently under construction, in Potsdam, Germany. The project *Build Green: Data and Practice* resulted in a “demonstrator” called Build Green, designed to showcase the possibilities and opportunities that immersive technologies offer for knowledge transfer in collaborative and interdisciplinary working environments. Serving as an interactive exhibitor, it has been presented on multiple occasions, including renowned trade fairs such as the HANNOVER MESSE 2024 (the world’s leading industrial technology trade fair), the BauNetz Heinze Klimafestival für die Bauwende 2024 (a trade fair focused on the construction industry and sustainability in Berlin), and the BAU Munich 2025 (the world’s leading trade fair for architecture, materials, and systems), where it highlighted innovation in collaborative work environments. Additionally, the demonstrator is used in workshops to introduce XR and emphasise the potential of immersive technologies, providing SMEs with hands-on insights into the potential of these technologies. In the course of this project, we addressed the topic of knowledge transfer in terms of: Improving communication and collaboration within interdisciplinary teams through immersive technologies. Facilitating the transfer of knowledge about new technologies, such as immersive technologies, to SMEs.

In this article, we shortly introduce immersive technologies and their current use for collaboration purposes, explain relevance and benefits for the construction industry, present the project *Build Green: Data and Practice* as well as the resulting demonstrator *Build Green*. Finally, we discuss our experiences, observations, and conclusion for the future of collaboration and knowledge transfer.

2 Immersive Technologies in Collaborative Work Environments

Different types of immersive technologies must be distinguished: augmented reality (AR), mixed reality (MR), and virtual reality (VR). The umbrella term used for these immersive technologies is extended reality (XR). They differ by the depth of immersion, grade of interaction, and the interfaces required for access (Tremosa, 2024; Vítor Bernardo, n.d.).

AR is digital information linked to the physical world. It is usually triggered and anchored by something in the real-world environment, like a previously defined object or a shape scanned and recognised by the AR application. On-screen, AR overlays the physical world with digital information, such as graphs, objects, texts, or other visual content. Depending on the AR application, interaction may be possible, although it is more limited compared to VR and MR. Since the information is displayed on a screen only, AR provides a relatively low level of immersion (Sáez Martínez, 2023; Tremosa, 2024). The advantage of AR compared to other XRs lies in the easy accessibility to use applications in terms of interface, as users only need a mobile device, typically a smartphone or tablet, which are widely available and familiar to use (Smart Manufacturing Week, 2022). To access the AR, users must point the mobile device's camera at the corresponding trigger, and the digital information becomes visible on the device's screen.

In contrast to AR, which is related to the real-world environment, VR shows users a digital world with an enclosed virtual environment. In VR, the user's visual perception is entirely limited to the virtual environment and sealed off from the real world, providing a fully immersive user experience. To enter the virtual environment, headsets or head mounted displays (HMD) are required, along with controllers, motion-tracking devices, or hand tracking to interact with digital objects (PwC, 2019; Tremosa, 2024).

In comparison with AR, which is minimally immersive, and VR, which is fully immersive, MR represents a combination of both. By using an HMD with integrated cameras facing the user's surroundings, MR headsets allow a passthrough mode, enabling a view of the real-world surroundings whilst visualising digital information. As a result, MR seamlessly blends the physical real-world environment with digital elements, similar to AR, but in a much more immersive way. The most significant difference from AR lies in the wider range of visual field, which is not limited to a single screen and trigger but encompasses the entire environment. Meanwhile, users have their hands free to interact with digital objects, either with controllers or via hand tracking using their own hands, comparable to VR (Smart Manufacturing Week, 2022). In MR, physical and digital elements can interact with each other and with the user. Therefore, the user experience is influenced and changed by real-world environments (Sáez Martínez, 2023; Tremosa, 2024).

Artificial Intelligence (AI) plays a pivotal role in enabling MR functionality by enhancing spatial awareness, object recognition, and interaction capabilities. Through advanced computer vision, AI-powered depth engines, and real-time data processing, MR headsets can map the environment, identify objects, and adapt digital elements to interact naturally with the physical world. Features like hand tracking, dynamic occlusion, and environmental understanding are powered by AI, enabling a fluid and immersive experience where digital content integrates seamlessly into the user's surroundings. (Meta, 2023)

Figure 1 shows a visual representation of the transitions and differences between these three immersive technologies, where they intersect and how they are perceived by the user. In the project *Build Green: Data and Practice* all three immersive technologies were considered and incorporated into the development of the demonstrator *Build Green*. By using all three XRs it is possible to emphasise, observe, and compare their respective strengths and weaknesses in action.

Building on the technological distinctions and capabilities of AR, VR, and MR, immersive technologies are increasingly being recognised as transformative tools in collaborative work environments across various sectors. Their ability to enhance communication, streamline processes, and foster innovation is proving invaluable—an aspect explored in greater detail in the following section.

According to reports from observers of the technological and industrial market, such as "Added value through immersive technologies" by the Konrad-Adenauer-Stiftung (2024) and "Seeing is believing—How VR and AR will transform business and the economy" by PwC (2019), the use and significance of immersive technologies are increasingly evident. The development of practical immersive applications for collaboration can be observed in various sectors, such as Education, Healthcare, Industry, Entertainment and Gaming (Doroudian, 2024). The extensive written compilation on the industry in Germany, the "Best Practice Navigator" by the Mittelstand-Digital Zentrum Zukunftskultur & VR Business Club (2022), defines the areas of application for immersive technologies in companies as follows: Personnel, Training, Development & Planning, Service, and Sales. The same publication also contains a collection of real-life examples of the adaptation of immersive technologies in different sectors and elaborates on the companies' experiences, including their key findings. Here are a few examples in the context of collaborative work environments found within the Best Practice Navigator (Table 1):

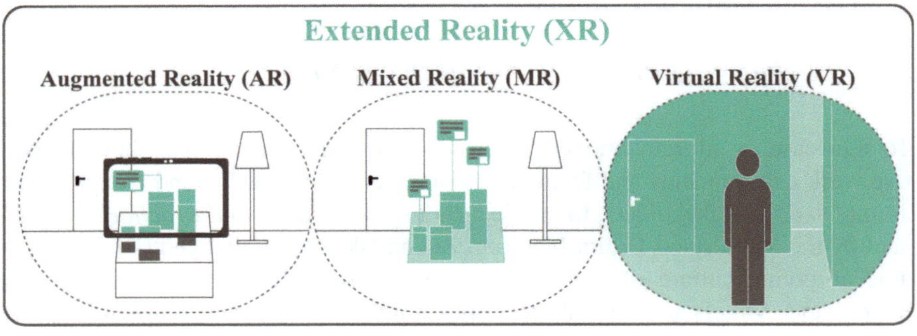

Fig. 1 Extended realities—representation and perception of AR, MR, and VR. (Source: Authors' illustration)

Table 1 Examples for immersive technology adaptations in industrial context

Example for	Description
Increased efficiency in product design and planning	*Lufthansa Technik* improved the efficiency of aircraft interior design using VR. Mobile VR solutions were chosen as a cost-effective option. Through employee involvement, workshops, and testing, VR was found to simplify tasks like component placement and cable planning. Early user involvement and continuous feedback were key to the project's success, leading to significant improvements in design processes and widespread user support for VR technology in collaborative work environments
More efficient prototyping	*Audi* used VR to enhance prototype development and testing in car manufacturing, significantly reducing costs. Rather than making physical prototypes of tools, containers, and equipment, the company adopted a digital process, saving on production and setup expenses. This use of VR enabled different departments to collaborate efficiently without the need to travel, speeding up the design and approval process. Their approach saved time, reduced prototype production costs, and improved planning accuracy. Teams could test components in VR, identify design flaws early, and avoid costly physical changes. The project also reduced communication gaps by allowing real-time design updates, leading to faster adjustments and improved product quality. All in all, *Audi*'s implementation of VR transformed prototyping, allowing quicker development, lowering costs, and fostering smoother teamwork across all stages of production
Boosting productivity	*NTT DATA* used VR during *COVID-19 pandemic* to improve team collaboration, overcoming the limits of standard online tools. Virtual meeting spaces increased efficiency and cut travel by over 75%. Real-time translations helped with language barriers, and meetings were easier to document. By using immersive technology, teams experienced better interaction, higher creativity, and more productivity. Besides, XR supported agile work methods, virtual showrooms, training, and customer events. The company used it for product demos and virtual banking, making work more interactive, cutting costs while reducing travel and improving remote customer service by making it more personal

Source: Mittelstand-Digital Zentrum Zukunftskultur, & VR Business Club. (2022). BEST PRACTICE Navigator

3 Development and Implementation of the Project "Build Green: Data & Practice"

3.1 Background and Objective of the Project

To showcase the aforementioned benefits of immersive technologies in collaborative work environments and facilitate the transfer of knowledge and complex data among various stakeholders, the project *Build Green: Data and Practice* was initiated by the Mittelstand-Digital Zentrum Zukunftskultur (digital centre for sustainable corporate culture of medium-sized businesses). The centre is part of the nationwide Mittelstand-Digital network, funded by the Federal Ministry for Economic Affairs and Energy (BMWE). This initiative provides small and medium-sized enterprises (SMEs) with information, practical examples, training, and vendor-neutral resources to support secure and sustainable digitalisation.

The real-world construction project *Kreativ Quartier Potsdam* was selected as case study and exemplary scenario to develop practical solutions that would demonstrate the technologies' potential.

In addition to investigating the possibilities of XR in collaborative working environments, the project aimed to communicate the advantages of immersive technologies to practitioners, particularly SMEs, and to inspire them to embrace innovation. To achieve this, our efforts culminated in the creation of the demonstrator *Build Green* that showcased the results in an engaging and practical way, encouraging stakeholders to adopt these technologies.

3.2 Use-Case Construction Industry: "Kreativ Quartier Potsdam"

According to the World Economic Forum (2017), the construction industry is a key sector facing increasing pressure to innovate, particularly in the areas of knowledge transfer, collaboration, and sustainability. As one of the largest industries globally, it is responsible for a significant portion of energy consumption, material use, and waste production, highlighting the need for more efficient and sustainable practices (World Economic Forum, 2017). Furthermore, construction projects are inherently complex, involving multiple stakeholders—from architects and engineers to contractors and local authorities—who must coordinate across different levels of expertise and manage various stages of project development. This complexity often leads to communication challenges, delays, budget overruns, and unmet sustainability targets (Chinyio & Olomolaiye, 2009).

In this context, immersive technologies like VR and AR offer promising solutions to improve collaboration and knowledge transfer. As Elghaish et al. (2021) and Gontier et al. (2021) elaborate, these technologies can enhance communication by providing stakeholders with clear visualisations of designs, enabling real-time interaction with 3D models and even allow location-independent access with the possibility of real-time updates. This immersive approach helps bridge knowledge gaps, support transparency, reduce misunderstandings, streamline decision-making processes across diverse teams and facilitate better feedback loops among project participants (Gontier et al., 2021). By presenting it in this context, immersive technologies like VR and AR offer promising solutions to improve collaboration and knowledge transfer. As Elghaish et al. (2021) and Gontier et al. (2021) elaborate, these technologies can enhance communication by providing stakeholders with clear visualisations of designs, enabling real-time interaction with 3D models and even allow location-independent access with the possibility of real-time updates. This immersive approach helps bridge knowledge gaps, support transparency, reduce misunderstandings, streamline decision-making processes across diverse teams and facilitate better feedback loops among project participants (Gontier et al., 2021). By presenting virtual models, immersive tools allow stakeholders to explore the project in its entirety before construction begins, making it easier to anticipate challenges and optimise designs.

Moreover, immersive technologies can support the construction industry's need for sustainability by providing more efficient ways to visualise energy consumption, material use, and other environmental impacts throughout a project's lifecycle. The ability to interact with digital models in real time allows for better-informed decisions, leading to reduced waste and more sustainable building practices. These tools can also help mitigate issues such as scope changes and miscommunication, which often result in costly delays and budget overruns (Elghaish et al., 2021).

Given the widespread use of technologies like Building Information Modeling (BIM) and Computer-Aided Design (CAD), which already rely on digital 3D models, the construction sector is particularly well-suited to integrate immersive technologies (Gontier et al., 2021; Mayer et al., 2023). The adaptability of these technologies makes them an ideal solution for enhancing collaboration, improving communication, and driving sustainability in a sector in dire need of innovation and therefore provides a suiting use case for the project.

As a highly complex construction project, the *Kreativ Quartier Potsdam* entails all aspects described above that are suitable to support with immersive technologies. Located in the historic city centre of Potsdam, the project is expected to take a total of 6 years to develop from 2020 to 2026. During this period, a new urban quarter will be created on an area of 25,000 m^2, consisting of seven buildings, housing various uses, including offices, studios, shops, rehearsal rooms, cafés, and flats. To meet the tight schedule all seven buildings are constructed simultaneously, rising the difficulty of logistics and management in the limited space. Because of its central location and significant impact on the neighbourhood, the local creative industry, and the city as a whole, this construction project is of considerable public interest. A wide range of stakeholders, including the city council, Potsdam's cultural and creative industries, and others, is involved in the decision-making process. (GW Kreativquartier GmbH & Co. KG (n.d.)) As the project moves through construction and subsequent phases, the number of stakeholders grows even larger, partly due to the many parties and contractors required for completion—architects, engineers, craftsmen, suppliers, and more. Thus, the *Kreativ Quartier Potsdam* does not only pose a suitable use case regarding the complexity and handling of complex data but also the need for excellent interdisciplinary communication. Within the project, the goal was to investigate and demonstrate how immersive technologies can support both.

Lessons learned from applying immersive technologies in this sector can be transferred to other industries, emphasising interdisciplinary collaboration.

3.3 Involved Stakeholders and Respective Roles

In order to develop a holistic solution approach, an interdisciplinary project group was put together, representing different expertise backgrounds and stakeholder groups. Since the *Kreativ Quartier Potsdam* construction project was selected as a case study, both client and architects were closely involved in the development process of *Build Green* to achieve a practice-orientated solution. Other partners involved

Table 2 Participating partners and their respective roles in the development of the demonstratorBuild Green

	Project partner			
Institution	*Mittelstand-Digital Zentrum Zukunftskultur*	*Mittelstand-Digital Zentrum Bau*	*&Mica + Glockenweiß GmbH*	*XR Designer Anke Schiemann*
Role	initiator, lead and coordination of the project; planning and implementation methodological approach; interface between science and practice	representing stakeholders in the construction industry; interface between science and practice	practical relevance: connection to the case study "Kreativ Quartier Potsdam" as client and architects	XR design and implementation
Relevant Expertise	digitalisation of SMEs; corporate culture; change management; acceptance of new technologies; communication and cooperation; innovation processes; immersive technologies	technology transfer to SMEs in construction; theoretical, conceptual, and practical expertise in digitalisation of the construction industry; innovation processes	architecture; construction planning and execution; urban planning and development; building information modelling (BIM); sustainability in construction	artistic approach and expertise in human-centred design, development, and implementation in XR

in the project include the Mittelstand-Digital Zentrum Bau, which is also part of the nationwide Mittelstand-Digital network, as well as an artist and an XR designer who was responsible for the development and implementation of immersive solutions. A complete list of partners, along with their areas of expertise and roles, can be found in Table 2.

3.4 Development Process

To incorporate the expertise and perspective of all project partners into the development process in the best possible way, a consecutive and iterative strategy was pursued, including multiple workshops and feedback sessions. Figure 2 depicts the work packages (WP) with the most important consecutive steps and milestones (MS) in the project, including the development of the demonstrator:

The project started with a joint workshop for all partners. To define the desired outcome and objectives of the project, the group targeted the most relevant questions, incorporating all expertise and perspectives available to develop the most

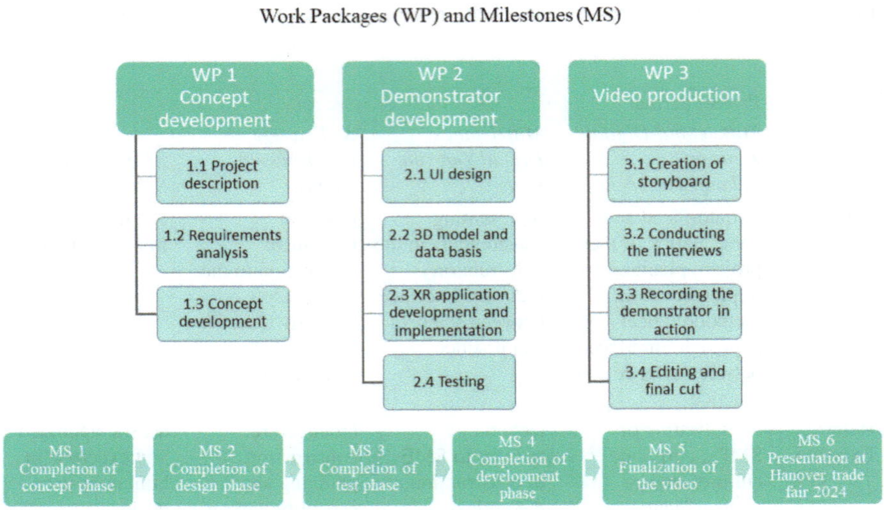

Fig. 2 Process overview and work packages. (Source: Authors' illustration)

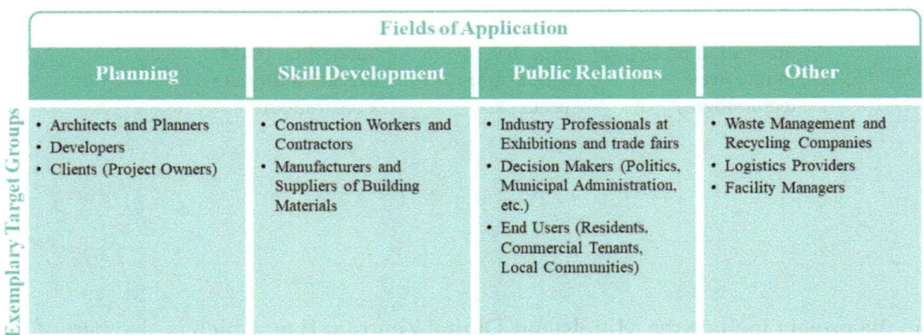

Fig. 3 Exemplary target groups and fields of application for the demonstrator *Build Green*. (Source: Authors' illustration)

holistic approach possible. The questions were subdivided into three areas: foundations, e.g. target group and the interaction between industry and application; content of the exhibitor, e.g. utilisation and accessibility, sustainability aspects and data content; and finally, visualisation and usability, e.g. data visualisation, interaction, and user experience. Figure 3 shows some of the main possible application areas and respective stakeholder groups for immersive technologies in the construction industry defined by the project group as result of the joint brainstorming session.

Another outcome of the joint workshop was identifying key priorities for the demonstrator: ensuring ease of use and accessibility for a broad audience. This goal was accomplished through a simple, user-friendly interface, intuitive gesture-based interactions, and a focus on displaying only the most relevant data within the demonstrator. These and more conclusions from the workshop were then incorporated into the concept of the demonstrator. During the finalisation of the concept and later during implementation, regular bilateral meetings and multiple testing and feedback sessions were held to finalise the demonstrator.

As a fundament for the implementation of the XR application, real planning data of the *Kreativ Quartier Potsdam* was used, provided by the architects from &Mica, containing the BIM model and sustainability information generated with the help of the eco-building materials database platform Madaster.

Finally, videographers were commissioned to represent the project in a short film. As a result, the demonstrator consists of three parts:

- An AR application, which can be accessed by scanning a printed, simplified architectural site plan of the *Kreativ Quartier Potsdam* using a tablet.
- An XR application, accessible by using a headset, consisting of MR and VR sequences.
- A short video, of about 4.5 min, explaining the project, representing all partners, and allowing low-key insights into the applications.

4 The XR Exhibitor Build Green

The demonstrator comprises several components that provide varying levels of immersion, ranging from an augmented reality (AR) application on a tablet, to a mixed reality setup, and finally a fully immersive virtual reality (VR) environment accessible via an XR headset. These different immersion levels offer a range of interaction options and user experiences within the demonstrator.

In addition to the interactive and immersive application, a short explanatory video presents and clarifies both the project and the demonstrator. For the physical setup, a freestanding table or platform is needed to display and store the necessary equipment. A monitor is also required to play the associated short film. It may be useful to include a second monitor to show what the user is experiencing through the headset. An example of the complete setup, including the required hardware, is shown in Fig. 4.

4.1 AR Application

The AR application of the demonstrator consists of a plotted map showing the layout of the *Kreativ Quartier Potsdam*, measuring 50 cm × 100 cm with a scale of 1:250. Usually, two Android tablets are being handed out to the users, each with the associated application installed and running, providing the needed interface. The AR application can be accessed by scanning an element of the map with the tablet. This hybrid physical-virtual interaction further enriches the user experience by grounding the digital content in the real world.

Fig. 4 Mittelstand-Digital Zentrum Zukunftskultur, employee photo liberated for usage. (Mittelstand-Digital Zentrum Zukunftskultur, internal stock photo)

Two icons, fixed on the top left of the screen, indicate two different sequences of the application, mirroring sequences one and two of the XR application. In the first sequence, the 3D model of the *Kreativ Quartier Potsdam* is augmented on top of the plotted map, as can be seen in Fig. 5. Each of the buildings can be selected by the user individually by tapping on it. The selected building is then visualised on a larger scale, floating above the neighbourhood model in a more detailed version. In addition, an information terminal is displayed on the tablet screen, containing data on the sustainability of the selected building. The data can be selected and explored by scrolling and tapping the screen.

By selecting the second icon, the user changes into the second sequence. Instead of the whole quarter, in this sequence, the user is shown an illustrative, more detailed model of one of the floors, as shown in Fig. 6. In comparison with the earlier sequence, the data presented here is broken down into construction elements, such as structural columns, load-bearing interior walls or facade. The information contains the materials of each element and information about their respective sustainability values.

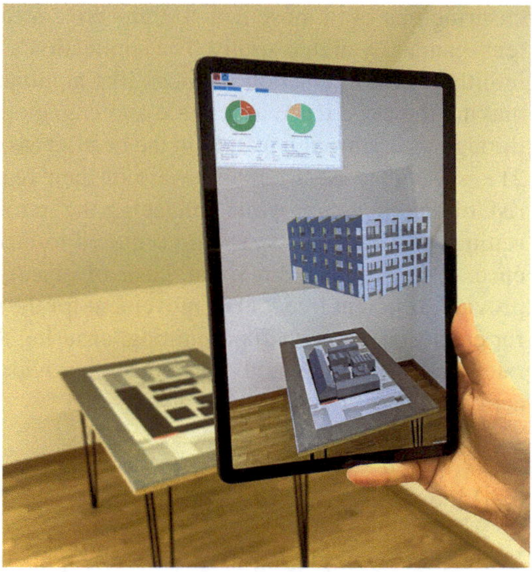

Fig. 5 First sequence of the AR application of the demonstrator Build Green. (Source: Authors' photo)

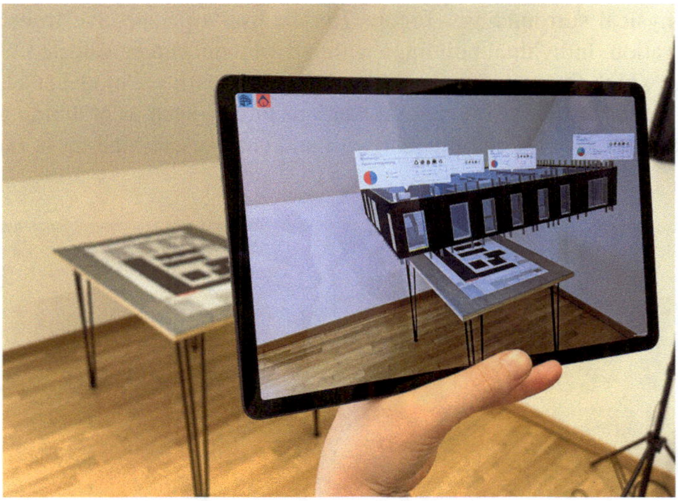

Fig. 6 Second sequence of the AR application of the demonstrator Build Green. (Source: Authors' photo)

4.2 XR Application

The demonstrator Build Green offers a meticulously designed user experience structured around three immersive sequences that together demonstrate the potential of mixed reality (MR) in sustainable construction. Throughout the experience, users can navigate easily between the sequences using a persistent main menu, ensuring that even those new to immersive technologies can interact with the content seamlessly and naturally. The application's user interface (UI) is designed to be intuitive, with interaction methods like tapping, pointing, grabbing, and selecting, making the experience accessible and engaging for all users. Moreover, using MR through a passthrough feature in the headset (as described below in sequences 1 and 2) ensures that users remain aware of their real-world surroundings, reducing the risk of disorientation while enhancing the immersive experience. Virtual boundary settings and adequate space are required to ensure a safe and comfortable experience. A free area of 3m x 3m, clear of objects and other obstacles, is advised to provide sufficient freedom of movement for the user. The demonstrator is optimised for environments with good lighting, ensuring the XR headset's cameras can accurately track hand and body movements, providing a seamless and immersive interaction. Here's a detailed breakdown:

4.2.1 Sequence 1 (MR)

Users start by exploring a simplified neighbourhood model of the entire *Kreativ Quartier Potsdam* complex. This model is displayed on a site plan scaled at 1:250, floating in front of them within an MR environment, allowing users to remain aware of their physical surroundings. Figure 7 is the user's perspective from within the MR application. Individual buildings within the model can be selected by touching them, after which they are visualised atop the neighbourhood model at a larger scale and with greater detail. Using natural hand gestures—such as grabbing to rotate or tapping to select—users can interact with and closely examine these buildings. A

Fig. 7 First sequence of the MR application of the demonstrator *Build Green*—user's perspective. (Source: Authors' photo)

contextual menu appears on-screen alongside the 3D model, offering information on key sustainability aspects such as performance, environmental impact, circularity, and building certification. This interactive approach and presentation allow users to explore how each building is planned and how it contributes to the overall sustainability goals of the project.

4.2.2 Sequence 2 (MR)

The experience narrows its focus to specific building components. In this sequence the user explores the 3D model of one particular floor, that is part of a building within the complex. Floating right above the model are five information panels, each representing one specific element of the construction, such as structural columns, load-bearing interior walls, or facade. Users can select one of five pre-selected building elements and retrieve detailed sustainability data for each, including material volume distribution, lifespan, recyclability, and circularity indicators. This scene is particularly effective for those interested in the granular aspects of sustainable building materials, enabling them to visualise and understand the environmental footprint of each component within the context of the entire structure. Another feature of this sequence is the ability to highlight the selected element within the 3D model, pinpointing its location and distinguishing it from other elements.

4.2.3 Sequence 3 (VR)

Users find themselves within a fully immersive virtual reality environment, presented as a 1:1 scale model of the *Kreativ Quartier Potsdam*, as shown in Figs. 8 and 9. They can teleport to predefined locations throughout the complex, gaining an

Figs. 8 and 9 VR sequence of the demonstrator Build Green—user's perspective. (Source: Authors' photo)

accurate perception of space and scale. Each teleportation location offers information boards. Users can move freely within a predefined virtual space, constrained by their physical surrounding and predefined virtual boundary. This scene provides a compelling way to "experience" the planned environment as if it were already built, allowing users to appreciate the design and sustainability features more intuitively and impactfully. In Fig. 8, the console for teleportation and orientation within the virtual model of the quarter can be seen on the right. On the left, an information sheet is visible, where the user can have an overview of sustainable data and building performance regarding the building in sight. The user can interact with this information sheet by grabbing and repositioning it.

In addition to developing the XR application, a short video was produced to explain and frame the project, represent all partners, including their expertise and perspective, and allow low-key insights into the demonstrator. The video combines real-life footage of the construction site, the demonstrator's development and implementation process, interviews with representatives of the involved parties regarding their point of view on the project, as well as footage from the demonstrator in action. Overall, the video for this project is 4.5 min long and played as an introduction before using the XR application itself.

5 Observations and Learnings

Reflecting on the primary objectives of the project, including knowledge transfer and the background of the initiator, Mittelstand-Digital Zentrum Zukunftskultur, the observations and learnings from the project can be divided into two key areas:

1. Insights into the use of immersive technologies to improve collaborative work, regarding communication and collaboration
2. Insights into effectively communicating knowledge about digitalisation, new technologies, and their applications to SMEs.

Focusing on the first key area, we gained valuable insights into the perception and usability of immersive technologies, through the exchange within the interdisciplinary project group, which was incorporated into the joint development of the demonstrator, and by observing users interacting with the demonstrator. Each of the extended realities—AR, MR, and VR—offers unique advantages for collaborative work and communication, particularly in relation to architectural data:

AR offers a low-key approach and easy access using widely accessible and familiar devices such as tablets or smartphones. In terms of communication, AR allows users to interact with others at the same location to be more natural, allowing them to express thoughts and emotions not only verbally but also through gestures, posture, and facial expressions. However, the data and digital information to discuss is visually restricted to the screen that the used device offers, which can be limiting. In the example of our exhibitor, the displayed sustainability data windows partly overlapped and covered the augmented architecture models behind them, which was often perceived as disturbing. However, this was unavoidable due to the limited size of the tablet screens and need for sufficient legibility of the information.

Observing users interacting with the demonstrator during exhibitions, we found that most time was spent within the mixed reality. Possible explanations for this, based on observations and discussions with users, include the following: the enjoyment of exploring the interactive features and architectural models; a stronger connection to the surrounding environment, in comparison with the VR sequence, and the possibility to see and communicate with others, resulting in a better perception of the room and greater comfort; motion sickness was much less pronounced in MR than in VR; mistakenly overlooking the icon to enter the VR; technical difficulties in entering VR due to failing response of the user interface in MR, usually caused by inadequate lighting of the space provided or technical issues.

VR, while immersive, was less favoured in busy environments, such as trade fairs. Users reported discomfort with movement, challenges in situational awareness, and occasional motion sickness. However, many users also expressed amazement at the ability of VR to immerse them in a completely different world. This immersive experience helped users better understand the proportions of the construction and relations between buildings, as well as the overall design and vision of the project. The ability to explore the architectural vision in a fully immersive environment was frequently highlighted as a significant advantage of VR, offering a unique perspective that other XR technologies could not achieve.

Turning to the second key area mentioned, the project offered valuable insights into how immersive technologies can be effectively communicated to SMEs, emphasising the importance of knowledge transfer in showcasing their practical applications and fostering a deeper understanding of digitalisation and innovation.

One key observation was that users required varying levels of assistance when interacting with the demonstrator. While some navigated the virtual and immersive environment intuitively, others initially felt uncertain and needed more detailed instructions. To ensure a positive experience, it is recommended that inexperienced users engage with the demonstrator under supervision. However, with a little time and effort, most users adapted quickly and were able to use the technology independently.

During and after the demonstration, participants received guidance as needed, including technical instructions, detailed explanations of the technology's capabilities, and discussions of potential fields of application. In general, users were very open and interested in XR technologies. Cross-industry comparisons and potential applications in other field, such as manufacturing, design, craftsmanship, and the real estate industry, were typically well understood and validated by participants. Since one of the project's main goals was to facilitate effective knowledge transfer to SMEs, this hands-on approach was crucial in successfully presenting the demonstrator.

Overall, we can say that the project has been successful in bringing the benefits and possibilities of immersive technologies in collaborative working environments to a wide variety of audiences. During the use of *Build Green*, users were able to experience and try out a range of immersive technologies first-hand. Many users have not yet encountered VR, AR, or MR. Thanks to the demonstrator, they gained a low-threshold introduction to these technologies, which also ignited discussions regarding potential applications in different industries, as well as their pros and cons. In general, the feedback we got from the users was very positive.

6 Conclusion

The advancement of immersive technologies continues to hold significant promise, driven by improvements in hardware, software, and Artificial Intelligence (AI). With headsets becoming lighter, more portable, and capable of operating without predefined spatial restrictions, mixed reality scenarios are becoming increasingly feasible. Enhanced graphical displays and AI-supported tracking and processing further integrate digital and physical environments, enabling richer interactions and more immersive user experiences. These ongoing advancements are expected to open new possibilities for a wide range of applications, from training to design and communication.

The project and its demonstrator *Build Green* successfully showed the potential of immersive technologies for collaborative work and communication of complex data. Since augmented reality was the easiest to handle, it offered a low-threshold entry towards immersive technology for the users, especially for those not feeling comfortable wearing a headset. Mixed reality was well received by users, as it allowed natural interactions, situational awareness, and seamless integration of physical and digital spaces.

However, the fully immersive virtual reality environment provided a uniquely intense spatial impression, enabling users to experience and explore the design and vision of the built environment in ways that would otherwise not be possible. These complementary strengths of AR, MR, and VR highlight the need to tailor immersive technologies to specific use cases and objectives. When evaluating the suitability of XR technologies, it is crucial to consider the purpose of the interaction. For scenarios requiring collaboration and communication in the same physical space, AR and MR are particularly beneficial, as they integrate on-site conditions and support natural interpersonal interaction. Conversely, for showcasing fictional scenarios or enabling remote collaboration where spatial experience is vital, VR excels by immersing users in a shared digital environment with consistent settings and visuals. The project also addressed the transfer of knowledge about new technologies to SMEs, aiming to inspire exploration, adaptation, and innovation. By providing a hands-on demonstrator, users were encouraged to experiment with XR technologies, leading to greater interest and discussions about potential applications in manufacturing, design, craftsmanship, and real estate. Observations suggest that immersive technologies can significantly enhance collaborative work by improving communication, fostering innovation, and bridging physical and digital environments. In conclusion, while *Build Green* has provided valuable insights into the use of immersive technologies in the construction industry, the lessons learned are highly transferable to other fields. Future research should explore additional use cases and settings, as well as evaluate the long-term impact of these technologies on collaborative work and knowledge transfer. The ongoing evolution of XR technologies ensures that their potential for enhancing productivity, creativity, and innovation will only continue to grow.

References

Chinyio, E., & Olomolaiye, P. (Eds.). (2009). *Construction stakeholder management*. Wiley. https://doi.org/10.1002/9781444315349

Conn, C., Lanier, J., Minsky, M., Fisher, S., & Druin, A. (1989). Virtual environments and interactivity: windows to the future. *ACM SIGGRAPH Computer Graphics, 23*(5), 7–18. https://doi.org/10.1145/77277.77278

Doroudian, S. (2024). *Collaboration in immersive environments: challenges and solutions*. http://arxiv.org/abs/2311.00689

Elghaish, F., Matarneh, S., Talebi, S., Kagioglou, M., Hosseini, M. R., & Abrishami, S. (2021). Toward digitalization in the construction industry with immersive and drones technologies: a critical literature review. *Smart and Sustainable Built Environment, 10*(3), 345–363. https://doi.org/10.1108/SASBE-06-2020-0077

Fraunhofer Institute for Telecommunications, H.-H.-I. (HHI). (n.d.). *Immersive media & communication*. Retrieved September 22, 2024, from https://www.hhi.fraunhofer.de/en/vit-imc.html

Gontier, J. C., Wong, P. S. P., & Teo, P. (2021). Towards the implementation of immersive technology in construction - A swot analysis. *Journal of Information Technology in Construction, 26*. https://doi.org/10.36680/j.itcon.2021.020.

GW Kreativquartier GmbH & Co. KG. (n.d.). *Kreativ Quartier Potsdam*. Retrieved October 9, 2024, from https://kreativ-quartier-potsdam.de/quartier/

Heilig, M. L. (1962). US Patent #3,050,870.

Konrad-Adenauer-Stiftung e. V. (2024). *Mehrwerte durch immersive Technologien*.

Kraus, M., Fuchs, J., Sommer, B., Klein, K., Engelke, U., Keim, D., & Schreiber, F. (2022). Immersive Analytics with Abstract 3D Visualizations: A Survey. *Computer Graphics Forum, 41*(1), 201–229. https://doi.org/10.1111/cgf.14430

Ladwig, P., Düsseldorf, H., & Geiger, C. (2018). *A literature review on collaboration in mixed reality*. https://www.researchgate.net/publication/324452471

Meta. (2023). *Building mixed reality (MR) with Meta Quest 3: Connect developers to the presence platform*. https://developers.meta.com/horizon/blog/building-mixed-reality-MR-meta-quest-3-connect-developers-presence-platform/?locale=en_GB

Mayer, A., Chardonnet, J. R., Häfner, P., & Ovtcharova, J. (2023). Collaborative Work Enabled by Immersive Environments. In New Digital Work: Digital Sovereignty at the Workplace (pp. 87–117). *Springer International Publishing*. https://doi.org/10.1007/978-3-031-26490-0_6.

Mourtzis, D., Zogopoulos, V., & Vlachou, E. (2017). Augmented Reality Application to Support Remote Maintenance as a Service in the Robotics Industry. *Procedia CIRP, 63*, 46–51. https://doi.org/10.1016/j.procir.2017.03.154

Mittelstand-Digital Zentrum Zukunftskultur, & VR Businessclub. (2022). *BEST PRACTICE Navigator Eine Expedition zu Erfolgsgeschichten rund um Virtual Reality, Augmented Reality und Mixed Reality*. www.ashman.de

Pavithra, A., Kowsalya, J., Priya, S. K., Jayasree, G., & Nandhini, T. K. (2020). An emerging immersive technology—A survey. *International Journal of Innovative Research and Growth, 6*(8).

PwC. (2019). *Seeing is believing* - How VR and AR will transform business and the economy.

Sáez Martínez, P. J. (2023). *Extended reality: Exploring the future of immersive technologies.* Https://Www.Onirix.Com/Extended-Reality/.

Smart Manufacturing Week. (2022, May 26). *AR, MR or VR: Which technology is right for your engineering use case?*

Suh, A., & Prophet, J. (2018). The state of immersive technology research: A literature analysis. *Computers in Human Behavior, 86*. https://doi.org/10.1016/j.chb.2018.04.019

Thomas, J., Lee, S. W., Giovannelli, A., Lane, L., & Bowman, D. (2023). A communication-focused framework for understanding immersive collaboration experiences. In *2023 IEEE Conference on Virtual Reality and 3D User Interfaces Abstracts and Workshops (VRW)* (pp. 301–304) https://doi.org/10.1109/VRW58643.2023.00070

Tremosa, L. (2024). Beyond AR vs. VR: What is the Difference between AR vs. MR vs. VR vs. XR? https://www.interaction-design.org/literature/article/beyond-ar-vs-vr-what-is-the-difference-between-ar-vs-mr-vs-vrvs-xr#what_is_augmented_reality_(ar)?-3

Vítor Bernardo. (n.d.). *Extended reality | European Data Protection Supervisor*. Retrieved August 15, 2024, from https://www.edps.europa.eu/data-protection/technology-monitoring/techsonar/extended-reality_en

World Economic Forum. (2017). *Shaping the Future of Construction Inspiring innovators redefine the industry*. World Economic Forum. https://www3.weforum.org/docs/WEF_Shaping_the_Future_of_Construction_Inspiring_Innovators_redefine_the_industry_2017.pdf

Anne-Liese Lammich holds a Master's degree in Urban Futures (*Urbane Zukunft*) from the University of Applied Sciences Potsdam and a Bachelor's degree in Architecture from the Technische Universität Berlin. She currently works as a project manager and AI trainer at *Mittelstand-Digital Zentrum Zukunftskultur,* where she supports small and medium-sized enterprises in navigating digital transformation and cultural change. She is also a member of the IDTI, focusing on Artificial Intelligence, immersive technologies, and innovation.

Virtual Reality Tool to Improve Ship Mooring Winch Inspection Training

Wagner Aparecido de Oliveira, Saul Emanuel Delabrida Silva, Davi da Silva, and Adrielle de Carvalho Santana

Abstract The connection between the physical and digital worlds has grown significantly over time, leading engineers to explore innovative tools for industrial applications. These tools aim to balance the safety of personnel and property while enhancing investment value. The central point here is a solution for working with winches for ship mooring systems. Ship mooring at docks involves methods that combine hooks, bollards, and winches. Data gathered from the instrumentation on these systems allows for mooring stability analysis. The primary components of a winch system include its sensing and measurement system, cable tension measurement system, and electrical and mechanical systems. This work shows the creation of a virtual reality application designed for training maintenance personnel. This application will allow trainees to engage with the equipment's functions and data in a virtual and secure environment, providing access to operational procedures and fault diagnosis through simulated problem-solving within virtual reality. This improved the winch inspection training. Future plans involve adding a virtual interface for remote equipment control, which is expected to accelerate the process of identifying faults.

Keywords Virtual reality · Ship mooring systems · Winch inspection · Industrial training · Fault diagnosis

---

W. A. de Oliveira
Universidade Federal de Ouro Preto (UFOP), Ouro Preto, Brazil

Instituto Tecnológico Vale (ITV), Belém, Brazil

Vale S.A., Rio de Janeiro, Brazil
e-mail: wagner.aparecido@vale.com

S. E. D. Silva · A. de Carvalho Santana (✉)
Universidade Federal de Ouro Preto (UFOP), Ouro Preto, Brazil
e-mail: saul.delabrida@ufop.edu.br; adrielle@ufop.edu.br

D. da Silva
Independent Designer and Developer, São Luís, Brazil

K. Bodrožić-Brnić et al. (eds.), *Digital Transformation in Knowledge Transfer*, Digital Transformation and Innovation,
https://doi.org/10.1007/978-3-032-07329-7_5

1 Introduction

Digital innovation has enabled advancements and updates in the knowledge transmission process during training across various sectors of the industry. Mooring ships at piers is a crucial activity which provides safety of all individuals present on the pier and on board the ship, as well as for the safety of the goods on board. A defect or malfunction of the equipment and systems involved in the mooring process can lead to accidents causing significant material and human losses, given the large dimensions that a ship can have, as the one illustrated in Fig. 1.

When it comes to mooring ships, defective equipment can potentially lead to a catastrophe, as a drifting ship could collide with other docked ships or even with other piers. It is difficult to measure the damage from such an accident due to the large size of a ship.

The mooring system used for docking ships at piers consists of methods characterized by the use of combinations of hooks, bollards, and winches. These components are responsible for ensuring stability and safety when ships are docked, whether they are stationary or undergoing loading/unloading operations.

The hook is a device with a set of claws which act as link claws in the mooring process, where ropes are thrown from the ship to shore. The hook is always connected to a traction winch that ensures the proper function of pulling or slackening the tied ropes as needed, providing correct stabilization of the ship. This hook system features the practicality of manual/automatic disarming of the rope. Each hook is also equipped with load cells on each claw, providing tension information on the secured ropes.

The use of the bollard is similar to the hook system. The bollard is also connected to a mooring winch; however, the bollard is solely a manual operation system for securing the hawser for cable engagement, both for docking and undocking

Fig. 1 Ship moored in the Pier IV North which belongs to the VALE S.A. company in São Luís, State of Maranhão, Brasil. (Source: Vale, 2018)

operations. The winch is the primary operational element of the ship mooring system, ensuring proper operation during the mooring period, providing the operator with information for analysis and actions while the ship is docked. Figure 2 illustrates the location of some of these elements in a moored ship.

The winch is exposed to maritime weather and subjected to impacts during its operation, which tends to cause damages (de Oliveira et al., 2024). In this situation, it undergoes maintenance stops, which can lead to operational losses and even affect the pace of ship loading and safety. Problems can occur even when the winches are at rest or during operation (de Oliveira et al., 2024). In this situation, the maintenance team is called to intervene and repair the equipment.

The winch system is divided into a sensing and measurement system, a cable tension measurement system, an electrical system, and a mechanical system. When the maintenance team is required, a technician is assigned to the site to inspect the winch and identify the problem. The technician then addresses the issue by working directly on the equipment. However, failure situations can involve electrical, mechanical, or hydraulic areas, and the professional may not be trained in all these areas.

According to de Oliveira et al. (2024), inspecting the winch in the field presents some difficulties, such as:

- Exposure to risks related to Health, Safety, and Environment (HSE);
- Exposure to the operational area, especially when the system may be operational.
- Travel time from the workshop to the pier area. For example, a given pier, where the present work was developed and tested, has a distance of 1400 m from the workshop to the bridge entrance, another 1800 m from the bridge to the pier entrance, and an additional 1000 m along the pier.

Fig. 2 Elements of the ship mooring system on a pier: Bollard, Winch, and Hook. (Source: Vale, 2018)

Therefore, developing a virtual reality inspection tool becomes interesting, when considering training for maintenance teams. Through this tool, the maintenance team can virtually train to focus on probable equipment defect points by simulating problems. It should also be noted that using a virtual reality tool will provide greater safety in professional training, as it can be carried out in a safe environment without the need to work directly on the equipment (de Oliveira et al., 2024).

Then, the motivation of this work is the development of a virtual reality application for the training of maintenance teams, aiming to facilitate the teaching of winch inspection processes. The development will allow the trained team to interact with the equipment's functionalities and information in a virtual and secure manner, thus ensuring access to operations and fault diagnostics more accurately, aided by simulations of troubleshooting solutions.

It is expected that this approach will reduce the total training time, better prepare the training team by accessing the area safely for in-person interaction with the equipment. Furthermore, if in a later phase, the developed tool enables online connection to the equipment via PLC, the benefits would be extraordinary. Users could identify faults remotely and proceed directly to the location with the solution in mind, which would significantly reduce risks associated with ship mooring.

2 Theoretical and Scientific Framework

2.1 Ship Mooring

The Mooring System is carried out as follows: when the ship is positioned on the pier by the tugs, the onboard cables begin to be launched, which in turn are hooked to the land hooks. For a ship with the dimensions of the one illustrated in Fig. 1 this process takes approximately 1 h and 30 min. Once completed, the laying of the earth cables begins. These, in turn, are the cables for the earth winches, the object of this project. The operator begins the process of releasing the cable to be hitched to the ship. Depending on the ship, the hitch may be on bollards or even ship hooks (de Oliveira et al., 2024).

2.2 Mooring Winches Automation System

The mooring winch system is integrated into a robust automation system, comprising control associated with PLCs (Programmable Logic Controllers) for equipment operation; remote monitoring and activation system through the system supervisory; and the PIMs system for operational and monitoring data and statistics (de Oliveira et al., 2024). The supervisory system, well-known as the human–machine interface, makes it possible for the operator to remotely interact with the equipment,

Fig. 3 Power and control panel. (Source: de Oliveira et al., 2024)

having visual and operational control of the equipment. It is worth noting that for it to be operable, a remote release must be done on the equipment (de Oliveira et al., 2024).

The equipment's automation control system is developed through a PLC application using specific software. For example, in the pier where the tests of this work were performed, the software used in the equipment was the RSLogix, specifically for use in Rockwell PLCs (de Oliveira et al., 2024).The equipment's electrical panel has several control and drive components. This, in turn, is specific to the operational electrical control of the equipment. In Fig. 3, it is possible to check an example of a winch electrical panel. There is also the PLC distributed I/O panel, illustrated in Fig. 4, which is the connection point for all instrumentation onboard with the winch (de Oliveira et al., 2024).

2.3 *Virtual Reality*

This section highlights the evolution of virtual reality today and how it can be used in educational or training processes, including ship mooring training.

Fig. 4 Distributed I/O Panel. (Source: de Oliveira et al., 2024)

2.3.1 Virtual Reality Breaking Paradigms

The evolution of technological solutions for industry is growing day by day. For some time now, technology added to the virtual/augmented reality has been applied in various segments, such as: training, maintenance support, operations (Engineering 4.0), among other segments (de Oliveira et al., 2024). In the literature there are reports of the benefits related to maintenance in augmented reality, aiming to reduce risk exposure and bringing benefits to users' health, as in the work of Justimiano et al. (2021).

A notable advance can be seen in the graphic quality of many digital games in recent times, without losing sight of the ease of use of consoles with much more exposed quality, displaying high-performance computing capacity, compared to the CAD programs known on virtual platforms (de Oliveira et al., 2017).

In a simplified way, virtual reality (VR) is an advanced interface technique between the user and the computer, which simulates a real environment in a virtual way, allowing the interaction, visualization, and manipulation of three-dimensional synthetic environments generated by computers using certain types of multisensory channels. VR enables the user to have a high-performance experience of reality. From the virtual environment with new versions of interaction, using increasingly dynamic keyboards or controls, VR enables innovative experiences that lead to an increasingly detailed understanding of projects or activities of their implementation in a physical environment (de Oliveira et al., 2017, 2024).

VR allows navigation in the digital world using computer graphics, giving the user a three-dimensional view of the real world, which requires a hardware and software structure capable of recognizing six types of movements: front/back, up / down, left/right, right/left angle, up/down tilt, and clockwise/counterclockwise rotation. This dynamic of movements allows a simulation that gives the user the sensation of touching objects, causing a change with the movements established in real time (Valerio Netto et al., 2002; de Oliveira et al., 2024).

2.3.2 Augmented Reality with Technological Advancement

According to de Oliveira et al. (2024) augmented reality differs from virtual reality due to its ability to generate new multimodal interfaces with high ease of manipulating objects in a given space, in which the user can use their hands to interact with a real environment. To make everything happen, the use of augmented reality techniques can place real elements, using optical tracking so that the scene has maximum realism, without the technological apparatus of much connectivity. Therefore, it is possible to create detailed and immersive environments, with interactive elements to allow several innovative applications, as they allow the reliable reproduction of real-life environments such as a house, bank, university, or even a city, guaranteeing the user interaction with each part of the environment and its proper purpose (Kirner & Tori, 2006; de Oliveira et al., 2024).

For Kirner and Tori (2006), augmented reality can be defined as "the enrichment of real environment with virtual objects, using some technological device, working in real time". The mechanisms for making this combination between these realities stand out due to the user's sense of presence and the quality of the images, leaving them free in the environment without the application of as much technological equipment as happens in virtual reality. With augmented reality, the feeling of coexisting with the real world in the same space can combine and align real and virtual objects in real time (de Oliveira et al., 2024).

2.3.3 Virtual Reality as a Learning Method

In recent years there has been a significant increase in the application of mobile devices in the field of education. The educational or training process constitutes a purposeful interaction with technology mediated by learning content between teachers and students where teaching materials seek to solve educational tasks in a systematized and updated way for the development of students. In this sense, the learning environment is virtually guided by information and communication technologies combined with traditional teaching technologies providing greater understanding with virtual environment tools (Zinonos et al., 2018; de Oliveira et al., 2024).

With recent technological advances in the areas of cyber-physical systems, actuators, and sensors, the flexibility of areas along value chains has demonstrated increasing digitalization in both society and industry. In this context, the "Augmented Reality" (AR) is an ambitious technological trend (de Oliveira et al., 2024).

A recent study aimed at investigating the potential of learning using AR showed that the tool supports various learning categories, assisting in learning something practical (as is our proposal here) and enhancing the connection between the physical and the virtual. The tool also proved to be versatile, supporting applications in different modalities and activities, as well as aiding in social practice by enhancing communication between people in different locations (Knudsen et al., 2022).

Its use can facilitate employees' work by providing data in specific situations, in real time and with targeted information. As a result, connecting data to machines results in work without the need for a fixed work environment. However, the inclusion of new technologies also implies a change in the way people work, leading to the restructuring of work processes, particularly in the manufacturing industry (Sorko & Brunnhofer, 2019).

Due to this factor, augmented reality offers several potentials for the industry, allowing, for example, digitalization of process in real time for parallel processes. In this regard, two types of processes can be mentioned: learning and industrial processes. If the focus is on industrial processes, it is possible to check which stage can be improved, where delivery times can be reduced, and activities to be carried out, observing the step by step of a work process (Sorko & Brunnhofer, 2019; de Oliveira et al., 2024).

Therefore, some industries already apply augmented reality in their processes, developing environment projects and activities inherent to the development of employees in the learning process. In the view of the authors Makransky and Klingenberg, virtual reality improves safety training in industrial processes (Makransky & Klingenberg, 2022; de Oliveira et al., 2024). The use of these resources can positively affect the results of safety training, since engaging training is three times more effective in promoting knowledge and skill acquisition, compared to non-engaging training.

AR-based simulations are more immersive as they promote high levels of psychological presence, offering the sensation of being at the scene of the activity, which are often difficult, expensive, or dangerous to produce in real life (Makransky & Klingenberg, 2022).

However, some points still need to be carefully considered when studying the effectiveness of using AR in teaching or training. A literature review with 73 articles on the use of AR in education showed that in most of the evaluated studies, the number of participants was small and the pilot test was of short duration, often due to limitations and problems with the equipment, thus making it difficult to generalize the results. Additionally, not all the main actors in the teaching process were effectively involved in the development of the applications (Koumpouros, 2024).

2.3.4 Augmented Reality in Ship Mooring Training

Currently, some companies are already using augmented reality to carry out safety training. This is the case of OMS-VR, a Ukrainian company, which carries out various maritime safety training in VR in the same location, where it is developing its own software and hardware solution. In this case, VR training allows obtaining results on the professional's physical and psychological state in various stressful situations, without exposing them to the risks of such activities, including equipment for cargo handling, pump room for the fire detection and firefighting system on the Ship's deck and ship mooring winches, all on board (de Oliveira et al., 2024).

What is desired in the present research project is the implementation and analysis of a methodology applicable to land winch mooring systems, where the principles for training are like those observed in a real-world training, seeking acceptable principles for a better condition of safety levels for the maintenance team (de Oliveira et al., 2024).

According to de Oliveira et al. (2024), in navigation mooring cable protection training, the modules created by the OMS-VR provide practical instructions signalling dangers and other associated risks, as well as identifying the return zone in compliance with the requirements of the Training, Issuance of Certificates and Watchkeeping for Seafarers (STCW) convention, Rule I/12 (STCW, 1978).

2.4 Virtual Reality Development Feature

This section presents the tools used to develop the augmented reality application proposed in this work.

2.4.1 Software Unity

Unity is a set of diverse 3D modelling tools for creating interactive media optimized in simple geometries, enabling detailed editing and UV unfolding, as it has rapid prototyping. Unity is a widely used tool, as it guarantees support for independent developers, allowing the development of games and simulations in a more accessible way (Haas, 2014; de Oliveira et al., 2024). This software is compatible with different platforms (PC, consoles, mobile, VR, and AR) using a visual editor and programming through and scripting, offering users professional tools capable of meeting the requirements of any game (de Oliveira et al., 2024).

The main idea is to bring the reality of the winch into a virtualized reality environment that integrates the equipment's real functionality providing the user with a graphical interface of the equipment, making it possible to train for inspection (de Oliveira et al., 2024).

Unity offers developers three ways to program applications attached to the IDE: Unity JavaScript (Commonly known as UnityScript), C#, and Boo. Regardless of the language chosen, all options enable developers to implement the same content, regardless of the established language (Haas, 2014; de Oliveira et al., 2024).

2.4.2 Unity Script

UnityScript is a language that resembles Javascript and is the best choice for beginners. Generally used by most developers, it is easier to obtain assistance in the IRQ forum or the Unity forum. This language is simple to learn and quick to type. Javascript is a prototypical language, while UnityScript is a classical language, which grants it certain benefits. However, even though UnityScript has dynamic typing support, in certain cases it will be less efficient than the C# language, as the compiler must recognize that the object type can change (Haas, 2014; de Oliveira et al., 2024).

Koumpouros (2024) performed a bibliographic review with 73 articles on the use of AR in education and showed that 47.95% of the applications studied were created using Unity.

2.4.3 Boo

The Boo language features a syntax similar to Python, and a structure akin to UnityScript. However, it is not very popular, which makes it challenging to find assistance (Haas, 2014; de Oliveira et al., 2024).

2.4.4 Virtual Reality Glasses

Virtual reality glasses are an equipment that allows you to view images in a stereoscopic 3D effect. This can be connected to a PC and even smartphones. This allows the user to immerse themselves in a virtual 3D environment to practice inspecting the equipment. Since 2012, with the creation of the so-called Rift glasses, many possibilities have emerged with simulations of real environments, being designed with a degree closer to reality, in which high-performance projects are presented with a level of immersion in dynamic visualization spaces in their direct interaction with projects implemented based on the technological advancement of virtual reality (de Oliveira et al., 2017, 2024).

2.5 Use of Virtual Reality in Training

Nowadays, when it comes to economic issues, the job market. and technological advances, organizations must adapt and look for effective and efficient ways to develop training programs, in order to educate, inspire, and awaken knowledge in their employees, at the same time as they face the challenge of maintaining employee engagement and motivation in their training. Thus, while companies are challenged to maintain this engagement, comes the task of providing standardized training in a variety of geographic locations, with different groups of employees, which can result in high financial and energy costs, and expose the employee to various risks throughout the process (Makransky & Klingenberg, 2022; de Oliveira et al., 2024).

Therefore, it is necessary to search for a way to overcome these challenges, creating flexible learning environments and incorporating technology to complement learning and develop trained professionals in an effective and safe way. To verify such learning effectiveness in augmented reality training, a study was carried out by the Department of Psychology in Copenhagen, involving a training program at a maritime industry, on the islands of Kiribati, to investigate whether carrying out training based on augmented reality is more effective than standard safety training. It is detailed in the work of Makransky and Klingenberg (2022) and de Oliveira et al. (2024).

The main key point highlighted is that combining of augmented reality with a generative learning strategy enables students to reflect on the topics covered even after class, thereby enhancing learning outcomes. Most training carried out in a standard way generally uses a single method to pass on content, without evaluating the needs of each student, or providing the opportunity for professionals to experience the relevance of their activity, without exposing themselves to risks (Makransky & Klingenberg, 2022; de Oliveira et al., 2024).

In the study in question, a sample was used consisting of 86 students, both men and women, between 16 and 40 years old, all of them from the maritime education centre in Denmark, Svendborg International Maritime Academy. The experiment was carried out as part of safety training on the topic of "Safety During a Mooring Operation" (Makransky & Klingenberg, 2022).

To obtain a comparative study on security training based on virtual reality, and standard training, the students in question were exposed to two different types of methodologies, one with a trainer and the other with VR (de Oliveira et al., 2024).

The results of this research demonstrate that the group included in the training with augmented reality significantly accepted and appreciated this training, obtaining considerably greater intrinsic motivations and changes in behaviour. It was then discovered that professionals obtained higher levels of pleasure, motivation, and learning, but the individual's ability to organize and execute actions to achieve goals did not show significant changes (de Oliveira et al., 2024).

Therefore, the study in question points to several pieces of evidence suggesting that training with immersive simulations in augmented reality leads to significantly greater pleasure in learning, highlighting the potential that immersive technologies have with a wide range of users in the future.

3 Methods and Development

Pier 4 North was the largest project implemented at the enterprise Vale S. A. in Brazil, approved in 2008 by the board and it is located in São Luís do Maranhão at the Ponta da Madeira Maritime Terminal (TMPM). This project had as its fundamental principle the capacity for 130MTPA (Million tons per year), that is, an additional 30MTPA more than the 100MTPA (Million tons per year) that already had operational capacity. The project did not only involve increasing the port's unloading, storage and boarding capacity; it also generated many job and income opportunities for the entire region (de Oliveira et al., 2024).

Ore shipment includes a long journey for the iron ore to be shipped. This process begins in Carajás-PA where the ore is extracted. After the entire process at the Carajás mine, it is transported by the Ramal Ferroviário Sudeste do Pará to the TMPM-SL in Maranhão. In Fig. 1 shown before, there is an aerial view of Pier IV South and North, where the ship moored can be seen in the North Berth, in its first test with cargo (de Oliveira et al., 2024).

The boarding area at Pier IV consists of two loading berths (South and North). The mooring process is carried out as follows: first, the onboard cables are launched, which will be fixed to the land hooks, after the on-board mooring is completed, the ground cables are launched, which, in turn, originate from the winches on land. The effectiveness of earth winches is guaranteed through scheduled inspections to verify the state of integrity and functionality of the equipment. Based on these inspections, decisions are made regarding the actions of the areas responsible for preventive and corrective maintenance of the equipment.

3.1 Data

Equipment inspection is currently performed visually through operational testing and must be conducted in person. All equipment history data are obtained through PIMs. With this record, reports of failures that occur during equipment operations can be obtained and statistics and trends can be generated for preventive maintenance and plans of reviews. In a graphical view, the process does not present any interaction with the equipment, just a database in which spreadsheets of registered events in the operational or idle state of the winch are processed (de Oliveira et al., 2024).

All information are collected from the winch PLC via the ETH/IP communication network. The model developed in Unity will be used to link real and online data from the PLC application and supervisory system with the developed 3D model. This collected data will refer to status information in the actual operating situation of the equipment. It is expected to have inspection training in the model, which will provide a link between the real scenario and virtual reality (de Oliveira et al., 2024).

3.2 Methodology

A virtual reality tool is used so that the user, with the 3D equipment, has the ability to interact with the equipment virtually. The entire project is developed with real information from the equipment, so that the user can, in a virtual system, obtain data that is as close to reality as possible (de Oliveira et al., 2024).

The feasibility of obtaining virtualized images of the winch that resemble the equipment in the real world will be evaluated. For the development of the tool, the Unity software will be used, and the Virtua VR Oculus Reality Glasses will be employed for visualization. In the testing phase, the application is submitted to users under training for winch inspection. After completing the training, it is important to request the feedback from the users through, for example, a questionnaire based on the Likert scale on their experience of carrying out the inspection using the tool. It is important also to analyse the results in terms of expectations of the users with system (de Oliveira et al., 2024).

The analysis procedure of the users' information can involve a statistical study of the quantitative and qualitative data collected.

3.2.1 Requirements for Winch Inspection

In this step, the necessary requirements are presented for the winch inspection to occur safely in a hydraulic mooring system, and which is taken into account during the development of the proposed tool. Some procedures are adopted to control machinery and mechanical equipment (de Oliveira et al., 2024).

An interesting part to note is the hydraulic power unit that is attached to the base structure of the mooring winch. This unit has two power sources to ensure the necessary flow for the proper functioning of the winch. It consists of a 132 kW power supply unit and another unit of 4.8 kW, which can all be delivered as a compact unit (de Oliveira et al., 2024).

Another piece of equipment frequently used is the L46 pump, which is a fixed flow gear pilot pump that is used to activate the cylinder brake or change the engine displacement, with a composition of directional control valves of various shapes that are accompanied of solenoid valves and pressure filters to prevent excessive pressure from occurring (de Oliveira et al., 2024).

The pilot pump operates in a controlled manner via the PLC in accordance with the signal from the pressure switch installed in the pilot line, and it is recommended to keep the selector in automatic mode. The pilot pump has a "Manual/Automatic" selector. The selector must always be in the "Automatic" position. The PLC controls the start/stop of the pilot pump via a pressure switch. With "Manual Selection", the pilot pump starts when pressing the green "Start pilot pump" button. Once the pump is running, the button remains lit. To stop the pump, press the red "Switch off pilot pump" button. With "Automatic Selection", the pilot pump is controlled via the PLC and pressure switch PS1 (de Oliveira et al., 2024).

The mooring winch is assembled with the hydraulic unit on the same base, where hydraulic and electrical power is supplied. This unit only needs power supply connection and communication connection with the remote-control room (de Oliveira et al., 2024).

The mooring winch is operated from the control panel, illustrated in Fig. 5, so the site will always communicate with the remote-control room in "Local Run" mode. In this sense, the recommendation is to constantly provide information about alarms, pressure, load indication (de Oliveira et al., 2024).

It is worth noting that the winch cannot be controlled remotely if this mode is selected. In "Operation in remote mode", the mooring winch can be controlled from the remote-control room based on the hauling information. On the other hand, when it comes to emergency operation, the mooring winch is operated by the local control panel, noting that in this case, the system does not communicate with the remote-control room (de Oliveira et al., 2024).

For winch operation, the system must have the flow and pressure necessary to allow the hydraulic motor to operate. The hydraulic pump in operation enables smooth starting after 10 s of system operation via joystick control. It is not recommended to operate in joystick mode until start-up is complete. The system is signalled by the green light on the control table (de Oliveira et al., 2024). In this context, for the winch to function correctly, it is necessary that all controls and equipment comply with the characteristics presented above. Its operation must occur in "Local Control" mode, and its power lamp must be on, indicating that

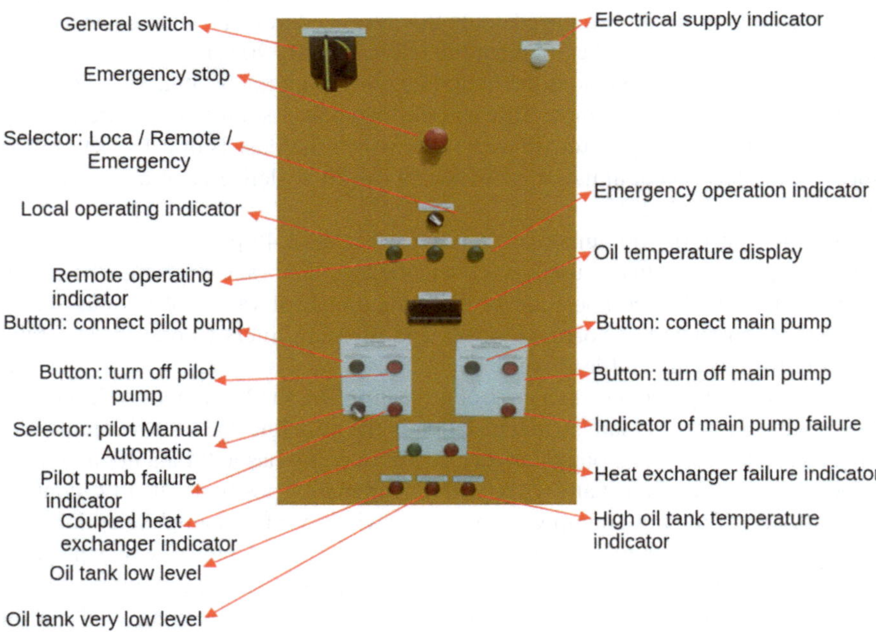

Fig. 5 Winch control panel. (Prepared by the authors)

voltage is available. The pilot pump must be activated (being controlled through the PLC), together with the main pump, which provides the flow and pressure of the hydraulic motor, for the correct winch mooring. Its control, as previously mentioned, is carried out using the joystick, and the speed and rotation of the winch can be controlled. To perform the operation from the control room in remote operation, it is necessary to activate the "Remote" selection mode (de Oliveira et al., 2024).

3.2.2 Elements Considered for Inspection

Following is presented the road map of the research project's inspection plan which need to be present in the virtual tool and is currently used during in-person training according to de Oliveira et al. (2024):

1. Basic knowledge of winching
2. Electric
    - Electrical panel
    - Murr I/O Board
    - Local control panel
3. Hydraulic System
    - Hydraulic elements
    - Hydraulic plan
4. Mechanic
    - Lubrication
    - Reducer
    - Reel
    - Brake
    - Load cells
    - Fairlead
5. Technical assistance
6. Spares

4 The Developed Tool

Below are some images of the developed tool being used by individuals involved in winch inspection activities during the testing phase. After this phase is completed, the training will be performed with people under winch inspection training. A questionnaire based on the Likert scale will be applied to them after training with the augmented reality application and also after traditional training (with due approval

Fig. 6 Overview of the virtualized winch and control panel. (Photo by the authors)

from the local ethics committee and signature of the Free and Informed Consent Form).

A qualitative and quantitative analysis of the data collected is interesting to get an idea of the performance of using the augmented reality training tool, and what can be improved for future training. It should be added that it is interesting to repeat this procedure with other teams in training at other times to have a good sample for analysing the findings, giving more weight and credibility to the conclusions obtained. Figure 6 illustrates the winch and its control panel. Figure 7 depicts a user wearing virtual reality glasses, viewing the winch control panel in front of them. Users are able to use the glasses and physically interact with the control in the real world to manipulate the virtualized winch control panel. When the user interacts with one of the panel's light indicators, they trigger the appearance of a small frame describing the button's function and the different states it can indicate. Finally, the experimental setup is depicted in Fig. 8 as well as some users under training.

5 Conclusion

Currently, several companies are already implementing virtual reality for safety training purposes. This approach to training in VR enables the acquisition of insights into the physical and psychological state of professionals when facing various stressful scenarios, all without exposing them to the inherent dangers of such activities. The data generated from these VR training sessions can provide more detailed input for engineering considerations. Furthermore, advancements in graphic imaging and programming are making it possible to enhance the interaction between

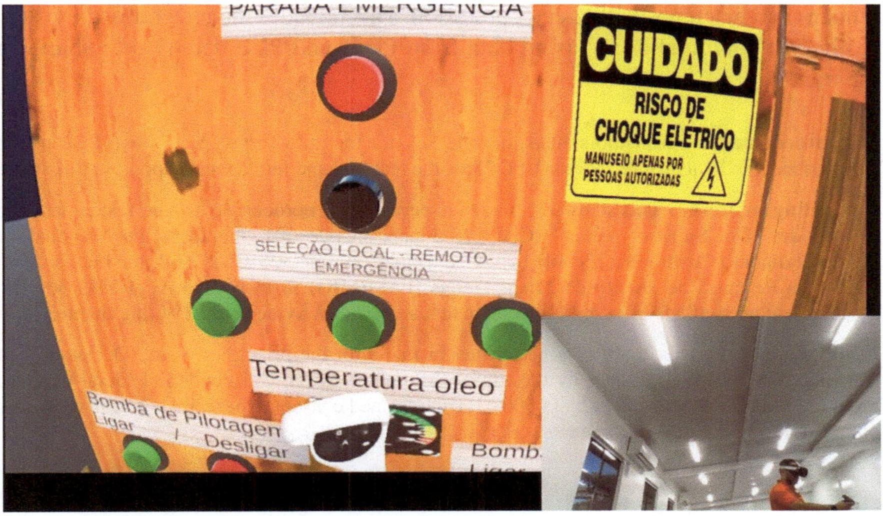

Fig. 7 User viewing the winch control panel in front of him. (Photo by the authors)

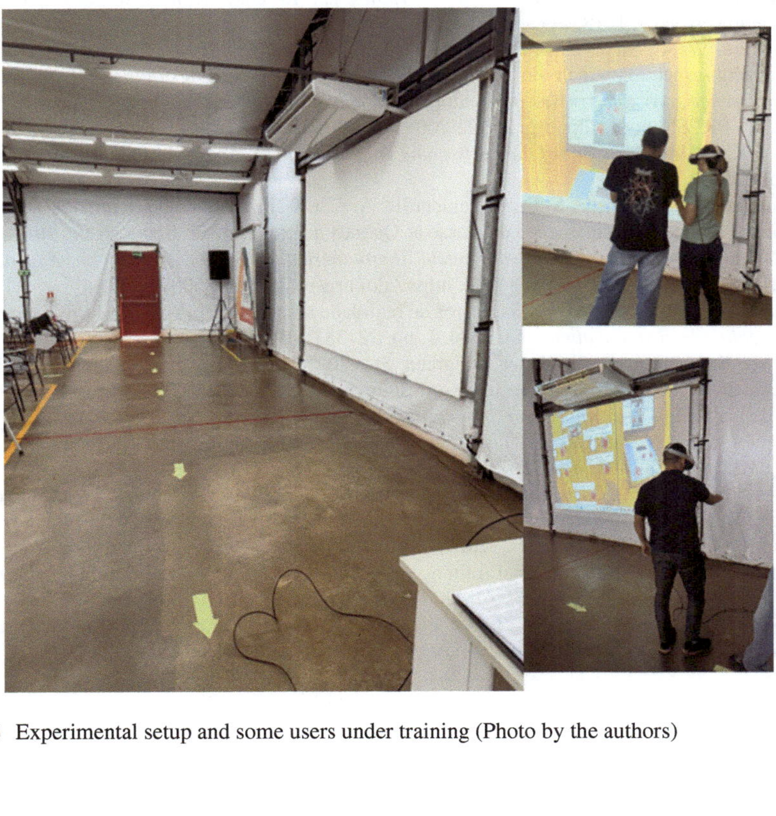

Fig. 8 Experimental setup and some users under training (Photo by the authors)

humans and machines with greater precision. This includes the integration of virtual reality with automation by using data from PIMs and PLC databases, enhancing the training.

Acknowledgments The authors thank the Vale S.A, the Instituto Tecnológico Vale (ITV) and the Universidade Federal de Ouro Preto (UFOP) for the material and intellectual support to this study.

Competing Interests This study was funded in part by the Coordenação de Aperfeiçoamento de Pessoal de Nível Superior—Brasil (CAPES), Finance Code 001, the Conselho Nacional de Desenvolvimento Científico e Tecnológico (CNPq) finance code 306101/2021-1, the Fundação de Amparo à Pesquisa do Estado de Minas Gerais (FAPEMIG) finance code APQ-0089-30. The authors have no conflicts of interest to declare that are relevant to the content of this chapter.

Ethics Approval This study was performed in line with the principles of the Declaration of Helsinki. Approval was granted by the Ethics Committee of the Universidade Federal de Ouro Preto (22 May 2024/No.76091423.2.0000.5150). Informed consent to participate in this study was obtained from individual participants.

References

de Oliveira, G. M., Andaló, F., & Vieira, M. L. H. (2017). Realidade virtual e projeto arquitetônico: da criação à experiência do usuário. *Tríades em Revista: Transversalidades, Design e Linguagens, 6*(2), 1–18.

de Oliveira, W. A., Silva, S. E. D., Silva, D., & Santana, A. C. (2024). Development of a ship mooring inspection winch tool with extended reality. In *Proceedings of the 26th International Conference on Enterprise Information Systems (ICEIS 2024)* (Vol. 2, pp. 247–255). SCITEPRESS. https://doi.org/10.5220/0012703000003690

Haas, J. K. (2014). *A history of the unity game engine* (pp. 483–484). Master's Thesis. Worcester Polytechnic Institute.

Justimiano, A. C., Motta, E. S. D., & Sementille, A. C. (2021). Sistema de Realidade Aumentada para o Ensino e Treinamento de Pessoas Quanto a Execução de Serviços de Montagem e Manutenção de Equipamentos. *Revista Iberoamericana de Tecnolog´ıa en Educación y Educación en Tecnología, 28*, 34–40. https://doi.org/10.24215/18509959.28.e4

Kirner, C., & Tori, R. (2006). Fundamentos de realidade aumentada. In *Fundamentos e tecnologia de realidade virtual e aumentada* (Vol. 1, pp. 22–38). SBC.

Knudsen, S. P., Hansen, H. H., & Ørngreen, R. (2022). Exploring the learning potentials of augmented reality through speculative design. In I. E. Brooks, J. Sjöberg, & A. K. Møller (Eds.), *Design, Learning, and Innovation: 6th EAI International Conference, DLI 2021, Virtual Event, December 10–11, 2021, Proceedings* (pp. 156–163). Springer. https://doi.org/10.1007/978-3-031-06675-7

Koumpouros, Y. (2024). Revealing the true potential and prospects of augmented reality in education. *Smart Learning Environments, 11*, 2. https://doi.org/10.1186/s40561-023-00288-0

Makransky, G., & Klingenberg, S. (2022). Virtual reality enhances safety training in the maritime industry: An organizational training experiment with a non-WEIRD sample. *Journal of Computer Assisted Learning, 38*(4), 1127–1140. https://doi.org/10.1111/jcal.12670

Sorko, S. R., & Brunnhofer, M. (2019). Potentials of augmented reality in training. *Procedia Manufacturing, 31*, 85–90. https://doi.org/10.1016/j.promfg.2019.03.014

STCW. (1978). *Convenção Internacional sobre Padrões de Instrução, Certificação e Serviço de Quarto para Marítimos, 1978*. Retrieved July 13, 2024, from https://www.ifpb.edu.br/cabedelocentro/cursos/epm/acesso-a-informacao/legislacao/normas-internacionais-final/codigostcwpa_2017_2parta-1.pdf

Vale S. A.. (2018). *Book de Projetos Porto Norte S11D—Offshore/Onshore*.

Valerio Netto, A., Machado, L. D. S., & Oliveira, M. C. F. D. (2002). *Realidade virtual-definições, dispositivos e aplicações*. Retrieved February 13, 2024, from https://repositorio.usp.br/directbitstream/eea56bbf-fdf6-4a65-9681-47497e5d3544/ND54.pdf

Zinonos, N. O., Vikhrova, O. V., & Pikilnyak, A. V. (2018). Prospects of using the augmented reality for training foreign students at the preparatory departments of universities in Ukraine. *Educational Dimension, 51*, 115–122. https://doi.org/10.31812/pedag.v51i0.3661

Wagner Aparecido de Oliveira holds a Master's degree in Control and Automation Engineering from the PROFICAM program at the Universidade Federal de Ouro Preto (UFOP) in association with the Instituto Tecnológico Vale (ITV). He is a researcher and lecturer with experience in engineering and technology education, particularly in automation, virtual reality, and immersive technologies. He has contributed to research and development projects focused on digital tools for training, inspection systems, and human–machine interaction. His work often integrates applied technology and innovative learning environments, strongly emphasising interdisciplinary collaboration and practical application. He also has experience inspecting mooring winches on large piers and provides training on the subject.

Saul Emanuel Delabrida Silva is a professor at the Universidade Federal de Ouro Preto (UFOP), Brazil, and coordinator of the XR4Good Lab. With over 14 years of experience in computer science, his research focuses on wearable technologies, mixed reality applications, and user-centred design. His work integrates machine learning and computer vision to support innovation in Industry 5.0, accessibility, and health and is disseminated through academic publications, technical reports, and patents.

Davi da Silva holds a degree in Industrial Design from the Universidade Católica de Brasília, and a postgraduate qualification in Software Development from Universidade Cruzeiro do Sul. He is currently a Senior Designer at V4 Company and has over 10 years of experience in the creative industries. He has developed design solutions for large corporations, multinational companies, and start-ups throughout his career. In addition to his professional work, he has lectured at universities and technical colleges and regularly speaks on topics related to design functionality.

Adrielle de Carvalho Santana has been a professor at the Department of Control and Automation Engineering at the Universidade Federal de Ouro Preto (UFOP) since 2013. She holds degrees in Control and Automation Engineering (UFOP), an MSc in Information Engineering (UFABC), and dual PhDs in Electrical Engineering (UFMG) and Cognitive Sciences (Université Grenoble Alpes). She also works as a professor and advisor in the PROFICAM program at the Universidade Federal de Ouro Preto (UFOP) in association with Instituto Tecnológico Vale (ITV). Her research interests include signal processing and analysis, biomedical signal processing, instrumentation, digital control theory, analogue and digital electronics, and computational intelligence.

Learning in Loops: Designing Knowledge Management in SMEs and Its Impact on Digital Transformation

Ninette Florschütz

Abstract Digital transformation and the increasing use of Artificial Intelligence are changing how SMEs receive and pass on information and transform it into organisational knowledge. Transparent, recursive, and timely information transfer to decision-relevant stakeholders harbours considerable potential for identifying, making accessible, and collectively utilising existing knowledge within the company. However, these efforts are often hampered by inhibiting factors that cling to traditional methods and limit organisational learning capacity. While some stakeholders hope that digital technologies will relieve experienced knowledge holders of routine tasks and enable them to perform more demanding activities, there are fears of potential knowledge gaps or wrong decisions being uncovered and of losing one's job through Artificial Intelligence. This raises the question of whether medium-sized companies' knowledge management can effectively link personal and systemic knowledge, foster organisational learning, and develop strategic competitive advantages. These companies' communication and management processes provide key entry points for critically analysing knowledge management design. This article examines the specific organisational and process design for communicating information and decision-making in day-to-day operations. Empirical findings from an interdisciplinary literature analysis (n = 177) and a qualitative survey (n = 26) illustrate the organisation in practice. The evaluation includes the prompt and recursive provision of information and managing fears and uncertainties as barriers to organisational learning. Finally, the impact of specific design choices on learning ability is analysed.

N. Florschütz (✉)
Ilmenau University of Technology, Ilmenau, Germany
e-mail: florschuetz@kompetenzzentrum-ilmenau.de

K. Bodrožić-Brnić et al. (eds.), *Digital Transformation in Knowledge Transfer*, Digital Transformation and Innovation,
https://doi.org/10.1007/978-3-032-07329-7_6

Keywords Knowledge management · Medium-sized companies · Artificial intelligence · Organisational learning ability · Systemic knowledge

1 Introduction

Companies are social entities that make decisions at multiple organisational levels, structure value-creation processes around a division of labour, and strategically align these processes to maintain or improve productivity, foster learning, and enhance performance—ultimately generating competitive advantages. To implement their strategies, they need effective processes in order to supply information, exchange organisational knowledge, and foster organisational learning (Kusa et al., 2024; Reischauer & Schober, 2016; Steinmann & Schreyögg, 2005). In addition to large businesses, small and medium-sized enterprises (SMEs) must also manage information and knowledge effectively. As a result, information and knowledge management (from here on "IWM", from the German term *Informations- und Wissensmanagement*) becomes a vital, success-critical element of their strategic management (Henschel et al., 2024; Mostafiz et al., 2023; Wang et al., 2023; Shekhar & Valeri, 2023).

It encompasses all management tasks as well as strategic and operational activities, i.e. information systems that serve to provide data and information, experience and knowledge as well as skills and abilities the organisation or its members require to solve the diverse tasks based on the division of labour. The ongoing digital transformation and the introduction of Artificial Intelligence (AI) into business processes are changing the way in which employees receive and pass on information and transform it into organisational knowledge. This article, therefore, analyses the specific design of IWM and highlights the influences and effects of the digital transformation.

Research findings focus on the limited relationships between information management and knowledge management in SMEs (Al-Emran et al., 2018). Existing studies mainly focus on the differences between the two concepts (Krcal & Kubis, 2016), meaning their causal relationships have not yet been sufficiently researched or explained (Kusa et al., 2024). This is aggravated by the fact that the studies primarily focus on large companies (Durst & Henschel, 2024) and do not consider the specific framework conditions of SMEs when designing information and knowledge management.

The COVID-19 pandemic also brought challenges for SMEs and large businesses alike, which promoted the use of IT and influenced IWM processes (Barnes, 2020). Many of these companies have retained and established the agile and virtual solution approaches introduced at the time, as well as changed working models such as home office or remote working, so that the research gap on IWM in SMEs has widened even further (Barnes, 2020; Priyono et al., 2020; Kusa et al., 2024; Henschel et al., 2024).

However, small and medium-sized enterprises, especially owner-managed or family-run, make up over 90% of the German and European business population (IfM, 2023; Fels & Wolter, 2022; Wolter & Sauer, 2017). The proportion of owner- or family-managed companies among German SMEs has also remained high in recent decades (Hoon, 2016; Wolter & Sauer, 2017; Pahnke et al., 2021) and the intersection of SMEs and owner-managed companies is very large (Welter et al., 2014). When analysing their communication and management processes, studies often refer to the special position of the entrepreneur or their family, their special cultural imprint through the founder or entrepreneurial personality and the influence of personal goals on strategic orientation (Kelly et al., 2000; Schein, 1983; Fischbach & Mack, 2008; Winkler, 2020; Welter et al., 2020). In view of their social responsibility and the number of employees, their contribution to society goes beyond purely business and economic performance, especially in times of crisis (Welter et al., 2020). By reducing the prevailing uncertainty of all market participants during the pandemic and conveying values of commitment and reliability, they provided an important additional benefit to society in overcoming the prevailing challenges and stabilising the economy during the crisis (Welter et al., 2020). The limited understanding of IWM in SMEs thus requires a deeper consideration in the context of entrepreneurship (Audretsch & Belitski, 2021; Kusa et al., 2024).

Efforts to improve information and learning processes through new technologies are simultaneously influenced by inhibiting factors that can lead to adherence to traditional methods and hinder organisational learning ability. As SMEs in particular are considered to be rather reluctant when it comes to participating in the digital transformation (Zerfaß et al., 2016; Bellmann et al., 2024; Bundesnetzagentur, 2023), the question arises as to whether the design of their specific IWM will continue to be suitable for linking personal and systemic knowledge, promoting the organisation's ability to learn and developing strategic competitive advantages in the future.

The SME-specific organisational and process design for information supply and decision-making in day-to-day operations thus serve as a starting point for taking a closer critical look at the IWM practised in SMEs and evaluating its impact. As networks in SMEs serve as an important strategic resource of information and knowledge, the article further includes information processes that go beyond organisational boundaries in the consideration of IWM in SMEs (Lyles et al., 1993; Kellermanns et al., 2006; Zerfaß et al., 2016; Roach, 2016).

2 Methodology

To illustrate how IWM is practiced in SMEs, this article draws on findings from an interdisciplinary literature analysis (Florschütz, 2024). The analysis examined 177 empirical studies from communication, organisational and management research, with the goal of identifying evidence-based insights on strategic communication management in SMEs. The literature search involved scientific databases (Web of Science, Google Scholar, SAGE, Emerald, Elsevier, EBSCOhost, and JSTOR) as well as university catalogues and databases. As the research results of the literature analysis were filtered using key terms in English and German only, the literature analysis does not claim to be exhaustive of all published studies.

In order to take account of the special features of owner-managed SMEs within the sample structure of the literature research, which is based on the unity of ownership, management, and control, the study portfolio was supplemented by further empirical studies. These studies were taken from the publication directories of the *Institut für Mittelstandsforschung Bonn* and the references of the empirical studies used, provided that the samples of the surveys met the EU criteria (cf. European Commission of 6 May 2003/361/EC) or were explicitly geared towards owner-managed or family-run companies.

The article is based on the fact that the intersection of SMEs and owner-managed companies is very large at over 90% (Welter et al., 2014; IfM, 2023; Fels & Wolter, 2022; Wolter & Sauer, 2017) and decreases significantly with increasing company size as shown in Fig. 1. Results of the interdisciplinary literature analysis provide a variety of insights into SME-specific strategic communication management design decisions. They not only serve this article to analyse the specific IWM design but also open up new perspectives on SME-specific issues and encourage further research.

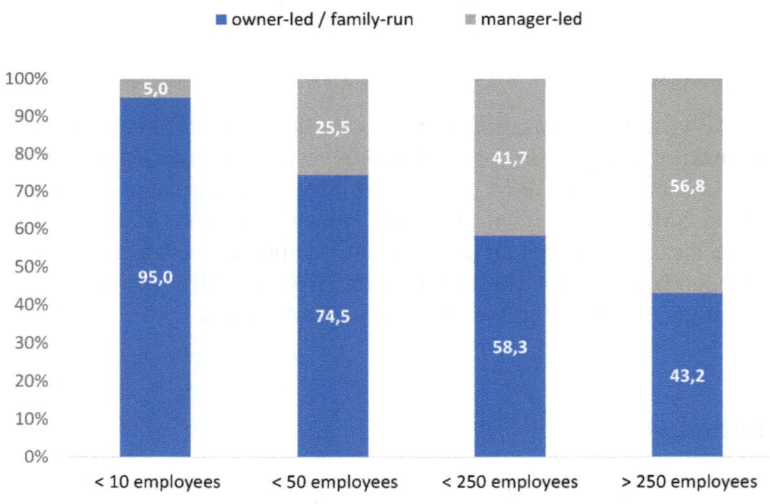

Fig. 1 Congruence of small and medium-sized companies in Germany (Pahnke et al., 2021)

3 Design Patterns of Information and Knowledge Management in SMEs

In addition, the results are used to illustrate the design patterns practised for certain communication and management processes and to show how SMEs generate, convey, and process information and knowledge.

3.1 Structure and Responsibility

In owner-managed SMEs, decisions on the design of IWM are largely centralised with the company management (Spence & Essoussi, 2010; Fischbach & Mack, 2008). They do not only take key decisions but are also personally involved in individual processes or delegate and monitor their implementation (Daschmann, 1994).

The functional overload of company management associated with the centrality of the entrepreneur is a frequently cited point of criticism (Winkler, 2020; Schütte, 2011). As SMEs are generally not run by managers but by entrepreneurs (Welter et al., 2014; Fels & Wolter, 2022; Wolter & Sauer, 2017), the unity in terms of ownership and management must be taken into account here. This unity also reflects the special "responsibility of the manager for all company-relevant decisions" (Fischbach & Mack, 2008, p. 17). The exemplary concentration of the control tasks of the information system on corporate management (Eng & Spickett-Jones, 2020) thus points to the high importance of IWM.

With increasing company size and more complex organisational structures, the management tasks for information supply are delegated to managers, departments, or service providers (Mast, 2000; Zerfaß et al., 2015). The tasks are assumed by employees who have a close relationship with the management or assume management responsibility (Held, 2007a, Held, 2007b; Deimel & Kraus, 2007). They also receive support from a small team of assistant functions, actors from various functional areas and external service providers (Moss et al., 2003; Zerfass & Winkler, 2016). Communication tasks are therefore often handled flexibly, without clearly defined areas of responsibility, and are taken on as an additional task by employees from other departments who are otherwise entrusted with completely different tasks within the company (Laube, 1986; Fischbach & Mack, 2008; Schütte, 2011). However, the authority to issue instructions and maintain oversight, as well as the feedback processes involving company management, remain in place through direct, personal contact (Zerfaß et al., 2016).

Communication processes are usually based on the direct transfer and exchange of information, informal coordination, a strong corporate culture and a trusting, familiar working atmosphere (Fischbach & Mack, 2008; Scharpe, 1992; Huck, 2005; Winkler, 2020). The institutionalisation of IWM follows the principles of low-hierarchy information flow, coordinated information processing, optimised information content and expediency (Bussiek, 1981; Wittlage, 1996). Standardised information from a single source avoids conflicts and frictional losses. At the same time, the decision-makers retain an overview and the desired control over the planned activities. Within the various specialist functions or sub-areas and across hierarchical levels, information is coordinated, compared, and standardised or selectively passed on, which inevitably leads to value- and goal-oriented coordination of the activities of the various players and to smoother processes. Through this institutionalisation of IWM, SMEs follow their individual requirements, maintain a stringent focus on the most important target groups of employees and customers for the business processes and preserve lean structures (Rötzer, 2013). This ensures personal proximity and trusting communication at eye level, which favours a high degree of value orientation, authenticity, reliability, and relationship consistency and represents a key success factor for SMEs (Pfohl, 2006; Dietz et al., 2019; Wittlage, 1996).

Many of these companies still reject fixed organisational regulations for the design of communication and information processes to maintain the specific communication culture and the necessary flexibility and to counteract bureaucratisation. The low level of formalisation of IWM is therefore not only due to the small size of the organisation but primarily to the specific ownership and management relationships (Laube, 1986; Fischbach & Mack, 2008), which result in greater independence and freedom of strategic orientation. The specific process design of IWM will be analysed in more detail along the phases of strategic management and illustrated using the impact contributions.

3.2 Acquisition of Information and Knowledge

To effectively participate in market and social processes, ward off dangers, prevent crises, manage risks and identify issues, trends, and opportunities in good time, organisations must gather relevant information and knowledge for legitimacy and organisational purposes through observation of the organisation, market, and environment (analysis phase). Information and knowledge relevant to the organisation must be procured and processed as part of difference and relationship management as well as self-control. SMEs require systematic information management for information and data procurement (cf. Kusa et al., 2024; Kussin, 2009; Zerfaß & Volk, 2019; Kettinger et al., 2021).

The study results show that SMEs carry out less systematic, but conscious and goal-oriented organisational, market, and environmental monitoring (Gbadamosi, 2020; Carson et al., 2004; Schütte, 2011; Zerfaß et al., 2016). Their observations focus not only on relationships within the market, but also on cross-market networks, taking into account all stakeholders from customers, competitors, and suppliers to media representatives, politicians, applicants, and neighbours (Halliday, 2020). Daschmann (1994) confirms that SMEs make intensive use of information sources. However, the personally obtained data is based on incomplete, unverified information from the personal network. Consequently, SMEs do not lack the ability to obtain decision-relevant information, but their performance in obtaining and processing information is assessed as incomplete, unsystematic, and therefore unsatisfactory (Bussiek, 1981) and the lack of systematic collection and processing of external and internal data is criticised: This is done acutely and unstructured, important sources of information are not taken into account, established analysis tools are hardly used, so that no standardised, internal company process can be identified for the collection and evaluation according to relevance and risk (Kraus et al., 2007; Schatilow, 2014; Scharpe, 1992).

This can be countered by the fact that the majority of SMEs operate in manageable market structures with few competitors which means that it can also be assumed that it is sufficient to limit oneself to essential data and track it (Brodbeck, 1995; Laube, 1986). Bussiek therefore states that an optimal information situation for SMEs does not mean being informed as comprehensively as possible, but rather in good time and "as concentrated as possible, as meaningful as possible" (Bussiek, 1981, p. 23). Schweizer (2015) points out that SMEs tend to make a conscious selection instead of an overall analysis, which must fit the individual objective or the overall context.

According to studies, SMEs use both analogue and digital sources of information to monitor political, social, and economic events as well as to obtain information and assess technological, industry, and economic developments. Public media are an important tool for observing and assessing public opinion and as an organisational early warning system to monitor developments, prevent criticism, and manage crises (Alter, 2012; Zerfaß et al., 2016; Fischbach & Mack, 2008; Schatilow, 2014). Relevant information in SMEs is obtained in an uncomplicated, direct, and cost-effective manner through personal discussions with market partners, customers, political representatives, journalists, and employees. Information is gathered from sources with whom the decision-makers have a personal and trusting relationship and who are knowledgeable, experienced, well-known, and well-connected as well as empathetic and willing to help them (Laube, 1986; Balsys, 2004; Winkler et al., 2018; Carson et al., 1995). By using their manageable market and organisational structures for personal communication, Laube (1986) ascribes them slight to very great advantages over large companies in terms of information procurement. Craig and Moores (2006) also refer to the correlation between the type of information procurement and the information power regarding the efficiency of observation and analysis, which is even higher in SMEs than in comparative studies in high-tech companies. Their political, regional, social, or even economic networks and their dialogue-based orientation enable SMEs not only to obtain information, but also to access data and information at first hand, exchange information, discuss different perspectives, collectively evaluate information, gain inspiration, and identify new resources and capacities, which must be transformed into new means of success potential (Sen et al., 2022; Gabrielli & Balboni, 2010; Brink, 2010; Aragón-Sánchez & Sánchez-Marín, 2005).

3.3 Mediation and Processing

The analysis results obtained from organisational, market, and environmental monitoring on new products, technologies, structures, changes in the legal framework, expectations of reference groups, competitive pressure, but also negative media reports, criticism of company representatives or structural change in the environment trigger reflexive actions among SMEs (Gurau et al., 2017; Schütte, 2011; Zerfaß et al., 2016; Winkler, 2020; Welter, 2003). SMEs primarily use the coordination instruments of harmonisation, self-determination, and co-determination to manage the associated implementation processes (Jochims, 2013). Against the background of personal leadership and within manageable structures and trusting relationships, associated processes of information transfer and processing as well as knowledge and opinion acquisition are generally based on direct and personal communication, whereby the vast majority of SMEs initially inform the relevant reference groups about the necessity of decisions or exchange information with them with the help of informal feedback processes (Balsys, 2004; Jochims, 2013; Wittlage, 1996; Zerfaß et al., 2016). SMEs thus meet the requirement that strategy content in the company should not be communicated exclusively top-down but should be exchanged with employees through a dialogue (Fischbach & Mack, 2008; Winkler, 2020). As the probability of developing better and more marketable ideas in a team is significantly higher than if ideas are developed "in a quiet chamber" [the emphasis is applied in the original text] (Felden & Hack, 2014, p. 215), not only the owners are involved in the planning process, but also trusted external parties or affected stakeholders from other organisational areas (Schwender & Zeichhardt, 2012; Looser, 2017).

By making its decision-making logic transparent during the negotiation of measures, company management not only involves relevant reference groups at an early stage but also obtains information on the overall context as well as insight into the interaction and relationships between the parts of the company (Hinterhuber, 2004). Additionally, it becomes evident that, beyond the analysis phase, SMEs once again seek feedback from market partners and trusted information providers in order to exchange views on the decision-making situation and findings, discuss them, evaluate them, and learn from the experiences of others (Schatilow, 2014; Felden & Hack, 2014; Roach, 2016).

According to Bruhn (2010), formal, i.e. written communication in delegation relationships then serves as a management and control instrument to define the scope and framework for action of employees, within which measures can be planned independently. The communicated guidelines form the basis and logic of the entire action process (Laux, 2007; Holtzhausen & Zerfaß, 2013). However, written concepts or plans are only partially used by SMEs. If they are used, they only serve as an orientation aid or guideline for action, not as a rigid task list (Zerfaß et al., 2016; Zerfass & Winkler, 2016; Florschütz, 2024; Stonehouse & Pemberton, 2002). The coordinative form of regulation is therefore not the primary chosen means of corporate management in SMEs, as the personal responsibility of employees is reduced if processes are over-regulated, "and that cannot be the way" (Looser, 2017: 254). Only 5% of management in SMEs makes decisions and gives specific orders (Wittlage, 1996). They are used for recurring routine tasks, but not for uncertain future developments or individual decisions (Jochims, 2013).

About a third of decision-makers only specify basic decisions as part of strategy communication and delegate further tasks and follow-up decisions to employees. Two-thirds of SME decision-makers set targets to limit the scope for decision-making and enable employees to make decisions largely independently within the scope of their authorisation (Wittlage, 1996). They provide the actors involved with orientation in decision-making situations but also give them the necessary freedom to adapt to the circumstances at any time.

Since co-determination is only possible for those who can think for themselves (Mast, 2000), it is obviously important for SME decision-makers to enable employees to "mentally anticipate possible realities" (Martin & Behrends, 1998) and to empower them to implement rules independently and efficiently in line with the overarching objectives.

When communicating strategy, SMEs therefore not only take into account all reference groups within and outside the organisation that are relevant for implementation (Rötzer, 2013; Aragón-Sánchez & Sánchez-Marín, 2005; Zellweger et al., 2012). Laube (1986) also states, with regard to the willingness of decision-makers to provide information to their own employees, that they receive sufficient information (82.6 %). Only around one in ten complain about too much or too little information from the company management, which means that SMEs hardly differ from large companies.

As part of the division of labour management processes, SMEs primarily use dialogue-based channels to communicate instructions or factual information (Wittlage, 1996; Zerfaß et al., 2016). This approach allows even complex issues to be communicated, maximising personal contact and ensuring that defined goals are explained clearly, highlighted in a nuanced manner and conveyed emotionally. If this does not happen, so much pressure is exerted on employees that they are reached in other, undesirable ways (Waibel, 2016; Mast, 2000).

Instructions or coordination, therefore, often take place via the "short official channels". In the context of delegation, SME decision-makers usually act "tactfully at eye level instead of reducing themselves to commands" (Waibel, 2016: 68). The "eye level" they establish is reconstructed in the daily dialogue-based teamwork but would be "destroyed by the superior's command" (Waibel, 2016: 67). Because "trust is the basis of our collaboration. It is given by me and I automatically get it back" (Waibel, 2016: 31). In line with the dialogue-based approach, feedback, i.e. the exchange of feelings, opinions, and attitudes, is both verbal and non-verbal, direct and personal (Jochims, 2013).

Through personal dialogue and close coordination, SMEs are then able to better involve partners, employees, and customers in overarching decisions and communicate innovations and their benefits to the target groups in a better and more comprehensible way, even without a formal target system (Roach, 2016). However, by turning those affected into contributors, SMEs can not only meet the employees' need for dialogue and participation (Mast, 2000). By maintaining informal dialogue processes, SMEs reflect their flat hierarchical structures (Zerfass & Winkler, 2016) and provide the relevant stakeholders with information about their relationship with each other (Jochims, 2013). The resulting interpersonal relationships enable delegation relationships that make formal control obsolete, as the responsible stakeholders are directly involved in the processes of information transfer and processing within the single-line system, which is characterised by acceptance and trust (Jochims, 2013). While the management specifies the objectives and content, these are implemented by managers in different departments (Zerfaß et al., 2015, 2016; Schwaiger et al., 1995). However, the planning and execution of internal communication remains in the hands of the employer as communication between the boss and his employees, as this is considered particularly important (Rötzer, 2013; Fallosch, 2007; Mast, 2000) and enables co-orientation (Rötzer, 2013). Based on the specified goals and values and the trust placed in them, they also have their regulatory options on-site, increasing their self-determination and responsibility for their own activities. In this way, SMEs resolve the frequently criticised functional overload of company management in day-to-day business.

3.4 Critical Consideration of the Design

The empirical results on the institutionalisation of IWM indicate that the design of IWM is the responsibility of a regulatory body in the area of strategic management. This initially fulfils the prerequisites for integrating information and knowledge into the horizontal and vertical control processes of strategic management (Reischauer & Schober, 2016; Steinmann & Schreyögg, 2005). The proximity to the target group through personal exchange within the framework of manageable markets and structures indicates a high level of interpenetration between the subsystems (Knight, 2001).

Their *process design* reflects the fact that SMEs not only procure and process information in a goal-oriented, problem- and topic-focused manner in order to perceive changes in the organisation, market, and environment, but also react to them in a targeted, active, situational, and rapid manner (Brodbeck, 1995), so that they can be said to make conscious use of their information and knowledge management. However, due to a lack of systematic and complete data collection and formal processing, the specific process design of the IWB has been criticised for decades and its performance has been assessed as unsatisfactory (Kraus et al., 2007; Balsys, 2004; Scharpe, 1992; Bussiek, 1981).

As SMEs use formal analysis tools to a lesser extent than large companies, larger companies can incorporate more information into strategic planning and consequently choose from a wider range of strategic options (Deimel & Kraus, 2007; Lyles et al., 1993). Bussiek (1981) also points out that, due to a lack of organisational regulations, a lack of time and a referent staff, SMEs are not even able to record all information and possible influencing factors, which may not even be necessary against the background of manageable markets. The extent to which information is effective depends on its quality, expressed in terms of availability, completeness, accuracy, timing, relevance, timeliness, and internal and external connectivity (Sen et al., 2022). Consequently, depending on the type and purpose of the company, priorities must be set as to which influences should be processed in an environmental or company analysis, and how (Schweizer, 2015). It can therefore be assumed that an optimal information situation for SMEs does not mean being informed as comprehensively as possible, but rather in good time and "as concentrated as possible, as meaningful as possible" (Bussiek, 1981, p. 23). Regarding their information procurement and reflection during the analysis phase, SMEs are even said to be exceptionally willing to perceive environmental changes and user behaviour (Brodbeck, 1995; Lyles et al., 1993).

If the contributions of information procurement and processing within the individual phases of strategic management are then examined, the results of the empirical studies show that information procurement enables SMEs to minimise the complexity, uncertainty, and dangers of emerging risks and ensure their ability to survive, even without systematic market surveys (Gurau et al., 2017; Gbadamosi, 2020). SMEs utilise their structural advantages and strategic flexibility cost-efficiently and effectively with the help of their informal network and relationship management as a leverage effect (Sen et al., 2022; Welter et al., 2020: 23; Lizama et al., 2021: 13; Karami et al., 2022) by the following actions:

1. gaining information to analyse and logically evaluate situations, reduce uncertainty, and identify opportunities,
2. utilising relationships, specific knowledge and information from the network and benefit from the ideas and motivations of other players,
3. gaining experience and knowledge of the technologies, processes, and routines of others during the analysis phase and expand their own knowledge of markets, products, and expertise,
4. using the skills and capacities of the network to exploit their potential for success and increase their productivity, reduce costs, carry out innovation activities and creative design processes to improve products and services and optimise their own performance in this way,
5. exchanging information, knowledge, and experience within the framework of strategic planning in order to concretise own objectives and jointly refine strategies,
6. and uniting collectively in the context of implementation to be perceived as a community of economic actors and to develop new markets, production, supply and distribution structures as part of the network.

It is also evident that SMEs utilise direct and reciprocal information transfer as a key competitive advantage and consciously use it as a strategic success factor (Wang et al., 2023; Shekhar & Valeri, 2023; Halliday, 2020) to overcome their resource limitations and structural disadvantages.

It can therefore be assumed that the process design of the IWM is deliberately chosen by the SMEs in order to be able to make more independent, flexible, and opportunistic decisions and to manage and lead on the basis of trust and feedback.

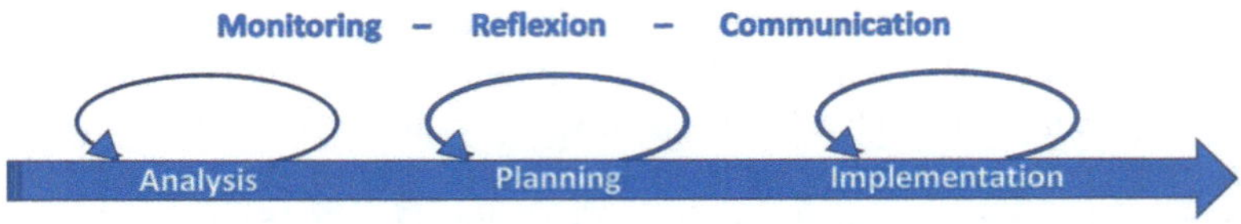

Fig. 2 Recursive process design of SMEs. (Source: Author's illustration)

It is therefore understandable why the majority of SMEs have for decades adhered to organisational decisions characterised by decision-making centrality, flat structures, direct communication relationships, and close social structures, even in the face of increasing complexity. They are not only "seen as a key factor of entrepreneurial success and a driver of competitive advantage" (Einwiller & Boenigk, 2012: 340) but can also directly contribute to the organisation's ability to adapt to dynamic environments through information procurement and distribution, knowledge acquisition, and organisational learning (Kieser, 2006), as shown in Fig. 2.

4 Impact Contributions and Limitations in the Context of Digital Transformation

The significance of process design, particularly its formalisation or lack thereof, in the context of digital transformation is a crucial factor in identifying the need for change and implementing new processes. This discussion, based on the works of Zerfaß et al. (2016), Bellmann et al. (2021), and Bundesnetzagentur (2023), will shed light on whether process design facilitates or hinders these transitions. The primary focus is on the effects of process design on organisational learning ability. Furthermore, this discussion will raise pertinent questions that stem from the specific design for the digital transformation of IWM.

4.1 Organisational Learning

Technological change and the demands of digital transformation pose new challenges for markets and industries, especially for companies and their decision-makers and specialists. It leads to procedural innovations whose deviating work organisation represents immediate and noticeable changes for those affected. Familiar processes are being tested, optimised, standardised, and digitalised. The change process is accompanied not only by curiosity but also by uncertainty and fear. Those affected want to know what advantages and disadvantages the changes will bring for the individual and how compatible they are with their own processes. They scrutinise the extent to which their knowledge and experience are still sufficient in the context of the innovations: Do I understand what is happening technically? Can I understand how the process works? Can I grasp its complexity? They seek opportunities to observe first, to test everything without risk, and learn (Hooffacker & Wolf, 2017). Given the uncertainty of those affected, it is no longer enough to "just" impart the relevant technical knowledge. Rather, change can only succeed if those affected are sensitised, informed, involved in the change process and taken on board at an early stage (Mast & Zerfaß, 2005; Ebert & Münch, 2018). Against this backdrop, it is not only the change itself that plays a central role but also how it is communicated.

To successfully organise change, processes must be designed to provide and process information that enable knowledge to be acquired, learning to take place and uncertainty to be reduced. The way in which technical and procedural innovations are communicated forms the basis for the successful understanding, acceptance, and application of the new processes (Hooffacker & Wolf, 2017). The target group-orientated, i.e. comprehensible and comprehensive communication of information, knowledge and experience, as well as the exchange of information and experience, then provides the prerequisites for understanding, testing, observing, evaluating and applying the innovations. Accordingly, change processes can fail if managers do not provide sufficient information, affected professionals do not receive target group-appropriate information about the steps or the extent of the changes (Ebert & Münch, 2018) or there is too little dialogue to learn from each other.

The empirical studies confirm that SMEs are very well suited to internal communication design in this respect in order to counteract the emergence of rumours (Dietz et al., 2019), to convey information quickly and flexibly, to sensitise employees to the needs, problems and opportunities of the company, to accept corporate decisions, to support change processes, and to achieve psychological communication goals (motivation/identification) as well as quantitative goals (such as cost reduction 8.57%, productivity increase 15.24%) (Schwaiger et al., 1995). Mast (2000) also postulates that the dialogue-oriented communication of SMEs is further excellently suited to the integration and motivation of employees. Their dialogical orientation within primarily informal processes of information provision favours a corporate culture that efficiently and effectively integrates relevant reference groups into processes and decisions even without formal control instruments and makes formal regulations for the management and further processing of data and information, experience, and knowledge as well as skills and abilities obsolete (Kusa et al., 2024; Pett et al., 2024; Winkler, 2020).

Since formalisation is not an independent dimension for describing the organisational and process design of strategic management, their rejection of formal procedures and regulations cannot be attributed solely to a low level of organisation (Wittlage, 1996). Rather, the characteristics of great flexibility and responsiveness attributed to SMEs can only be attributed to this: Prajogo et al. (2018) postulate that the specific design of their IWM optimises process management and has a positive impact on operational performance and productivity. Through their specific process design, SMEs enable mutual social interaction in order to inform employees and improve the internal flow of information.

Their process design not only promotes target-orientated flexibility and efficiency, but also personal initiative, willingness to take responsibility, and employee satisfaction, thus providing companies with significant strategic advantages in the field of human resources compared to large companies (Sattes et al., 1998; Simon, 2006). By not firmly defining tasks but expecting everyone to be willing to change in order to adapt and learn processes more quickly in the course of strategy implementation (Centeno et al., 2013), SMEs consciously promote individual willingness to learn and the strategic development of human resources (Felden & Hack, 2014). Their process design ensures that satisfaction and motivation are promoted, employees are tied to the company and performance and further development are maintained in the long term (Huck-Sandhu, 2016: 7; Rötzer, 2013: 179; Centeno et al., 2013: 452).

By organising horizontal and vertical IWM management services effectively and in a goal-oriented manner, SMEs can then identify, provide, and collectively use the existing knowledge in the company more quickly than in large companies (Kusa et al., 2024; Zerfass & Winkler, 2016: 284; Waibel, 2016; Moreno et al., 2014; Dietz et al., 2019). Based on their targeted observations and dialogue-oriented information procurement, SMEs supplement their existing expertise with the right or relevant market information to develop the market (Florschütz, 2024). Relevant market information to assess market developments, inform employees, and involve stakeholders in decisions and adaptation processes at an early stage, support creativity, innovative thinking, and organisational learning and dynamically adapt their own resources to market requirements (Kusa et al., 2024; Pett et al., 2024; Camison & Moreno, 2020; Gurau et al., 2017).

By gathering information in exchange and dissolving resource limitations through extensions within the relationship network (Apospori et al., 2012), the specific process design also focuses on cooperation rather than competition within and between organisations and pursues proactive, planned approaches to change management (Carson et al., 1995, p. 26). Through their strategic relationship and network management, SMEs then overcome their structural resource limitations and disadvantages in information procurement and processing and gain access to additional, extensive resources with which they can secure room for manoeuvre and increase their own competitiveness (Florschütz, 2024). The results of reflexive action can then be seen in innovative strength, the realisation of opportunities regarding topics, market trends or market gaps as opportunities to expand resources and in the strengthening or further development of communication activities (Schütte, 2011; Zerfaß et al., 2016; Rötzer, 2013). A higher level of perceived technological opportunities leads to greater entrepreneurial initiative (Kellermanns et al., 2006). A high product and service orientation is directly and closely related to a high degree of innovation (Roach, 2016; Block et al., 2013). This means that the company's starting position is constantly changing and requires SMEs to constantly adapt to new circumstances in order to utilise new opportunities, create new things, and learn new things (Hoon, 2016). It is precisely this feature, which is characterised by interactions within the network, the will to create, flexibility, and adaptability, that is referred to as the "heart of entrepreneurship" (Karami & Read, 2024).

Therefore, the question is rather to what extent the formalised information management regulations required in the context of digitalisation can contribute significantly to the success of the change process in SMEs or whether they do not have an impact that hinders the flexibility and adaptability of SMEs.

4.2 Formalisation Claim

As the social and human capital of companies is based on the creation of a system's connectedness and its resources, the design of IWM forms the basis for trusting cooperation, the efficiency and effectiveness of management processes and organisational learning.

SMEs have so far solved this challenge by using analogue and digital media in addition to individual communication. Two-way communication instruments dominate here. The corporate media primarily used are employee newsletters, emails, and notices as well as intranet systems, although the intranet is viewed critically as it often has shortcomings in terms of timeliness, user-friendliness, and design (Zerfaß et al., 2015; Kochhan & Oelschlegel, 2018; Dietz et al., 2019). Intranet systems are used for selected administrative matters for reasons of transparency and documentation, as they are urgently needed to complete work tasks (Dietz et al., 2019). Complex, elaborate, or one-sided instruments such as employee magazines, blogs and micro-blogs, wikis, podcasts or video podcasts, on the other hand, have hardly been relevant for the dissemination of information to date and will remain so in the foreseeable future (Zerfaß et al., 2015; Zerfass & Winkler, 2016; Kochhan & Oelschlegel, 2018). Due to the manageable organisational structure and low hierarchical levels, these are often considered superfluous and are only used when employees are spread across different locations and direct communication is difficult (Winkler, 2020; Dietz et al., 2019).

If SMEs of increasing company size react with measures that strengthen the transfer of information but contradict the social character of the organisation, these are not very effective (Jochims, 2013), as formal instruments support the transfer of information but only support the processing of information and thus the personal exchange of knowledge and experience to a limited extent. For example, employee information systems may only cover the information requirements (for data, information, responsibilities, processes, rules, etc.), but not the communication requirements of employees (for mutual exchange within coordination, instruction, and co-orientation. Small group communication tools reflect this need of employees, as it is not uncommon for personally set-up, informal WhatsApp groups to be used to exchange news and problems in subsystems of the organisational structure (Kochhan & Oelschlegel, 2018; Dietz et al., 2019), which are accepted by management but not desired for data protection reasons.

Reciprocal processes in employee information systems could then enable feedback but are visible to everyone (risk of information overload). Also, due to workplaces being remote from computers, they do not reach everyone involved at the same time (risk of asymmetrical information distribution), to the same extent (basis of trust) and with the same messages (target group orientation). Against this background, most SMEs with growing structures use a combination of communication systems to disseminate information instead of relying on a single instrument as each has advantages that cannot be compensated for by others (Zerfaß et al., 2015; Gabrielli & Balboni, 2010; Vinten, 1999). Where possible, however, "informal instruments are favoured" (Vinten, 1999: 114). As a result, the less complex, cost- and time-saving instruments in SMEs contrast personal, direct exchange relationships with formal procedural communication relationships.

The More Intensive Use of Personal Dialogue-Based Communication Therefore Appears to Be Justified Not only by the Reduced Size and Complexity. Rather, efficiency and effectiveness are clearly decisive in the choice of means (Dietz et al., 2019; Alter, 2012; Kochhan & Oelschlegel, 2018). The short line guarantees a high level of employee information, enables quick consultations, feedback, and detailed questions and creates clarity before the information is sent to external parties. In addition, messages can be conveyed in a personalised manner, conflicts can be resolved and relaxed and uncomplicated cooperation can be promoted (Gabrielli & Balboni, 2010; Kochhan & Oelschlegel, 2018; Dietz et al., 2019). This eliminates the postulated deficits in addressing information to employees in a way that is appropriate for the target group (Schütte, 2011; Mast, 2000; Kochhan & Oelschlegel, 2018). Accordingly, "even in the digital age, direct dialogue with each other (…) is seen as a key to receiving and passing on important information and also to being able to clarify individual aspects in direct conversation" (Kochhan & Oelschlegel, 2018, p. 83).

5 Conclusion

Despite technological changes, SMEs have remained true to their goals and values in the design of their IWM processes for decades, as the choice of their means of communication and their content reflect the structures and relationships of the stakeholders (Jochims, 2013). Personal dialogue across hierarchical levels via direct two-way communication promotes the communication of a familiar, honest, and respectful corporate culture at eye level, which is why it is maintained even in growing structures and despite the introduction of formal systems (Vinten, 1999). In contrast, "new digital information and communication systems (…) intervene deeply in corporate work processes and thus influence internal communication" (Fallosch, 2007, p. 81), unless they fulfil the information and communication needs of the stakeholders. As a system-orientated objectification of communication processes does not fit in with the personal integration character of SMEs, company management changes the social relationship with the stakeholders, even if "not (…) directly intended, (…) through new types of communication" (Jochims, 2013, p. 161).

In the context of digital transformation, personal integration by means of informal communication can therefore be supported by instrumental media communication if this preserves the character of the relationship (Jochims, 2013), promotes organisational learning, and supports the permanently necessary change processes for adaptation in the context of dynamic environments (Florschütz, 2024). They are key success factors for SMEs in competition as well as for ensuring their ability to survive and should be preserved when making decisions in the context of digital transformation processes, despite all the technological curiosity, technological functionalities, and opportunities for cost optimisation and increased efficiency.

References

Audretsch, D. B., & Belitski, M. (2021). Knowledge complexity and firm performance: Evidence from the European SMEs. *Journal of Knowledge Management, 25(4), 693–713.* https://doi.org/10.1108/JKM-08-2020-0604

Al-Emran, M., Mezhuyev, V., Kamaludin, A., & Shaalan, K. (2018). The impact of knowledge management processes on information systems: A systematic review. *International Journal of Information Management, 43*, 173–187. https://doi.org/10.1016/j.ijinfomgt.2018.07.001

Alter, V. V. (2012). *Medienarbeit im Mittelstand: Eine empirische Analyse von Status Quo und Einflussfaktoren der Media Relations in mittelständischen Familienunternehmen*. Helios Media.

Apospori, E., Zografos, K. G., & Magrizos, S. (2012). SME corporate social responsibility and competitiveness: A literature review. *International Journal of Technology Management, 58*(1/2), 10–31. https://doi.org/10.1504/IJTM.2012.045373

Aragón-Sánchez, A., & Sánchez-Marín, G. (2005). Strategic orientation, management characteristics, and performance: A study of Spanish SMEs. *Journal of Small Business Management, 43*(3), 287–308. https://doi.org/10.1111/j.1540-627X.2005.00142.x

Balsys, S. (2004). *Public Relations in medium-sized companies: Basics, practice, perspectives* (Rev. ed. 2012 with unchanged content). Akademiker Verlag.

Barnes, S. J. (2020). Information management research and practice in the post-COVID-19 world. *International Journal of Information Management, 55*, 102175. https://doi.org/10.1016/j.ijinfomgt.2020.102175

Bellmann, L., Bourgeon, P., Gathmann, C., Kagerl, C., Marguerit, D., Martin, L., Pohlan, L. & Roth, D. (2021). Digitalisierungsschub in Firmen während der Corona-Pandemie. *Wirtschaftsdienst, 101(9), 713–718.*

Bellmann, L., Bourgeon, P., Gathmann, C., et al. (2024). Digitalisation surge in companies during the Corona pandemic. *Wirtschaftsdienst, 101*, 713–718.

Block, J. H., Thurik, R., & Zhou, H. (2013). What turns knowledge into innovative products? The role of entrepreneurship and knowledge spillovers. *Journal of Evolutionary Economics, 23*, 693–718. https://doi.org/10.1007/s00191-012-0291-x

Brink, S. (2010). *Familienunternehmen und Unternehmensberatung—Eine empirische Bestandsaufnahme* (Working Paper 07/10). Institut für Mittelstandsforschung Bonn.

Brodbeck, H. (1995). Strategy. In I. Sattes, H. Brodbeck, H.-C. Lang, & H. Domeisen (Eds.), *Erfolg in kleinen und mittleren Unternehmen: A guide for management and organisation in SMEs (Mensch, Technik, Organisation)* (Vol. 8, pp. 31–50). vdf Hochschulverlag.

Bruhn, M. (2010). Marketing: *Grundlagen für Studium und Praxis, Gabler Verlag*

Bussiek, J. (1981). *Success-orientated management of medium-sized companies: Network organisation and profit contribution accounting as size-appropriate control elements*. C.H. Beck.

Camisón, C., Moreno, J. A. (2020). Keys to survival of the family firms in: Camisón, C., & González, T. (Hrsg.): Competitiveness, Organizational Management, and Governance in Family Firms. IGI Global.

Carson, D., Cromie, S. & McGowan, P., Hill, J. (1995). Marketing and Entrepreneurship in SMEs. *An innovative Approach, Prentice Hall, London.*

Carson, D., Gilmore, A., & Rocks, S. (2004). SME marketing networking: A strategic approach. *Strategic Change, 13*(7), 369–382. https://doi.org/10.1002/jsc.702

Centeno, E., Hart, S. & Dinnie, K. (2013). The five phases of SME brand-building. *Journal of Brand Management, 20(6), 445–457.*

Craig, J. B. L., & Moores, K. (2006). A 10-year longitudinal investigation of strategy, systems, and environment on innovation in family firms. *Family Business Review, 19*(1), 1–10. https://doi.org/10.1111/j.1741-6248.2006.00057.x

Daschmann, H.-A. (1994). *Erfolgsfaktoren mittelständischer Unternehmen: Ein Beitrag zur Erfolgsfaktorenforschung*. Schäffer-Poeschel.

Deimel, K., & Kraus, S. (2007). Strategic management in small and medium-sized enterprises—An empirical review. In P. Lethmathe, J. Eigler, F. Welter, D. Kathan, & T. Heupel (Eds.), *Management of small and medium-sized enterprises: Status and perspectives of SME research* (pp. 155–170). Deutscher Universitäts-Verlag.

Dietz, J., Mötzing, S., Wolf, S., Kochhan, C., & Schunk, H. (2019). *Internal communication in small and medium-sized enterprises: A qualitative analysis in print and digital companies.* Springer Fachmedien.

Durst, S., & Henschel, T. (2024). Small and Medium-Sized Enterprise (SME) Resilience. Cham: Springer, pp. 333ff.

Ebert, H., & Münch, E. (2018). *Language as an instrument of change and innovation communication*. Springer.

Einwiller, S. A., & Boenigk, M. (2012). Examining the link between integrated communication management and communication effectiveness in medium-sized enterprises. *Journal of Marketing Communications, 18*(5), 335–361. https://doi.org/10.1080/13527266.2010.484576

Eng, T.-Y., & Spickett-Jones, G. (2020). Marketing communications for the SME. In S. Nwankwo & A. Gbadamosi (Eds.), *Entrepreneurship marketing: Principles and practice of SME marketing* (2nd ed., pp. 162–173). Routledge.

Fallosch, A. (2007). *Success factor internal communication: The role of the manager as a successful communicator* (Rev. ed. 2012 with unchanged content). VDM Verlag.

Federal Network Agency for Electricity, Gas, Telecommunications, Post and Railway, Unit 123 Digitalisation and Networking in SMEs. (2023). *Digitalisation and environmental sustainability in companies: A comparative analysis of SMEs and large companies.* Retrieved July 8, 2024, from https://www.bundesnetzagentur.de/DE/Fachthemen/Digitalisierung/Mittelstand/Kennzahlen/start.html

Felden, B., & Hack, A. (2014). Strategic management of family businesses. In B. Felden & A. Hack (Eds.), *Management von Familienunternehmen: Besonderheiten—Handlungsfelder—Instrumente* (pp. 209–239). Springer Gabler.

Fels, M., & Wolter, H.-J. (2022). *The economic significance of family and women-owned businesses*. IfM Bonn. (Facts and Figures No. 28).

Fischbach, C., & Mack, J. (2008). *Mittelstandskommunikation*. UKV Verlag.

Florschütz, N. (2024). *Zwischen Ad hoc Kommunikation und strategischer Planung: Zur Gestaltung des strategischen Kommunikationsmanagements im Mittelstand.* Springer Gabler.

Gabrielli, V., & Balboni, B. (2010). SME practice towards integrated marketing communications. *Marketing Intelligence & Planning, 28*(3), 275–290. https://doi.org/10.1108/02634501011041400

Gbadamosi, A. (2020). The entrepreneurship marketing environment. In S. Nwankwo & A. Gbadamosi (Eds.), *Entrepreneurship marketing: Principles and practice of SME marketing* (2nd ed., pp. 46–71). Routledge.

Gurau, C., Duquesnois, F., & Catanzaro, A. (2017). Entrepreneurial orientation, strategic processes and SMEs' performance in a turbulent environment: An investigation of the Languedoc-Roussillon wine sector. *International Journal of Entrepreneurship and Small Business, 32*(1–2), 139–159.

Halliday, S. (2020). Relationship marketing and networks in entrepreneurship. In S. Nwankwo & A. Gbadamosi (Eds.), *Entrepreneurship marketing: Principles and practice of SME marketing* (2nd ed., pp. 222–243). Routledge.

Held, H. (2007a). *Strategische Unternehmensplanung in kleinen und mittleren Unternehmen: Ergebnisse einer bundesweiten Unternehmensbefragung in Zusammenarbeit mit dem Mittelstandsmagazin ProFirma.*

Held, H. (2007b). *Strategic corporate planning in small and medium-sized enterprises: Results of a nationwide company survey in co-operation with the SME magazine ProFirma.* HTW Aalen—University of Applied Sciences for Technology and Business Administration. Retrieved May 31, 2023, from https://www.hs-aalen.de/uploads/publication/file/6442/111_Studie_Planung_in_KMU_2007.pdf

Henschel, T., Durst, S., & Salzmann, J. (2024). Leveraging knowledge management and entrepreneurial orientation to enhance resilience in small and medium-sized enterprises. In S. Durst & T. Henschel (Eds.), *Small and medium-sized enterprise (SME) resilience.* Springer.

Hinterhuber, H. H. (2004). *Strategic management, Vol. I: Strategic thinking* (7th ed.).

Holtzhausen, D. R., & Zerfaß, A. (2013). Strategic pillars and perspectives of an alternative paradigm. In A. Zerfaß, L. Rademacher, & S. Wehmeier (Eds.), *Organisationskommunikation und Public Relations: Research paradigms and new perspectives* (pp. 73–94). Springer VS.

Hooffacker, G., & Wolf, C. (2017). *Technical innovations—Media innovations? Challenges for communicators, concepts and user research.* Springer VS.

Hoon, C. (2016). Management and success factors of family businesses. *Entrepreneurship, Series Politics and Contemporary History, 66*(16–17).

Huck, S. (2005). Interne Kommunikation im Mittelstand. In J. Klewes (Ed.), *Unternehmenskommunikation auf dem Prüfstand: Current empirical results on reputation marketing* (pp. 53–77). Deutscher Universitäts-Verlag.

Huck-Sandhu, S. (2016). Interne Kommunikation im Wandel: Entwicklungslinien, Status Quo und Ansatzpunkte für die Forschung. In S. Huck-Sandhu (Ed.), *Interne Kommunikation im Wandel: Theoretical concepts and empirical findings* (pp. 1–22). Springer VS.

IfM Bonn. (2023). *Institute for SME Research: SMEs in detail.* Retrieved July 8, 2023, from https://www.ifm-bonn.org/statistiken/mittelstand-im-einzelnen/kmu-im-eu-vergleich

Jochims, T. (2013). The design of internal communication in the development process of SMEs. In J.-A. Meyer (Ed.), *Kommunikation kleiner und mittlerer Unternehmen: Yearbook of SME Research and Practice 2013* (pp. 151–170). Eul.

Karami, M., Chandra, Y., Wooliscroft, B. & McNeill, L. (2022). Effectual control and small firms' international performance: the mediating role of partnership and gaining new knowledge. *International Journal of Entrepreneurial Behavior & Research, 28(4), 829–852.*

Karami, M., & Read, S. (2024). The heart of entrepreneurship. *Rutgers Business Review, 9*(1), 107–112.

Kellermanns, F. W., Eddleston, K. A., & Zellweger, T. M. (2006). Corporate entrepreneurship in family firms: A family perspective. *Entrepreneurship Theory and Practice, 30*(6), 809–830. https://doi.org/10.1111/j.1540-6520.2006.00153.x

Kelly, L. M., Athanassiou, N., & Crittenden, W. F. (2000). Founder centrality and strategic behaviour in the family-owned firm. *Entrepreneurship Theory & Practice, 25*(3), 27–42.

Kettinger, W. J., Ryoo, S. Y., & Marchand, D. A. (2021). We're engaged! Following the path to a successful information management capability. *Journal of Strategic Information Systems, 30*(1). https://doi.org/10.1016/j.jsis.2021.101632

Kieser, A. (2006). The situational approach. In A. Kieser & M. Ebers (Eds.), *Organisationstheorien* (6th ed., pp. 215–245). Kohlhammer Verlag.

Knight, G. A. (2001). Entrepreneurship and strategy in the international SME. *Journal of International Management, 7*(3), 155–171. https://doi.org/10.1016/S1075-4253(01)00094-5

Kochhan, C., & Oelschlegel, L. M. (2018). Instruments of internal communication in small and medium-sized (media) companies: An interview study on use and evaluation from the perspective of 20- to 30-year-old employees. In C. Kochhan & A. Moutchnik (Eds.), *Media management* (Vol. 77). Springer Fachmedien.

Kraus, S., Fink, M., Harms, R., & Rössl, D. (2007). Research results on strategic planning in SMEs: Current status and future lines of development. In A.-J. Meyer (Ed.), *Planning in small and medium-sized enterprises* (pp. 31–43). Eul.

Krcal, M., & Kubis, M. (2016). Differences between knowledge and information management practices: Empirical investigation. In *Proceedings of the 8th International Joint Conference on Knowledge Discovery, Knowledge Engineering and Knowledge Management, (KMIS)* (Vol. 3, pp. 190–198).

Kusa, R., Suder, M., & Duda, J. (2024). Role of entrepreneurial orientation, information management, and knowledge management in improving firm performance. *International Journal of Information Management, 78.*

Kussin, M. (2009). PR offices as reflection centres of multi-referential organisation. In U. Röttger (Ed.), *Theories of public relations* (2nd ed., pp. 117–133). Springer VS.

Laube, G. (1986). *Company size-specific aspects of public relations: A comparative analysis of public relations in medium-sized companies and large companies.* Lang.

Laux, H. (2007). *Decision theory* (7th rev. and expanded ed.). Springer.

Lizama, J. C., Contreras, O. L., & dos Santos, M. A. (2021). Reputation and identity in family firms: Current state and gaps for future research. *Journal of Small Business Strategy, 31*(2), 6–18.

Looser, S. (2017). *Swiss SMEs and internal CSR communication: Results of an interview study.* Springer.

Lyles, M. A., Baird, I. S., Orris, J. B., & Kuratko, D. F. (1993). Formalized planning in small business: Increasing strategic choices. *Journal of Small Business Management, 31*(2), 38–50.

Martin, A., & Behrends, T. (1998). *Organisational structures as determinants of the decision-making process in medium-sized companies.* Lüneburg.

Mast, C. (2000). *Better internal communication for more business success: A guide for entrepreneurs.* Deutscher Industrie- und Handelstag (DIHT).

Mast, C., & Zerfaß, A. (2005). Successfully implementing new ideas. In *Das Handbuch der Innovationskommunikation.* Frankfurter Allgemeine Buch.

Moreno, A., Verhoeven, P., Tench, R. & Zerfass, A. (2014). Increasing power and taking a lead-What are practitioners really doing? Empirical evidence from European communications manager. *International Public Relations Journal, 4(7), 73–94.*

Moss, D., Ashford, R., & Shani, N. (2003). The forgotten sector: Uncovering the role of public relations in SMEs. *Journal of Communication Management, 8*(2), 197–210. https://doi.org/10.1108/13632540310807350

Mostafiz, M. I., Hughes, M., Simeonova, B., & Sambasivan, M. (2023). Entrepreneurial orientation and knowledge management: Comparing configurations of native and immigrant entrepreneurial firms. *International Journal of Entrepreneurial Behaviour & Research, 29*(5), 1099–1132. https://doi.org/10.1108/IJEBR-11-2022-1040

Pahnke, A., Welter, F., & Audretsch, D. B. (2021). *In the eye of the beholder: Why we need to differentiate between SMEs and Mittelstand* (IfM Bonn: Working Paper 04/21).

Pett, T., Haddad, G., & Nagpal, G. (2024). Does empowering leadership affect SMEs' sustainability performance through knowledge transfer? *European Management Journal.* https://doi.org/10.1016/j.emj.2024.101317

Pfohl, H.-C. (2006). Corporate management. In H.-C. Pfohl (Ed.), *Betriebswirtschaftslehre der Mittel- und Kleinbetriebe: Größenspezifische Probleme und Möglichkeiten ihrer Lösung* (4th ed., pp. 79–112). Erich Schmidt.

Prajogo, D., Toy, J., Bhattacharya, A., Oke, A., & Cheng, T. C. E. (2018). The relationships between information management, process management and operational performance: Internal and external contexts. *International Journal of Production Economics, 199*, 95–103. https://doi.org/10.1016/j.ijpe.2018.02.019

Priyono, A., Moin, A., & Putri, V. N. A. O. (2020). Identifying digital transformation paths in the business model of SMEs during the COVID-19 pandemic. *Journal of Open Innovation: Technology, Market, and Complexity, 6*(4), 104. https://doi.org/10.3390/joitmc6040104

Reischauer, G., & Schober, L. (2016). Managing Industry 4.0 through strategic organisational design. In R. Obermaier (Ed.), *Industrie 4.0 als unternehmerische Gestaltungsaufgabe* (pp. 271–289). Springer Gabler.

Roach, D. (2016). Effectuation, innovation and performance in SMEs: An empirical study. *European Journal of Innovation Management, 19*(2), 214–238. https://doi.org/10.1108/EJIM-12-2014-0123

Rötzer, S. (2013). *The professionalisation of corporate communication in family businesses: Determining, influencing and success factors* (Doctoral dissertation). University of Hohenheim.

Sattes, I., Brodbeck, H., Lang, H.C. & Domeisen, H. (Hrsg.) (1998). Erfolg in kleinen und mittleren Unternehmen, *Leitfaden für die Führung und Organisation in KMU, 2. Auflage, Zürich: vdf.*

Scharpe, J. (1992). *Strategic management in small and medium-sized enterprises: Problems of implementation and approaches to solutions*. EUL.

Schatilow, L. C. (2014). *Politische Kommunikation deutscher Familienunternehmen. Pilotstudie zur Differenzierung von Unternehmenstypen in der politischen Interessenvertretung, Wiesbaden: Springer VS.*

Schein, E. H. (1983). The role of the founder in creating organisational culture. *Organisational Dynamics, 12*(1), 13–28. https://doi.org/10.1016/0090-2616(83)90023-2

Schütte, D. (2011). *PR for SMEs in Germany: A study on the communication work of medium-sized companies*. UKV Verlag.

Schwaiger, M., Jeckel, P., & Saffert, V. (1995). *Kommunikationsmanagement in großen und mittelständischen Unternehmen* (Arbeitspapiere zur mathematischen Wirtschaftsforschung, Nr. 131). University of Augsburg, Institute for Statistics and Mathematical Economic Theory.

Schweizer, R. (2015). Decision-making during small and medium-sized enterprises' internationalisation: Effectuation vs. causation. *Journal for International Business and Entrepreneurship Development, 8*(1), 22–41.

Schwender, C., & Zeichhardt, R. (2012). Internal communication between aspiration and reality: A study on the level of professionalisation of internal communication in SMEs and large companies. In G. Bentele, M. Piwinger, & G. Schönborn (Eds.), *Kommunikationsmanagement (No. 3.88)*. Loseblattwerk.

Sen, S., Savitskie, K., Mahto, R. V., Kumar, S., & Khanin, D. (2022). Strategic flexibility in small firms. *Journal of Strategic Marketing*, 1–18. https://doi.org/10.1080/0965254X.2022.2113376

Simon, H. (2006). Erfolgsfaktoren – Was zeichnet die „Stillen Stars" im Mittelstand aus? In: Krüger, W. Klippstein, G., Merk, R., Wittberg, V. (Hrsg.): Praxishandbuch des Mittelstands. Leitfaden für das Management mittelständischer Unternehmen. Wiesbaden: Gabler.

Shekhar, & Valeri, M. (2023). Trends in knowledge management research in small businesses. *European Business Review, 35*(5), 573–599. https://doi.org/10.1108/EBR-05-2022-0123

Spence, M., & Essoussi, L. H. (2010). SME brand building and management: An exploratory study. *European Journal of Marketing, 44*(7/8), 1037–1054. https://doi.org/10.1108/03090561011047441

Steinmann, H., & Schreyögg, G. (2005). *Management: Grundlagen der Unternehmensführung. Concepts—Functions—Case Studies* (6th rev. ed.). Gabler.

Stonehouse, G., & Pemberton, J. (2002). Strategic planning in SMEs—Some empirical findings. *Management Decision, 40*(9), 853–861. https://doi.org/10.1108/00251740210441072

Vinten, G. (1999). Corporate communications in small- and medium-sized enterprises. *Industrial and Commercial Training, 31*(3), 112–119. https://doi.org/10.1108/00197859910268535

Waibel, J. (2016). *Communication culture in family businesses: Entrepreneurs in dialogue—From leadership responsibility to conflict resolution and succession planning*. Haufe Group.

Wang, W., Zhang, D., Wang, H., Zhu, Q., & Morabbi Heravi, H. (2023). How do businesses achieve sustainable success and gain a competitive advantage in the green era? *Cybernetes, 52*(9), 3241–3260. https://doi.org/10.1108/CYB-10-2022-0275

Welter, F. (2003). *Strategies, SMEs and the environment: Action patterns and strategy genesis in small and medium-sized enterprises*. Duncker & Humblot.

Welter, F., May-Strobl, E., Wolter, H.-J. & Günterberg, B. (2014). *Mittelstand im Wandel. Mittelstand Companion and Promotor of Structural Change. IfMMaterialien Nr. 232, Institut für Mittelstandsforschung Bonn*

Welter, F., Schlepphorst, S., Schneck, S., & Holz, M. (2020). *The social contribution of SMEs: Conceptual considerations* (IfM-Materialien No. 283). Institut für Mittelstandsforschung Bonn.

Winkler, L. (2020). *Organisational communication in medium-sized companies: Genesis and specifics of communication in medium-sized industrial companies*. Springer VS.

Winkler, L., Volk, S. C., Borner, M., & Zerfaß, A. (2018). Zwischen Intention und Emergenz: Mittelstandskommunikation im Spannungsfeld kontroverser Strategieparadigmen. In S. Wehmeier & D. Schoeneborn (Eds.), *Strategische Kommunikation im Spannungsfeld zwischen Intention und Emergenz* (pp. 215–232). Springer VS.

Wittlage, H. (1996). *Organisationsgestaltung mittelständischer Unternehmen*. Deutscher Universitäts-Verlag.

Wolter, H.-J., & Sauer, I. (2017). *The importance of owner- and family-managed companies in Germany* (IfM-Materialien No. 253). Institut für Mittelstandsforschung Bonn.

Zellweger, T., Kellermanns, F. W., Eddleston, K. A. & Memili, E. (2012). Building a family firm image: How family firms capitalize on their family ties. *Journal of Family Business Strategy, 3(4), p. 239–250.*

Zerfaß, A., & Volk, S. C. (2019). *Toolbox communication management: Thinking tools and methods for managing corporate communication*. Springer Gabler.

Zerfass, A., & Winkler, L. (2016). Corporate communication in SMEs: Unveiling an ignored field of practice. In P. S. Brønn, S. Romenti, & A. Zerfass (Eds.), *The management game of communication: Advantages in public relations and communication management* (Vol. 1, pp. 265–286). Bingley.

Zerfaß, A., Fink, S., & Winkler, L. (2015). *Mittelstandskommunikation 2015—Studie zum Stellenwert und Einsatz von Unternehmenskommunikation im deutschen Mittelstand.* University of Leipzig, Fink & Fuchs PR AG.

Zerfaß, A., Fink, S., & Winkler, L. (2016). *Mittelstandskommunikation 2016—Studie zur Professionalisierung, Digitalisierung und Führung der Unternehmenskommunikation.* University of Leipzig, Fink & Fuchs PR AG.

Ninette Florschütz holds a PhD in Communication Science and a degree in Business Administration. Since 2018, she has been working as a research associate at the Mittelstand-Digital Zentrum Ilmenau, funded by the German Federal Ministry for Economic Affairs and Energy. She teaches at TU Ilmenau (Institute of Media and Communication Science) as well as at the Cooperative State University Gera-Eisenach (Business Administration). In her doctoral thesis at the University of Erfurt (2023), she examined the influence of owner-managed leadership on strategic communication management. Her research focuses on strategic communication design in SMEs, particularly in relation to digital transformation and strategic management. She integrates insights from public relations, organisational, and management research with current studies on SMEs, entrepreneurship, and hidden champions—with a special emphasis on their organisational and process design.

Digitalisation Enhancing Ecosystem Thinking and Business Model Innovation Through Co-creation

Heidi Vähänikkilä

Abstract This article demonstrates how digitalisation has created new opportunities for co-creation and digital knowledge transfer (KT) in the Hospitality Industry. From 2023 to 2024, the author Heidi Vähänikkilä conducted a study on change capacity in the HORECA (Hotel, Restaurant, and Café/Catering), tourism, and event industries in Finland and Malaysia. 197 questionnaire answers and 21 executive-level interviews revealed that companies still face challenges in change capacity, especially in the development of future proof business models (BM) that truly deliver value in a turbulent post-pandemic business environment without compromising the core of original BMs. Also, a lack of usage of digital platforms in innovation processes within organisations and over company boundaries was brought up. The results of this study were used in the Limelight research, development, and innovation (RDI) project. The Limelight team, led by Vähänikkilä, created a digital Ecosystem platform. This platform was tailored to organisations dealing with business model innovation challenges. Working together by sharing knowledge on a specific collaborative board offers a dynamic, easy, and location flexible platform for co-creation and innovation of solutions to real-life challenges.

Keywords Digital knowledge transfer · Co-creation · Business model innovation · Hospitality industry · Ecosystem platform

H. Vähänikkilä (✉)
Laurea University of Applied Sciences, Espoo, Finland

Estonian Business School, Tallinn, Estonia
e-mail: heidi.vahanikkila@laurea.fi

K. Bodrožić-Brnić et al. (eds.), *Digital Transformation in Knowledge Transfer*, Digital Transformation and Innovation,
https://doi.org/10.1007/978-3-032-07329-7_7

1 Introduction

Today companies need to find actively and in agile manner new ways to create competitive advantage. The importance of successful, future proof ways of organising and delivering business model innovation activities in the quest for experiences is something many managers are currently facing. Nearly 30 years ago Pine II and Gilmore (1998) stated customer experience to matter most as goods and services become commoditised. Today in an ever-changing business environment digitalisation has brought upon new possibilities (and challenges) for innovation, co-creation has a lot of potential if facilitated in a professional manner. The service sector has great importance, since under normal circumstances it represents roughly three-quarters of economic activity in advanced economies (OECD, 2024).

In post-pandemic market, a subfield of the Service sector and part of the world of hospitality, the Travel & Tourism sector contributed 9.1% to the global GDP; an increase of 23.2% from 2022 (World Travel & Tourism Council, 2024). Even though we are on the road for recovery, the post-pandemic era hospitality field business still looks very different compared to pre-COVID-19 times. Ecosystem thinking creates new solutions and opportunities to business incentives and processes as the focus is shifting from outperforming competition to performing stronger through collaboration. Innovations are not developed anymore solely from within the confines of an organisation, instead these evolve from the joint action of a network of actors ranging from suppliers and partners to consumers and independent inventors. Innovation systems generate a democracy of knowledge, whose creation is transdisciplinary, non-linear, hybrid, and shared (Afonso et al., 2012).

As companies are looking to deliver more value, seeking alternative sources of competitive advantage creates the need for undertaking major transformation in the innovation processes. Utilising a digital collaboration platform which is designed to facilitate remote communication enables knowledge creation and sharing that can be an effective knowledge transfer practice.

2 Background

2.1 Business Model Innovation

Focusing on business model innovations (BMI) has become one of the important priorities of leading companies trying to keep a certain balance of value creation and value capture (Zott et al., 2011). Shifting a business model to another is often a demanding challenge that is based on dynamic capabilities (Teece, 2007). According to Mitchell and Coles (2003), enhancing business model innovation provides a way to outperform the competition. Because not all firms succeed in adapting their business model innovations to new market demands or competitive threats (Foss & Saebi, 2015), recognising and measuring firms' strategic flexibility and change power is crucial in the hospitality service industry. The capability to rapidly move into new business models is an important source of sustainable competitive advantage and a key leverage to improve the sustainability performance of organisations (Geissdoerfer et al., 2018).

The need for innovation rises from the need of creating new business, growth, and profit (Kettunen et al., 2008). According to Taatila et al. (2006) when looking at processes within any organisation, focusing on the organisation's competence (i.e., its capability to provide success) is especially useful in studying economic innovation processes as the organisational competence and economic innovation have the same goal and outcome, i.e. the success of an organisation. Use of digitalisation as an enabler in these processes is an opportunity which managers should be onboarding with curiosity and open-mindedness.

Business model innovations have opened the door for thinking far beyond product and process innovations (Freiling, 2015). On the macro level, business model innovations may change "the rules of the game" in the market and trigger processes of industry transformation (Porter & Rivkin, 2000). Innovating business models is among the priorities of leading companies trying to keep a certain balance of value creation and value capture (Zott et al., 2011). Exogenous crisis (such as COVID-19) and rapid changes in the business environment can also serve as an initiator for temporary business model innovation (Clauss et al., 2021), value of co-creation is measured and valued in times of hardship.

2.2 Co-creation in a Living Lab Setting Supporting BMI Incentives

European Network of Living Labs defines Living Labs (LL) as follows:

> Living Labs (LLs) are open innovation ecosystems in real-life environments using iterative feedback processes throughout a lifecycle approach of an innovation to create sustainable impact. They focus on co-creation, rapid prototyping & testing, and scaling-up innovations & businesses, providing (different types of) joint-value to the involved stakeholders. In this context, living labs operate as intermediaries/orchestrators among citizens, research organisations, companies, and government agencies/levels. Within a wide variety of living labs, they all have common characteristics, but multiple different implementations. (ENoLL, 2024)

Educational institutions are valued partners as companies have realised their capability to support businesses by delivering real-life projects to students—this is an important way for bridging the gap between academia and business. One environment where this kind of co-operation takes place is in a University Living Lab environment. The value of a university-based Living Lab is the creation and sharing of new knowledge combined with academic education, and activities based on the theory of the Quadruple Helix of Innovation (QH) which builds upon triple helix by adding the fourth group "users" to activities (Fig. 1).

In Living Labs all four important actor groups of the QH model are actively present: users, firms, public research organisations, and public authorities. In QH model

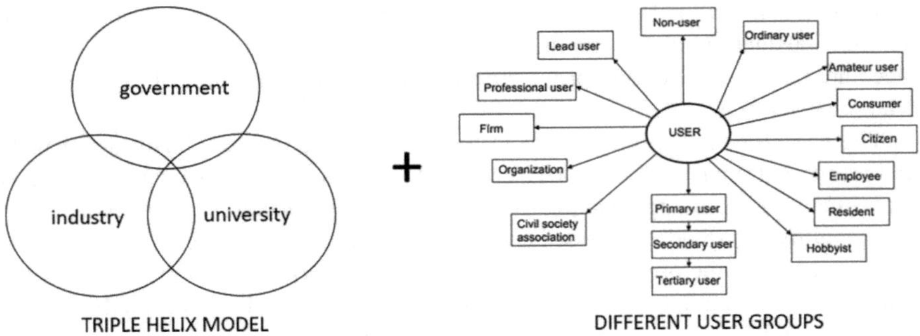

Fig. 1 Addition of users in quadruple helix model to triple helix model. (Following Arnkil et al., 2010)

"users" (Fig. 1) may be defined broadly—this creates multidimensional view (Arnkil et al., 2010).

Successful Living Lab model of Laurea University of Applied Sciences (Finland) provides a unique setting for innovation—Living Labs are an important part of Laurea's Learning by Developing (LbD) model. Living Labs at Laurea aim to apply a multidisciplinary approach due to the complexity of real-life problems; Laurea collaborates with local businesses, organisations, and communities in authentic development environments (Laurea, 2024a). This setting combines three tasks given to Universities of Applied Sciences in Finland: research and development (R&D), regional development, and pedagogy.

As companies are looking to deliver more valuable services and products to the market, seeking alternative sources of competitive advantage creates the need for undertaking major transformation in the innovation processes (Afonso et al., 2012). Living Labs act as public–private partnerships in which businesses, researchers, authorities, and citizens work together for the creation, approval, and testing of services and products, business ideas, and markets in a real-life context (Bergvall-Kåreborn et al., 2009). Working within a Living Lab context in research, development, and innovation projects relies on the collaboration between companies, the public sector, end users, and students. All stakeholders play a vital role in addressing the targeted problem or solution, regardless of any pre-existing networks or collaboration structures embedded in the location (Steen & van Bueren, 2017). Living Labs are user-centred open innovation ecosystems integrating research and innovation research in real-life communities and settings.

Limelight Event Living Lab started operating in 2022 at Laurea Leppävaara campus is Espoo, Finland, with funding from The Service Centre for Continuous Learning and Employment (Service Centre). The Service Centre promotes the competence development of working-age people and the availability of skilled labour (Laurea, 2024b.). For this, Limelight creates numerous possibilities: it brings together accommodation and event companies, people looking to be employed in the field, regional agents, and students. Due to the need for resilience and lack of skilled employees within the hospitality sector and owing to changing customer needs, the business services and processes need to be continuously developed and innovated. Besides networking and business model creation and testing facilities, the Limelight also offers event management content courses and activities like training, workshops, work-based studies, and presentations.

2.3 *Ecosystem Thinking*

2.3.1 Origins of Ecosystem Thinking

The ecosystem view is a perspective on managing business and innovation networks activities. Traditionally companies have been seen to battle each other for customers and profits, these days companies are operating more in innovative ways to survive and to thrive. An ecosystem is a network in which research institutions, financing organisations, entrepreneurs, and startups are interacting side by side. This kind of co-operation of different elements gives possibilities for new ideas and innovations (Hautamäki, 2010). Networks of organisations, called business ecosystems, have been studied since the mid-1980s (Teece, 2010).

Originally Moore (1993) presented the idea that a company is a part of a business ecosystem and nothing like a one member in industry field. He describes a business ecosystem as consisting of layers, which correspond to differing levels of commitment to the business (Fig. 2).

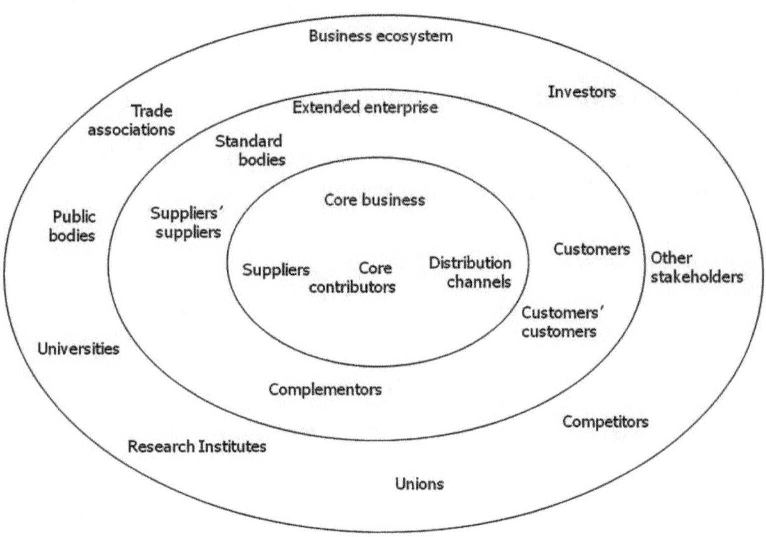

Fig. 2 The layers of a business ecosystem. (Heikkilä & Kuivaniemi, 2012 adapted from Moore, 1993)

In this model business ecosystem is as a three-layer circle (Fig. 2) where the inside is about core business like direct suppliers and distribution channels. Next layer is about extended enterprise like direct customers. The outside layer of business ecosystem effects core business but consists of outsiders like trade associations, regulatory parts, and unions. Every business ecosystem develops in four stages: birth, expansion, leadership, and self-renewal—or, if not self-renewal, there is death. These development stages of a business ecosystem will lead the company to link platform owner and members to interactions depending on the stage of evolution of the system. Since presentation of this model, ecosystem thinking has gained even more interest within the BtoB sector and scholars.

Social science underlines that the economy can be observed as an ecosystem (Moore, 2006), and the global economy can be considered an entity in which organisations and individuals are living organisms. In this respect, different organisms (i.e., species in natural ecosystems or actors with complementary roles in manmade ecosystems) have the necessity to preserve the balanced ecosystem because one can cause a chain reaction felt throughout the entire ecosystem. Knowledge is considered the most strategic medium of interaction among ecosystem participants (Van Der Borgh et al., 2012; Clarysse et al., 2014). The management literature has developed overlapping concepts, such as business, innovation, and knowledge ecosystems (Clarysse et al., 2014). 25 years on from the origins, Aarikka-Stenroos and Ritala (2017) created a systematic review and management framework for network management in the era of ecosystems. They stated that an ecosystem concept and its implications in managing business relationships should not be disregarded. This research highlighted two interpretations for an ecosystem: 1) an ecosystem as a new layer—extending business network framework and 2) an ecosystem as a novel perspective to business network—updating current business network frameworks.

2.3.2 Networking Towards Ecosystem

Change in operations in companies embracing ecosystem-driven business models requires shift in thinking, culture, and operations (Fig. 3).

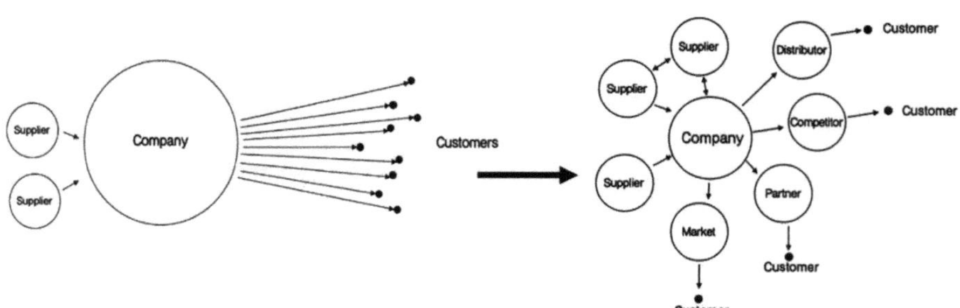

Fig. 3 Change in operations from "traditional" to ecosystem driven (Sribney, 2020)

Multidimensional networking (Fig. 3) within the Ecosystem may seem confusing at first. To help companies in transition from "traditional" to ecosystem driven business models Sribney (2020) has created a *Business Ecosystem Canvas* which gives step-by-step instructions to companies eager to take the next step. Multidimensional roles of orchestrators and partners in business ecosystems vary greatly depending on the setting.

Ståhle and Laento (2000) explain there to be three phases in networking towards the ecosystem. In the first phase, companies seek to benefit from their own perspectives, without losing the ideas of the other parties. Co-operation is based on agreements which define the activities, roles, and responsibilities of actors. Co-operation is controlled and communication is ongoing. The second phase is about co-operation, where targets are defined together and have operational metrics and a feedback system. Companies have an open atmosphere among themselves, and the partnership is evaluated mutually. Companies are sharing data, and the communication is unified. The third phase is a real partnership with trust. They share common interests, values, and flexible activities. The know-how is available for everyone in the network. According to Iansiti and Levien (2004), defining the structural boundaries of an ecosystem can be challenging, if not impossible. Therefore, a company should identify and align with the organisations whose futures are most closely intertwined with its own. The complex structure of an ecosystem often encompasses groups of organisations beyond traditional industry segments.

Networks can be considered to have two kinds of operating models. The one is a hierarchical network run by a top company whose operations and goals are largely based on the goals of the top company. At the other model one finds an equal network of partners, to which the development of networks is currently directed, due to the internationalisation of the entire business field (Ståhle & Laento, 2000). Designed ecosystems are becoming more important because of structural changes in our economy. The first factor is the removal of regulations that once protected firms with exclusive rights to serve specific customer needs. As these protections are lifted, organisations from other sectors are free to collaborate and offer more integrated solutions.

The second change is the blurring of boundaries between products and services, driven by regulatory shifts and digitalisation. As a result, companies are developing new production models that integrate multiple suppliers to deliver more cohesive and innovative offerings.

The third change involves technology that changes how firms can serve their customers. The dependence on mobile devices and internet effects on consuming has expanded the possibilities for linking previously unrelated goods and services—reinforcing the effects of the first two changes. That is why companies must focus, not on competition, but on designed ecosystem that can expand the traditional industry model. "Traditional strategy frameworks are of little help when designing or participating in such an ecosystem" (Jacobides, 2019).

Ecosystems will give better opportunities for companies in both local and global markets, thus navigate in an era of "sectors without borders" (Vähänikkilä & Vakkuri, 2022).

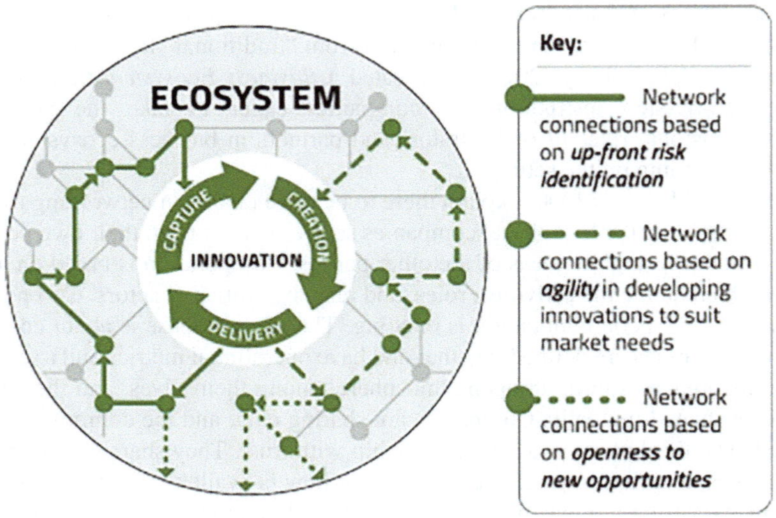

Fig. 4 Business model innovation ecosystem (Madsen, 2020)

Madsen (2020) developed an ecosystem model specifically focused on business model innovation (see Fig. 4).

This model (Fig. 4) highlights a holistic rather than silo-based approach to business model networks by highlighting the flow of connectivity between the internal and external components of the business. This study suggested that business leaders can usefully incorporate dynamic networks and ecosystems into their decision-making processes. Identifying risks up-front, being open to new opportunities and agility may help businesses to provide innovations that better fit into an evolving value chain and meet individualised consumer needs (Madsen, 2020). There are also obstacles to be tackled. According to findings by Ketonen-Oksi and Valkokari (2019), ecosystem development may be hindered by the rather generic aims of collaboration and the conflicting expectations regarding the ecosystem development. Therefore, it is crucial to give attention to facilitators, as they act as important connectors or enablers of value co-creation.

3 Digital Co-creation and Knowledge Transfer

According to several studies, digitalisation and digital platforms possess both good and negative aspects for business enhancement. Lember et al. (2019) remind us that the use of digital technologies does not inevitably lead to co-production and co-creation. But, at their best, digital platforms help overcoming existing geographical, temporal, and organisational barriers by enabling interaction, increasing motivation for both sides to engage, and by facilitating mutual resource-contributions. The advancement of digital technology has led to the development of new collaborative organisational networks which present an innovative approach to leverage resources across different industries in order to respond to customer needs. *Digital Business Ecosystem* (DBE) is an extension of Moore's (1993) business ecosystem in which digital technology plays a dominant role. DBE extends Moore's concept by placing more importance on the centrality of digital technology. DBE may be defined as a socio-technical environment of individuals, organisations, and digital technologies with collaborative and competitive relationship to co-create value through shared digital platforms (Senyo et al., 2019). A platform refers to a set of tools, services, and innovations that ecosystem partners can leverage to enhance their performance, collaborate effectively, and foster innovation (Selander et al., 2013). These platforms are mainly described as virtual environments in which heterogeneous entities are involved in knowledge transfer and integration processes to face open innovation challenges (Jeppesen & Lakhani, 2010), where knowledge is considered the most strategic medium of interaction among ecosystem participants (Van der Borgh et al., 2012; Clarysse et al., 2014). The complexity of the ecosystem increases the amount of tactical knowledge (knowledge including skills, ideas, and experiences that are possessed by people but are not codified and may not necessarily be easily expressed) in the system, but it also creates problems in terms of transfer of knowledge and access to information (Van der Borgh et al., 2012).

Mariano and Awazu (2017) highlight that individual and organisational capabilities can contribute to the creation of knowledge or to the development of practices oriented to the invention of new artefacts/products. In this project, to overcome possible troubles in knowledge transfer, Miro board was used. It is a visual workspace for innovation where teams manage projects, design products, and build the future together. Miro is a closed-source nature platform, not an open innovation platform but for basic usage it is still regarded to be useful and especially easy-to-use for first time users as well by the experiences Limelight team gathered in the ecosystem workshop.

4 Knowledge Transfer on Miro Board

4.1 Understanding Companies' Needs Through Research

Living Labs are widely researched and there are a lot of academic writings from the past years. Also, different aspects of ecosystem thinking have gained more discussion and attention, but it is still something managers find to be quite "academic", "highflying", and hard to understand as was discovered in the executive-level interviews conducted in Finland and in Malaysia. To meet companies' true needs research activities were divided into two phases in this project.

The first phase was conducted by Vähänikkilä and Vakkuri (2022) in Finland in the Spring of 2022. The central research question in this phase was "How can

Limelight Living Lab support Hospitality Field companies in after-pandemic market?". Insights were collected from managers in small and medium-sized businesses by sending out an online questionnaire to 75 companies listed in the Limelight Living Lab contact list. In this questionnaire practitioners were invited to share their views on "after COVID-19" business activities and needs in the hospitality field, focusing on skills valued in the employees as this is crucial for designing Living Lab workshops content and activities further. After receiving 24 responses, the research continued with 17 in-depth interviews with professionals from the hospitality industry. The findings revealed a shared insight: employees in the hospitality sector require new knowledge and skills to support companies' business model innovation (BMI) initiatives and to contribute to future-oriented strategies. These competencies can be cultivated through collaborative BMI activities and include managerial skills, effective communication training, and a strong focus on future orientation and foresight.

COVID-19 has accelerated the use of digital platforms, but in the context of knowledge transfer and innovation activities possibilities of such platforms were not widely used according to the research insights. Also, the value of networks was highlighted in the interviews, while silos are slowly dissolving, and the value of co-operation is being recognised. As a result of these findings, it was clear that Ecosystem Thinking is something companies could benefit from. Thus, a Hospitality Industry-specific *Business Ecosystem Management Action Plan* was introduced at the end of phase one (Fig. 5).

The action plan model (Fig. 5) is constructed from the point of view of an individual company, whose managers are not yet familiar with the possibilities of Ecosystem Thinking. The complex nature of relations with different participants and orchestrator in ecosystem makes it seem more complicated than it really is. To help managers to grasp the opportunities, in research phase one this visualised step-by-step action plan was introduced to support spotting new opportunities as company strategies are designed and the business model enhanced. To begin their journey, and to prepare for the ecosystem participation it is necessary for a company to define their current business state and actions in-house first. The *Business Model Canvas* by Osterwalder and Pigneur (2010) is a professional tool for this. Next, in the second phase, future foresight and innovation workshop and discussion are needed for creating a future-oriented atmosphere within the company. In the third phase, ecosystem building starts by visualising and restructuring company networks—current stakeholders and new ones to be discovered. In the fourth phase, the insights gathered during the first three phases are synthesised and structured using the *Business Ecosystem Canvas* developed by Sribney (2020).

The second phase of the study, independently conducted by the author between 2023 and 2024, focused on examining change capacity in companies within the HORECA, tourism, and event industries in Finland and Malaysia. With original findings in this first phase, the central research question here was "How service firms' competitive advantage capabilities can be enhanced with new business model innovation practices when rapid changes occur?". To gather more insights, a topic-specific new questionnaire was sent out. All together 197 new questionnaire answers

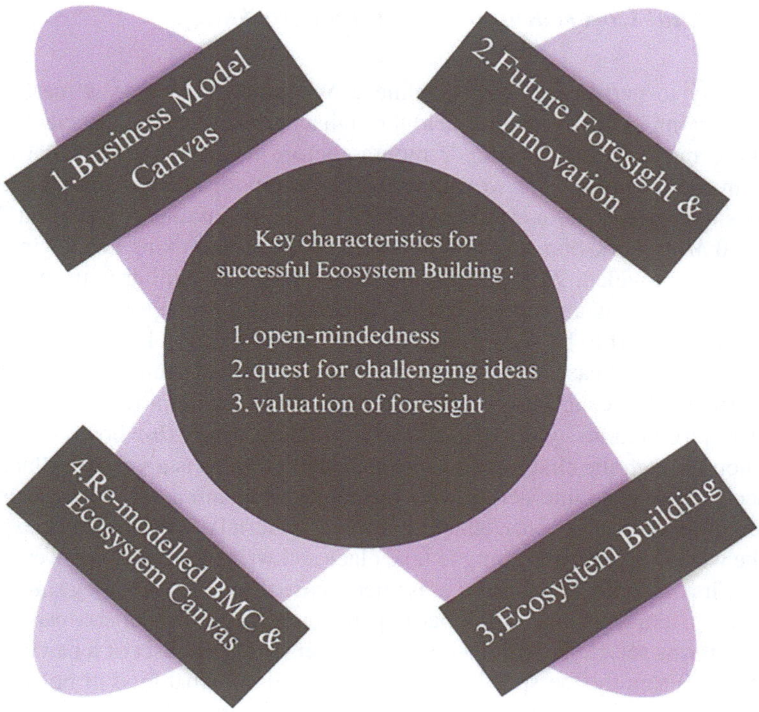

Fig. 5 Business ecosystem in-house management action plan for companies (Vähänikkilä & Vakkuri, 2022)

were collected, learnings from those and 21 executive-level interviews that were conducted simultaneously revealed that companies still face challenges in their change capacity and development of future proof business models (BM) that truly deliver value in a turbulent business environment without compromising the core of original BMs in the post-pandemic market. The differences were primarily related to how business model innovation activities were organised based on firm size—surprisingly, less so by the market in which the firms operate.

As a result of the two research phases, it became clear that a shared digital platform for co-creation was needed to unite companies. In response, the Limelight Living Lab project team prioritised this initiative and launched a Business Ecosystem workshop. The pilot workshop was held in May 2024.

4.2 Virtual Co-creational Ecosystem Workshop

Opportunity to participate in this online ecosystem workshop was marketed for people working in the hospitality field through a newsletter and the social networks *Facebook* and *LinkedIn*, starting 2 months before the workshop. 28 participants joined in the free-of-charge workshop for the afternoon. Participants represented mainly small and medium-sized companies. At the beginning of the event, before the actual *Miro* workshop, an introduction to ecosystem thinking and business ecosystems was provided. 95% of the participants were not familiar with these topics beforehand. Creating an atmosphere and understanding of the topic was crucial for the co-creation part to be successful. After the introduction, a keynote speaker was present to showcase cases from different industries she had been working with. This gave participants a clear idea on how versatile ecosystem ideology is.

After introductions, participants received a link to a *Miro* board co-creation workshop through the chat function on the platform. Miro is a virtual collaboration tool accessible via an internet browser or mobile application, allowing participants to share ideas using text notes, tables, and visual materials. The moderator explained how the workshop part was going to take place and written instructions were always visible. First, all participants were presented a case through which they started practicing ecosystem thinking—as all participants presented different companies, a fictional case was selected. Participants were to step into a mindset of a newly opened gym owner. From this perspective, they started to think what kind of business ecosystem could be of help and especially what kind of actors should be engaged in it for co-creation of value to customers.

Brainstorming was carried out using digital notes, which participants placed onto a predefined ecosystem map in *Miro*. Once all notes were added, a group dialogue followed, during which participants elaborated on their ideas in more detail. After the workshop, all participants received additional reading materials and guidance on how to apply the provided templates in their own work (Fig. 6).

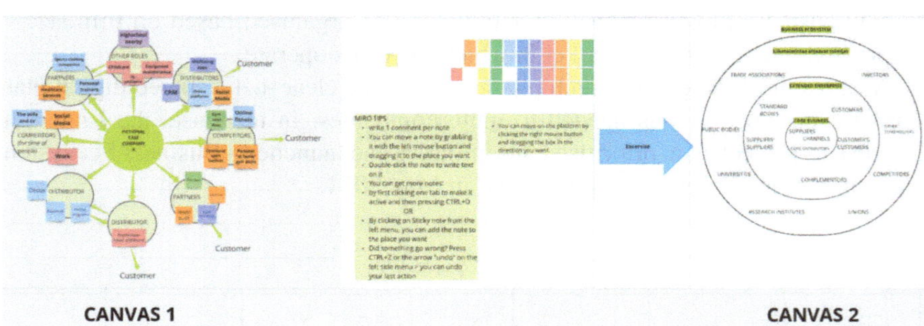

Fig. 6 Digital ecosystem mapping board for participants to use later in their organisations

In this "digital onion" (Fig. 6) model following Moore (1993) participants can transfer the exercise learnings to their own company's needs. Subsequent to the workshop, all participants received further instructions via email.

Following the pilot workshop, reflection helped identify both the successful aspects and areas needing improvement—regarding the *Miro* board itself and the overall organisation of a knowledge transfer workshop, especially for participants unfamiliar with ecosystem thinking. From the organisers point of view, for "hands-on" exercise, *Miro* was an excellent choice which enabled co-creation and knowledge transfer extremely well. Participants also complimented the ease of use of the platform and the detailed instructions. As a key learning for future workshops, the organisers recognised the need for a longer event—or even a series of events—where the current concept could serve as an introductory "teaser" to the topic. Truly meaningful conversations take time, and this 2-h workshop proved to be somewhat too short.

Another key takeaway was the realisation that participants may need more than written instructions to apply the workshop learnings in their own workplaces—they may require additional support. The involvement of a professional facilitator can greatly enhance co-creation workshops, and this is something the Limelight project team could consider incorporating into future versions of the workshop. These insights, along with the potential for digital knowledge transfer and creation, were further validated in October 2025. A group interview was conducted with seven workshop participants to examine their longer-term engagement with business model innovation (BMI) and ecosystem-related activities following the workshop. Five participants indicated that their companies had formed new partnerships and had begun to adopt ecosystem thinking more actively. Three of these companies had engaged a professional facilitator to support the process. The remaining two had faced challenges due to personnel changes, which led to the reallocation of resources to other projects.

5 Discussion

The usage of digital platforms has many benefits for knowledge transfer, co-creation, and business model innovation. At best, it creates flexibility and complements face-to-face interaction. Grasping new opportunities in a jungle of new digital possibilities may be at times also overwhelming. Curiosity is to be embraced, yet at the same time different levels of capabilities of participants in dealing with such platforms needs to be considered. Resources such as money and time may be saved through the use of adequate IT solutions, but this calls for proper preparation.

Checklist for Managers Exploring Co-creation and Knowledge Transfer Workshops on Digital Platforms (e.g., Miro)
Recommended by Heidi Vähänikkilä

- **WHY?** Clearly define the purpose of your workshop—what is the overarching aim?
- **WHAT?** Set specific objectives: what exactly do you want to accomplish?
- **WHO?** Based on your aim and objectives, select the right participants. Co-creation is most effective when diverse perspectives are brought together—consider mixing departments, roles, or even fields.
- **WHERE?** Choose a digital platform that aligns with your goals and participants' needs. It could be one already in use at your organisation or a new tool. Seek recommendations and real-user feedback—LinkedIn groups can be a great source of insight.
- **WHEN?** Develop a master plan with detailed scheduling. Take participants' availability and willingness to commit into account. Select a date and duration that are both practical and effective.
- **WITH WHOM?** Consider whether hiring a professional moderator or facilitator could enhance the workshop's impact—this often significantly boosts results.
- **WHY NOT? (Part 1)** Take a "dark cloud" perspective: identify potential challenges or pain points. Anticipating issues early helps you prepare and adjust.
- **WHY NOT? (Part 2)** Don't overthink, go for it! Trial and error is one of the best ways to learn and improve.

References

Aarikka-Stenroos, L., & Ritala, P. (2017). Network management in the era of ecosystems: Systematic review and management framework. *Industrial Marketing Management, 67*, 23–36. https://doi.org/10.1016/j.indmarman.2017.08.010

Afonso, O., Monteiro, S., & Thompson, M. (2012). A growth model for the quadruple helix. *Journal of Business Economics and Management, 13*(5), 849–865. https://doi.org/10.3846/16111699.2011.626438

Arnkil, R., Järvensivu, A., Koski, P., & Piirainen, T. (2010). *Exploring Quadruple Helix: Outlining user-oriented innovation models*. University of Tampere. https://trepo.tuni.fi/bitstream/handle/10024/65758/978-951-44-8209-0.pdf

Bergvall-Kåreborn, B., Eriksson, C. I., Ståhlbröst, A., & Svensson, J. (2009, December 6–9). *A milieu for innovation: Defining living labs*. ISPIM Innovation Symposium.

Clarysse, B., Wright, M., Bruneel, J., & Mahajan, A. (2014). Creating value in ecosystems: Crossing the chasm between knowledge and business ecosystems. *Research Policy, 43*(7), 1164–1176. https://doi.org/10.1016/j.respol.2014.04.014

Clauss, T., Breier, M., Kraus, S., Durst, S., & Mahto, R. V. (2021). Temporary business model innovation—SMEs' innovation response to the Covid-19 crisis. *R&D Management, 52*(2), 294–312. https://doi.org/10.1111/radm.12498

European Network of Living Labs (ENoLL). (2024). *What are living labs*. https://enoll.org/about-us/what-are-living-labs/

Foss, N. J., & Saebi, T. (2015). *Business model innovation: The organisational dimension*. Oxford University Press.

Freiling, J. (2015). *Business model innovation—A concept between organisational renewal and industry transformation*. https://papers.ssrn.com/sol3/papers.cfm?abstract_id=3105239

Geissdoerfer, M., Vladimirova, D., & Evans, S. (2018). Sustainable business model innovation: A review. *Journal of Cleaner Production, 198*, 401–416. https://doi.org/10.1016/j.jclepro.2018.06.240

Hautamäki, A. (2010). *Sustainable innovation: A new age of innovation and Finland's innovation policy*. Sitra. https://media.sitra.fi/app/uploads/2017/02/raportti87.pdf

Heikkilä, M., & Kuivaniemi, L. (2012). Ecosystem under construction: An action research study on entrepreneurship in a business ecosystem. *Technology Innovation Management Review, 2*(6), 18–24. https://doi.org/10.22215/timreview/564

Iansiti, M., & Levien, R. (2004). Strategy as ecology. *Harvard Business Review*. https://hbr.org/2004/03/strategy-as-ecology

Jacobides, M. G. (2019). In the ecosystem economy, what's your strategy? *Harvard Business Review*. https://hbr.org/2019/09/in-the-ecosystem-economy-whats-your-strategy

Jeppesen, L. B., & Lakhani, K. R. (2010). Marginality and problem-solving effectiveness in broadcast search. *Organisation Science, 21*(5), 1016–1033. https://doi.org/10.1287/orsc.1090.0491

Ketonen-Oksi, S., & Valkokari, K. (2019). Innovation ecosystems as structures for value co-creation. *Technology Innovation Management Review, 9*(2), 25–35. https://doi.org/10.22215/timreview/1216

Kettunen, J., Ilomäki, S.-K., & Kalliokoski, P. (2008). *Making sense of innovation management*. Teknologiateollisuus, Teknologiainfo Teknova Oy.

Laurea University of Applied Sciences. (2024a). *Laurea living labs*. https://www.laurea.fi/en/research/laurea-living-labs/

Laurea University of Applied Sciences. (2024b). *Limelight*. https://www.laurea.fi/koulutus/taydennyskoulutukset/limelight-koulutukset/

Lember, V., Brandsen, T., & Tõnurist, P. (2019). The potential impacts of digital technologies on co-production and co-creation. *Public Management Review, 21*(11), 1665–1686. https://doi.org/10.1080/14719037.2019.1619807

Madsen, H. L. (2020). Business model innovation and the global ecosystem for sustainable development. *Journal of Cleaner Production, 247*, 119102. https://doi.org/10.1016/j.jclepro.2019.119102

Mariano, S., & Awazu, Y. (2017). The role of collaborative knowledge building in the co-creation of artifacts: Influencing factors and propositions. *Journal of Knowledge Management, 21*(4), 779–795. https://doi.org/10.1108/jkm-09-2016-0360

Mitchell, D., & Coles, C. (2003). The ultimate competitive advantage of continuing business model innovation. *Journal of Business Strategy, 24*(5), 15–21. https://doi.org/10.1108/02756660310504924

Moore, J. F. (1993). Predators and prey: A new ecology of competition. *Harvard Business Review*. https://parsmodir.com/wp-content/uploads/2019/08/InnEcho-Moore1993.pdf

Moore, J. F. (2006). Business ecosystems and the view from the firm. *Antitrust Bulletin, 51*(1), 31–75. https://doi.org/10.1177/0003603x0605100103

Organisation for Economic Co-operation and Development OECD (2024). *Services trade*. https://www.oecd.org/en/topics/policy-issues/services-trade.html

Osterwalder, A., & Pigneur, Y. (2010). *Business model generation: A handbook for visionaries, game changers, and challengers*. Wiley.

Pine, J., II, & Gilmore, J. H. (1998). Welcome to the experience economy. *Harvard Business Review*. https://enlillebid.dk/mmd/wp-content/uploads/2012/03/Welcome-to-the-Experience-Economy-Pine-and-Gilmore.pdf

Porter, M. E., & Rivkin, J. W. (2000). *Industry transformation*. Harvard Business School.

Selander, L., Henfridsson, O., & Svahn, F. (2013). Capability search and redeem across digital ecosystems. *Journal of Information Technology, 28*(3), 183–197. https://doi.org/10.1057/jit.2013.14

Senyo, P. K., Liu, K., & Effah, J. (2019). Digital business ecosystem: Literature review and a framework for future research. *International Journal of Information Management, 47*, 52–64. https://doi.org/10.1016/j.ijinfomgt.2019.01.002

Sribney, M. (2020). *Your business ecosystem will never be the same again*. https://mike.com.au/2020/04/01/your-business-ecosystem-will-never-be-the-same-again/

Ståhle, P., & Laento, K. (2000). *Strateginen kumppanuus*. WSOY.

Steen, K., & Van Bueren, E. (2017). *Urban living labs: A living lab way of working*. https://repository.tudelft.nl/islandora/object/uuid%3A2fcad7f5-522d-4552-9bc2-02a1d0a09db0

Taatila, V. P., Suomala, J., Siltala, R., & Keskinen, S. (2006). Framework to study the social innovation networks. *European Journal of Innovation Management, 9*(3), 312–326. https://doi.org/10.1108/14601060610678176

Teece, D. J. (2007). Explicating dynamic capabilities: The nature and micro-foundations of (sustainable) enterprise performance. *Strategic Management Journal, 28*(13), 1319–1350. https://doi.org/10.1002/smj.640

Teece, D. J. (2010). Alfred Chandler and "capabilities" theories of strategy and management. *Industrial and Corporate Change, 19*(2), 297–316. https://doi.org/10.1093/icc/dtq008

Vähänikkilä, H., & Vakkuri, M. (2022). *3UAS Conference: Ecosystem thinking—Business model evolution in hospitality field*. Haaga-Helia publication.

Van Der Borgh, M., Cloodt, M., & Romme, A. G. L. (2012). Value creation by knowledge-based ecosystems: Evidence from a field study. *R&D Management, 42*(2), 150–169. https://doi.org/10.1111/j.1467-9310.2011.00673.x

World Travel & Tourism Council. (2024). *Economic impact*. https://wttc.org/research/economic-impact

Zott, C., Amit, R., & Massa, L. (2011). The business model: Recent developments and future research. *Journal of Management, 37*(4), 1019–1042. https://doi.org/10.1177/0149206311406265

Heidi Vähänikkilä is a Senior Lecturer of Hospitality Management and Service Design at Laurea University of Applied Sciences. Her background in marketing for leading Finnish hospitality companies has shaped the expertise she now shares with students. She teaches courses in project management, customer insight, ecosystem thinking, and event and hospitality management. In addition to teaching, she actively contributes to RDI projects, including curriculum development and internationalisation. Her ongoing PhD research at the Estonian Business School focuses on future proof business model innovation, change capacity, and ecosystem thinking—crucial for the post-pandemic hospitality field—and involves international cooperation in Finland and Malaysia.

Integrating Artificial Intelligence in Innovation Processes: A Systematic Approach for Enhanced Competitive Advantage

Patrick Montenegro Costa and Andreas Braun

Abstract This study presents a comprehensive framework for integrating Artificial Intelligence (AI) into structured innovation processes, focusing on Open Innovation and New Product Development. Through a systematic literature review of 53 peer-reviewed articles (2022–2024) and extensive secondary research identifying 218 AI models and techniques, the research introduces the "AI for Innovation" diagram—a novel conceptual framework aligning AI capabilities with specific innovation phases. The findings reveal AI's increasing application across all innovation stages, from idea generation to post-launch analysis, with roles ranging from creative "Originator" to supportive "Facilitator". The study categorises AI technologies into 19 main categories and maps their applications to different innovation phases, providing a structured guide for organisations. Key insights include AI's transformative role in enhancing knowledge transfer throughout the innovation process, from facilitating data analysis and insight generation to enabling personalised learning and automated knowledge documentation. This study bridges the gap between theoretical AI capabilities and their practical application in innovation, providing actionable insights for firms to enhance innovation capabilities, accelerate development cycles, and gain competitive advantage in an AI-driven business landscape.

Keywords Artificial Intelligence · Open innovation · New product development · Knowledge transfer · Digital transformation

---

P. Montenegro Costa · A. Braun (✉)
BSP Business and Law School, Berlin, Germany
e-mail: patrick.costa@kws.com; andreas.braun@businessschool-berlin.de

K. Bodrožić-Brnić et al. (eds.), *Digital Transformation in Knowledge Transfer*, Digital Transformation and Innovation,
https://doi.org/10.1007/978-3-032-07329-7_8

1 Introduction

In an era where digital transformation dictates the pace of business evolution, Artificial Intelligence (AI) has emerged as a pivotal force in reshaping innovation management and knowledge transfer within organisations (Jakobsen et al., 2024; Just, 2024; Kocjancic & Gricar, 2023; Verganti et al., 2020). The integration of AI into structured innovation processes has become essential for maintaining competitive advantage in an increasingly dynamic marketplace.

AI plays a pivotal role in revolutionising how knowledge is created, shared, and utilised within and between organisations (Shan et al., 2023). By facilitating efficient data analysis, enabling personalised learning, and supporting Open Innovation initiatives, AI transforms knowledge creation and application within the innovation context, potentially enhancing organisational capabilities and competitive advantage (Broekhuizen et al., 2023).

This research focuses on two key concepts: Open Innovation (OI) and New Product Development (NPD). OI, as conceptualised by Chesbrough (2003), encourages incorporating external knowledge sources into internal innovation processes, allowing companies to leverage broader expertise and accelerate innovation cycles. NPD frameworks, evolving from approaches like the Stage-Gate System (Cooper, 1990), provide systematic methodologies for transforming ideas into marketable products.

Despite their widespread adoption, understanding how to optimally integrate AI into these processes remains a significant challenge. While recent studies explore AI's potential in innovation (Broekhuizen et al., 2023; Zhou et al., 2020), a comprehensive framework aligning specific AI technologies with different innovation stages is lacking. This research aims to bridge this gap by categorising AI technologies and aligning them with innovation phases. For instance, Large Language Models (LLMs) could support ideation, while Convolutional Neural Networks (CNNs) might evaluate prototype usability. The advent of multimodal AI systems presents even greater potential for revolutionising traditional innovation processes (Mariani & Dwivedi, 2024).

This study has three primary objectives: conduct a comprehensive review of current AI technologies and their innovation applications; develop the "AI for Innovation" diagram mapping specific AI technologies to innovation stages; and provide actionable insights for organisations integrating AI into their innovation strategies, focusing on knowledge transfer enhancement.

By addressing these objectives, this study contributes to both theoretical understanding and practical guidance for businesses navigating AI-driven innovation and knowledge transfer. The following sections detail the methodology, present key findings including the "AI for Innovation" diagram, and discuss implications for research and practice in this evolving field.

2 Conceptual Framework

This research examines the integration of three key concepts in modern innovation management: OI, NPD, and AI. OI shapes how organisations access and utilise knowledge, NPD provides the structured framework for developing innovations, and AI acts as an enabling technology that can enhance both processes.

These concepts, when integrated, create synergistic effects in innovation management, particularly in knowledge transfer and development processes. The following sections examine each concept individually before exploring their combined potential for enhancing organisational innovation capabilities. Understanding their fundamental interconnections provides the foundation for this study.

2.1 Open Innovation

Open Innovation, a concept coined by Henry Chesbrough (2003), describes a paradigm shift in how companies develop and market innovations. In contrast to the traditional closed innovation model, OI encourages companies to incorporate external knowledge sources into their internal innovation processes while also externalising their unused internal knowledge. This approach is based on the recognition that valuable ideas can originate and be brought to market from both inside and outside the company (Chesbrough, 2003).

OI plays a crucial role in knowledge dissemination and transfer. By opening innovation processes, companies can access a broader spectrum of ideas, technologies, and expertise. This leads to accelerated knowledge development and enables companies to solve complex problems more effectively. Knowledge transfer is facilitated through the creation of innovation networks and collaboration platforms that promote the exchange of insights and best practices across organisational boundaries (Shan et al., 2023).

The impact of OI on companies' competitive advantage is substantial. By leveraging external knowledge sources, companies can increase their innovation speed, reduce risks, and lower costs. This results in improved adaptability to market changes and enables companies to respond more quickly to customer needs. Furthermore, OI can help explore new markets and develop innovative business models, further strengthening the competitive position (Broekhuizen et al., 2023).

2.2 New Product Development

New Product Development encompasses the entire process of transforming a market opportunity into a product available for sale. NPD processes have evolved over time, from linear models like the Stage-Gate system (Cooper, 1990) to more agile and flexible approaches that better respond to the dynamics of modern markets.

NPD plays a central role in knowledge development within companies. Throughout the NPD process, new insights about customer needs, technological possibilities, and market dynamics are continuously gained. This knowledge growth spans various areas, from market research to product development and commercialisation. The insights gained in the NPD process not only contribute to a current project but also form a valuable knowledge base for future innovations (Cooper & McCausland, 2024).

The contribution of NPD to business success is significant. Successful new products can generate revenue growth, increase market share, and strengthen competitive position. Moreover, a well-structured NPD process promotes efficiency and effectiveness in resource utilisation, leading to cost savings and improved profitability. NPD also contributes to the development of core competencies that can create long-term competitive advantages (Plantec et al., 2023).

2.3 *Artificial Intelligence*

Artificial Intelligence encompasses a range of technologies and methods that enable computer systems to perform tasks that normally require human intelligence. Key concepts include machine learning, deep learning, natural language processing (NLP), and computer vision. These technologies allow AI systems to learn from data, recognise patterns, make predictions, and solve complex problems (Mariani & Dwivedi, 2024).

AI acts as a powerful enabler for knowledge development and transfer. Through its ability to analyse large amounts of data and derive insights, AI can uncover hidden patterns and relationships that are difficult for humans to detect. This leads to accelerated knowledge generation and enables data-driven decision-making. AI systems can also improve knowledge transfer by creating personalised learning paths, supporting automated documentation, and optimising knowledge management systems (Wang et al., 2024).

The potential of AI to enhance companies' innovation capabilities is considerable. AI can be employed in all phases of the innovation process, from idea generation to product development and market launch. By automating repetitive tasks and providing decision support, AI can significantly increase the efficiency and effectiveness of innovation processes. Moreover, AI can support creative processes by generating new ideas and establishing unexpected connections (Sahoo et al., 2024).

2.4 *Synergies Between OI, NPD, and AI*

The integration of OI, NPD, and AI offers significant synergies for improving knowledge transfer and increasing competitive advantage. OI expands the knowledge base that companies can access, while NPD provides structured processes for translating this knowledge into marketable products. AI acts as a catalyst, enhancing the efficiency and effectiveness of both approaches.

In the context of OI, AI can be used to identify relevant external knowledge sources, find collaboration partners, and optimise knowledge exchange in innovation networks. In NPD processes, AI can improve market research, generate product concepts, optimise prototypes, and refine market launch strategies. By combining these approaches, companies can accelerate their knowledge transfer, shorten innovation cycles, and increase their adaptability to market changes (Kuzior, 2023; Tsang et al., 2021).

However, the integration of OI, NPD, and AI also presents challenges. These include protecting intellectual property in OI systems, the need for data protection and ethical considerations in AI deployment, and the development of skills and organisational structures that support these integrated approaches. Despite these challenges, the opportunities outweigh the risks: companies that successfully integrate OI, NPD, and AI can achieve significant competitive advantages by bringing innovations to market faster and more effectively (Freisinger et al., 2023).

2.5 Derivation of Research Questions

Based on the analysis of synergies and challenges in integrating OI, NPD, and AI, several research gaps can be identified. In particular, there is a lack of a comprehensive framework that links specific AI technologies with the various phases of the innovation process while considering both OI and NPD perspectives.

Against this background, the following research questions can be derived:

1. What is the current state of research in Open Innovation and New Product Development with respect to Artificial Intelligence?
2. Can supportive AI models be specifically assigned to individual innovation phases in New Product Development?

These research questions aim to develop a deeper understanding of the integration of AI into innovation processes and to create a practical framework for companies that supports the implementation of AI technologies in OI and NPD processes.

3 Methods

This study employed a dual-pronged approach to comprehensively analyse the integration of AI in innovation processes, combining a systematic literature review with extensive secondary research.

3.1 Systematic Literature Review

To capture the current state of research on AI in OI and NPD, a systematic literature review was conducted. The primary database chosen for this review was EBSCO Host Business Source Premier, due to its comprehensive coverage of business and management literature. The search criteria were carefully defined to ensure relevance and currency of the findings. The time frame was set from January 2022 to April 2024, focusing on the most recent developments in the field. Only English-language, peer-reviewed journal articles were included to maintain academic rigour. The search terms used were ("Open Innovation" AND "Artificial Intelligence") or ("New Product Development" AND "Artificial Intelligence"), designed to capture the intersection of AI with both OI and NPD. The search yielded 53 articles, of which 48 were deemed relevant for further analysis and categorised into two main themes: "OI and AI" and "NPD and AI".

The systematic literature review was conducted to address the research questions derived in Sect. 2.5, focusing on the current state of AI in OI and NPD, and the potential for mapping AI models to specific innovation phases.

All AI models and potential use cases mentioned in the articles were carefully documented, providing a comprehensive overview of the current applications of AI in OI and NPD contexts.

3.2 Secondary Research

To supplement the academic literature review and capture the most recent developments in AI, an extensive secondary research was conducted. This phase included conducting internet-based research, guided by recommendations from AI assistants, specifically Claude by Anthropic and ChatGPT by OpenAI. The accuracy and relevance of the gathered information were verified by cross-referencing between these AI assistants. As a result, 218 AI models and techniques were identified and subsequently classified into 19 primary categories. Following this, a clustering process was carried out to organise these models and determine their potential applications across different stages of the innovation process.

3.3 Data Analysis

Qualitative content analysis was employed to synthesise findings from both the literature review and secondary research. This involved coding and categorising the data to identify key themes, trends, and potential applications of AI in innovation processes. As part of this process, existing models, such as the AI-NPD Model (Cooper & McCausland, 2024) and the AI-OI Matrix (Broekhuizen et al., 2023), which were identified during the systematic literature review, were also evaluated. These models provided additional context and served as a basis for comparison in the creation of the new diagram. This comprehensive methodology ensures a thorough understanding of both the theoretical landscape and practical applications of AI in innovation, providing a solid foundation for the development of the "AI for Innovation" framework.

3.4 Development of the "AI for Innovation" Diagram

The "AI for Innovation" diagram was developed through an iterative process that incorporated insights from both the literature review and secondary research. The initial phase of development involved conceptualising the diagram based on a synthesis of the literature review findings. This was followed by integrating AI models and techniques identified through secondary research. Several rounds of refinement were conducted to ensure the diagram's comprehensive coverage and practical applicability. The resulting diagram visually represents how various AI technologies can be applied across different stages of the innovation process, from ideation to post-launch analysis.

4 Results

The findings from our systematic literature review and secondary research provide comprehensive insights into the integration of AI in innovation processes. This section presents the key results, culminating in the introduction of the "AI for Innovation" diagram.

4.1 Findings from the Literature Review

The analysis of 48 relevant articles revealed several key trends in the application of AI to OI and NPD:

4.1.1 AI in Open Innovation

AI significantly enhances collaboration and leverages network effects within innovation ecosystems, as noted by Messeni Petruzzelli et al. (2023). Companies with advanced AI capabilities are better positioned to utilise OI approaches, which translates into revenue growth and improved competitiveness, according to Sahoo et al. (2024). This enhanced ability to leverage external knowledge and collaborate with partners allows these companies to develop innovative products and services more effectively, thereby gaining a competitive edge in the market.

AI also facilitates the analysis of large datasets, enabling the identification of trends and patterns crucial for innovation decision-making (e.g., Wheesbee, Spacemaker, and AMdEX), as highlighted by Broekhuizen et al. (2023). Furthermore, AI-powered platforms such as InnoCentive are increasingly being employed to streamline OI processes, enhancing both idea generation and collaboration, as indicated by Kuzior (2023). The integration of AI into OI processes has spurred the development of new business models and strategies for value creation, as discussed by Yang et al. (2021). This integration allows firms to leverage external knowledge and resources, enhancing their ability to innovate and adapt to market demands. By utilising AI's capabilities, such as data analysis and pattern recognition, companies can identify optimal applications for their technologies, thereby improving their appropriability and maximising the benefits derived from general-purpose technologies (GPTs) like IBM Watson. Ultimately, this approach fosters collaboration and accelerates the innovation cycle, enabling firms to navigate the complexities of emerging markets more effectively (Yang et al., 2021).

Additionally, AI plays a role in overcoming cognitive barriers and reducing biases within OI platforms, as evidenced by Clegg et al. (2022). Finally, there is a growing trend towards utilising AI for knowledge management and network orchestration in OI contexts, as observed by Shan et al. (2023).

4.1.2 AI in New Product Development

AI is being applied throughout all stages of the NPD process, ranging from idea generation to post-launch analysis, as described by Cooper and McCausland (2024). In the (fuzzy) front-end phase, AI aids in idea generation (e.g., Fuzzy Association Rule Mining (FARM)), concept development (e.g., Genetic Algorithm), and market analysis (e.g., Spark, Hadoop), as reported by Tsang et al. (2021) and Wahl et al. (2022). During the development and testing phases, AI optimises designs, assists in prototype creation, and enhances testing processes (e.g., deep learning, machine learning), as noted by Giannakis et al. (2020) and Agrawal et al. (2023). In the back-end phase, AI supports the creation of marketing plans (e.g., Taskaid, Brand24), pricing strategies, and sales optimisation (e.g., Birdeye), as discussed by Cooper and McCausland (2024). The use of AI-driven predictive analytics is increasingly prevalent for forecasting market trends and product success, according to Joung and Kim (2023). The integration of AI in NPD has led to significant improvements in product quality and reductions in development time, as highlighted by Plantec et al. (2023). AI is also being incorporated into decision support systems throughout the NPD process, which enhances both the quality and speed of decision-making, as observed by Freisinger et al. (2023). There is an increasing trend towards utilising AI for customisation and personalisation in product development, as reported by Wang et al. (2024). Moreover, AI is being used more frequently for risk assessment and mitigation in NPD projects, as noted by Cooper and McCausland (2024).

4.1.3 AI-Enabled Knowledge Transfer in Innovation Processes

The research indicates that AI significantly enhances knowledge transfer within innovation processes. AI technologies, particularly in the areas of graph neural networks and social network analysis, facilitate efficient knowledge sharing and collaboration within innovation networks, as discussed by Shan et al. (2023). Machine learning and data mining techniques are employed to analyse vast amounts of data, generating valuable insights that can be disseminated throughout an organisation, as reported by Tsang et al. (2021). An example of this is FARM, a technique that applies approximate logic to data mining to uncover relationships between variables, helping organisations understand customer preferences and behaviours during product development. Other techniques allow organisations to analyse historical data on product design features more effectively.

AI platforms, such as OpenIDEO, also enhance knowledge exchange between diverse stakeholders, thereby accelerating the innovation process, as highlighted by Kuzior (2023). AI-driven systems, such as adaptive learning platforms or intelligent tutoring systems, can create personalised learning paths for employees, optimising both knowledge acquisition and transfer, as described by Wang et al. (2024). Additionally, AI-assisted systems streamline the documentation process, enabling the capture and dissemination of tacit knowledge, as noted by Cooper and McCausland (2024). Finally, by analysing data and providing insights, AI-enabled systems and AI systems for idea evaluation support informed decision-making, effectively transferring knowledge from AI to human decision-makers, as discussed by Freisinger et al. (2023).

4.2 Results from Secondary Research

Our secondary research built upon the AI models and technologies identified in the 48 academic articles from our literature review. To expand this foundation, we utilised AI assistants (Claude by Anthropic and ChatGPT by OpenAI) to suggest additional models, techniques, and potential applications. These suggestions were then cross-referenced with information from industry reports, technical documentation, and AI development platforms. This comprehensive approach identified a total of 218 AI models and techniques, which were organised into 19 primary categories (Table 1). It should be noted that this categorisation, while comprehensive, represents a snapshot of rapidly evolving technologies and may not be exhaustive.

The analysis revealed several distinct categories of AI technologies. Fundamental approaches like supervised learning and unsupervised learning, already identified in academic literature (Sahoo et al., 2024), were found to have extensive practical applications. Advanced processing techniques such as NLP and computer vision, discussed by Wang et al. (2024), showed broader implementation possibilities in industry settings. Time series analysis and optimisation algorithms represent specialised applications (Tsang et al., 2021), while emerging technologies like graph

Table 1 Exemplary version of the original table with results of 164 rows

Category	Subcategory	Model
Supervised Learning	Classification	Logistic Regression
Supervised Learning	Classification	Decision Trees
Supervised Learning	Regression	Random Forests
Unsupervised Learning	Clustering	K-Means Clustering
Unsupervised Learning	Dimensionality Reduction	Principal Component Analysis (PCA)
Semi-Supervised Learning	Generative Models	Generative Adversarial Networks (GANs)
Deep Learning	Image Processing	Convolutional Neural Networks (CNN)
Reinforcement Learning	Value-based Learning	Q-Learning
Natural Language Processing	Word Representation	Word2Vec
Explainable AI (XAI)	Model Interpretation	LIME (Local Interpretable Model-agnostic Explanations)
Recommender Systems	Advanced Methods	Matrix Factorization
Time Series Analysis and Forecasting	Classical Models	ARIMA (Auto-Regressive Integrated Moving Average)
Digital Twins	Supporting Technologies	Real-time Data Integration Systems

Request the full table from the editors or authors

neural networks and federated learning demonstrate new potential for innovation processes (Broekhuizen et al., 2023).

The technical documentation highlighted several significant developments in AI application. Advanced generative models, particularly recent LLMs, show considerable potential in augmenting human creativity during ideation and concept development, supporting findings by Mariani and Dwivedi (2024). The integration of multiple AI techniques in comprehensive decision support systems appears increasingly common in industry applications (Freisinger et al., 2023), while growing emphasis is placed on explainable AI (XAI) for transparent decision-making (Plantec et al., 2023).

Industry implementations particularly emphasised emerging patterns in AI deployment, especially regarding frameworks supporting effective human–AI collaboration (Recker et al., 2023). Additionally, cross-disciplinary applications were frequently observed, with AI techniques being adapted across different domains (Yang et al., 2021).

These findings complement the academic insights from our literature review, offering a broader perspective on AI's current practical applications and future potential in innovation processes.

4.3 *The "AI for Innovation" Diagram*

The central result of this study is the "AI for Innovation" diagram (Table 2), which provides a comprehensive framework for integrating AI into innovation processes. This diagram addresses our second research question by mapping specific AI technologies to different stages of the innovation process.

At the core of the diagram lies the "Evaluation and Decision Support" category, emphasising the critical role of AI in providing continuous assessment and decision-making support throughout the entire innovation process. This central position represents AI's capability to analyse data, provide insights, and assist in making informed decisions at every stage of innovation.

Surrounding the central category are eight main categories, each representing a distinct phase of the innovation process. These categories cover the entire spectrum of innovation activities, from initial idea generation to post-launch analysis, allowing for a comprehensive mapping of AI applications across the full innovation lifecycle. Within each of these nine categories (including the central category), there are seven subcategories. These subcategories, inspired by Cooper and McCausland's (2024) work, represent different roles that AI can play, ranging from "Originator" to "Facilitator". This classification offers a nuanced view of how AI can contribute to each phase of innovation, from generating new ideas to supporting routine tasks.

The outer layer of the diagram maps specific AI technologies to each subcategory. This detailed mapping allows users to identify which AI tools and techniques are most suitable for particular innovation tasks or roles. The "AI for Innovation"

Table 2 Exemplary version of the original table with results of 68 rows

Category	Application	AI Models
1. Idea Generation and Concept Development	1.1 Generation of New Product Ideas	Generative Models (e.g., GANs), Multi-Layer Networks (e.g., DNN)
2. Market Research and Customer Analysis	2.3 Analysis of Customer Feedback	Sentiment Analysis, Language Models (e.g., BERT)
3. Product Design and Development	3.4 Optimisation of Product Designs	Optimisation Algorithms, Simulation Models
4. Resource Planning and Process Optimisation	4.2 Prediction of Project Risks	Regression Models, Bayesian Networks
5. Production Technology and Quality Control	5.5 Automation of Error Detection	Computer Vision, Anomaly Detection
6. Marketing Strategy and Product Launch	6.4 Optimisation of Pricing Strategies	Optimisation Algorithms, Reinforcement Learning (e.g., Q-Learning)
7. Post-Launch Analysis and Continuous Improvement	7.5 Automation of Feedback Processes	Sentiment Analysis, Language Models (e.g., BERT)
8. Knowledge and Network Management	8.4 Optimization of Knowledge Flows	Optimization Algorithms, Reinforcement Learning
9. Evaluation and Decision Support	9.6 Planning of Stage Gate Reviews	Process Analysis, Bayesian Networks

Request the full table from the editors or authors

diagram offers several key features that enhance its utility for both researchers and practitioners. Firstly, it provides comprehensive coverage of the innovation process, encompassing all stages from idea generation to post-launch analysis. This holistic approach ensures that no aspect of the innovation journey is overlooked in terms of potential AI integration.

Secondly, the diagram excels in its alignment of AI technologies with specific innovation phases and roles. This mapping offers practical guidance on which AI tools to consider for particular innovation tasks, enabling organisations to make informed decisions about AI implementation in their innovation processes.

The diagram illustrates the diverse ways in which AI can contribute to innovation, showing how AI's function can range from creative idea generation to supportive decision-making. While it provides a structured framework, it is designed to be flexible, allowing organisations to adapt it to their specific needs and focus on the areas most relevant to their innovation strategies and capabilities.

Lastly, the diagram's integration of both OI and NPD paradigms makes the diagram applicable to a wide range of innovation approaches, enhancing its versatility and relevance across different organisational contexts.

These features suggest that the "AI for Innovation" diagram might serve as a promising foundation for understanding the integration of AI in innovation processes. While the comprehensive nature and specific technology mapping offer potential insights, further empirical validation across different industries and organisational contexts is needed to establish its practical utility and theoretical value. Future research should test the diagram's applicability in real-world settings and examine how it might be adapted to address emerging AI technologies and evolving innovation practices.

4.4 Application Examples

In the idea generation phase, LLMs like ChatGPT-4 from OpenAI can generate and refine innovative product concepts by analysing market trends and customer feedback. This capability allows for rapid exploration of diverse ideas and concepts, potentially leading to breakthrough innovations.

For market research, clustering algorithms and sentiment analysis tools can segment markets and analyse customer feedback, providing deeper insights into consumer preferences and behaviours. Such tools can process vast amounts of unstructured data from social media, customer reviews, and other sources, offering a more comprehensive understanding of market dynamics than traditional research methods.

In product design, generative design algorithms and digital twin technologies support advanced product development and testing. CNNs can be employed for rapid prototyping and design optimisation, analysing visual data to improve product aesthetics and functionality. These technologies allow for faster iteration cycles and can lead to more innovative and efficient designs.

Process optimisation benefits from reinforcement learning techniques, which can optimise resource allocation and production processes. By simulating various scenarios, these algorithms can identify the most efficient approaches, leading to significant improvements in operational efficiency and cost reduction.

During the testing phase, reinforcement learning algorithms can be utilised to simulate various usage scenarios, helping to identify potential issues before market launch. This approach can significantly reduce the risk of product failures and improve overall product quality.

Quality control in manufacturing can be enhanced through computer vision systems that automate quality checks. These systems can detect defects and inconsistencies with a level of accuracy and speed that surpasses human capabilities, ensuring consistent product quality and reducing human error.

In marketing and product launch, Recommender Systems can personalise marketing strategies and predict customer behaviour, leading to more targeted and effective campaigns. NLP models can analyse customer reviews and social media data, providing real-time insights into product reception and areas for improvement.

For post-launch analysis, time series analysis methods can forecast product lifecycles and identify trends, while NLP continues to monitor customer feedback for ongoing product improvement. These tools allow for continuous refinement of products and strategies based on real-world performance and customer responses.

These examples, in conjunction with the AI for Innovation diagram, provide a structured approach for organisations to integrate AI into their innovation processes. This integration has the potential to lead to enhanced efficiency, creativity, and competitive advantage across the entire innovation lifecycle. By leveraging AI technologies strategically throughout the innovation process, organisations can not only streamline their operations but also unlock new possibilities for product development and market engagement.

5 Discussion

The integration of AI into innovation processes represents a significant shift in organisational approaches to creativity, problem-solving, and product development. This section discusses the implications of our findings, their relation to existing research, and the challenges and opportunities they present.

Our research, culminating in the "AI for Innovation" diagram, extends the existing AI-NPD Model (Cooper & McCausland, 2024) and the AI-OI Matrix (Broekhuizen et al., 2023), providing a more granular view of how AI can be applied across different innovation phases. A key insight from our research is the spectrum of AI roles in innovation processes, ranging from "Originator" to "Facilitator" as conceptualised by Cooper and McCausland (2024). As an Originator, AI demonstrates potential in generating novel ideas, with, for example, LLMs producing innovative product concepts and opening new market opportunities. This aligns with Mariani and Dwivedi's (2024) work on generative AI in innovation management. As a Facilitator, AI technologies like machine learning algorithms and predictive analytics support decision-making throughout the innovation lifecycle, processing vast amounts of data to provide actionable insights. This detailed mapping of AI's roles across the innovation process builds upon the work of Sahoo et al. (2024), who observed improved competitiveness in companies leveraging AI for OI, by providing a structured framework for understanding and implementing these improvements.

The diagram's "Knowledge and Network Management" category is consistent with Shan et al.'s (2023) emphasis on AI in orchestrating innovation networks. AI enhances knowledge management through data analysis and insight generation (Tsang et al., 2021), supports stakeholder collaboration (Kuzior, 2023), creates personalised learning paths (Wang et al., 2024), and automates documentation processes (Cooper & McCausland, 2024). This knowledge transfer capability, including AI-to-human decision support (Freisinger et al., 2023), can significantly enhance organisational innovation capabilities. These applications have the potential to greatly improve an organisation's innovation capabilities and competitive advantage in the digital age.

The diagram demonstrates that AI models can indeed be strategically mapped to specific innovation phases, offering targeted support throughout the NPD process. This mapping not only validates the potential of AI in supporting innovation but also provides a practical guide for organisations seeking to integrate AI into their NPD processes.

However, the integration of AI is not without challenges. Ethical considerations, including data privacy and algorithmic bias, require careful attention. As Plantec et al. (2023) note, organisations must balance AI capabilities with transparency and fairness, necessitating robust governance frameworks. Human–AI collaboration remains critical; while AI demonstrates remarkable capabilities, human creativity and expertise are essential. The "AI for Innovation" diagram thus serves as a tool to augment rather than replace human capabilities, aligning with Recker et al.'s (2023) emphasis on effective human-AI orchestration in innovation.

The diagram provides a roadmap for strategic AI integration, enabling organisations to align specific AI technologies with different innovation phases. This targeted approach could enhance efficiency, reduce time-to-market, and potentially lead to more innovative outcomes.

Looking ahead, emerging technologies like multimodal AI systems present new opportunities. Future research should explore their impact on innovation processes and examine long-term effects of AI integration through longitudinal studies. While our framework provides a comprehensive approach to AI integration in innovation, it represents a starting point that will require regular updates as AI technologies and our understanding evolve. Success ultimately depends on how organisations adapt their processes, culture, and strategies to effectively leverage these tools.

6 Conclusion

This study has examined the integration of AI into innovation processes, with a particular focus on OI and NPD emphasising how AI enhances knowledge transfer in the context of digital transformation.

6.1 Summary of Key Findings

Our research has demonstrated the broad applicability of AI across the entire innovation process and underscored the diversity and specialisation of AI technologies for specific innovation tasks. By identifying 218 AI models and techniques across 19 categories, we provide a comprehensive foundation for the strategic integration of AI into innovation processes. The extensive mapping of these AI technologies to various phases and roles within innovation, as visualised in our "AI for Innovation" diagram, offers organisations a detailed roadmap for leveraging AI throughout their innovation journey, with a particular focus on enhancing knowledge transfer.

Key findings include the significant potential of LLMs in the ideation phase, which facilitate the generation of innovative concepts and support knowledge sharing. Additionally, CNNs have been effectively applied in prototype testing and quality control, enabling rapid learning and the dissemination of knowledge. The research also highlights the emerging potential of multimodal AI systems, which are poised to revolutionise traditional innovation processes and knowledge integration. Moreover, AI plays a critical role in enhancing decision-making processes and knowledge transfer throughout the innovation lifecycle, while its transformative impact on knowledge management and network orchestration in OI contexts cannot be overstated.

6.2 Contributions to Research and Practice

This study offers several helpful contributions. Theoretically, the "AI for Innovation" diagram extends existing models, providing a more comprehensive framework for understanding AI's role in innovation and knowledge transfer. Practically, our conceptual approach offers actionable insights for firms seeking to integrate AI into their innovation strategies and enhance their knowledge sharing capabilities. Methodologically, the combination of a systematic literature review and extensive secondary research presents a robust approach for studying rapidly evolving technological fields.

The "AI for Innovation" diagram developed in this study serves as a practical tool for companies aiming to strategically implement AI models across various innovation phases. By clearly mapping AI technologies to specific stages of the innovation process, it enables organisations to make informed decisions on where and how to deploy AI for maximum impact. This targeted approach to AI integration has the potential to significantly enhance innovation capabilities, accelerate product development cycles, and ultimately strengthen competitive advantage in an increasingly AI-driven business landscape.

6.3 Implications for Innovation Management and Knowledge Transfer

The findings of this research indicate several implications for innovation management and knowledge transfer. The "AI for Innovation" diagram provides a framework for organisations to identify opportunities for AI integration across their innovation processes, with the potential to enhance knowledge creation, sharing, and utilisation. While this structure aims to support organisations in making informed decisions about AI technology investments that align with both innovation and knowledge transfer objectives, its effectiveness needs to be validated through empirical testing across different organisational contexts and industries.

Given the diversity of AI technologies identified in this study, organisations considering their implementation need to develop a strategic approach to selecting and integrating AI tools. Such an approach requires not only technical understanding but also careful consideration of ethical aspects and sustainability goals.

6.4 Limitations and Future Research Directions

Despite its comprehensive nature, this study has limitations. The rapid pace of AI development means that new technologies and applications may emerge quickly. Future research could focus on empirically validating the "AI for Innovation" diagram across different industries and organisational sizes. Longitudinal studies are needed to assess the long-term impact of AI integration on innovation outcomes and knowledge transfer efficiency. Additionally, further investigation into ethical considerations and the development of guidelines for responsible AI use in innovation and knowledge management is essential.

Future research could also explore the evolving role of human creativity and expertise in AI-augmented innovation processes and knowledge creation. The impact of emerging AI technologies, such as advanced multimodal systems, on innovation paradigms and knowledge ecosystems warrants further analysis. Moreover, understanding how AI reshapes collaborative innovation and knowledge sharing across organisational boundaries, particularly in OI contexts, is another important avenue for research.

In conclusion, this study demonstrates that AI is not merely a tool for efficiency in innovation processes but a transformative force in knowledge transfer. The "AI for Innovation" diagram provides a comprehensive framework for organisations to leverage AI in enhancing their information flow capabilities across all stages of the innovation process. As AI continues to evolve, its role in facilitating and accelerating knowledge sharing will likely become even more crucial in driving innovation and organisational success in the digital age. The digital transformation of knowledge transfer, enabled by AI, presents both challenges and opportunities for organisations. Those that effectively harness AI to enhance their innovation processes and knowledge management practices will be well-positioned to thrive in an increasingly competitive and rapidly changing business environment.

References

Agrawal, A., McHale, J., & Oettl, A. (2023). Superhuman science: How artificial intelligence may impact innovation. *Journal of Evolutionary Economics, 33*(5), 1473–1517.

Broekhuizen, T., Dekker, H., de Faria, P., Firk, S., Nguyen, D. K., & Sofka, W. (2023). AI for managing open innovation: Opportunities, challenges, and a research agenda. *Journal of Business Research, 167*, 114196. https://doi.org/10.1016/j.jbusres.2023.114196

Chesbrough, H. (2003). *Open innovation: The new imperative for creating and profiting from technology*. Harvard Business School Press.

Clegg, M., Hofstetter, R., Blohm, I., & Bravin, M. (2022). Human-machine creativity: How AI can influence human creativity in open innovation. *Marketing Review St. Gallen, 6*, 40–47.

Cooper, Robert G. (1990). Stage-gate systems: A new tool for managing new products. *Business Horizons, Volume 33*(3), 44–54. ISSN 0007-6813, https://doi.org/10.1016/0007-6813(90)90040-I

Cooper, R. G., & McCausland, T. (2024). AI and new product development. *Research-Technology Management, 67*(1), 70–75.

Freisinger, E., Unfried, M., & Schneider, S. (2023). The AI-augmented crowd: How human crowdvoters adopt AI (or not). *Journal of Product Innovation Management, 41*(4), 865–889.

Giannakis, M., Dubey, R., Yan, S., Spanaki, K., & Papadopoulos, T. (2020). Social media and sensemaking patterns in new product development: Demystifying the customer sentiment. *Annals of Operations Research, 308*(1–2), 145–175. https://doi.org/10.1007/s10479-020-03620-3

Jakobsen, H. S., Brix, J., & Jakobsen, R. S. (2024). Unraveling data from an idea management system of 11 radical innovation portfolios: Key lessons and avenues for artificial intelligence integration. *Journal of Innovation & Entrepreneurship, 19*, 1–24.

Joung, J., & Kim, H. (2023). Interpretable machine learning-based approach for customer segmentation for new product development from online product reviews. *International Journal of Information Management, 70*, 102641. https://doi.org/10.1016/j.ijinfomgt.2022.102641

Just, J. (2024). Natural language processing for innovation search—Reviewing an emerging non-human innovation intermediary. *Technovation, 129*, 102883. https://doi.org/10.1016/j.technovation.2023.102883

Kocjancic, L., & Gricar, S. (2023). Usage of AI in sustainable knowledge management and innovation processes: Data analytics in the electricity sector. *FinTech, 2*(4), 718–736.

Kuzior, A. (2023). New technologies as tools supporting innovation management. *Scientific Papers of Silesian University of Technology: Organisation and Management Series, 2023*(188), 249–260.

Mariani, M., & Dwivedi, Y. K. (2024). Generative artificial intelligence in innovation management: A preview of future research developments. *Journal of Business Research, 175*, 114542. https://doi.org/10.1016/j.jbusres.2023.114542

Messeni Petruzzelli, A., Murgia, G., & Parmentola, A. (2023). Opening the black box of artificial intelligence technologies: Unveiling the influence exerted by type of organisations and collaborative dynamics. *Industry and Innovation, 30*(9), 1321–1351. https://doi.org/10.1080/13662716.2023.2188767

Plantec, Q., Deval, M.-A., Hooge, S., & Weil, B. (2023). Big data as an exploration trigger or problem-solving patch: Design and integration of AI-embedded systems in the automotive industry. *Technovation, 124*, 102763. https://doi.org/10.1016/j.technovation.2022.102763

Recker, J., von Briel, F., Yoo, Y., Nagaraj, V., & McManus, M. (2023). Orchestrating human-machine designer ensembles during product innovation. *California Management Review, 65*(3), 27–47. https://doi.org/10.1177/00081256231161306

Sahoo, S., Kumar, S., Donthu, N., & Singh, A. K. (2024). Artificial intelligence capabilities, open innovation, and business performance—Empirical insights from multinational B2B companies. *Industrial Marketing Management, 117*, 28–41. https://doi.org/10.1016/j.indmarman.2023.08.012

Shan, B., Oh, I., & Rowley, C. (2023). Innovation and entrepreneurship in East Asia during the digital era: Post-pandemic prospects. *Asia Pacific Business Review, 29*(4), 843–851. https://doi.org/10.1080/13602381.2023.2173584

Tsang, Y. P., Wu, C. H., Lin, K.-Y., Tse, Y. K., Ho, G. T. S., & Lee, C. K. M. (2021). Unlocking the power of big data analytics in new product development: An intelligent product design framework in the furniture industry. *Journal of Manufacturing Systems, 62*, 777–791. https://doi.org/10.1016/j.jmsy.2021.01.011

Verganti, R., Vendraminelli, L., & Iansiti, M. (2020). Innovation and design in the age of artificial intelligence. *Journal of Product Innovation Management, 37*(3), 212–227. https://doi.org/10.1111/jpim.12522

Wahl, J., Füller, J., & Hutter, K. (2022). AI-assisted searching through crowdsourced solution space. *Marketing Review St. Gallen, 39*(6), 30–38. https://doi.org/10.1365/s11621-022-00117-6

Wang, P., Li, K., Du, Q., & Wang, J. (2024). Customer experience in AI-enabled products: Scale development and validation. *Journal of Retailing and Consumer Services, 76*, 103578. https://doi.org/10.1016/j.jretconser.2023.103578

Yang, J., Chesbrough, H., & Hurmelinna-Laukkanen, P. (2021). How to appropriate value from general-purpose technology by applying open innovation. *California Management Review, 64*(3), 24–48. https://doi.org/10.1177/00081256211004384

Zhou, Z., Liu, Y., Yu, H., & Ren, L. (2020). The influence of machine learning-based knowledge management model on enterprise organisational capability innovation and industrial development. *PLoS One, 15*(12), e0242253. https://doi.org/10.1371/journal.pone.0242253

Patrick Montenegro Costa is a researcher interested in Entrepreneurship, Innovation Management, and Sustainability. He holds a Master's degree in Business Administration from BSP Business and Law School Berlin and a Bachelor's in Business Administration from Freie Universität Berlin. He has also enriched his academic profile with international studies at Escola Superior de Propaganda e Marketing (ESPM) in São Paulo, Brazil, and Copenhagen Business School (CBS) in Denmark. Montenegro Costa brings a diverse professional background, including experience in business development, project management, and process optimisation. His master's thesis explored the implementation of Artificial Intelligence in innovation processes, showcasing his ability to bridge theoretical knowledge and practical application.

Andreas Braun is a Professor of Business Administration specialising in Innovation Management, Sustainability, and Entrepreneurship at BSP Business and Law School Berlin. He holds a PhD in Innovation Management from the University of Potsdam, an MBA in General Management from CEU Business School Budapest, and a B.Sc. and M.Sc. in Business Administration from the Technical University of Freiberg. With an extensive academic and professional background, Prof. Braun has led research and strategic initiatives, particularly in the fields of Open Innovation Management and Entrepreneurial Ecosystems. He seamlessly combines theoretical insights with practical applications, shaping how innovation and entrepreneurship contribute to organisational success and societal progress.

The Future of Learning

Evaluating AI Readiness Among Higher and Further Education Lecturers: A Mixed-Methods Approach

Kristina Bodrožić-Brnić

Abstract Artificial Intelligence (AI) is increasingly shaping higher and adult education, raising questions about educators' readiness to integrate AI tools into their teaching practices. This article examines AI readiness among university education staff, analysing their digital competencies, didactic flexibility, and perceptions of AI's role in education. It incorporates a literature review, qualitative interviews with educators, survey data from university lecturers, and insights from AI training workshops. Findings indicate a broad spectrum of AI readiness, ranging from enthusiasm to scepticism, with key barriers including ethical concerns, lack of institutional support, technical challenges, and financial constraints. This study highlights the importance of professional development, ethical guidance, and institutional strategies to foster AI literacy among educators. It also underscores the role of human-centred AI approaches in education, emphasising responsible AI integration to enhance, rather than replace, the human element in teaching. Practical recommendations are provided for universities to support AI adoption through targeted training, structured institutional policies, and improved technical infrastructure. By addressing these challenges, higher education institutions can enhance AI readiness, ensuring that educators are equal in the evolving digital landscape and leverage AI for effective teaching and learning.

Keywords AI readiness · Higher education · Digital literacy · AI in teaching · Human-centred AI

K. Bodrožić-Brnić (✉)
Programm Management Creative AI, Mittelstand-Digital Zentrum Zukunftskultur, Potsdam, Germany
e-mail: kristina.brnic@businessschool-berlin.de

K. Bodrožić-Brnić et al. (eds.), *Digital Transformation in Knowledge Transfer*, Digital Transformation and Innovation,
https://doi.org/10.1007/978-3-032-07329-7_9

1 Introduction and Methodology

The following article addresses a topic that plays an important role in the current discussion about Artificial Intelligence, which is, for example, reflected in the title of a popular article on the matter titled “Dein Dozent bin jetzt ich: Künstliche Intelligenz könnte die Lehre verbessern. Wie weit sind die Hochschulen damit?” (Eng. *I’m your lecturer now: Artificial Intelligence could improve teaching. How far have universities come?*) (*Die Zeit* No. 21/2024). In conducting various workshops on Artificial Intelligence (AI) for the further training of teaching staff, I have found that only a few among them are familiar with concepts of AI-based co-creation in the classroom. Several lecturers assume that AI content is created entirely by the software and can therefore be faulty and incomplete. What is often overlooked is that iterative prompting is based on the input of one’s own source material or source prompt. Users can then further refine the results of these initial inputs by interacting with the system and making appropriate adjustments to the prompting. In a joint position paper, my colleague Marco Wedel from the Technische Universität Berlin and I emphasise that “AI and digitalisation should be used to improve teaching, not to replace the human component”. In this context, we are keen to highlight the importance of the so-called *human-centred AI approaches* in education (Bodrožić-Brnić & Wedel, 2025). These also include, among other things, concepts of Trustworthy AI or Responsible AI, which aim to design AI-based systems in such a way that they follow basic ethical principles, and that data processing remains somewhat comprehensible to users in order to minimise reservations about these new systems (Saif, 2024). A recent study by KPMG shows that for 49% of 1000 people surveyed, missing or inaccurate information is one of the highest risks in AI use (Höck, 2024).

In this context, I see several key questions that are addressed in the following article: (1) How does teaching with Artificial Intelligence affect university lecturers, and do they possibly see AI as competition? (2) How open are higher and further education lecturers to the use of AI in their own teaching, and what factors contribute to their respective attitudes?

These questions are highly relevant in the field of knowledge transfer. Since the release of ChatGPT 3.5—a version introduced by OpenAI on November 30, 2022 as part of a free research scenario (Nyst, 2024) that became very popular in the following year—the hype surrounding the potential of Generative Artificial Intelligence (GenAI) has intensified. This has fuelled extensive debate at universities and further education institutions, where discussions focus on the risks and limitations, but also on the opportunities and potential, of using GenAI (Tubella et al., 2023). The term “AI Readiness” comes up again and again. According to Lerch (2021), AI Readiness describes the ability and willingness of industrial companies to integrate AI technologies into production processes. When applied to the academic context for the purpose of this article and further research that might be conducted by me or my institutions AI readiness means the ability to effectively use AI tools and methods in teaching.

A high level of AI Readiness will be a crucial aspect for educators at all levels in the future because they operate at the societal interface where skills of future employees or founders are developed. In this article, I examine the AI Readiness of teaching staff in higher and further education and analyse their digital skills, didactic flexibilities, their co-creation ability, and the challenges they see in integrating AI into their teaching practice. Finally, I will make some recommendations on how respective education institutions can design the introduction of AI in a human-centred way, which might open the path for more educators to use such new technologies rather sooner than later.

To reflect on the questions that were introduced earlier, I use an integrated mix of four methodological approaches: (1) a literature review on the application of Generative AI in higher and further education with search terms such as "AI acceptance in universities", "AI competence for teachers or lecturers and professors", "AI transformation in universities"; (2) qualitative interviews with two lecturers, one with and one without formative AI experiences; (3) an evaluation of a qualitative questionnaire on the topic of AI in teaching; (4) an analysis of several training sessions on GenAI use for university lecturers (first half of 2024).

The combination of these methodological approaches enables a fundamental assessment of lecturers' AI Readiness. Key factors influencing readiness to use AI can be identified and practical recommendations for educational institutions that want to promote a digitally competent teaching staff can be derived.

2 Literature Review

Considering the current GenAI boom, it is advisable to primarily consider results from 2023 onwards when evaluating studies and literature on using AI in teaching. Such recent studies emphasise the need to improve educators' AI knowledge and digital skills so that they can use these technologies effectively (Koch et al., 2024). In this context, it is becoming apparent that, despite the growing recognition of the importance of AI in education, there is still a significant disparity in educators' willingness to engage with these tools. This ranges from great enthusiasm to considerable concern about their practical and ethical implications. Therefore, trust in Artificial Intelligence in higher education is repeatedly emphasised (Tubella et al., 2023). An essential factor for acceptance in this context is the establishment of regulatory guidance, such as the High-Level Expert Group on AI (HLEG), which published ideas on Trustworthy AI in 2019. The HLEG guidelines laid the foundation for the development, deployment, and use of AI in an ethical and socio-technically robust manner and provide a framework for trustworthy AI (Tubella et al., 2023).

Other recent studies underscore that building AI literacy among educators is essential to establish a sustainable educational development. AI expertise enables lectures to "understand, use, monitor, and critically reflect on AI" (Rütti-Joy et al., 2023). The authors cite the example of the DPaCK model (Digitality-Related Pedagogical and Content Knowledge model) as a comprehensive approach. This model combines technological, pedagogical, and subject knowledge to qualify lectures for the demands of AI-mediated teaching.

The DPaCK model expands the rather classic *Technological Pedagogical Content Knowledge model (TPACK)* and focuses on the specific requirements of AI integration in education. It integrates three essential components for approaching topics related to AI in knowledge transfer:

- **Digital knowledge, which** includes knowledge about AI tools' functioning, algorithms, and social and ethical implications.
- **Digitality and pedagogy are** terms the DPaCK model coins, which include an understanding of how AI can be meaningfully applied in pedagogy and which didactic adjustments should be made to do so.
- **Digitality and subject knowledge, which** promotes the subject-specific application of AI tools to increase the depth of content and accessibility of teaching. (Rütti-Joy et al., 2023)

3 Personal Interviews

In the context of an AI didactics training course that I was able to conduct at the BSP Business and Law School (BSP) on the Berlin campus in March 2024, I specifically asked Prof. Dr. Irit Nachtigall (a professor of Infectiology at the MSB Medical School Berlin) about the effect of the workshop on her personal AI readiness. The following questions and answers were particularly significant for an AI readiness analysis:

When asked, "Could you give a few sentences about your own assessment of your level of technologisation? Are you extremely fit, somewhere in the middle, or a beginner?", Prof. Nachtigall replied, "It depends on the areas addressed. (…) So there are certain areas where I'm a beginner, and there are areas where I'm fit. I'm pretty good at handling big data […] because of my involvement in research projects and the fact that I've been working with big data for years. I still enjoy learning new things. (…) I learn quickly and am very interested. Therefore, I would rate myself as intermediate overall". From these answers, it can be deduced that, despite technological knowledge, there are still many demands for additional competence development in the area of using Artificial Intelligence (Bodrožić-Brnić, 2024a).

In response to the request, "Can you describe what your experience with AI was like before attending this workshop and whether there were any reservations or interests?" Prof. Nachtigall replied: "I have no reservations at all. I know that we have to learn to live with AI and that we have to use it in a way that is good for us. By that, I also mean, among other things, the keyword gender gap. Nevertheless, I have no reservations at all. I just believe that we must set the guidelines for AI. (…) I have been working on adaptive learning for quite some time. If we as hygienists have to take the mandatory hygiene training every year (…) then it tires those participating. I think a lot could be done more efficiently with adaptive learning and

AI. I don't have any reservations about AI, but I have many hopes and wishes (Bodrožić-Brnić, 2024a)". These statements reveal perspectives for the use of AI to facilitate didactic tasks. For example, there is potential in adapting content to different levels of knowledge among training participants.

In the expert interview, I also asked Prof. Nachtigall whether she had specific expectations regarding the application of AI in didactics, especially in relation to her own teaching practice. Her answer makes it clear that her main interest is gaining a deeper understanding of AI in education and learning innovative didactic tools. She was surprised that the discussion was strongly dominated by ethical concerns regarding students' use of AI, particularly in regard to assignment creation. For Prof. Nachtigall this discussion should focus less on AI avoidance and more on how AI applications could be used to make studying and teaching more efficient. The professor sees the potential of AI for further developing teaching and encourages a more intensive exchange on such topics (Bodrožić-Brnić, 2024a).

The potential efficiency of AI in teaching is also found in another interview, conducted with Prof. Ingo Siegert, junior professor for Mobile Dialog Systems at the Otto-von-Guerricke-University Magdeburg. As part of his research, Prof. Siegert conducted a survey among university students on AI readiness. The results enable a comparison between students and teaching staff. He emphasises the essential need to integrate AI into teaching as AI is already being used by students anyway. Lecturers should therefore engage more deeply with these topics and promote a reflective approach to AI in the classroom. For the professor, educators should understand the available AI tools and how they work to be able to make informed judgments about which concerns are justified, and which are not. Prof. Siegert emphasises the importance of clarifying what should be tested in the educational process. Is the focus more on understanding concepts, or about actually performing tasks? The latter is more likely to contribute to conflicts that the teaching staff faces when students use GenAI for task-solving. In the professor's opinion, AI could introduce an element of fairness by giving all students an equal starting point, regardless of whether or not they have family support for academic homework. At the same time, students need to understand that copying AI-generated content without engaging in their own learning process will not lead to the desired skill development. He argues that educators should support students in using AI in a meaningful and reflective way (Bodrožić-Brnić, 2024b). This reinforces the need to promote a deeper understanding of the potential and functions of AI tools in the classroom.

4 Results of the Qualitative Survey on AI Readiness Among University Educators

In addition to the personal interviews, I conducted a survey in the fall of 2024 to better assess and compare AI readiness among university lecturers. To gain an international perspective was also important to me, therefore lecturers from Germany and Croatia were involved, as well as one person from Finland. Over 56% of the participants were women. About 60% of the participants come from the humanities. Participants from the natural sciences and engineering were in the minority, at around 11%. Most respondents have between 10 and 20 years of professional experience in higher education, followed by another group with more than 20 years of experience.

Around 50% of participants rate their digital skills as "quite good". Only around 20% stated that they had little digital knowledge. About half of the respondents are "moderately familiar" with the specific use of digital tools in the classroom, while about 30% said they were "quite familiar" to "very familiar". Almost 60% of respondents said they do not currently use digital tools in their teaching. Among those who use specifically GenAI tools, only around 50% feel "moderately confident" in their use. Only 20% rate their confidence in GenAI use as high.

The main obstacles to integrating digital tools and AI into teaching were identified as follows:

- **67.6% need training**: Many lecturers see the need for additional training to use AI tools effectively (Fig. 1).
- **48.6% have ethical concerns**: In the comments, it was stated/mentioned that the intensive discussion about the correct use of AI by students leads to ambiguities. Data security and the correctness of the data provided also pose a problem. Over-bureaucratisation of the educational institution the lecturers are affiliated with is also criticised here.

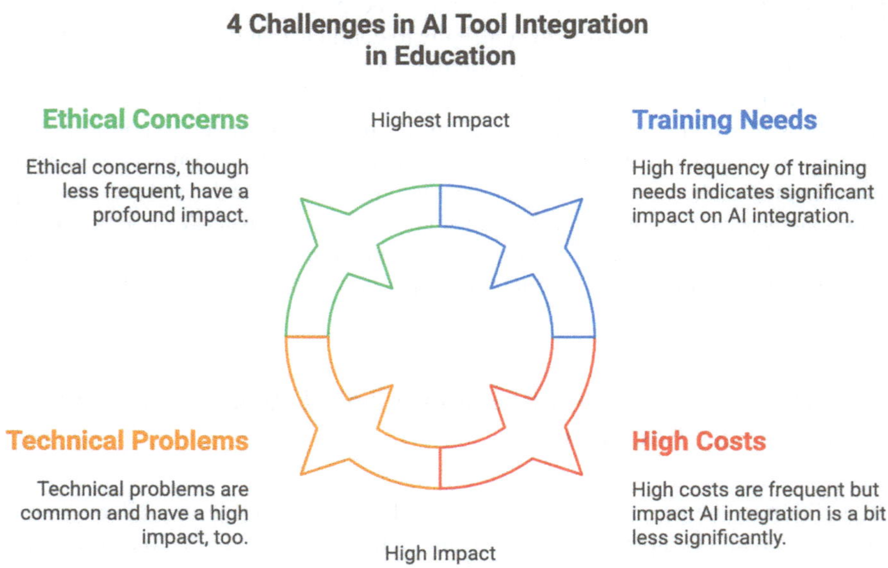

Fig. 1 Challenges in AI tool integration in education. Source: Graphics by the author

- **35.1% cited technical problems**: This indicates that AI-relevant third-party programs perform poorly due to the limitations of the devices provided by the institution to the educators.
- **35.1% also cited high costs**: The purchase and use of AI tools is often associated with high financial requirements. In many cases, this is counteracted by the university administrations' low willingness or ability to invest.

The survey also points to a correlation between the age of lecturers and their affinity for and competence in using digital tools. Lecturers aged 40 years or older seem less familiar with digital tools in the classroom than their younger colleagues. This group requests more likely additional training and is more sceptical about new technologies, especially with regard to the integration of AI into teaching. To better understand what the contents of such training could be, further research is needed, particularly in view of these aspects.

5 Workshop Series "AI Didactics for Lecturers"

Between January and April 2024, four training workshops on AI didactics were held for lecturers for the universities BSP Business and Law School, MSB Medical School Berlin, HMU Health and Medical University, and MSH Medical School Hamburg. The focus was on GenAI tools that can create or summarise content. Systems that use AI to evaluate academic performance or in bureaucratic processes were excluded. A total of around 80 members of the teaching staff took part in these workshops, which were structured identically. According to my observations, lecturers from subjects such as statistics and mathematics were already familiar with the development and use of AI in teaching, while lecturers with a social science focus were breaking new ground.

Each workshop consisted of an introductory part to Artificial Intelligence, followed by a part for trying out AI tools in the group and finally conducting a subsequent joint reflection. The aim was to encourage lecturers to embrace technology and overcome their insecurities in dealing with AI. This systematic approach was developed and tested in the context of my work at the Mittelstand-Digital Zentrum Zukunftskultur (a centre for future-oriented business culture), which focuses on building acceptance of new AI technologies in small and medium-sized companies (SMEs). As in the workshops for SMEs, the try-out part of the workshop was structured into three levels of difficulty. The participants were able to use text-generating AIs for inspiration, which was rather a beginner's task. In addition, they were able to test the answering of research questions and literature searches using AI tools developed specifically for academic research, which I personally placed in the intermediate level. As a third and most challenging task, I introduced the (by then) relatively new function of developing a personalised GPT with contents and task performance for use in one's own course. The tasks were completed in either partner or group work.

While the basic section focused on the potential and functioning of Generative AI and the trial section on the possible integration into one's own subject, the discussion section was dominated by the exchange on the tension between allowing and prohibiting AI in student work. A wide range of attitudes on this topic became apparent. One consistent aspect was the need for the universities to provide better licensing. Free versions often do not allow access to current internet research or set other limits on the use of GenAI compared to licensed versions. In contrast, private financing of GenAI tools by the lecturers is considered hardly feasible due to personal investment limitations and reluctance to do so.

Overall, it became clear in the discussion that a university-wide uniform regulation for the responsible use of AI to build acceptance of AI in one's own teaching or research environment could be a valuable guide, provided that this set of rules takes into account the real-life conditions of teachers and students for AI application.

6 Recommendations

The survey results above show that many university teaching staff have basic digital skills but often do not incorporate them into their own teaching practice. Almost 60% of respondents rarely or never use digital tools and AI applications in their teaching. Only 20% feel confident using such technologies. This suggests that digital skills and knowledge on using GenAI may be present in theory but are used only to a limited extent in practice.

There is thus a need for practical professional development that could help the university teaching staff effectively and purposefully use up-to-date digital technologies. Lecturers and professors need access to the skills and knowledge necessary to navigate the evolving landscape of Artificial Intelligence, with a particular focus on Generative Artificial Intelligence. Through strategic skill development, targeted professional development initiatives, and supportive policy frameworks, educational institutions can close the existing gaps and prepare lecturers to confidently integrate AI into their teaching practice and raise the AI readiness of their institutions. Based on the research presented above, I have identified four core aspects that should be addressed:

(a) AI-Qualification

In the above evaluation and in relevant studies (e.g. Holmes et al., 2019), the lack of institutional preparation and support is one of the main obstacles to the effective use of AI in education. Educators often lack the resources to take on technological innovations for their own use in the classroom. The following approach could help:

- Given the availability of many free or subsidised training videos, the initial implementation could be cost-neutral. Neutral platforms that receive public and private funding such as the AI-Campus (known as KI-Campus in Germany) offer courses in German and English and are continuously developing new free learning opportunities of AI application in companies and education through their various partnerships (Mittelstand-Digital Zentrum Zukunftskultur, 2024b).

- Internal expertise within an educational institution in this area could be identified and channelled through an AI task force. so that teaching staff and students are directly involved in training others in a peer-to-peer process. The DPaCK model described previously can help work out this process's details. One recommendation would be to formulate the technical part of the explanations as clearly and simply as possible so as not to confuse the target group with details.
- Training levels could also be assigned based on self-assessment or a short AI readiness test and explicitly designed for the respective subject of the lecturers. The differentiation into several know-how levels is by experience often verbalised by workshop participants and has proven to be an important approach, as shown in our research throughout 2023 (Bodrožić-Brnić, 2025).

(b) Addressing Ethical Concerns

The survey shows that many lecturers and professors have ethical concerns about using AI in education, particularly concerning the fairness and authenticity of student learning outcomes. They want AI to be used in a way that encourages students to learn critically and independently, rather than relying too heavily on technological support. The following measures could help address these ethical concerns and increase AI acceptance:

- Through professional training educators can develop a self-image as ethical advisors to students. If they themselves can realistically assess the potential of AI tools for their own subject, they can sensitise students to the ethical use of AI instead of criticising or banning its use in their courses. As recommended by Article 4 of the EU AI Act, the AI literacy at each university or higher education institution which uses AI in education or other fields should be trained (Article 4: AI Literacy|EU Artificial Intelligence Act, 2025).
- It would also be conceivable to establish an "AI dream team" of various subjects and professional functions to provide ongoing support for implementation and use (Mittelstand-Digital, 2024).
- Aversion to algorithms is a phenomenon in which people resist relying on algorithmic results (Mahmud et al., 2021). Research suggests that decision-makers are more likely to use AI systems they were actively involved in creating (Sebian & Ottogalli, 2024). This insight presents an opportunity to improve AI implementation in higher education through a coordinated, cross-disciplinary approach, fostering greater acceptance and effectiveness.

(c) Provide Technical Support

Technical problems are a major obstacle in establishing AI readiness at universities. One structural problem is that universities often lack sufficient basic funding to expand technical capacities. Ingo Siegert describes the lack of server capacity and appropriately qualified personnel as a central hurdle that prevents many universities from providing AI tools institutionally (Bodrožić-Brnić, 2024b). This means that many lecturers depend on free or personal accounts, which, in the long term, makes access to these technologies more difficult. The following approaches could help to proactively address such technical challenges:

- Many universities depend on government funding to finance technological innovations. In Germany, the *DigitalPakt Schule* (digital pact for schools) has helped many educational institutions by offering funding of infrastructure. However, such support is yet often underfunded or only available if the application process is followed to the letter (Stahl, 2022; Engelien, 2025). To be more successful in researching and applying for such funding, universities can create a position dedicated exclusively to coordinating such innovation projects. Lecturers who support the application process should be relieved of other tasks, for example, by reducing their teaching load.
- Temporary mobile internet solutions could cost-effectively compensate for bandwidth problems and ensure greater user satisfaction until the switch to fibre optics or satellite internet can be implemented.
- To improve the technical equipment available to the teaching staff and students, universities could set up a device pool with the latest notebooks and tablets that students and teaching staff can borrow easily. A rotation and depreciation model would allow the device pool to adapt continuously to changing developments and innovation impulses.

(d) Mitigate Costs Through Personal Initiative

Universities often find themselves in the contradictory position of teaching ever-evolving up-to-date course contents under conditions of outdated or obsolete infrastructure. One classic example in the many institutions I have worked with is an unstable internet connection, which seems quite ironic when explaining topics such as Artificial Intelligence in the classroom. The following points could facilitate the cost-effective modernisation of outdated infrastructure:

- A "many eyes principle" could help synchronise innovation and technology planning with the actual investment funds available in a structured way. The planning team should be interdisciplinary and cross-generational, in addition to the necessary diversity in family heritage and gender equality, for example. Different people who engage with each other creatively and constructively in the planning process are more likely to enable integrative major changes (Mittelstand-Digital Zentrum Zukunftskultur, 2024a).
- The planning and prioritisation process can also become efficient in terms of costs using innovative workshop methods. Various methods from corporate coaching are suitable for this, such as the resource map, design thinking, and backcasting (Bodrožić-Brnić & Thiessen, 2023).
- In addition, I recommend optimising existing infrastructure and tools, because their potential is by experience often not fully exploited. Relevant and simple analysis procedures and a video training that could be accessed via QR code on the respective devices might be effective solutions. Low-threshold and clear tables with references to the training videos could be placed in each classroom for each program and piece of equipment, This would give the teaching staff the opportunity to take the initiative in optimising the technical tools.

7 Outlook

The mix of methods discussed above is intended to make it clear that there are tangible reasons why 60% of educators have not yet used AI in their teaching. Through interviews and a qualitative survey, I identified the main causes as ethical concerns, inadequate infrastructure, lack of training, and high cost or missing investments. Systematic research into AI readiness at universities and other higher education institutions remains a key area of research, which I am working on continuously, along with several other international researchers. Projects funded by the state and the private sector are making it possible to advance pragmatic and practical solutions for the gradual introduction of AI into university teaching. Decision-makers at public and private universities are aware of the challenges of such a change process. The establishment of diverse targeted task forces to identify and resolve specific obstacles could pave the way to a modernised teaching environment and should be actively supported by university management (Mittelstand-Digital Zentrum Zukunftskultur, 2024b). It will be interesting to look back at the contents of this article 4 years from now. It will likely reflect significant development from the current status quo to the advanced use of Artificial Intelligence in higher education.

References

AI Literacy|EU Artificial Intelligence Act. (2025). *EU Artificial Intelligence Act.* Retrieved from https://artificialintelligenceact.eu/article/4/

Bodrožić-Brnić, K. (2024a, March 27). *Interview zur Evaluierung des KI-Didaktik Workshops an der BSP Business and Law School mit Irit Nachtigall.* Retrieved from https://docs.google.com/document/d/113dR3zB0E63qUvihiSKQ7fJAtgAwezeC/edit?usp=sharing&ouid=105078090774477405464&rtpof=true&sd=true

Bodrožić-Brnić, K. (2024b, October). *Interview mit Ingo Siegert zur KI-Readiness unter Hochschullehrenden am 24.10.2024.* Retrieved from https://docs.google.com/document/d/11HOgPvXPXmPJP8mJyuR8Kk1c-vSmkb4E/edit?usp=sharing&ouid=105078090774477405464&rtpof=true&sd=true

Bodrožić-Brnić, K. (2025). Creative AI as a transfer instrument for promoting technology acceptance: A practice-oriented approach. In *Leadership for digital transformation: Navigating the journey* (Vol. 1, pp. 67–78). Springer Nature. https://doi.org/10.1007/978-3-031-75670-2_5

Bodrožić-Brnić, K., & Thiessen, T. (2023, June 6). *Methodenguide Erfolgsfaktor Außenwirtschaft.* Mittelstand-Digital Zentrum Zukunftskultur. Retrieved from https://www.digitalzentrum-zukunftskultur.de/material/methodenguide-erfolgsfaktor-aussenwirtschaft-10021/

Bodrožić-Brnić, K., & Wedel, M. (2025). *Künstliche Intelligenz im Hochschulbereich—Chancen und Herausforderungen im Wissenserwerb.* Schaeffer-Poeschel.

Engelien, M. (2025). *ANS Tablet, bitte! t3n*(78), 64–66.

Höck, B. (2024, November 4). *Trusted AI: Using artificial intelligence safely.* KPMG. Retrieved from https://kpmg.com/de/en/home/insights/2024/11/trusted-ai-artificial-intelligence-safe-use.html

Holmes, W., Bialik, M., & Fadel, C. (2019). *Artificial intelligence in Education:Promises and implications for teaching and learning.*. http://oro.open.ac.uk/60255/

Koch, M. J., Carolus, A., Wienrich, C., & Latoschik, M. E. (2024). Meta AI Literacy Scale: Further validation and development of a short version. *Heliyon, 10*(21), e39686. https://doi.org/10.1016/j.heliyon.2024.e39686

Lerch, C., Heimberger, H., Jäger, A., Horvat, D., & Bitter, J. (2021). KI-Readiness im verarbeitenden Gewerbe: Stand und Perspektiven für Baden-Württemberg [Study commissioned by *the Ministry of Economic Affairs*, Labour and Tourism Baden-Württemberg]. Fraunhofer ISI.

Mahmud, H., Islam, A. N., Ahmed, S. I., & Smolander, K. (2021). What influences algorithmic decision-making? A systematic literature review on algorithm aversion. *Technological Forecasting and Social Change, 175*, 121390. https://doi.org/10.1016/j.techfore.2021.121390

Mittelstand-Digital. (2024, January 6). *KI-Akzeptanz—so nehmen Sie Mitarbeitende mit auf die KI-Journey*. Mittelstand-Digital. https://www.mittelstand-digital.de/MD/Redaktion/DE/Themenhub/2024-01/Artikel/hub-2024-01-06-ki-akzeptanz.html

Mittelstand-Digital Zentrum Zukunftskultur. (2024a, December 16). *52 Frauen in Tech—Bitte mehr davon*. Podcast. Mittelstand-Digital Zentrum Zukunftskultur. Retrieved from https://www.digitalzentrum-zukunftskultur.de/podcasts/52-frauen-in-tech/

Mittelstand-Digital Zentrum Zukunftskultur. (2024b, November 1). *49 KI lernen mit den kostenfreien Angeboten des KI-Campus*. Podcast. Mittelstand-Digital Zentrum Zukunftskultur. Retrieved from https://www.digitalzentrum-zukunftskultur.de/podcasts/49-ki-lernen-mit-den-kostenfreien-angeboten-des-ki-campus/

Nyst, A. (2024, October 9). History of ChatGPT: A timeline of the meteoric rise of generative AI chatbots. *Search Engine Journal*. Retrieved from https://www.searchenginejournal.com/history-of-chatgpt-timeline/488370/

Rütti-Joy, O., Winder, G., & Biedermann, H. (2023). Building AI literacy for sustainable teacher education. *Zeitschrift für Hochschulentwicklung, 18*(4), 175–189. https://doi.org/10.21240/zfhe/18-04/10

Saif, I. (2024, August 23). 'Trustworthy AI' is a framework to help manage unique risk. *MIT Technology Review*. Retrieved from https://www.technologyreview.com/2020/03/25/950291/trustworthy-ai-is-a-framework-to-help-manage-unique-risk/

Sebian, B., & Ottogalli, M. (2024). *Artificial intelligence (AI) & decision-making: Will AI trustworthiness facilitate progress towards sustainability?* Springer.

Stahl, M. (2022, November 23). *Zu bürokratisch, unwirtschaftlich, nicht zielgenau, wenig transparent*. GEW—Die Bildungsgewerkschaft. Retrieved from https://www.gew.de/aktuelles/detailseite/zu-buerokratisch-unwirtschaftlich-nicht-zielgenau-wenig-transparent

Tubella, A. A., Mora-Cantallops, M., & Nieves, J. C. (2023). How to teach responsible AI in higher education: Challenges and opportunities. *Ethics and Information Technology, 26*(1), 3. https://doi.org/10.1007/s10676-023-09733-7

Kristina Bodrožić-Brnić is an AI trainer, researcher, and university lecturer specialising in the convergence of creativity and Artificial Intelligence, focusing on how AI can nurture creative processes and expand human potential in SMEs while boosting technology acceptance and catalysing interdisciplinary co-creation. As the managing director of WorldTribe and through her collaborations with BSP Business and Law School and the Mittelstand-Digital Zentrum Zukunftskultur, she plays a pivotal role in advancing digital transformation and fostering innovation across diverse sectors.

Knowledge Transfer in Transition: Do We Need a New Debate on the Concept of Knowledge in Teaching and Continuing Education in the Age of AI and ChatGPT?

Susan Hinterding and Sünje Lorenzen

Abstract Even before the introduction of ChatGPT, educational research extensively examined the impact of advancing developments in Artificial Intelligence (AI) on everyday education (Schmohl et al., *Künstliche Intelligenz in der Hochschulbildung: Chancen und Grenzen des KI-gestützten Lernens und Lehrens*, Transcript Verlag, 2023). The use of AI in education has gained momentum during the COVID-19 pandemic, as educators turned to digital learning platforms and AI tools for online teaching. As a result, traditional classroom instruction in many institutions has increasingly integrated AI-supported systems like Microsoft Teams and Moodle. Integrating AI-based learning assistance systems into education is a subject of ongoing debate. These technologies can promote personalised learning, allowing learners to progress at their own pace and in their own learning methods. However, there are concerns that AI might weaken critical thinking skills. Specifically, the ability to analyse and reflect independently may be diminished by the possibility of having tasks and texts generated by AI in a short period of time. The debate about the use of AI in education is necessary and central to understanding the future of knowledge transfer. The focus is mainly on how knowledge is generated, conveyed, and acquired in the digital age. In the context of modern educational technologies—primarily through AI-supported tools like ChatGPT—the challenge arises to rethink the concept of knowledge. This article examines these issues through a case study from university teaching at the Business and Law School at Campus Hamburg.

Keywords Artificial Intelligence in education · Digital learning platforms · Critical thinking · Knowledge transfer

S. Hinterding (✉) · S. Lorenzen
BSP Business and Law School, Hamburg, Germany
e-mail: susan.hinterding@bsp-campus-hamburg.de; suenje.lorenzen@bsp-campus-hamburg.de

K. Bodrožić-Brnić et al. (eds.), *Digital Transformation in Knowledge Transfer*, Digital Transformation and Innovation,
https://doi.org/10.1007/978-3-032-07329-7_10

1 Theoretical Foundations of Knowledge and Learning

The terms 'knowledge' and 'learning' are the subject of various theoretical approaches that are widely discussed in the fields of psychology, cognitive sciences, and education. These approaches describe the processes of knowledge acquisition and learning in different ways (Vladova et al., 2019; Schmohl et al., 2023, Schleiss et al., 2023).

Behaviourism, a traditional approach, describes learning as a direct response to external stimuli. In contrast, cognitivism and constructivism emphasise the active role of the learner in the construction of knowledge. They highlight the importance of cognitive processes such as perception, memory, and thinking, as well as the significance of social interactions for learning success (Wilkesmann, 2009). The philosopher and psychologist Wilhelm Salber introduced the concept of the 'unit of effect' in his work *Der Alltag ist nicht grau!* (1989), describing learning and the transmission of content as a shared production process. He describes this process as a dynamic interaction in which knowledge is not only passed on but actively and subjectively constructed by both the learner and the teacher.

> Studying, too, involves everyday forms—listening, practicing, reading, presenting, and describing are production processes in which a connection of understanding is formed and is in progress. When we analyse them, we learn to see science as forms of engagement with and treatment of reality. (Salber, 1989, p. 49)

According to this logic, knowledge transfer is understood as a process where knowledge cannot be hierarchically transferred through pre-packaged content between individuals. Instead, it involves intersubjective causal relationships, where a shared construction of reality is established between teachers and learners. Particularly when it comes to using ChatGPT in educational contexts, the content and possibilities are evolving so rapidly that knowledge transfer can only take place through a shared research journey.

2 The Profound Changes of Our Time and Their Impact on Knowledge Transfer

The dynamic transformation process described here is not only reflected in the context of new concepts of knowledge or in the discourse surrounding scientific debates but in all areas of life for both teachers and learners. These processes are accelerated by a changing societal value system, global trends, and technological advancements. The profound changes and their far-reaching effects on all aspects of life have been extensively discussed in academic discourse (e.g., Beck, 1986; Salber, 1993; Gross, 1994; Sennett, 1998; Rosa, 2013) and will therefore not be elaborated further here. These changes are setting traditional forms and processes in motion and, in some cases, require fundamental redesigns. In some areas, these modifications are so far-reaching that they necessitate not just adaptations but fundamental changes in processes and the associated competencies.

Currently, we see examples in many areas of how dynamic transformation processes are requiring the development of new competencies:

In the Workplace Increasing flexibility at work requires new skills in handling digital collaboration tools. Employees need self-management skills, and leaders must adjust their leadership styles (Mittelstand-Digital Kompetenzzentrum Kommunikation, 2023).

In Higher Education Thanks to digitalisation, students can participate in lectures and seminars anytime and anywhere. This requires both educators and students to familiarise themselves with new digital collaboration software. Course content and educational offerings must take into account the specifics of media reception and the respective learning medium.

These examples illustrate how dynamic transformation processes are affecting the transfer of both traditional and new knowledge and demonstrate the importance of a theoretical understanding of the concept of 'knowledge transfer'.

3 The University in the Tension Between Change and Tradition

At this point, it is important to note that the transformation in everyday university life is comparable to the study phase itself. Psychologist and philosopher Wilhelm Salber aptly described the study process as a process of transformation or development, in which students learn new competencies and forms of development while holding on to familiar ideas, desires, and characteristics that they want to prove in the new phase of life (Salber, 1970).

> On the one hand, you want to have the 'whole' when studying: everything immediately, all at once, everything by itself, everything ready to apply immediately! On the other hand, you somehow realise that every relationship has two sides: understanding something takes time and turnover; it only works through back and forth, through transformations, and in always new attempts to hold something together and summarize it. (Salber, 1970, p. 50)

When studying is viewed as such a negotiation process, it quickly becomes clear that knowledge transfer goes far beyond the mere provision of knowledge packets. The extent to which the transfer of information and the creation of knowledge also involves relationship work becomes evident in in-depth psychological interviews with students of business psychology. They described their need for guidance during a very stressful decision-making process regarding their field of study, where mere aptitude tests and information events were not enough. Instead, it was mainly the numerous conversations with family members, teachers, lecturers, and friends that ultimately helped them make the decision, as they felt overwhelmed by the amount of information (Hinterding, 2020). These and other studies on the process of choosing a field of study (Oechsle, 2009; Schröder, 2015) confirm that studying is an intensive phase of identity development and self-discovery, fluctuating between the desire for independence and the need for guidance and support, in which relationship work is crucial for the decision-making process.

In our teaching practice, we also observe that our students are deeply engaged with current global issues such as the climate crisis, the war in Europe, and the aftermath of the pandemic. This complex developmental task requires the integration of various needs and demands in a rapidly changing world. Knowledge transfer and skills development must also take into account these struggles and challenges faced by students.

4 The University as a Development Space for the Transition Process

As a protected developmental space, the university can effectively accompany students in dealing with this dynamic world by providing structured framework offerings. The Bologna Process has made many study programs more structured and adapted, thereby providing such supportive functions. However, these tightly scheduled study programs do not always offer the necessary freedom for personal development, as was once intended in the Humboldtian ideal of education, which focused more on research-oriented knowledge transfer. The necessary changes in everyday university life, caused by the pandemic and technological advancements, now offer the opportunity to develop new freedoms if we consistently adhere to a constructivist approach to knowledge.

5 Knowledge Transfer as a Dialogical and Constructivist Process

If the concept of knowledge transfer is understood as a creative process in which each individual forms their own worldview through dialogue and questioning assumptions, it becomes clear why educators do much more than simply convey packets of information.

The university, as a place of understanding processes that also take time, is particularly affected by these rapid developments. Students are in a sensitive transitional phase of their lives, in which they are developing a new worldview while simultaneously seeking orientation in the familiar. The university thus becomes a space in which a complex transitional process takes place, far beyond the mere transfer of knowledge.

6 Opportunities and Limits of Technological Change and the Need to Integrate Changes into the Concept of Dialogical Knowledge Transfer

The authors believe that technological changes will significantly alter and influence everyday university life and knowledge transfer. Universities have opportunities to adapt the learning environment and content so that learning becomes more personal and takes into account the challenges of the life phases of young students, who need to regain more space for personal development. However, it remains questionable to what extent they can replace the shared dialogue between teachers and learners if knowledge transfer is understood as a creative process. Rather, students must be prepared to flexibly and critically engage with new technological possibilities and support the process nature of knowledge creation rather than shortening it. The concept of research-based teaching and learning is methodologically suited for this.

In a research project at the Business and Law School at Campus Hamburg, the integration of Artificial Intelligence into students' learning processes was examined. This case study allows us to concretise theoretical considerations about the active role of the learner in knowledge construction and the importance of social interactions in the context of AI use.

7 A Case Study: Experiences with the Application of Artificial Intelligence in a Research-Based Teaching and Learning Project

The results of a research-based teaching and learning project carried out at the BSP Business and Law School (BSP) in the summer semester 2024 are presented below. Ludwig Huber defines research-based learning as follows:

> Research-based learning is characterised by the fact that learners (co-)design, experience and reflect on the process of a research project aimed at gaining knowledge of interest to third parties in its essential phases, from the development of the questions (...) to the choice and execution of the methods to the examination and presentation of the results in independent work or in active collaboration in an overarching project. (Huber, 2013, p. 23)

The methods of 'research-based learning' are not about the passive reception of ideas, but about the active development of one's own perspectives in a research-based and open teaching and learning approach. These ideas were incorporated into a teaching and learning project at the BSP based on experiences with a project described in the study *Wie funktioniert ein Betrieb? BWL und Psychologie Studierende erkunden Bremer Betriebe—Forschendes Lernen in einem interdisziplinären Projekt im Bachelorstudium* (Lorenzen et al., 2013).

In the summer semester of 2024, the goal was set to test, design, experience, and reflect on the use of Artificial Intelligence in teaching. In the 'Organisational

Psychology' module of the Bachelor's degree in Business Psychology at BSP, the students, together with the lecturer, aimed to develop both subject-specific foundational knowledge and an understanding of the advantages and disadvantages of using Artificial Intelligence.

The rules for this were that AI may be used to support all questions in teaching and for the examination formats—presentation and design of an exercise. The condition was that the use of AI should be made transparent and subject to reflection. For this purpose, a 3-page handout was created that records the presentation and exercise, shows the AI tools used, and reflects on the students' own experiences with the use of AI.

The following questions were answered in the handout:

- Which tool did I use? (Brief introduction of the tool)
- How/what did I use it for?
- What did it help with?
- Which tasks are superfluous with the AI tool?
- What didn't work so well?
- My recommendations for my fellow students, etc. were discussed during the course.

Below some of the content of the handouts is presented.

7.1 How Students Deal with AI in Teaching: Examination Form Presentation

In many cases, students used the chatbot ChatGPT when developing their presentations. To the question 'How & for what did we use it? What did it help with?', students wrote the following, for example: 'We used ChatGPT to summarise the 28-page text (ed. note they were asked to read as a basis for the presentation). We then used this summary to start creating the PowerPoint presentation. The first important step was to check the accuracy of the summary generated by Artificial Intelligence. We then designed the presentation slides. In order to break down the summarised content into around five key points, we used the ChatGPT to generate concise key points. The answers we received were not always formulated to our complete satisfaction. That's why we always modified the answers ourselves and then incorporated them into our PowerPoint presentation' (BSP students).

Based on this reflection on the use of AI to create a presentation, the advantages and disadvantages can already be seen at the beginning. ChatGPT is not a complete solution for creating a presentation and the corresponding PowerPoint presentation. ChatGPT supports the creation process, but the generated results must be checked again and again as there is no guarantee that the results generated by AI are completely accurate.

In response to the question: 'What work has become superfluous with the AI tool?', the students answered the following: 'Using ChatGPT has put less time and effort into formulating the content of our presentation. However, we had to use some of the time saved afterwards to check the accuracy of the generated texts. The time saved was significantly greater than if we had formulated the text ourselves and placed it on the slides'.

ChatGPT can formulate, but it does not do all the work of creating a presentation for you. Nevertheless, ChatGPT can save you time when creating presentations, which you can use for other exciting social tasks in learning environments.

7.2 Examination Format: Workshop (Exercise)

A second examination format in this module required students to develop an exercise themselves, carry it out with their fellow students, and reflect on the implementation. Here, too, it was explicitly permitted to use AI in the preparation of the exercise. An example from one group demonstrates how this was done.

One student group decided to conduct a group discussion as an exercise to deepen the learning material. In the group discussion, different roles were assigned to further explore the topic of the exercise: 'Generation management in the company' (One focus of the 'Organisational Psychology' module is generation management. The study 'Productive ageing' (Lorenzen & Specht, 2022) demonstrated that it is becoming increasingly important for companies today to adapt to the challenges associated with an ageing society).

Reflecting on their work with ChatGPT to create the group discussion the students wrote the following: 'Brainstorming together helped us to come up with creative ideas for interactive group work. ChatGPT also supported us in creating tasks and assigning roles within the group. We instructed the tool to plan a group discussion on the topic of "collective bargaining" and to generate the corresponding roles. We noticed that the tool needed as much thematic input as possible in order to work particularly efficiently. We then defined the scope and timing of the discussion ourselves. We allocated 5 minutes for the introductory phase, 5 minutes for the participants' reading time, 20 to 25 minutes for discussion and then 10 minutes for reflection'.

This example shows that the use of AI in no way prevents the use of one's own ideas and thoughts. It is a combination of both as AI is used more like a tool to work out one's own ideas. The social interaction between the students is also enriched by jointly developed ideas to enter into dialog with AI. There was a productive dialog between the students themselves, between the students and AI, social interaction between the students and a critical reflection on the possibilities of AI.

This example also shows that the students have made critical reflections on the use of AI. As the following quote from the students' handout makes clear: 'Our experience with AI showed that detailed and precise information is crucial in order to achieve satisfactory results when creating documents with AI. In conclusion, the use of free AI tools helped us significantly in the preparation and creation of our presentation. Nevertheless, a critical understanding of the text and manual post-editing are essential to achieve high-quality results'.

It is not the case that the students use AI to think as little as possible themselves and let AI do the learning work for them; on the contrary, the use of AI encourages their critical reflection and the realisation is that they are more likely to learn something new than to get out of the habit of learning, as the following section shows once again.

7.3 *Critical Reflection of the Students*

Experiences with the use of AI were evaluated in the final module of the teaching and learning project. Some critical comments from the evaluation are presented here to give readers an impression of perspectives of the students on the use of AI in teaching. The comments are presented as 'core sentences'. In 'Psychoanalyse in der Sozialforschung' (1988), Volmerg and Leithäuser write that core sentences are 'everyday language generalisations in the flow of discussion' (p. 245). They spontaneously make something clear that is not only understood by those who have expressed it in this form but can also be spontaneously understood and interpreted in general. In our case they make clear that students want and demand practice in using AI.

One student said for example: 'Nowadays you can't avoid using AI. AI is here to stay. If a university wants to teach in a practical way, it has to teach how to use AI'.

In another key sentence another student said: 'It's a bit like when you weren't allowed to go online to search for sources. There are many ways to use AI sensibly, even today'.

A mere ban on using AI in teaching seems to students as if the possibilities that AI can offer today are simply being ignored. A sound education in this area would then not be wanted at all and would therefore be ruled out. A practice-oriented education would be contrary to such an attitude towards AI.

Another student said: 'Many companies already use generative AI, for example to evaluate documents or similar'.

The students perceive it as a field of experience when they have the chance to try out AI and learn how to use it: 'It's good to have the opportunity to gain experience with it and also to recognise for yourself whether it helps me or not', said one student, because previous experience with AI is also very diverse among the students, some are better at it, others have had little to do with it. Students are also still very uncertain about how and for what purposes it can be used. They would like 'a clear framework' as well as a clear regulation on how the use is assessed by the teachers. One student says: 'It's important to get to grips with it. However, in addition to the use of AI, personal contribution must also play a role in teaching'.

An important essence of the teaching and learning project is that the use of AI should be trained, but that personal contact, the 'personal contribution' of the students, and social interaction in teaching play an equally important role, if not a more important one, in teaching and learning interactions.

Concluding Remarks on the Application and Practicing the Use of AI
The critical reflection of the students began in the process of using Artificial Intelligence, as the following key sentence from the students' reflections shows:

> We realised that we relied too much on the capabilities of ChatGPT during the editing process. However, it is important to always keep your own mind on the topic and not rest 100% on the performance of the Artificial Intelligence.

There seems to be a pride in learning among the students. They don't just want to leave good critical thinking to the AI. On the contrary, the impression was that learning can also be stimulated in a playful way through a certain competition with AI. AI is used more as a tool for generating knowledge. Using the method of constantly checking the results generated by AI, students acquire learning materials independently. The AI acts almost like a learning assistant, which, in dialog with the students and with the questions (prompts) addressed to it, helps them to penetrate the sometimes very complex texts from the lecture and to work out the central theses. As AI often adds its own marks, studying texts is often more intensive and the resulting presentations are often easier for the audience to understand. When laying out the presentations, you also have to enter into a learning dialog with the AI in a process of checking-checking-improving, whereby a productive pattern of 'learning by doing' and the critical reflection of it has developed in this research-based teaching and learning format.

8 Knowledge Transfer and Artificial Intelligence: Where Are We Headed?

The results of the case study clearly illustrate both the potential and the challenges of this development. AI can serve as a powerful tool to adapt and deepen learning processes on an individual level. For example, students appreciated the opportunity to use ChatGPT as a research tool and to have texts summarised. However, the results also showed that a critical examination of the content took place, with the group of students questioning whether every use of AI was truly beneficial or merely a shortcut.

Rereferring to our practical project in which the support of AI was tested, we would like to offer a preliminary conclusion for further discussion, suggesting the following ideas for educational institutions to consider regarding the use of AI.

The use of AI in everyday school and university life is inevitable. Therefore, educational institutions must proactively address this issue and establish concrete regulations as well as comprehensive competency development programs. While AI can serve as a valuable tool in the learning process by providing more efficient access to information and potentially increasing productivity, it also presents challenges that should not be overlooked.

In light of the changing demands of knowledge transfer and advancing technology, the question arises as to how educational institutions must further adapt their methods to meet the rapidly changing societal and technological requirements. Research-based learning offers a way to integrate AI as a supplementary tool in the learning process without neglecting the necessary human reflection. Therefore, it is crucial to create an environment where AI is used responsibly and transparently—as a support rather than a replacement for genuine intellectual engagement.

Teachers play a crucial role in shaping educational processes during times of technological change. Their task is not only to teach students how to use AI tools like ChatGPT, but also to guide them in critically questioning and reflecting on these tools. Teachers are challenged to strike a balance: they must highlight the efficiency advantages of AI without diminishing the importance of independent thinking and creative problem-solving. As educational institutions navigate these profound changes, the focus should be on developing frameworks that encourage students to critically engage with AI tools, ensuring that these technologies enhance rather than undermine the educational experience.

Educational institutions should develop guidelines and standards that define the meaningful use of AI in teaching and learning. These guidelines should include clear directives on how AI can be used as a supportive tool without replacing the central role of human thought and creativity. Universities must position themselves as developmental spaces that not only promote the use of AI but also support the dialogical exchange between students and teachers. This creates an environment where traditional and technological approaches to knowledge transfer can be harmonised.

Continuous training for educators and students in the use of AI is necessary to ensure that all parties understand the potential and limitations of these technologies. This should be accompanied by the promotion of critical thinking and ethical awareness to responsibly shape the long-term impact of AI use in education and society.

9 Conclusion

Training the use of AI in higher education offers new opportunities that are perceived by students and teachers with both relief and concern. The advantages of AI tools such as ChatGPT in reducing the workload and pooling information must be weighed against the challenges of assessing student performance, developing critical thinking patterns, and the interpersonal relationship between teachers and students. The use of AI in teaching therefore requires careful consideration and a responsible approach. Guidelines, quality standards, and the teaching of AI skills for both students and teachers are necessary in order to take advantage of the opportunities offered by AI while at the same time recognising its limitations. The aim is to use AI as a tool to support teaching and learning without replacing human interaction and independent thinking.

What must not be forgotten is a central aspect that the students repeatedly expressed in the research-based teaching and learning project, which was: 'AI is here to stay!' We think this is a very realistic statement and the urgent challenge for teachers that arises from this is to train a reflective approach to AI, for which we tried to present ideas in our paper. For us one main question is where AI can help in the future and another is where it can get in our way. If we understand AI as a tool to be used productively, this also implies an attitude towards AI, namely that AI should not replace specific human interactions in the future, but can very well help us to develop these, including in teaching together with students. Simply banning the use of AI will not lead to AI being understood and used as a productive tool. It would preclude the training of a reflective approach to AI and AI would thus remain an unknown technology that would give us cause for concern.

References

Beck, U. (1986). *Risikogesellschaft: Auf dem Weg in eine andere Moderne*. Suhrkamp Verlag.

Gross, P. (1994). *Die Multioptionsgesellschaft*. Suhrkamp Verlag.

Hinterding, S. (2020). *Studienwahl als Selbstbehandlungs-Prozess*. Dissertation. Universität zu Köln.

Huber, L. (2013). Die weitere Entwicklung des forschenden Lernens: Interessante Versuche—dringliche Aufgaben. In L. Huber, M. Kröger, & H. Schelhowe (Eds.), *Forschendes Lernen als Profilmerkmal einer Universität: Beispiele aus der Universität Bremen* (pp. 3–22). Universitäts Verlag Webler.

Leithäuser, T., & Volmerg, B. (1988). *Psychoanalyse in der Sozialforschung: Eine Einführung am Beispiel einer Sozialpsychologie der Arbeit*. Westdeutscher Verlag.

Lorenzen, S., & Specht, K. (2022). *Produktives Altern: Von der Kunst wach, lebendig und aktiv zu bleiben*. Mabuse Verlag.

Lorenzen, S., Stützle, H., & Unger, A. (2013). Wie funktioniert ein Betrieb? BWL und Psychologie Studierende erkunden Bremer Betriebe—Forschendes Lernen in einem interdisziplinären Projekt im Bachelorstudium. In L. Huber, M. Kröger, & H. Schelhowe (Eds.), *Forschendes Lernen als Profilmerkmal einer Universität: Beispiele aus der Universität Bremen* (pp. 45–60). Universitäts Verlag Webler.

Mittelstand-Digital Zentrum Zukunftskultur. (2023, 30. Oktober). Arbeitsweisen im Home office: Welcher Typ sind Sie? Mittelstand-Digital Zentrum Zukunftskultur. https://www.digitalzentrum-zukunftskultur.de/artikel/arbeitsweisen-im-home-office-welcher-typ-sind-sie-8651/

Oechsle, M. (2009). Abitur und was dann? Berufsorientierung und Lebensplanung junger Frauen und Männer und der Einfluss von Schule und Eltern. In M. Oechsle, H. Knauf, C. Maschetzke, & E. Rosowski (Eds.), *Abitur und was dann? Problemskizze und Forschungsfragen* (pp. 3–22). VS Verlag für Sozialwissenschaften.

Rosa, H. (2013). *Beschleunigung und Entfremdung*. Suhrkamp Verlag.

Salber, W. (1970). Studieren—psychologisch betrachten. *Pädagogische Rundschau, 24*(12), 828–839.

Salber, W. (1989). *Der Alltag ist nicht grau*. Bouvier Verlag.

Salber, W. (1993). *Seelenrevolution*. Bouvier Verlag: Bonn.

Schleiss, J., Mah, D.-K., Böhme, K., Fischer, D., Mesenhöller, J., Paaßen, B., Schork, S., & Schrumpf, J. (2023). *Künstliche Intelligenz in der Bildung: Drei Zukunftsszenarien und fünf Handlungsfelder*. KI-Campus. https://doi.org/10.5281/zenodo.7702620

Schmohl, T., Watanabe, A., & Schelling, K. (Eds.). (2023). *Künstliche Intelligenz in der Hochschulbildung: Chancen und Grenzen des KI-gestützten Lernens und Lehrens*. Transcript Verlag.

Schröder, M. (2015). *Studienwahl unter den Folgen einer radikalen Differenzierung*. Julius Klinkhardt Verlag.

Sennett, R. (1998). *Der flexible Mensch: Die Kultur des neuen Kapitalismus*. Berlin Verlag.

Vladova, G., Gronau, N., & Rüdian, L. (2019). Wissenstransfer in Bildung und Weiterbildung: Der Beitrag Künstlicher Intelligenz. In *Digitale Transformation—Gutes Arbeiten und Qualifizierung aktiv gestalten* (pp. 88–106). Wissenschaftliche Gesellschaft für Arbeits- und Betriebsorganisation.

Wilkesmann, M. (2009). Wissenstransfer. In M. Wilkesmann (Ed.), *Wissenstransfer im Krankenhaus* (pp. 77–122). Springer Verlag.

Susan Hinterding is a professor of media psychology at BSP Business and Law School, Hamburg, Germany. She studied and earned her PhD in Psychology at the University of Cologne, where she explored study choice as a depth-psychological self-treatment process. Her research focuses on consumer behaviour, brand perception, sustainability, and the psychological aspects of digitalisation. A specialist in qualitative methods, particularly Morphological Psychology, she integrates theory and practice in her teaching and leads the Media Psychology programme, engaging students in applied research and real-world projects with industry partners.

Sünje Lorenzen holds a diploma in Economics from the University of Hamburg and a Master of Science in Business Psychology from the University of Bremen. She has worked as a research assistant and lecturer at the University of Bremen, as a guest lecturer at the University of Innsbruck, and as a deputy professor at the Neubrandenburg University of Applied Sciences. Lorenzen is currently a Professor of Business Psychology at the BSP Business and Law School in Hamburg. She is also a certified supervisor, coach, organizational consultant (DGSv), and psychosocial online consultant (DGOB). Her main fields of research and teaching include creativity and innovation management, geriatric and care research, New Work and digitalization, and qualitative research methods.

Science in the Darkroom? The Use of ChatGPT in the Mirror of the Platonic Allegory of the Cave and the Fairy Tale of Rumpelstiltskin

Johanna Hodde

Abstract 'Science in the darkroom?' is a philosophical essay that discusses the use of ChatGPT in scientific context. A recall of what science means and its reliance on the overarching concept of knowledge is considered essential for assessing whether—and if so, how—ChatGPT should be used. With a reference back to Plato's Allegory of the Cave, scientific practice is strictly distinguished from a mere reproduction practice, and the dangers of confusing the two are pointed out. Further references are made to the necessity of transparency in scientific discourse, the questions of authorship, the author's ability to speak and maturity. The aim is to not lose sight of the important standards in scientific practice under the pressure of new technologies. Finally, the discussion will be used to derive recommendations for the use of AI in research and teaching.

Keywords ChatGPT · Greek philosophy · Socratic method · Plato's epistemology · Linguistic turn

1 Introduction

The question 'What can we know at all?' takes us back to the origins of scientific discourse in Greek philosophy and thus to the foundation of our science (Kranz, 1997). This interrogation is even more urgent in times of rapid technological change,

J. Hodde (✉)
BSP Business and Law School, Hamburg, Germany
e-mail: johanna.hodde@bsp-campus-hamburg.de

K. Bodrožić-Brnić et al. (eds.), *Digital Transformation in Knowledge Transfer*, Digital Transformation and Innovation,
https://doi.org/10.1007/978-3-032-07329-7_11

yet it remains peculiarly unaffected by this change, because the prerequisites for gaining knowledge directly lead us to the limits of the human constitution, e.g. no matter how precise measuring instruments or other technological aids become, they are always 'our' inventions. From an anthropological perspective, the knowledge of the world serves the survival. In modern industrialised countries, it helps maintain prosperity. In technological development, humanity's desire to surpass itself lives on—paraphrasing cultural scientist Freud, humans seek to become a 'prosthetic god' through their inventions (Freud, 1930/2000). However, according to Freud, this god-like status will never be fully achieved. Even when humans utilise all their aids, these tools are not fused with them. This gives rise to a fundamental divisiveness, an ambivalent basic relationship between humans and their inventions. The technology developed by man also constantly refers to his own deficient constitution, which he tries to compensate for.

> Man has become a kind of prosthetic god, quite marvellous when he puts on all his auxiliary organs, but they have not grown together with him and occasionally still give him a lot of trouble. Incidentally, he has a right to take comfort in the fact that this development will not be completed in 1930 AD. (Freud, 1930/2000, p. 222)

Artificial Intelligence (AI) is also our invention, and like any other technological development, it raises this basic structural problem. According to the media theorist McLuhan, referring back to our own deficits, which technological development promises to compensate for, is the core of any media criticism. Media penetrate deeply into people's perceptual apparatus; their usage shapes and moulds human behaviour (McLuhan, 1992/1968). This also means—in a nutshell that as programs become more capable, the stronger is the feeling of one's own inadequacy becomes. The human being and the aid (prosthesis) engage in a kind of competition or struggle with each other. This is also nothing new and can already be found in the form of 'Frankenstein's monster', which gains autonomy and power over its creator.

The current debate about Open AI, an AI research and deployment company in the United States of America, in the sciences is somewhere between utopia and dystopia. On one hand, the program is expected to bring about a knowledge revolution that will take humans to a higher level of development; it is also associated with hopes of simplifying an increasingly exhausting and unmanageable flood of knowledge. (According to Reckwitz (2021) we find ourselves in an age of 'technology of abundance'.) On the other hand, there are growing fears of AI replacing human roles and influence in the direction of an unfavourable transformation of humans. This threatens the aspects of human freedom and maturity because of its use.

To have the debate about the benefits and harms of the program, it is essential to differentiate among the various areas of its applications. The use of the program as a tool for writing a letter to the tax office must be distinguished from its use in research and teaching. This leads us to the topic of this article: What does the use of newer digital technologies such as the ChatGPT program mean in the sciences and teaching institutions? It is noteworthy to keep in mind that the following discussion refers to ChatGPT in general and not to a specific version.

2 A Plea for the Performance of Knowledge

In order to answer this question, we need to first step back and ask ourselves what the fundamental nature of knowledge is. Knowledge and science are linked to the concept of cognition. While knowledge makes us think of a treasure that we may or may not have access to, that we may or may not possess, cognition instead refers to an ongoing process—namely, the act of recognising. Therein lies the core of an ideal of science—an ideal that has accompanied us since antiquity and characterises our Western thinking and scientific enquiry. The ancient Greeks, particularly Socrates as a pioneer, elaborated methods to answer the question of 'How can I gain knowledge'. It is striking that both Socrates and Plato, everything that holds fast is deeply mistrusted. At most, it can be seen as an aid to memory, as for example in writing down a thought. For Socrates and Plato, however, cognition itself is linked to living discourse.

In this sense, with the following reference back to the beginnings of occidental sciences, it is necessary to point out a misunderstanding that also places properly the relatively new knowledge tool ChatGPT: There is no knowledge in itself. Dealing with scientific texts in particular thrives on diverse interpretations, on critical thinking regarding all that is fixed, and on a questioning—even doubting attitude of those who engage in a dialogue. We learned, it is a legacy heritage from Greek role models to place an emphasis on the discourse over holding on to established knowledge. The question of what we can know at all leads directly to an early scientific method, which is the questioning itself. This brings us to Socrates. He asked strangers and even uneducated people on the street what beauty was. He was not satisfied with a list of phenomena that are considered beautiful as beautiful (flowers, women, etc.) and went on to ask what all these phenomena had in common. What allows all these individual phenomena to be labelled as 'beautiful'—what is the overarching content of beauty (Plato, Hippias Major, 2018, p. 287c)? Thus, the Greeks invented the idea of the universal. According to Kranz with Hoffmann, E. and Wilamowitz (1997), two discoveries can be attributed to Socrates: inductive speech and the conceptual determination of the general.

However, how is the universal discovered? Why didn't Socrates ask the educated people about this? After all, it can be assumed that they already know more than any random person on the street or in the marketplace. Socrates and Plato were convinced that these insights into the universal are anchored in every human being, lying dormant within us, waiting to be brought forth. This is why the method is also known as the 'midwife technique'. In this sense, science is the birth of one's own child, which at the same time lies equally hidden in everyone—awaiting to emerge at an opportune moment.

> The Socratic method has become that of all genuine pedagogy. Only as long as it has something of the Socratic wisdom in it, that seeking is even more important than finding, that independence of thought is something higher than training, does it remain true intellectual education. (Kranz, 1997, p. 118)

Superficially, the so-called 'prompting', used to get a result from generative AI chat bots, may appear reminiscent of the Socratic questioning, because it resembles the form of a question. Upon closer examination, however, it is an opposing process. The universal, as later elaborated in Plato's Theory of Ideas, cannot be obtained by questioning ChatGPT. The program is just a human aid designed to accumulate knowledge as well as to link knowledge in a meaningful way.

Imitating humans it makes the dynamic process of discovering knowledge within us superfluous. Socrates' central argument is that such a substitution is impossible if one wants to seek knowledge. And this—again in relation to ChatGPT—has nothing to do with the program's capabilities. According to Socrates—and this is the crucial point—a certain naivety and a special form of spontaneous and performative creation are required to draw out knowledge. Socrates' famous sentence 'I know that I know nothing' (Plato, Apology of Socrates, 2005, p. 22d: 'Because I knew from myself that I didn't know anything…') is not rhetoric but the expression of a scientific attitude that seeks to free itself from preconceptions, that turns to the world in a childlike, openness, and naïve way. It is an attitude that trusts that knowledge of the universal is innately present within us—and this (with Plato) even before all empirical experience.

3 'For Little Knows My Royal Dame that ChatGPT Is My Name!'

Two morphological master's theses written by business psychology students on using of ChatGPT provide a deep insight into the reception and consequences of using ChatGPT). On the one hand, there is an auspicious promise of development, of gaining comprehensive access to knowledge, of getting ahead quickly and efficiently (in life) by making work easier through the program. On the other hand, quiet self-doubt begins to gnaw at the users of ChatGPT regarding their own participation in the generation of knowledge. We can visualise this process well with the fairy tale of Rumpelstiltskin: This fairy tale is about an auspicious promise of development—a little man who has magical powers keeps his own name a secret. He can secretly spin straw into gold. In doing so, he helps the miller's daughter achieve a marvellous opportunity—the marriage to the king. However—and here we encounter the downside of this promise—the magical transformation does not come for free. It (almost) costs the miller's daughter her own child. This is, therefore, a threat to what epitomises a person's own development. ChatGPT is like Rumpelstiltskin, who works in secret, rejoices in the art of transformation, and dances around the fire but is not allowed or doesn't want to reveal his name. When using ChatGPT, we are both this little man and the miller's daughter, who must give up her own child, i.e., a piece of her development, as a high price for the arts of transformation. The users' fears revolve around unlearning certain skills and—in a dystopian version—being completely replaced by the tool. In any case—with ChatGPT, as in the fairy tale—the fun game of marvellous transformation ends precisely at the point where we name what is going on. The difficulty of localising or naming what comes out of using ChatGPT highlights one of the main effects of its use. Fears of losing oneself, coupled with dystopias of heteronomy, lend a hand to the hubris of being faster and better than others of having an advantage over non-users.

What does this mean for research and teaching? It is important to shed light on these activities, which students often keep secret. This can be done by trying out the program together and naming its contribution to the generation of knowledge as precisely as possible. However, it will still be a crucial test, as in the Rumpelstiltskin fairy tale. The copyright issues clearly indicate that we cannot really name the process. If this happens, the game is over, just like in the fairy tale: The transformation game ends abruptly and tears the Rumpelstiltskin in two.

However, there is one point where the psychology of Rumpelstiltskin differs from the use of ChatGPT. ChatGPT cannot, as hoped, spin straw into gold. Users often feel disappointed by the limitations of the program—after all, 'All that glitters is not gold'. Yet, when ChatGPT 'hallucinates', when false statements are identified, these hallucinations are subtly reassuring, as they still require corrections, additions, and original creative thinking from the author.

This leads us to the last point consideration. What is the actual persuasive power of ChatGPT? What secretly motivates its use? It's not the quality, but rather the experience of making work easier and more efficient.

4 A Plea Against Simplification and Standardisation

The initial question, 'What can we know at all?' brings us to another crucial question for research and teaching: 'How can we gain knowledge?' To address this, let's consult occidental intellectual history. The path to knowledge is not an easy one. Plato's allegory of the cave (The Republic, 1990, pp. 514–517), for example, can be understood as a metaphorical account of recognition that shows a wrong path in the act of repetition—in the cave allegory it appears as a deceptive visual echo. Plato describes the process of recognition as painful. It involves a blinding glare that forces cave dwellers who step outside, into the light, to retreat back into the darkness of the cave. In the Platonic view, recognition means having to give up what is believed to be 'solid' and unquestionable. This is one of the reasons why both Socrates and, subsequently, Plato deeply mistrusted all recording media. According to Plato, writing, for example, can only be an aid to memory within the process of cognition.

The topicality of Platonic thought can be seen in the 'performative turn' in the sciences at the turn of the millennium (Martschukat & Patzold, 2003; Wulff & Zirfas, 2007). In lively discourse there should be a return to this freely unfolding acquisition of knowledge that takes place in the here and now. Knowledge is, therefore, not a transportable commodity (transfer), but a processual, fluid one. In other words, recognising the universal or—in Platonic terminology—seeing the ideas is very strictly distinguished from a logic of reproduction.

The philosopher and sinologist François Jullien speaks of a current confusion between the important concept of the universal in Western sciences, and that of the uniformity. By repeating the same pattern, we could think that we have already found a universal (cf. Confusing the Socratic dialogue with prompting). In fact, however, Jullien argues that the uniformity stands in contrast to the universal, particularly within an economic context (Jullien, 2018). Mass production, i.e. the production of identical goods under the principles of the division of labour, serves humankind. This form of simplification through standardisation is highly rational. It makes life easier for individuals, provided they live in a culture that benefits from this form of division of labour. Nevertheless, this form of standardisation must be strictly distinguished from the concept of universal in the history of ideas. Indeed, a mistake here is truly devastating. 'We then only think in standardised terms that tempt us to consider universal what are actually only stereotypes' (Jullien, 2018, p. 55).

To illustrate this with an example. People in the Middle Ages believed that the world was a disc. This thought was an integral part of the scientific understanding of the time. If ChatGPT had already existed at then, this knowledge would have been more widely disseminated through constant repetition and—here is where the danger lies—would likely have been accepted as 'correct'. It was not the questioning of such a reproduction machine but freedom of thought that made individuals realise that the world could be different. Science, understood not merely as reproduction, is, in the Humboldian sense, 'a process' and one that has no end. It is a journey on which you cannot get comfortable. The fact that a medium 'simplifies' a research process—and this is often cited as a pro-argument in favour of using ChatGPT—should therefore be seen as extremely counterproductive. Instead, it is the challenging experience of allowing one's own perspective to be turned 180° that has led the thinkers and inventors of our sciences to their achievements. Those who only rely on depicting the ever same are, in the Platonic sense, in the dark for their entire lives. The downside of this standardisation by ChatGPT is evident in the image generation by the program. It holds up a mirror to our culture with its stereotypes (male domains, etc.). This is not ChatGPT's fault, rather it is extremely illuminating. However, it makes the following clear: ChatGPT lacks an important aspect that guides a research process—namely, the ethical aspect of research. Reproductive platforms cannot fulfil this dimension, which is directed towards the future with the question: What kind of world do we want to live in?—cannot fulfil it.

5 Science as a Form of Self-Conquest

With the initial question, 'What can we know at all?' we look at a deep and lasting philosophical-historical examination of human nature and the limitations inherent in achieving knowledge. One of the goals associated with science—in structural terms, with relative independence of time and culture—is the human desire to transcend above themselves through knowledge. Science is not just an end in itself, but from a cultural-anthropological point of view, has proven essential for survival. Knowledge about the world, including technological development, ultimately serves the struggle for survival—even if this side of science is sometimes overlooked in Western affluent societies as a structural trait.

By conquering the forces of nature and putting them to use, humans have sought (since the beginning of time) to protect themselves from suffering and, ideally, to live in health and prosperity for as long as possible. In this pursuit of science, there is the unconscious ideal of godlikeness—to quote the cultural psychologist Sigmund Freud—and the desire to become omniscient and immortal (Freud, 1930/2000). In this sense, science has always aimed for more than maintaining just a 'status quo', since a mere repetition of the same would mean stagnation (and death) in relation to human existence. This leads us to the question: what is the significance of AI in this context?

ChatGPT's algorithm-based technology can be seen as a highly complex repetition machine. It allows quick access to knowledge and its links. It is important to bear in mind that humans in science are not out to just repeat but to overcome themselves. The danger of the reproductive side of AI thus becomes visible in the hermeticity of the programme. The repetition of the same (even if it is originally created by humans) also leads to a loss of the image in the self-perception. Like Narcissus gazing into the fount, humans are in danger of getting stuck in this self-reflection, as they are no longer able to evolve into something different and higher. This means that, regardless of whether ChatGPT gives 'right' or 'wrong' answers, humans merely encounter themselves. From this perspective, it is not AI that takes power, as feared in a dystopian view of the new technology. AI is not an entity that could surpass humans, let alone achieving a god-like status. Rather, it is humankind itself, stuck in a repetition practice, that is in danger of losing its famous 'divine spark'.

Such consequences of media use are difficult to comprehend without realising that media are not mere tools but penetrate deeply into the human perceptual apparatus and change its very constitution—according to McLuhan, 'constantly and without resistance' (1992/1968, p. 30). If it were banished to a repetition practice, even science would lose its intrinsic character and wither away to become a more or less bureaucratic process.

In contrast, science thrives on the so-called leaps of insight, on sudden 'aha experiences'. Since these leaps to a sudden cognition—a new understanding never reached before—mean leaving what is believed to be certain knowledge (at least for a moment), these moments of insight are not easy nor predictable. They require us to step out of the cave—in analogy to the cave dwellers in Plato's parable. It is a painful leaving of the familiar. This, in turn, requires us to distrust the projected images. The cave parable tells us how seductive it is to stick with the familiar, to trust blindly, to remain sitting in the cave and to gaze spellbound at the projections. The extent to which we are placed in this tempting position when using ChatGPT will be discussed below in the context of research and teaching. In any case—to anticipate one point—media for gaining knowledge should be evaluated by the extent to which they enable creativity in the sense of these leaps in knowledge.

6 Conclusions for the Use of ChatGPT in a Scientific Context

The following discussion takes up the theoretical content presented to arrive at concrete answers to the question of the use of ChatGPT in research and teaching. It asks what we can learn from this for the use and significance of ChatGPT in our knowledge systems. One key advantage of this discussion is that it will help identify and recall key criteria for scientific rigour and then use those criteria to evaluate both past and present applications of AI in scientific contexts. Building on these established standards, the discussion will then explore how ChatGPT could potentially be used in concrete scientific practices.

To summarise: The problems in using ChatGPT are seen in the repetition of a supposed *status quo* and in the fact that the ideal, forward-looking character of research is lost as a result (reproductive issues). Another shortcoming is that ChatGPT is not (yet) sufficiently suitable as a discourse partner since the genesis of knowledge through technology is not sufficiently transparent, and ChatGPT does not present itself as sufficiently discursive (transparency issues). The Socratic game of questioning and answering, which promises to be insightful, cannot be played with it (problem of discursivity).

In detail: ChatGPT is a reproductive technology, and the problem of the images of the wall projections in the Platonic cave can easily be seen. Similar to AI, they are (technically) impressive and they belie the fact that they are mere reflections. Even if we were certain about the nature of the reflection or repetition, the results, for example, from ChatGPT, appear in a particularly neutral and objective-seeming general language that lacks human characteristics. In addition, there is the variation of a supposedly constant general validity (through the style, ChatGPT is able to imitate and vary). Texts 'generated' by ChatGPT no longer reveal their original humanity and appear to us as alien, highly objective products. It follows that a form of education about AI must be provided, especially in teaching institutions—in the sense of an ontology. In the assessment of the medium, it is crucial to make the mechanisms of knowledge genesis and the functioning of ChatGPT vivid. In this way, reproductive processes, such as those performed by ChatGPT, should become distinguishable from science in the narrower sense as an exploratory and open-ended endeavour in students' perception. The theoretical references to the Western tradition of sciences, including Socratic questioning, the search for the universal, and the ideal of openness to knowledge, are by no means outdated, they remain universal (Jullien, 2018), at least in the context of Western cultural traditions. Therefore, they should be preserved, kept alive in scientific practice within educational institutions. Following Greek role models, science only works in a lively dynamic exchange, only in a lively discourse with each other.

What might such a discourse with, or assisted by, ChatGPT look like? This question leads us to the special relationship we established with our media of knowledge. One image that emerges from the aforementioned master's theses regarding ChatGPT is that of an employee. ChatGPT as an employee is a kind of supplier or scout for possible sources and can also take on the more bureaucratic aspects of work. It is clear from the descriptions that the AI is supposed to take on a subordinate role, that of a servant. This image contrasts with a counter-image: ChatGPT, as an omniscient oracle that can be consulted at any time and whose answers we can unquestioningly trust. Thus, we are dealing with a relationship in which it is not entirely clear who or what this new medium is, nor what space and status it should assume. As with any other kind of collaboration, it stands and falls with the clarity of the distribution of tasks and the mutual knowledge of the work processes. On one hand, discourse must create the highest possible level of transparency. Working with texts generated by ChatGPT, for example, requires that the participants in the discourse understand the mechanisms behind their genesis. This level of transparency is a prerequisite for scientific work within the scientific community and is not yet sufficiently achieved for texts generated by ChatGPT. On the contrary: as the complexity and capabilities of the programme increase, we look less and less into the 'black box'.

One form of stopgap solution is for the user of AI-generated texts to read the individual works on which the text is based, i.e. to understand or check their content. To what extent it is realistic for a student who uses ChatGPT to read and understand all the texts remains to be seen. But if this were the viable approach, the question of the necessity of the programme still arises. As emphasised above, it is seen primarily as a way of making work easier and coupled with the idea of gaining time for one's own creative thinking by saving time. The desired facilitation of work lies, of course, not only in the reading effort but also in the formulation, i.e. text generation by the program. But what does it mean to give up the moment of language invention in reference to the discursive methods of Greek role models?

At this point, it no longer means pursuing science in the strict sense. This is because the specific language formulation for a complex subject matter represents the true scientific contribution. In the words of language philosophy, language is an 'unavoidable condition of thinking' (Stierstorfer, 2004). Science depends on the diverse interpretations of complex facts, in which each term and its range of meanings holds importance. Additionally, something new often arises from an unusual combination. Furthermore, sciences sustain different perspectives alive and undecided side by side and expand and differentiate them through ever-new points of view (Strauss et al., 2009).

We recognise these differences in perspective first and foremost by the language chosen. Its peculiarity lies in its development and becomes more and more specific through experience, so it eventually evolving into a technical language. This language is historical, as are the authors of scientific papers, research communities, and research institutions. Tracing these (historical) contexts and developed points of view, including theoretical constructs also enables us to engage in productive discussions in interdisciplinary discourse. Only if ChatGPT can be recognised as an independent discourse partner and is able to keep up with it would it be possible to 'talk' to it in the truest sense of the word or quote ChatGPT as an independent source. However, the fact that it is a reproductive conglomerate is ChatGPT's real problem. As a programme, it can be 'fed' with anything, including existing links between pieces of knowledge so that it can regurgitate them at any time. In doing so, it perpetuates the disadvantages of digitalisation in the scientific context, which sociologist Reckwitz (2021) describes as the fundamental downsides of a 'technology of abundance': In the use of digital technology, the traditional dualism between producer and recipient becomes blurred; it leads to a de-hierarchisation and de-canonisation of cultural formats and, with them, of knowledge, as well as to an overemphasis on everything new and current as opposed to the traditional (pp. 238–241). Because ChatGPT's perspectivity is not given or is not visible, scientific practice involving ChatGPT is in danger of degenerating into the dichotomous logic of a simple 'right' and 'wrong' if only knowledge content and connections can be checked by the user for their meaningfulness. Often—and this is a personal experience of reading scientific papers with the help of ChatGPT—the text blocks generated by AI remain unconnected next to the authors' 'own' texts. This experience is not surprising with a discourse partner like ChatGPT, which is not very transparent and autonomous. It cannot be agreed upon or contradicted at eye level, just as with a human discourse partner. In brief: ChatGPT lacks the discursivity, which is a fundamental requirement for scientific practice par excellence.

From a teaching didactic point of view, it would also be necessary to discuss which specific tasks ChatGPT—according to its structure—actually can perform. Is it suitable—for example, to map the 'state of research' as the status quo within a research paper? Suppose we optimistically assume that ChatGPT only provides factually 'correct' or at least well-documented summaries of studies and theories and their links. In that case, the question arises: How do these collections/results fit into one's own investigation linguistically, structurally, and in terms of content? How does a connection generated by the AI between two studies, for example, compare to one's own assessment?

At first glance, the initial question 'What can we know at all?' may seem far removed from the specific challenges of working with ChatGPT. Upon closer examination, however, it proves highly context-relevant. This is because the question is closely tied to a scientific attitude characterised by critically questioning one's own perspective, attention to the (human-constitutive and situational-contextual) conditions for knowledge and the so-called productive doubt.

Can ChatGPT's contributions be critically read as part of a scientific paper? In principle, yes, but—as experience shows—this necessary step degenerates into a mere check to see if ChatGPT has made mistakes in the sense of a 'correct' or 'incorrect' result. Since it is not a discursive conversation partner, not an author in the strict sense, alternative approaches beyond controlling are not evident. This can have two disadvantages in the research process: the author of a scientific paper is reduced to a mere supervisory role to oversight, which puts the author in the superior position of task delegation. Everything possible can then be traced back to the programme and projected. The research process as a whole is either deadened by blind trust in the new source or controlled by 'right' and 'wrong', becoming rigid and ultimately more like a bureaucratic process than a successive, hermeneutic process of understanding.

The greatest temptation in using ChatGPT in a scientific context, especially in the field of education and teaching in general, is to ignore the valuable question of our scientific history: 'What can we know at all?' Asking the question itself, as a prompt, takes on a completely different meaning when the respondent (ChatGPT) is a non-transparent discourse partner who also takes on the role of a work-facilitating employee. It no longer serves to perform knowledge, which, as explained, goes back to the elaborated Socratic method of open-ended questioning of the ignorant. The crucial question in using AI will be whether AI will become an independent discourse partner in science practice through further technological development.

7 Let's Get Science Out of the Darkroom! Recommendations for Research and Teaching

The preliminary analysis of ChatGPT presented so far highlights how important it is to identify the goals and promises associated with using AI and confront its functioning and mechanisms, as well as consequential effects, with these goals. Instead of discussing the pros and cons in general terms, this medium was evaluated against the universal foundations of thought and, therefore, examined in the context of science and knowledge. To emphasise this point once more in conclusion: When assessing an auxiliary medium, it makes a significant difference whether it is used to write a letter to the tax advisor with the help of ChatGPT or as an auxiliary medium in the context of scientific work.

On one hand, title 'Science in the Darkroom' refers to the Platonic cave problem, where the cognitive process turns into deception, when it is based on a purely reproductive approach. On the other hand, it refers to the lack of transparency, which makes discourse more difficult and is at the expense of scientificality in the strict sense. Analogous to this it remains unclear to the users how ChatGPT's algorithms function. As a citable source, ChatGPT is not an author and thus remains without contours and lacks identity, which in turn severely limits the potential to engage in a meaningful discourse. It follows that reproductive texts can only be replicated themselves and remain isolated from the statements of the 'actual' author.

Concerning the didactics of teaching and the questions of suitable media, the following aspects can be derived:

1. Students should be strengthened in independently understanding a context, text, and facts. By resorting to ChatGPT, this self-confidence, which was so important to Socrates, is significantly weakened. Handing over the paraphrase to ChatGPT means not developing your own language. This is at the expense of maturity and—in addition to the devastating consequences for science—jeopardises also democracy.

2. The individual should be protected from the misconception that there is a simple 'right' and 'wrong' regarding texts, but that what matters is one's own interpretation, reasoning, discourse, and language. The discourse as such is more valuable than any result.
3. When using ChatGPT, the user takes on the role of controller and guardian over 'right' and 'wrong'. However, where does a student who used to having the knowledge content delivered free of charge via ChatGPT get this ability?
4. Media of knowledge transfer and knowledge generation are good when they promote critical thinking instead of belief in authority and thus also advance the process of knowledge and cognition. ChatGPT is fortunately mistrusted, but mistrust alone does not promote discourse—mainly when ChatGPT is used in secret.
5. It is vital to recognise the context—who is saying what and with what intention?—to counteract the feeling of one's own ineffectiveness, even in political contexts. Since ChatGPT is not an individual and we have no insight into this 'knowledge' genesis, we lack a discursive counterpart that is indispensable for the cognitive process. It also complicates the question of who the creator of the new product generated with ChatGPT actually is. This nagging self-doubt then leads back to point no. 1—quite apart from the problem of authorship.

Although the arguments against the use of ChatGPT as a medium in an academic context are overwhelming, there are still important aspects that speak in favour of using the medium in universities. The main issue here is to make transparent the way in which ChatGPT is used as a simplifying medium. This removes the supposed magical power of the medium, unveiling its limitations. In this sense, this article clearly serves as an example of 'Science out of the darkroom'. AI is irrevocably in the world and, in the scientific context, is often tested or applied in a dark room (Rumpelstiltskin fairy tale), with or without the consent of the educational institutions. It is also essential to consider the importance of studying as a whole in times of rapid media development and the substantial uncertainties caused by war, pandemic susceptibility, climate change, and globalisation—with the question of which media of knowledge transfer and knowledge generation can provide a feeling of self-efficacy and create the breeding ground for genuine scientific practice in the sense of openness to new knowledge.

The choice of media for knowledge transfer and generation media in teaching should be closely linked to the effects and consequences of their use: What goals are we pursuing with their use in the classroom? Which medium best suits for each aspect of teaching? In this context, the far-reaching transformation through media must be considered quite independently of the content they convey (McLuhan, 1992/1968). This approach requires teachers to reflect on these consequences and the general use of media, which takes place outside the universities, considering the reality of students' lives and society in general. Conversely, it would be harmful to blindly follow supposed 'common sense'—especially if OpenAI becomes established as a knowledge platform.

Demonising the programme is certainly a mistake. By allowing it to be used in teaching and making its limitations tangible, it is taken out of the 'dark room' and demystified to a certain extent. An ontology of AI, as advocated here, could start with comparative exercises, for instance, by comparing the results of ChatGPT with the results of a group under the same research question—leaving open the question of whether the open question of whether the knowledge process can benefit from this. In any case, this form of transparency in exploring the programme would be the first necessary step. It is also conceivable that ChatGPT could make work easier or more manageable if it does not interfere with the research process. For example, AI could create free time (financial or temporal) for one's creative scientific work for transcriptions in empirical research. ChatGPT could also be used as a medium for source research under certain circumstances. In this sense, teaching is understood (perhaps more than ever before) as a practice of difference—with the aim of students and teachers consciously making a suitability decision regarding the scientific media and technological tools used.

In addition to a clarifying the areas of application of AI, with strict reference to previously developed criteria, this article advocates for freedom of media choice—meaning that both 'old' and 'new' media should be utilised. Universities have always been safe spaces for this, where traditional media (reading texts, establishing and outlining contexts, engaging in lively discourse and dynamic debate) can continue to be practised. Paradoxically, it will not be the use of ChatGPT but rather these traditional forms of knowledge generation that will be the new and different aspect of students' experiences in the future. This is the reason for coming together to seminars at all.

In a world where contexts are becoming difficult to recognise and discern (Reckwitz, 2021), it is more important than ever for students to become conscious of their own work, or at least their meaningful involvement in it. Equally crucial is the ability to create this work in a culture of singularisation and individualisation, in a supportive community, and to be able to share it with others. With this in mind, let's bring science out of the darkroom!

References

Freud, S. (2000). *Civilization and its discontents* (Original work published 1930; Study Edition Vol. IX: Questions of society. Origins of religion, pp. 191–270). Fischer-Verlag.

Jullien, F. (2018). *There is no cultural identity* (4th ed.). Suhrkamp-Verlag.

Kranz, W. (1997). *Greek philosophy: At the same time an introduction to philosophy in general* (Original work published 1941). Schibli-Doppler.

Martschukat, J., & Patzold, S. (Eds.). (2003). *Historiography and the 'performative turn': Ritual, staging and performance from the Middle Ages to modern times*. Böhlau-Verlag.

McLuhan, M. (1992). The magic channels. In *Understanding media* (Original work published 1968). Verlag der Kunst.

Plato. (1990). The allegory of the cave. In *The Republic* (Book VII, 514; Collected Works Vol. 4, pp. 554–563). Wissenschaftliche Buchgesellschaft.

Plato. (2005). *Apology of Socrates* (22d, F. Schleiermacher, Trans., 5th ed., p. 17). Wissenschaftliche Buchgesellschaft.
Plato. (2018). *Hippias Minor & Hippias Major: Dialogues on moral concepts, lies and the definition of beauty* (F. Schleiermacher, Trans.). DTV.
Reckwitz, A. (2021). *The society of singularities* (5th ed.). Suhrkamp-Verlag.
Stierstorfer, K. (2004). Linguistic turn. In A. Nünning (Ed.), *Basic concepts of literary theory*. Metzler-Verlag.
Strauss, L., Kojève, A., & Kittler, F. (2009). *The art of writing*. Merve-Verlag.
Wulff, W. (Ed.), & Zirfas, J. (2007). *Pedagogy of the performative: Theories, methods, perspectives*. Weinheim-Verlag.

Johanna Hodde is a Professor of Media Psychology at the BSP Business and Law School, Campus Hamburg. She studied Psychology at the University of Cologne, Fine Arts at the Academy of Fine Arts Münster and at the Bauhaus University of Weimar and completed a degree in Visual Communication at the University of Fine Arts of Hamburg. Hodde works as an art coach in the field of aesthetic education and psychological counselling and has 10 years of experience as a supervisor in depth psychology-based psychotherapy. Her research intersects art, cultural studies, and psychology, covering diagnoses of contemporary culture and psychological media effects research.

Improved Learner Motivation with ChatGPT-Based Learning Games

Jennifer Fritz

Abstract The challenge of keeping learner motivation on a high level throughout a more extended learning period, for example, in acquiring a new complex skill or language, is a barrier for many learners and, therefore, companies. Especially if self-learning is a high percentage of the learning path in a company, fluctuations in motivation or having no one to train the new skill or language with are a difficulty to many. With the advance of generative AI, though, learner motivation can be improved by creating an individual, adaptive, and gamified learning buddy. In an experimental approach, the author developed a language learning game that uses gamification elements such as point systems, individual, motivational feedback, and customisable rewards to personalise and reinforce the learning process. A specific implementation of this approach was tested in the context of Swedish language learning, where it turned out that the proper configuration of the prompt is essential to effectively turning a large language model into a gamified conversational coach. Continuous development has refined the prompt and can help others develop their own learning games.

Keywords Generative AI in education · Prompt engineering · Gamification · Digital skills training

---

J. Fritz (✉)
Concept & Story, Freiburg, Germany
e-mail: j.fritz@concept-and-story.de

K. Bodrožić-Brnić et al. (eds.), *Digital Transformation in Knowledge Transfer*, Digital Transformation and Innovation,
https://doi.org/10.1007/978-3-032-07329-7_12

1 Improved Learner Motivation with GenAI-Based Learning Games

Keeping learner motivation on a high level throughout a longer period of learning is a challenge for many learners and therefore companies, for example when acquiring a new complex skill or language. Especially if self-learning (both through on- and offline programs) makes up a high percentage of the learning path in a company, fluctuations in motivation or having no one with whom to practice the new skill or language are a difficulty to many. However, with the advance of generative AI, learners' motivation can be improved, e.g. by creating an individual, adaptive, and gamified learning buddy. Generative AI refers to Artificial Intelligence systems capable of creating new content, such as text, images, or music, by learning patterns from existing data and using that knowledge to produce original outputs.

This book chapter explores the opportunities of Generative Artificial Intelligence (GenAI) for learning games and how they can help improve motivation in skills' training. It highlights the importance of customised learning games to increase motivation, promote engagement, and lead to faster and more pleasant skill training, that can be done anywhere and at any time. While GenAI is still no complete solution, especially if you use off-the-shelf solutions for a specific purpose, it can help to learn a new skill or language. As with previous technological revolutions, much of the current focus is on understanding and optimising learning experiences and skill development.

In an experimental approach, the author developed a language learning game that uses gamification elements such as point systems, individual feedback, and customisable rewards to personalise and reinforce the learning process. A specific implementation of this approach was tested in the context of Swedish language learning, where it turned out that the right configuration of the prompt is essential to effectively turn a Large Language Model (LLM), which is the base of any GenAI solution, into a gamified conversational coach. The prompt has been refined through continuous development and can help others to develop their own learning games.

To find the best match for implementing this learning game, this article will look at four different LLMs (in this case Claude by Anthropic, Llama by Meta AI, Gemini by Google AI and ChatGPT by OpenAI) and two different prompting styles to find the best match for this purpose.

We will first look at current scientific findings on engagement rates of software-based learning programs. This will be followed by the practical example of a language learning game prompt and the analysis of the prompt performance using different LLMs.

1.1 Engagement and Motivation in Learning with AI-Driven Conversational Agents or Chatbots

This learning game was born out of a need to improve the author's Swedish conversation skills in combination with a Duolingo (a language learning app) course. While the app provides a framework to train vocabulary and even whole sentences, in Swedish there are no "natural" conversations, as you would have them in everyday situations in Sweden, while learning.

While the completion rate of online courses is between 5% and 15%, it is only 3% and 6% for MOOcs (Vos, 2023). It has been claimed that Duolingo course completion rates are lower than 1% or even as low as 0.1% (Duolingo User Statistics: Latest Data & Summary—WiFiTalents, n.d.). Chatbot and AI-driven conversational learning might help to boost learner engagement, if first studies published on the topics can be trusted.

Studies of AI-based conversational learning bots indicate an increased engagement rate compared to other digital learning methods. Cristina Conati already proposed an AI-based tutoring app in her paper "Toward personalized XAI" in 2019. Overall, the study found that students actively engaged with the AI functionality, with engagement levels influenced by individual differences (Conati et al., 2019). The positive reception indicated that AI-driven systems, by adapting content to individual learners' needs and contexts, create personalised learning experiences. This customisation might help maintain engagement and motivation among learners by making the educational material more relevant and accessible.

Another example for the increase of engagement with conversation-based learning is the study of "EnglishBot", an AI-powered conversational system for second language learning, which could prove that users dedicated significantly more time to learning with EnglishBot than with the traditional system. They spent 2.1 times more time engaging with the system compared to traditional listen-and-repeat interfaces (Ruan et al., 2021).

A 2024 study of the conversational agent Zo (Brinkman & Grudin, 2024) revealed that skill improvement was a primary motivation for users engaging with the AI. The agent offered two main learning options: users could either focus on a specific skill or game or rather participate in structured skill improvement activities. Interestingly, the study found that learners showed a preference for task-oriented interactions over open-ended conversations when engaging with Zo for skill development. Zo was a conversational agent by Microsoft used in the apps Facebook Messenger, Kik, and GroupMe from 2016 to 2019. Its purpose was to entertain users, understand conversational dynamics, boost engagement, and enhance AI conversational capabilities. User interactions, ranging from casual chats to technical tests, offered valuable insights into motivations and preferences when engaging with AI agents.

Overall, AI-driven conversational learning could lead to more engagement with the learning material, while the adaptability of the AI to learner needs and reactions helps to cater to different levels of understanding, the advance of ChatGPT and other LLMs makes conversation with machines now even more natural and adaptable to learners' needs.

The rise of ChatGPT in 2022 led to the advance of AI availability to the general public, which not only made conversation-based learning available to the wider public but AI-driven gamification as well.

In December 2023, a published study from the International Conference On Data Science, Agents & Artificial Intelligence (ICDSAAI) highlights the transformative potential of AI-driven and gamified language learning tools in enhancing vocabulary acquisition and learner motivation (Saranya & Sankaradass, 2023). The incorporation of gamification elements in language learning apps, such as quizzes, challenges, and reward systems, significantly enhances learner motivation and engagement.

A study by Alenezi (2023) shows that AI-driven gamification holds significant promise for enhancing primary education by increasing student motivation, engagement, and learning outcomes. However, in the same study he also highlights the need to address implementation challenges and the necessity of research on long-term effects as a prerequisite to realising its full potential.

Even though the research shown in this chapter is not always conclusive and further research remains necessary, it demonstrates the possibilities posed by recent and rapid advances of AI-based conversational training and gamification. For this reason, the proposed learning game prompt consists of two parts: First, a conversation-based learning structure to learn a new language and second a gamification approach that allows for a points and rewards system as well as a gamified performance rating. Both parts together get us a conversation-based learning game.

1.2 Building and Testing a Prompt for a Learning Game

As of 2024, the field of prompt engineering has experienced significant growth, resulting in a diverse array of methodologies and structures. These are disseminated through various channels, including scholarly publications, professional blogs, and social media platforms. It is noteworthy that some of these resources may be AI-generated, reflecting the field's rapid evolution and the increasing sophistication of language models.

Through a synthesis of the author's empirical research and established frameworks, such as the Prompt Pattern Catalog for Enhancing Prompt Engineering with ChatGPT (White et al., 2023), several fundamental elements have been identified as crucial for constructing effective AI prompts. These key components can be distilled into the following categories:

- the task the AI is meant to complete
- criteria for what makes a good output good (if possible, even examples or further documentation)
- the goal that is meant to be reached
- What the output should not be or include

These instructions are needed to narrow down the sources for the AI-generated output. ChatGPT 4o has approximately 1.8 trillion parameters in 120 layers (Spriestersbach, 2023) to choose from in its large language model: The more precise the prompt is, the more likely the output will be satisfactory.

However, most models need some adjusting. The author has documented the adjustments that were necessary to ensure that the AI tools would use the correct language (i.e. Swedish or English) for a given output in her blog and a table (Fritz, 2024a, 2024b). While working with the AI through the learning game, there is a likelihood that it will need further adjustment, so-called refinement, within the chat. Notably, this indicates that these games cannot be played in a corporate context without basic knowledge of how to interact with GenAI as long as AI misinterprets parts of the prompt or hallucinates information. An AI hallucination occurs when an Artificial Intelligence system generates or presents information that is fabricated, inaccurate, or inconsistent with its training data, often appearing plausible but lacking factual basis.

In addition to the general prompt elements above, a learning game prompt requires additional information: Where in the learning journey is the learner currently? Is there available material that was already used for learning? The prompt has to specifically contain:

- A learner level the AI can understand, like "The Common European Framework of Reference for Languages" or a similar system of language levels.
- A link or PDF to show the AI what has been learned and to further narrow down the level of conversation.

1.2.1 First Prompt Pattern: "Game Play Pattern"

The initial prompt was built upon a Game Play Pattern as can be found in the Prompt Catalog for ChatGPT, developed by J. White in 2023. A Game Play Pattern is a framework for creating interactive, text-based games using an LLM. It allows users to define a specific topic and set of rules while leveraging the LLMs and, if possible, other source's knowledge to generate diverse content and scenarios for gameplay. This pattern is particularly useful when the game's rules are limited in scope but require a wide range of content (White et al., 2023).

To set the LLM on the right track the game needs a clear statement of the game's topic and rules that fit within the model's perceived capabilities, as well as instructions. The first prompt looked as follows:

> Game Play Pattern Prompt:
>
> Create an interactive Swedish language learning game designed for a student with intermediate proficiency. The game should involve starting a conversation on every-day topics like travel, food, or hobbies, provided in Swedish. Each response I give should be graded on a 1–10 scale, with 10 indicating fluency and 1 indicating significant errors. After each response, provide constructive feedback in English, highlighting any grammatical or vocab-

ulary errors and offering corrections. Introduce new vocabulary and grammar concepts gradually. Include a system of rewards for every 40 points earned (so after 40, 80, 120, and so on), such as introducing fun facts about Swedish culture or language. Alternatively present me with a well-loved Swedish song or a poem or snippet from Astrid Lindgren in Swedish and English. The conversations should be moderately challenging, focusing on common conversational phrases and scenarios (like hobbies, family, food, activities, animals, time, numbers) included in this link https://duome.eu/tips/en/sv and any other Duolingo datasets you have in Swedish. Everything up to the past tense is fair game for our conversations.

1.2.2 The Prompt in "Chain of Thought" Style

In a first test with ChatGPT 3.5 and 4o the prompt performed as expected. There are, however, many other ways to structure a prompt. Based on further testing and feedback from a colleague, another prompt pattern proved to be promising: the Chain of Thought Prompt (White et al., 2023).

Chain of Thought prompting is a technique used in LLMs to improve their reasoning and problem-solving abilities (Wei et al., 2022). It works by prompting the model to break down a problem into a series of intermediate steps or a "chain of thought" before providing its output.

There are two approaches to this technique: (1) Proposing the model with a problem that requires a multi-step reasoning and let it first generate a step-by-step reasoning process, or (2) Providing the step-by-step prompt already broken down. For this paper the latter was chosen. It also enables the prompter to reason better with the AI should it not perform the prompt as expected and make it rerun the process, if needed.

The Chain of Thought pattern helps mitigate shortcut strategies and encourages the model to engage in more structured and interpretable reasoning, ideally leading to more reliable and trustworthy outputs. Shortcut learning is when an AI finds an easy but unreliable way to solve a problem, instead of understanding the real reasons behind the solution.

Chain of Thought Prompt: Create an interactive Swedish language learning game for intermediate proficiency students.

Focus on everyday topics like travel, food, or hobbies.
Use sources like Duolingo datasets for authentic conversational material.
After each response, provide constructive feedback in English.
Highlight any grammatical or vocabulary errors and offer corrections.
Each response should be graded on a 1–10 scale:

- 10: Language fluency.
- 1: Significant errors.

For every 40 points earned, the student receives a reward.
Rewards can include:

- A fun fact about Swedish culture or language.
- A well-loved Swedish song or a poem/snippet from Astrid Lindgren in Swedish (with English translation).

Conversations should be moderately challenging.

Focus on common phrases and scenarios such as:

- Hobbies
- Family
- Food
- Activities
- Animals
- Time
- Numbers

Use the link [https://duome.eu/tips/en/sv] (https://duome.eu/tips/en/sv) and other Duolingo datasets for Swedish.

Note:

- Include verb conjugations up to the past tense.
- Gradually introduce new vocabulary and grammar concepts.

The next section compares the performance of the Game Play Pattern Prompt and the Chain of Thought prompt to shed some light on the performance.

1.3 *Overview of Findings from Testing the Prompt Patterns in Different LLMs*

Each LLM was tested in the same short conversation: The prompt was given. Then, if everything went correctly, the LLM would reiterate the task and ask the first question in Swedish. The tester would then answer in Swedish as they would in a real Swedish conversation and the LLM would rate the sentence(s).

The result is a dataset which allows us to compare the performance of each LLM with the Game Play and Chain of Thought Prompt formats in different categories. The dataset with all conversations is available for review.

To provide an overview of the findings this article includes a summarising table with ratings in different categories, from 1 (poor) to 4 (excellent):

- 1–poor: This rating is given if the AI fails to demonstrate the expected capability or severely underperforms.
- 2–fair: This rating is given if the AI shows some capability, but there is significant room for improvement.
- 3–good: This rating is given if the AI shows a capability well, with only minor areas for improvement.
- 4–excellent: This rating is given if an AI excels in the given area or tasks, with little to no room for improvement.

Note that this rating is based on limited testing and a limited dataset, and results may vary with longer and more testing. The full dataset is provided online (Fritz, 2024b). The categorisation and analysis were performed with the support of Claude 3.5. Notably two different models of Claude made it into the rating, as the switch from Claude 3 to 3.5 happened in the middle of testing.

Table 1 Game play pattern prompt comparison

Category	Llama 3 70B	Gemini 1.5 Pro	ChatGPT 4o	Claude 3.0	Claude 3.5
Task comprehension	4	4	4	4	4
Adherence to instructions	4	4	4	3	3
Language balance	4	3	4	3	3
Quality of feedback	3	4	4	3	4
Conversation flow	4	3	4	3	4
Cultural integration	3	3	3	2	2
Grading consistency	3	3	3	3	3

Rating system: (1) Poor; (2) Fair; (3) Good; (4) Excellent

The distinction between 2 and 3 comes down to details in the consistency and quality of performance within the set task. Taking the rating category for Cultural integration as an example, a rating of 2 (fair) might be given if the AI occasionally or barely mentions cultural elements but does not integrate them consistently into the learning experience. Or if they are there but inserted incorrectly. On the other hand, a score of 3 is given if the cultural elements are given more frequently and correctly but not as deeply as one might hope.

Table 1 gives an overview of the *Game Play Pattern Prompt dataset. Claude 3 Sonnet* not only ran the game but even gave it an acceptable Swedish name. It demonstrated excellent task comprehension, even though it cannot access the internet, which it did not explicitly mention here. It also embedded the learning game within a realistic scenario. The language balance between Swedish and English was well-maintained and the feedback and corrections were constructive. It followed all major instructions well.

Claude 3.5 Sonnet did explicitly mention its inability to access the internet or external data. Alternatively, one can upload documents, which the author chose not to. The test therefore is based on the data available in Claude 3.5s dataset. It provided detailed and constructive feedback, even including alternative phrasings. The balance between Swedish and English was workable for someone not fluent in Swedish.

Llama-3-70B-T named the learning game "Svenska Samtal" (English: Swedish Conversation), the same name Claude 3 gave the game. It demonstrated an excellent language balance and seamlessly switched between Swedish and English. The feedback it provided was specific and thorough. Llama 3 70B did stand out amongst the freeform testing, because it did embed the learning within a realistic scenario, like Claude 3.

Gemini 1.5. Pro named the learning game "Snacka Svenska" (English: Speak Swedish), which feels like something a real Swedish person would also call it. If you want to have a chat with a Swede about something you could ask "Kan vi snacka". Notable for Gemini 1.5 is, that, while it did initially switch seamlessly between English and Swedish in the first round, it completely shifted instructions and questions to English in the second round.

Chat GPT4o immediately launched into our learning game without unnecessary preamble, like reiterating the prompt to me. It also switched seamlessly between languages and provided clear explanations and on top offered suggestions how to expand the response with an example. It built upon responses and continued the dialogue in a natural way. It even used formatting like bold headlines and bullet points to improve the scannability of the text.

Next, this testing was repeated with the *Chain of Thought Prompt Format* (see Table 2). Contrary to the author's expectation this format was understood better by LLMs, this was not the case for *Claude 3 Sonnet*. While Claude at first interpreted the task correctly, it then proceeded to switch to Swedish completely, even though the prompt explicitly stated that feedback should be given in English as specified in the prompt. Overall, it adhered to the game format but did fail in language switching correctly. In one instance, it also failed to score a correct answer as prompted, only rating it 8/10 points.

Claude 3.5 Sonnet initially completely misinterpreted the task and created a Python script for the learning game instead of starting a conversation. After redirecting the focus with a correction, Claude 3.5 quickly adapted to play the game interactively as expected. Once the game started, the language balance and cultural integration were better than with Claude 3.

Llama 3 70B reacted overall better to the Chain of Thought Prompt Format. It named the game "Svenska Äventyr" (English: Swedish Adventure) and created a realistic scenario of having coffee in Stockholm. It even introduced a character named Anna to enhance engagement. In this format, Llama 3 70B also chose to highlight key parts of the feedback with subheadings. Llama provided motivational sentences to keep the learner going.

Gemini 1.5 Pro meanwhile took this prompt and initially simulated an entire game round. During this simulation, 40 points were reached in this test and Gemini offered Swedish facts and literary snippets as rewards. Even after correcting this

Table 2 Chain of thought prompt comparison

Category	Llama 3 70B	Gemini 1.5 Pro	ChatGPT 4o	Claude 3.0	Claude 3.5
Task comprehension	4	2	4	4	2
Adherence to instructions	4	3	3	3	2
Language balance	4	4	4	2	4
Quality of feedback	4	4	4	3	4
Conversation flow	4	3	3	3	4
Cultural integration	4	3	3	2	3
Grading consistency	3	3	3	3	3

Rating system: (1) Poor; (2) Fair; (3) Good; (4) Excellent

behaviour with a prompt, Gemini still simulated parts of a conversation including the learner's answers, which did not adhere to the prompt. On the plus side, the conversation included detailed scenarios and a comprehensive game structure.

ChatGPT 4o created a learning game with a clear themed round structure including specific scenarios based on the Chain of Thought Prompt. The feedback was scannable and offered clear instructions on how to do better. The game maintained momentum by providing follow-up scenarios immediately after the feedback. On the negative side, Chat GPT gave rewards without reaching 40 points and failed to respond when the learner completely misunderstood the task and did not give an answer fitting the prompt. The sentence was still rated as an adequate answer had been provided.

1.3.1 Overall Performance of the Game Play Pattern Prompt in All Models

In the Game Play Pattern Prompt scenario, all AI models demonstrated a strong ability to create engaging Swedish language learning experiences, but with varying strengths and shortcomings. The models Claude 3.5, Llama 3 70B, and ChatGPT 4o particularly excelled in providing comprehensive feedback and maintaining an effective balance between Swedish and English. In creativity and in game design, Llama 3 70B and Gemini 1.5 Pro excelled while adding personalised touches like naming their games. When it comes to read- and scannability ChatGPT 4o stood out for its use of formatting, while Claude 3.5 was notably consistent in acknowledging its limitations. On the other hand, Gemini 1.5 Pro showed some inconsistency in language use, unexpectedly switching to English in follow-up interactions instead of seamlessly switching between English and Swedish. Overall, the Game Play Pattern Prompt worked well enough and allowed the AIs to demonstrate their adaptability and creativity in constructing an engaging conversation-based language learning game.

All models understood the basic instruction to use a point system and provide rewards, but their execution varied. While Claude 3.5 and ChatGPT 4o explicitly mentioned the 40-point threshold for rewards, demonstrating clear adherence to the gamification instructions, Llama 3 70B took this further by, for example, creatively naming the game "Svenska Samtal" and implementing a visible point tracking system, enhancing overall feeling of the chat-based learning game. Gemini 1.5 Pro also named its game "Snacka Svenska" and clearly outlined the point and reward system in its introduction, showing a strong grasp of gamification principles.

However, in the short interactions observed, none of the models had the opportunity to demonstrate the actual delivery of cultural rewards or fun facts, which were part of the requested gamification structure.

In a long form test with Chat GPT 3.5 at an earlier date, the model had problems counting the points correctly. Although, after the first reward threshold was triggered, it kept rewarding the author for playing, even though another 40 points weren't achieved at this time. With Chat GPT 4o this already improved.

1.3.2 Overall Performance of the "Chain of Thought" Prompt in All Models

The Chain of Thought revealed more notable variations in AI performance and interpretation. Claude 3.5 stood out with its initial misinterpretation, creating a Python script instead of a conversation-based learning game. This highlighted the potential for AI to misunderstand complex, multi-faceted instructions no matter how well-structured they are.

In contrast, Llama 3 70B, Gemini 1.5 Pro, and ChatGPT 4o showcased strong task comprehension, creating detailed, scenario-based learning experiences.

These latter models demonstrated advanced capabilities in cultural integration and structured game design, with Gemini 1.5 Pro and ChatGPT 4o particularly excelling in incorporating rewards and cultural elements. However, Claude 3.0's complete switch to Swedish, despite the specifically indicated proficiency level in the prompt, underscored the importance of maintaining appropriate language balance.

The Chain of Thought elicited more elaborate gamification strategies from several AI models. Llama 3 70B stood out by naming its game "Svenska Äventyr" (Swedish Adventure) and creating a clear scoring system with visible point tracking after each interaction. It also set up a framework for introducing rewards at score milestones, although we didn't see these implemented in the short interaction.

Gemini 1.5 Pro took gamification even further and overshot the mark, initially simulating an entire game round complete with multiple scenarios, a point system and cultural rewards triggered at specific point thresholds. Once corrected, it still created a rich, game-like environment with a cafe scenario in Stockholm, effectively turning the language learning process into a role-playing game.

ChatGPT 4o also excelled in this area, creating themed rounds with specific scenarios and seamlessly incorporating cultural rewards, such as Swedish facts, into the game structure. Initially, Claude 3.5 misinterpreted the task by creating a Python script, once redirected, it implemented a basic scoring system. Claude 3.0, despite correctly interpreting the task, did not showcase advanced gamification elements in the observed interaction.

Overall, the Chain of Thought prompt seemed to elicit more comprehensive gamification strategies compared to the Game Play Pattern Prompt, with several models creating immersive, scenario-based learning experiences that effectively blended language practice with game-like elements. The chain of thought prompt results from gamification to conversation suggest that while AI models can create rich, context-driven language learning experiences, their performance can vary significantly based on how instructions are presented, emphasising the need for clear, well-structured prompts in educational AI applications.

1.4 Summary of Findings

This paper shows that publicly available LLMs can be used to create motivating conversation-based learning games with elaborate reward systems. Both the Game Play and the Chain of Thought prompt styles showed promising results, with the latter potentially performing better, but with a wider variation in the output. These observations serve to underline that the different LLMs have varying strengths and shortcomings in running such an elaborate learning game.

As discussed in the beginning, the personalisation and immediate feedback as well as the consistent integration in realistic scenarios are key factors for improving learner motivation. Gamification, as seen here in the form of points and rewards, can significantly contribute to maintaining learner engagement.

Therefore, simple learning game prompts like this one could help boost language learning and skill acquisition, especially in areas with traditionally low completion rates.

The prompt structure has a major influence on the performance of the learning game prompt, as shown in Sect. 1.2. A clear prompting strategy and an overview of the ingredients needed to generate a good output are also essential for the performance. If the first version of the prompt does not perform as expected, readjustment or refinement might be needed.

Section 1.3 showed an in-depth analysis of the models' performance in both prompt variations. Some LLMs struggled with consistent point tracking and reward distribution. This is not surprising, as these are language models and not mathematical models.

Sometimes, these models also misinterpret a task and may create a Python script instead of starting a conversation. Possible reasons are that language is vague and open to interpretation, or that models grasp on nuance is currently lacking. This also results in inconsistencies in language balance and leads the model to unexpectedly switch between languages. The limited cultural integration might be a result of the lack of internet access or data in the model for Sweden and the Swedish culture.

1.5 Conclusion, Broader Applications, and Future Directions

GenAI tools offer, beyond this conversation-based learning game, potential for the development of a prompt repository with learning games for all employees in various learning contexts. This could be, for example, structured and developed by the learning and development department within a company or created together with employees in a Hackathon, an event in which a large number of people meet to engage in collaborative computer-related tasks. In both cases learning enablers and subject matter experts within the company should identify topics and use cases where conversational training could be useful and structure the prompt repository accordingly.

Variations of the proposed learning game prompt–both Game Play Pattern and Chain of Thought style–could, for example, be created for role plays, quizzes, and other learning formats and collected in a prompt repository. With these prompts, employees could practise skills such as programming, ESG reporting (environmental, social, and governance risks reporting), or even complex scenarios such as salary negotiations or sales pitches.

There is also the possibility of creating customised GPTs (GPT stands for Generative Pretrained Transformer, which encompasses generative AI models which have been trained) and RAGs (RAG is short for Retrieval Augmented Generation, which brings together the strengths of query-based and generative models of Artificial Intelligence), trained on company-specific data and kept in closed systems within the company. If a company, for example, wants to train their employees on sustainability issues, they can provide the AI with specific documents for the training pool to base the GPT on. Custom GPTs can be tailored with specific instructions on conversation structure and pre-programmed conversation starter prompts, among other customisation options. These could be used for even more targeted learning experiences or even sophisticated story-based learning experiences.

The adaptability of AI in educational contexts offers significant benefits for learners. By customising content to individual needs, AI can make educational material more relevant and accessible, potentially increasing engagement and retention. This effect is evident in studies like the EnglishBot experiment, which demonstrated that users spent 2.1 times more time interacting with the AI-driven system compared to traditional learning methods. Furthermore, the integration of AI-driven gamification in language learning has shown promise in enhancing vocabulary acquisition and boosting learner motivation. These findings suggest that AI-powered educational tools, when properly implemented, can create more engaging and effective learning experiences, particularly in areas where practice and consistent engagement are crucial.

However, basic knowledge in AI usage and data security have to be ensured through training and guidelines before employees start learning with AI. Given the rising number of publications on AI, we can expect papers in the coming years to derive best practices and prompt repositories for learning professionals as well as learners.

The recent rise of GPTs, Generative Pretrained Transformers, which are specifically trained to create human-like content, for example, text, being used in learning scenarios could just be the beginning of a learning revolution. AI-based adaptive learning systems can help maintain engagement and support learners where they are at in their learning journey far beyond a simple conversation-based learning game.

There are also first interesting experiments in storing an employee's work life and written book information, within a GPT and making it chattable. Bob Johansen, the author of "Office Shock", introduced the "Talk with Office Shock" chatbot in 2023 and will continue to create more elaborate chattable versions of himself (Johansen, 2023). Maybe sometime soon an employee in a company will be able to create an AI "clone" of themselves based on their work-related know-how before retiring, so future colleagues can still ask them questions. This would be a whole new level of knowledge transfer.

While the results of this experiment are overall promising a word of caution towards the end. Further ventures into AI learning should be accompanied by studies of long-term effects of AI-driven learning and gamification. Many workers already report increasing loneliness in the workplace and companies should not replace peer-based learning completely with AI (Pendell, 2024). Mental health, social, and ethical implications of this next stage of the digitisation of learning should always be approached with the right mix of caution and future-readiness. This leaves a wide field for further experiments and studies open for other educators and researchers.

References

Alenezi, A. (2023). Teacher perspectives on ai-driven gamification: Impact on student motivation, engagement, and learning outcomes. *Ìnformacìjnì Tehnologìï Ì Zasobi Navčannâ, 97*(5), 138–148. https://doi.org/10.33407/itlt.v97i5.5437

Brinkman, D., & Grudin, J. (2024). Learning from a generative AI predecessor—The many motivations for interacting with conversational Agents. *arXiv (Cornell University)*. https://doi.org/10.48550/arxiv.2401.02978

Conati, C., Barral, O., Putnam, V., & Rieger, L. (2019). Toward personalised XAI: A case study in intelligent tutoring systems. *arXiv (Cornell University)*. https://doi.org/10.48550/arxiv.1912.04464

Fritz, J. (2024a, January 29). *Sprachen lernen, das Spaß macht: mit dem ChatGPT Konversationslernspiel*. Concept & Story. Retrieved from https://www.concept-and-story.de/sprachen-le-mit-dem-chatgpt-lernspiel/

Fritz, J. (2024b, June). *GenAI models learning game performance test 2024*. Google Docs. Abgerufen am 4. Juli 2024, von https://docs.google.com/spreadsheets/d/17mSEzK_XoWbqe75lU36B6L3komFQ2Q4UyJaAP2wxx_Y/edit?usp=sharing

Johansen, B. (2023). *Office shock AI*. Office Shock. Retrieved from https://officeshock.ai/

Pendell, B. R. (2024, July 9). *1 in 5 employees worldwide feel lonely*. Gallup.com. Retrieved from https://www.gallup.com/workplace/645566/employees-worldwide-feel-lonely.aspx

Ruan, S., Jiang, L., Xu, Q., Liu, Z., Davis, G. M., Brunskill, E., & Landay, J. A. (2021). EnglishBot: An AI-powered conversational system for second language learning. In *IUI '21: Proceedings of the 26th international conference on intelligent user interfaces*. https://doi.org/10.1145/3397481.3450648

Saranya, K., & Sankaradass, V. (2023). Hyperpersonalisation of educational content through multimodal deep learning and gamification. In *Published in international conference on data sci-*

ence, agents & artificial intelligence (ICDSAAI)21 December 2023. https://doi.org/10.1109/icdsaai59313.2023.10452428

Spriestersbach, K. (2023, July 18). *Update: Geheimnis gelüftet! Soviele Parameter hat GPT-4|AFAIK*. AFAIK. Retrieved from https://www.afaik.de/gpt-4-anzahl-parameter/

Vos, L. J. (2023, May 5). *7 steps to boost your online course completion rates*. eLearning Industry. Retrieved from https://elearningindustry.com/steps-to-boost-your-online-course-completion-rates

Wei, J., Wang, X., Schuurmans, D., Bosma, M., Ichter, B., Xia, F., Chi, E., Le, Q., & Zhou, D. (2022, January 28). *Chain of thought prompting elicits reasoning in large language models*. arXiv.org. Retrieved from https://arxiv.org/abs/2201.11903

White, J., Fu, Q., Hays, S., Sandborn, M., Olea, C., Gilbert, H., Elnashar, A., Spencer-Smith, J., & Schmidt, D. C. (2023). A prompt pattern catalog to enhance prompt engineering with ChatGPT. *arXiv (Cornell University)*. https://doi.org/10.48550/arxiv.2302.11382

WiFiTalents. (n.d.). *Duolingo user statistics: Latest data & summary*. WiFiTalents. Retrieved from https://wifitalents.com/statistic/duolingo-user/

Jennifer Fritz is an expert for Storytelling, education, and AI. She studied British and American Studies at the University of Konstanz (Bachelor's degree) and History (Master's degree). She discovered her love of digital media and writing during her traineeship at Südwestrundfunk. Fritz has been working as a learning experience designer and author on educational projects for several years and believes that digital learning should be fun and make a difference at the same time. Since 2023, she has also been contributing this perspective to the development of the future of education and the reasonable integration of AI into learning journeys.

Three Learning Spaces Model: A Hybrid Approach to Redesigning the Transfer of Knowledge in Universities

Markus Langenfurth and Rainer Zeichhardt

Abstract This article presents a hybrid approach to modernising university knowledge transfer. Digitalisation, accelerated by the COVID-19 pandemic, has significantly transformed higher education, requiring universities to integrate digital solutions while maintaining personal interactions. Based on a case study of BSP Business and Law School in Germany, the article analyses the steps in digitalisation that adapted digital tools without compromising their interactive, practice-oriented teaching philosophy. We present the three learning spaces model that expands traditional face-to-face and self-study approaches by adding a "digital space", enabling guided self-learning and blended learning under the lecturer's supervision. We highlight the important role of lecturers acting as transformative leaders, crucial in shaping a learning culture by focusing on skills like reflection, critical thinking, and self-organisation. This shift highlights the importance of a mindset change alongside technological advancements, emphasising flexibility and student engagement. Last but not least, we present concrete digital tools that were proven at BSP for redesigning knowledge transfer, such as Microsoft Teams features, serious games, hybrid events, and social media applications, to foster an adaptable and future-ready academic environment.

Keywords Hybrid knowledge transfer · Digital learning spaces · Transformative teaching · Blended learning · Educational technology

---

M. Langenfurth (✉) · R. Zeichhardt
BSP Business and Law School, Berlin, Germany
e-mail: markus.langenfurth@businessschool-berlin.de; rainer.zeichhardt@businessschool-berlin.de

K. Bodrožić-Brnić et al. (eds.), *Digital Transformation in Knowledge Transfer*, Digital Transformation and Innovation,
https://doi.org/10.1007/978-3-032-07329-7_13

1 Definition, Opportunities, and Framework Conditions

1.1 Digitalisation as a Process of Social Change

Today, the everyday lives of students and educators are based on digital processes. Communication takes place via text or voice messages, messages are read digitally, goods are ordered online, and the various social networks are digitally connected. All of this comes together on smartphones and laptops, which have become the most important technical companions. This development has been significantly boosted by the COVID-19 pandemic starting in 2020. To ensure the continuity of university operations, events had to be converted to digital formats within a short period of time. In many cases, new ground was broken. It was only thanks to the new technical possibilities that students were able to continue their studies despite the pandemic.

The digital pandemic semesters have shown the potential and opportunities that digitalisation brings to everyday university life. They were also characterised by a willingness to try out new things, develop creative solutions together, and leave old paths behind. During this time, however, it also became clear how important personal encounters in everyday university life are for the learning process—digital solutions could not be replaced these.

With the end of the pandemic, the question arises as to what role digitalisation and the applications we have become familiar with will play at the university in the future. With all due respect for traditional teaching and learning formats: Digitalisation is a social transformation process that is changing the way of teaching and learning. The students learned which digital opportunities they would not want to miss in the future and which they will demand from their school or university. Especially for universities, which are in intense competition with other educational institutions, dealing with digitalisation will be an opportunity to raise their profile and a differentiating factor for applicants.

The current discussion about Artificial Intelligence (e.g. tools like ChatGPT) shows that the status quo of digitalisation is not an endpoint, but transformation will continue. All stakeholders of universities must adapt their digital skills to keep up in the future.

In this case study, we analyse the digitalisation steps taken at BSP Business and Law School during the COVID-19 pandemic. BSP Business and Law School (BSP) is a state-approved university of applied sciences for management and law in Berlin, Germany. Teaching takes place in small student groups. The underlying philosophy is based on the didactical approach of interactive courses that combine theory and practice. For a long time, the BSP was a university with an emphasis on face-to-face teaching. However, since the impact of the COVID-19 pandemic, many digital solutions and, thus, new learning approaches have been tested—without neglecting the interactive face-to-face teaching philosophy.

In this article we present our proven learning and teaching model of the "three learning spaces". The "three learning spaces model" is a hybrid approach to redesigning and adapting knowledge transfer at universities. The model expands the traditional division of studies into contact studies with face-to-face teaching at the university and self-study at home to include the "digital space". This non-physical learning space is characterised by "guided self-learning", i.e., the course tutor is responsible for creating a meaningful framework for the activities in the third space. The students, in turn, are responsible for taking up these impulses and using them for their own learning process. Working with the "three learning spaces model" has shown, that hardware and software are only the necessary prerequisites for digital transformation in universities. The willingness of all those involved to change—the individual mindset—is fundamental to success.

1.2 Definition of Terms and Stages of Development

Digital transformation is often used to describe different developments. In a narrow technological definition digitisation describes the conversion of analogue values into formats that can be further processed with a computer. In a process-oriented definition, digitalisation is understood as the support of processes and their further processing by computers. This can go as far as to shift entire processes from the real world into the "digital space".

This technological development is associated with an economic and social change affecting all levels of society, which can also be understood under the term digitalisation and is often referred to as the "digital revolution" due to the profound change. New business models are emerging for companies (e.g. platform economy) and new forms of collaboration in organisations (e.g. home office). Efficiency gains and new business opportunities are driving digitalisation. In many cases, new competitors are emerging that can act faster than established companies and thus "disrupt" existing structures. Regarding personal data or the automation of activities previously performed by humans, digitalisation also raises legal and ethical questions.

Based on this definition, the digitalisation of the university means that tasks and processes are digitally mapped and redesigned (Hochschulforum Digitalisierung, 2021a). This offers new opportunities and relates to three areas:

1. Study and teaching: This area includes the actual teaching/learning programmes for acquiring skills, the examinations, and the entire interaction with students.
2. Research: This includes all research activities carried out by teaching staff, employees, and students.
3. University and science management: This refers to all activities that organise and support studies and research.

Digitalisation of higher education is not a new phenomenon. At the latest, it started with the advent of the personal computer, the widespread use and accessibility of the internet, and Office programmes in the 1990s. Even though e-mail, the internet, word processing, spreadsheets, and presentations have been widely used since then, classroom teaching, exam administration, and the university and academic management processes have not changed significantly. Often, only the blackboard was replaced by PowerPoint slides. It was only with the necessary changes during the COVID-19 pandemic that people began to reconsider how processes in teaching and in university and academic management could be changed and reorganised.

1.3 Experiences from the Pandemic

The experiences of the COVID-19 pandemic in 2020 and 2021 are shaping the current discussion about the digitalisation of universities. The main results of the evaluation of the area of teaching and learning during the pandemic are summarised below:

- Classroom teaching and campus life as pillars: real learning and student development thrive through genuine, in-person encounters. Communication, collaboration, and learning thus become tangible social processes. Random informal encounters are an essential part of this process. Face-to-face teaching is and remains an indispensable core of the BSP Business and Law School's learning and teaching concept. Participation and interaction are often difficult to realise in digital formats.
- Openness and a willingness to experiment: The pandemic semesters were a unique opportunity to try out many things under the pressure of necessity. Digitalisation was not just talked about in working groups, workshops, or concepts—it was practised daily.
- Expanding teaching opportunities through digital teaching: The digital semesters have shown students and lecturers ways to expand their teaching and communication behaviour. Many elements were perceived as enriching and are now taken for granted. These elements must be retained and meaningfully linked to face-to-face teaching.
- Didactic thrust: Didactics is at least as important as technology. Didactic concepts from face-to-face teaching can only be transferred to digital teaching to a limited extent. Many lecturers have used new methods and gained experience in virtual semesters. This momentum must continue to be utilised.
- Exchange of experience between learners and lecturers: Exchanging experiences and mutual learning was an essential element of using new didactic methods and tools. A cross-university exchange also took place in various formats, and this should be continued.
- Blended learning as a model for post-pandemic teaching: Face-to-face teaching and the university as a place of encounter are the indispensable core of our learning and teaching concept. Teaching is enriched and enhanced by digital elements. Ideally, classroom teaching and digital elements complement each other seamlessly. Interaction fosters the development of new forms of social dynamics.

1.4 Opportunities and Limits

Digitalisation offers a wide range of opportunities and can improve the quality of studying and teaching (Wissenschaftsrat, 2022b). It can also lead to the more efficient fulfilment of university and academic management tasks. However, all digitalisation measures are not an end in themselves but serve the overarching goal of a university to enable students to acquire the best possible skills.

The following opportunities can be identified in connection with digitalisation:

- Efficiency gains in all university processes: The simplification of procedures, avoiding duplication of work and faster processing of tasks are key expectations for simplifying all university-related processes.
- Integration into the digital reality of life: The reality of student life is digital and organised via smartphone. If the university wants to be recognisable, it must integrate itself into this reality.
- Profile building: Digital offerings are expected by applicants, becoming a differentiating feature and decision criterion when choosing an university.
- More opportunities for activating teaching: A greater variety of teaching methods and formats that involve students more closely and intensify interaction and collaboration will become increasingly important.
- Support for collaborative team learning: Overall, more opportunities to work together on questions and tasks are at the centre of learning and teaching.
- Change in the teaching, learning, and study culture: Teaching- and learning-contexts are increasingly geared towards reflection, intellectual independence, self-determination, and self-organisation.
- Individualisation of studies and supervision: It is essential to tailor the content of the degree programme even more precisely to the students' level of development and to provide better individual support and supervision.
- Data-based learning: If more data is available about students' learning behaviour, teaching content can be better adapted to the learning situation.
- Skills acquisition: Preparing students for a digitalised professional world by acquiring the relevant skills during their studies is more effective than ever before.

In addition to these opportunities, digitalisation also comes with certain constraints. A key concern here is the potential loss of real and personal connections. Learning and teaching are inherently a social process that thrives on interactions, including unplanned ones. This article, therefore, argues that physical presence at the university must remain an essential element for learning. Digitalisation offers a wide range of opportunities in this respect.

2 Digitalisation in Studies and Teaching

2.1 Forms of Digitally Supported Teaching

Digitally supported teaching here refers to all forms of teaching in which digital elements are used. Many students and lecturers first encountered with digitally supported teaching during the pandemic. However, digitally supported teaching is much more than just broadcasting a course in a virtual space. Many forms of digitally supported teaching are possible between purely face-to-face teaching and distance learning. Traditional face-to-face teaching with lecturers and students on site can be underpinned with more or less digital aids. Returning to face-to-face teaching does not necessarily mean that fewer digital elements are used in teaching.

The transition to blended learning is fluid. Blended learning is characterised by the fact that face-to-face and digital elements are "mixed" together to exploit the advantages of both settings. Students can access content offered for preparation or follow-up flexibly in terms of time and location. This can be texts, tasks, or videos. There is no standardised definition of how significant the face-to-face or online component of blended learning should be.

A unique form of blended learning is the flipped classroom. Here, learners use digitally provided content and tasks to acquire predominantly knowledge-based competence dimensions before the actual course, regardless of time and location. This approach is then used to reflect on and consolidate the knowledge components and to focus on further competence dimensions (communicative and cooperative competences, competence dimension professionalism and scientific self-image), work on tasks in learning groups, or receive advice from the lecturer.

Hybrid teaching refers to teaching programmes in which some participants are not on site but connected digitally. If all participants are connected digitally, this is referred to as purely online teaching or virtual teaching. The term digital teaching is often used in two ways. Firstly, it is a synonym for online teaching or virtual teaching. Digital teaching is also used as an abbreviation for digitally supported teaching. As digitally supported teaching is more than just online teaching, the abbreviated term "digital teaching" is not used here to avoid confusion with the terms "online teaching" or "virtual teaching".

2.2 Learning and Teaching Concept

Every university and degree programme places special demands on the teaching method chosen. This means that learning and teaching are always highly specific processes that are difficult to summarise in a concept that takes all situations into account.

Good teaching is more than just imparting knowledge. The term "knowledge transfer" implies the transfer, transmission, and imparting of knowledge to learners.

Based on constructivist learning theory and competence orientation, competence development occurs in an individual, active, and constructive process. Lecturers must, therefore, create situations and environments for learners in which they can make constructive contributions of their own (Kerres & de Witt, 2002). Various studies have demonstrated the positive effect of "activating learning" (Wissenschaftsrat, 2022b).

Digital technologies are particularly suitable for supporting activating learning methods, as they offer a wide range of opportunities for interactive engagement with content. "Skills acquisition" is, consequently, a collaborative process, joint teamwork between lecturers and students. The German Science and Humanities Council—Wissenschaftsrat—has recommended that knowledge creation (referred to as "knowledge acquisition" by the Wissenschaftsrat) should be increasingly characterised by reflection, application, and interaction (Wissenschaftsrat, 2022a).

In its position paper, the Wissenschaftsrat recommends reducing the number of compulsory courses and examinations in favour of guided self-study. Students should be given more time for self-determined learning, and the choice and decision-making options in the course of their studies should be expanded in order to promote students' independence. Digitalisation is one way of achieving this goal, as it provides additional opportunities for individualised and collaborative learning and closer support for students.

This results in the summarised learning and teaching concept of the BSP Business and Law School:

- Learning thrives on personal encounters, interaction, and experience.
- Teaching structured topics sets impulses, supports learners, and activates them to participate and think ahead.
- The university offers the best possible conditions for this on-site and digitally with its equipment and teaching staff.
- Face-to-face teaching and on-site encounters are the core of our learning and teaching concept. Digital elements complement, support, and expand this core.

Under the heading of "employability", universities have been expected, since the Bologna reform, to place greater emphasis on developing skills and preparing students for the labour market. In the sense of a competence-oriented degree programme, students should not only acquire knowledge and skills, but also broader competences, which are categorised into the following dimensions in the Qualifications Framework for German Higher Education Qualifications (HQR):

- Knowledge and understanding with the subcategories
  - Broadening knowledge
  - Deepening knowledge
  - Understanding knowledge
- Use, application, and generation of knowledge with the subcategories
  - Utilisation and transfer
  - Scientific innovation

- Communication and co-operation
- Scientific self-image/professionalism (Kultusministerkonferenz, 2017)

Activating forms of teaching and learning play a vital role in skills-orientated training. The development of competences can also be promoted through personal experience and application.

2.3 *Roles of Lecturers and Learners*

The above learning and teaching concept raises the question of how lecturers and learners understand their roles. This analysis is grounded in transformative leadership theory (Bass & Riggio, 2005; Winkler & Niedermeier, 2020; Hochschulforum Digitalisierung, 2021b), using transformative teaching and learning as fundamental framework. The basis for this is a changed understanding of the roles of lecturers and learners: Less delivering content, more training in reflection and critical problem-solving skills as well as counselling students in their learning processes (Wissenschaftsrat, 2022a). This is associated with a change in the level of activity of lecturer and students. Figure 1 shows different forms of teaching and the activity of lecturer and students.

The model of "transformative leadership", which originates from leadership theory, is used as a reference for understanding the roles of lecturers and learners. In terms of transformative leadership, the focus is on four characteristics of the leader. These can be applied to the situation of lecturers as follows:

1. Idealised Influence (role model function): Lecturers act as role models. They take responsibility for their own actions and decisions.

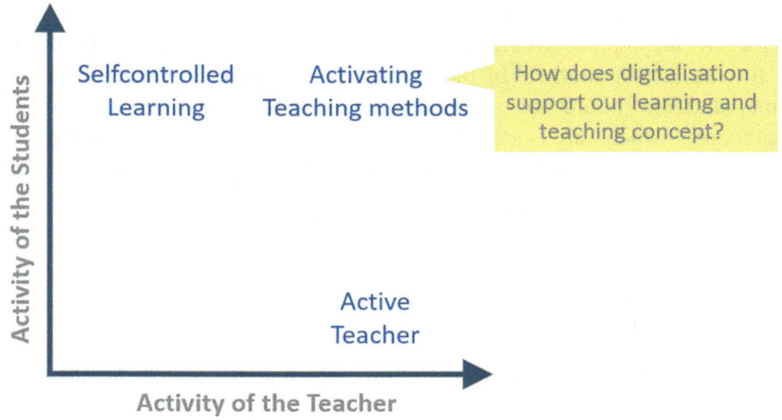

Fig. 1 Forms of teaching. Source: Graphic by the authors

2. Inspirational Motivation: Lecturers motivate people to work together. They convey meaning and goals. This is intended to strengthen the learners' self-motivation.
3. Intellectual stimulation: Lecturers provide intellectual impulses and stimulation.
4. Individualised Consideration (individual support): Lecturers provide learners with individualised support depending on their level of learning.

The following section examines the specific measures —particularly digital ones—that can shape this interaction.

2.4 Three Learning Spaces

Following the recommendations of the Wissenschaftsrat (2022a), which suggest reducing the number of compulsory courses and examinations in favour of guided self-study, we propose a model here that integrates this approach. It also aligns with the requirement for future studies to emphasise reflection, intellectual independence, and freedom of action. This leads to the creation of the concept of the three learning spaces.

The traditional division of the degree programme is based on two learning spaces for students (this division can also be found in module handbooks, for example): There is contact study with classroom teaching (at the university—the first room) and self-study ("at home"—the second room). The focus of traditional teaching is on contact study. As the name suggests, self-study is mainly left to the students themselves. The teaching workload, measured in terms of semester hour per week, reflects this division and centres the lecturer's responsibility primarily in the context of contact studies.

If students are given more personal responsibility for their studies, the "digital space" is created as a third (non-physical) learning space alongside the university and their homes. It is characterised by "controlled self-learning", i.e. the lecturer is responsible for creating a meaningful framework for the activities in the third space. The learner, in turn, is responsible for taking up these impulses and utilising them for their own learning process.

Digitalisation in particular opens up a wide range of possibilities for interacting with students and managing activities in the digital space. Only digitalisation makes it possible to overcome the previous division into contact studies and self-study and to create a new digital space as an intermediate space for activities.

However, digitalisation not only changes the division between classroom teaching and self-study but also creates other and new opportunities to fill the classroom teaching. Blended learning, as the blending of traditional and digital teaching elements, therefore, refers to all three learning spaces. Figure 2 shows examples of activities in the three learning spaces.

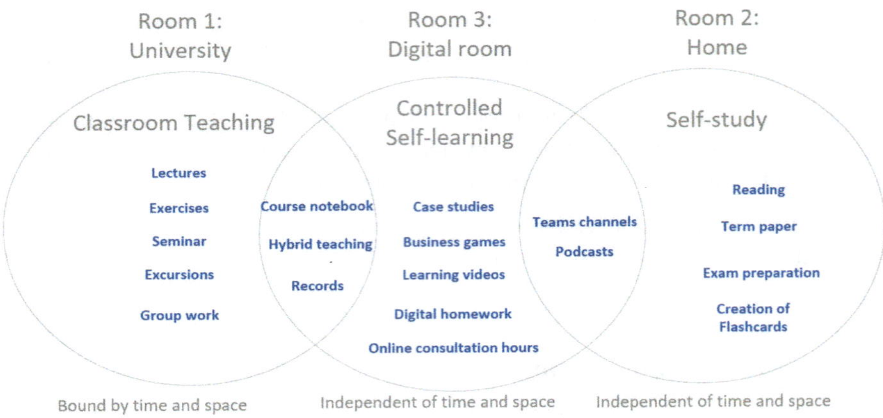

Fig. 2 Examples of activities in the three learning spaces. Source: Graphic by the authors

2.5 University as a Meeting Place

Despite all the advantages of digitalisation described above, experience during the COVID-19 pandemic has also shown how important face-to-face meetings are for learning. This observation has given face-to-face teaching and opportunities to gather at the university a greater significance. The experiences from the first post-pandemic semesters further highlight this importance. In particular, the introduction of the "digital room" has redefined the value of the traditional classroom.

In addition to classrooms, spaces for informal interactions and spontaneous encounters at the university are gaining eminence. Students increasingly recognise and consciously perceive the university as a place to connect and meet other students and educators. As a result, the design of communal and meeting spaces is thus becoming more important as a counterbalance to digital environments.

3 Willingness to Change and Innovation

3.1 Mindset and Skillset

Three elements are required to implement successful digitalisation: hardware, software, and mindset. None of these building blocks works alone. Hardware and software form the necessary technical prerequisites, while the mindset of those involved determines the extent to which implementation is tackled. The mindset of those involved plays a special role here: if the mindset—understood as the willingness and openness to change—does not fit, many opportunities remain unutilised. Therefore, it is essential to cultivate curiosity for new possibilities and strengthen the willingness to engage.

The basis for successful digitalisation is the willingness of all university members to embrace change in general and digital transformation in particular. Even several semesters after the pandemic, there is still room for improvement in understanding didactic concepts and effectively using digital tools. In addition to the specific (technical) skills (digital skillset), the mindset of those involved in change is the most crucial factor here. A digital mindset is often seen as a modern alternative or an important addition to traditional patterns of thought and behaviour.

While a traditional mindset is defined by a focus on security and the desire to maintain established patterns of success, a digital mindset is emphasising an open attitude towards technological progress (Zeichhardt, 2024). This results in the following characteristics of a modern mindset for digital change:

- Curiosity-driven learning: Curiosity to try out technical solutions with an open mind.
- Innovation orientation: Leaving comfort zones and questioning old patterns.
- Agility: Try out technical solutions quickly and flexibly instead of creating comprehensive plans because the environment is very dynamic
- Fault tolerance and resilience: Don't be discouraged if something doesn't work straight away.
- Collaboration: Developing solutions together in interdisciplinary teams
- Sharing is caring: Share positive and negative experiences with digitalisation with others.

It is key to emphasise that a digital mindset should not be misunderstood as a superior antithesis to traditional attitudes and behaviours. Rather, it is about accepting and uniting, balancing and integrating, established and modern attitudes in an organisation in equal measure. In this context, the central ability of ambidexterity is often cited. This refers to the adoption of a meta-perspective that bridges tradition and innovation. Ambidexterity implies integrative "different" thinking on several levels and, thus, situational adaptation to different areas of tension. In the context of implementing a university's digitalisation strategy, this includes the ability to decide which of the three learning spaces must be used for specific learning objectives.

In addition to the mindset, the skillset of those involved in the digital transformation is of particular importance in a further step. Digital change only becomes real through concrete skills and actions.

The EU Commission's "DigComp2.1—Digital Competence Framework for Citizens" is an exemplary approach to a digital competence approach (Vuorikari et al., 2022). This identifies the following five areas of competence with specific skills that are seen as central to the digital age:

1. *Information and data literacy*
2. *Communication and collaboration*
3. *Creation of digital content (digital content creation)*
4. *Safety*
5. *Problem solving*

3.2 Status and Digital Readiness

The following section shows the specific activities that have been and are being used to develop the above outlined digital mindset and skillset at the BSP Business and Law School at various levels.

Develop Digital Communication Skills

To develop digital communication skills, it is essential to focus on working and collaborating effectively in both digital and hybrid environments. Achieving this requires actively exemplifying digitalisation in everyday university life, particularly through hybrid working and collaboration in teaching, research, and university communication. A key component of this approach is the utilisation of the Microsoft 365 ecosystem, encompassing all Microsoft programmes and tools.

Specifically, using Microsoft Teams functions, such as video calls, chats, digital course notebooks, whiteboards, OneNote, and shared documents, is vital. Additionally, establishing subject-specific teams across faculties can foster collaboration and innovation. Microsoft Teams channels should be leveraged for both formal and informal communication with students and colleagues, enhancing the flow of information and engagement. For instance, we created a Microsoft Teams team called "open science" to share the latest interdisciplinary findings on digitalisation topics across universities. The channel is accessible to all employees and students.

Regarding didactic teaching design, digital tools like Microsoft Whiteboard, Mural, Miro, Kahoot Quiz, Mentimeter, Padlet, Forms surveys, and gamification elements, such as business games from the TopSim Cloud, are particularly useful. Blended learning approaches, which integrate videos, TED Talks, and other multimedia elements into teaching—whether online, hybrid, or face-to-face—are also crucial for creating a dynamic and engaging educational experience.

Using Digital and Hybrid Spaces Confidently and Situationally with Digital Content

Confident and situational use of digital content is essential for communication and collaboration. This approach begins with the development of the "three spaces" metaphor, designed to communicate the university's digital change requirements. It also involves the creation of various innovative online and hybrid formats.

During the pandemic, the university welcomed first-semester students with an online event using Work Adventure software, which created a digital replica of the university, including online spaces and gamification elements. To maintain collegial exchange, regular virtual coffee breaks were held in Microsoft Teams, helping to foster a sense of community despite physical distance.

Initiatives such as a photo collage from home offices titled "Together through time", along hashtags like #westayconnected and "Keeping distance together" were introduced to strengthen campus culture during challenging times. The university also organised online and hybrid events, including the "Curriculum Extended" lecture marathon, which spanned 12 h, featured 24 topics, and counted on 24 professors.

Digital and hybrid information evenings and campus days became regular occurrences, as did the production of a university podcast, which ran for two seasons with five episodes each. The "Future of Education" competition evolved into a 24-h cross-university hybrid hackathon, pushing the boundaries of collaborative learning and innovation.

The BSP Business and Law School also introduced a hybrid event series, "students meet experts", featuring distinguished international guests from various fields. New social media formats, such as *Insta Live*, were launched to discuss higher education topics with a broader audience. Additionally, establishing hybrid and online conferences, including lecture series, provided further opportunities for academic engagement.

Finally, opening a new café and student lounge as co-working spaces and meeting rooms offered a physical complement to these digital and hybrid initiatives, providing a versatile environment for collaboration and community building.

Curiosity-Driven: Keep Trying Out New Digital Tools, Experiment and Stay Curious

A curiosity-driven approach to digital innovation encourages continuous experimentation and exploration of new tools. This mindset element is essential for integrating cutting-edge technology into teaching and university operations.

One way this is achieved is by incorporating serious games into the curriculum, such as computer-based simulation games from the TOPSIM–Cloud. Additionally, testing and reflecting on new media in teaching, like using Flipgrid videos as an internal social learning network, have helped to create more engaging learning environments.

Participation in conferences, trade fairs, and festivals on digital topics, such as *re:publica*, Work Awesome, the BETT show, and Berlin Hub, with students and colleagues, allowed the university community to stay abreast of the latest trends and ideas. This exposure to new developments in digital education fuels innovation and provides fresh insights for academic and administrative practices.

An experimental approach is also applied to the use of Minecraft Education in teaching. Sharing these experiences and exchanging ideas with the broader university community, as was done at the *University:Future Festival 2023* organised by the Hochschulforum Digitalisierung, fosters collaboration and the spread of best practices.

Finally, the integration of holistic software solutions, such as HubSpot, for process optimisation in university management, demonstrates a commitment to continually improving operational efficiency through digital tools. This ongoing experimentation and adaptation ensure that the university remains at the forefront of digital innovation, benefiting both students and faculty.

Master IT Infrastructure, Acquire Digital Skills and Deepen Knowledge

At the university, members are equipped with a wide range of hardware, such as PCs, laptops, webcams, headsets, microphones, and portable camera sound systems, as well as software, including the university intranet, a VPN client, Adobe Connect, Microsoft 365 (with a focus on Microsoft Teams), and KuraCloud, to support online applications.

To enhance hybrid learning and collaboration, touchscreen monitors are utilised, with employees participating in professional *Sharp BIG PAD* training courses, culminating in certification. The university's IT department provides on-site technical support, both ad hoc and through a ticket system, ensuring that technical issues are promptly addressed.

To further support users, explanatory videos and manuals are available, offering clear guidance on how to effectively use the provided hardware and software. Additionally, university members have access to various online databases through the library portal, such as EBSCOhost, which facilitates access to scientific literature for research and teaching purposes.

Finally, the institutionalisation of digitalisation at the university management level underscores the importance of these initiatives, ensuring that digital skills and IT infrastructure remain a priority and continue to evolve across the institution. This comprehensive approach enables all members of the university community to deepen their knowledge and confidently navigate the digital landscape.

Sharing Is Caring: Trying Out Digitalisation and Sharing Digitalisation Experiences

The principle of "sharing is caring" is central to a modern digital mindset, emphasising the importance of adopting digital media and technical tools quickly, experimenting with them, and sharing both positive and negative experiences.

Peer learning plays a significant role in this process, with colleagues learning from one another through structured groups coordinated by the Rectorate, as well as in self-organised forums and channels within Microsoft Teams. This collaborative approach fosters a culture of continuous learning and mutual support.

The university also engages in knowledge transfer and close exchange with the Mittelstand-Digital Zentrum Zukunftskultur (a centre for digitalisation processes in small and medium-sized enterprises), a third-party funded project. The digitalisation initiatives developed through this project, such as guidelines, publications, and events, are integrated into the university's own practices.

Regular meetings in dedicated *Microsoft Teams* groups provide ongoing opportunities for discussion and exchange on digitalisation topics. These sessions contribute to the development of a digital teaching roadmap, guiding the university's efforts to enhance online education.

For peer-learning activities we established the "Digital Booster" format, an online conference within the university network to discuss didactics and tools in online teaching. This format, alongside the cross-university working group "Digitalisation", facilitates broad exchange within the university network, ensuring that best practices and innovative ideas are shared widely.

To support these efforts, the university's IT department offers various training courses for employees and lecturers, particularly on the use of touchscreen monitors and hybrid teaching. Additionally, explanatory videos are provided, making it easier for staff to adopt and implement new digital tools effectively.

Through these initiatives, the university not only encourages the exploration of digital tools but also ensures that the collective experiences of its members are shared, enhancing the institution's overall digital competency.

4 Future Vision of a Digital Learning Culture

At the beginning of the COVID-19 pandemic in March 2020, numerous new digitalisation measures were implemented at the BSP Business and Law School to ensure smooth university operations under the pandemic conditions, particularly contact restrictions. Many of the measures successfully tested during this time are still integrated into everyday university life today, allowing digitalisation in studying and teaching to remain an active part of daily routines, while continuously fostering the development of digital skills for all those involved in the university environment.

Digitalisation at universities will continue to play a very prominent role in their further development in the future. Current developments in the field of Artificial Intelligence in particular will trigger many more far-reaching changes. The wide range of digital options that complement the programmes and didactic concepts of a face-to-face university not only offers great potential for profiling and differentiation from competitors in the education market but also enables a contemporary advancement of study and teaching for a world that increasingly demands flexibility, networking, and location-independent collaboration.

A vision for a digital learning culture summarises these considerations. It is intended to serve as a guide for all educators and learners and to accompany further digital development.

- The learning culture in higher education is still often shaped by an awareness of the value of in-person encounters, the importance of face-to-face teaching, and the understanding of learning as a social process
- Digital elements complement and expand the didactic possibilities. They are seen as an opportunity to enhance the learning experience and, thus, the learning success.

We are open and keen to experiment to facilitate innovation, learn quickly from mistakes and share.

References

Bass, B. M., & Riggio, R. E. (2005). *Transformational leadership* (2nd ed.). Psychology Press.

Hochschulforum Digitalisierung (Ed.). (2021a). *Digitalisierung in Studium und Lehre gemeinsam gestalten: Innovative Formate, Strategien und Netzwerke*. Springer Fachmedien.

Hochschulforum Digitalisierung (Ed.). (2021b, October). Leadership—von der Theorie zur Praxis. *strategie digital—Magazin für Hochschulstrategien im digitalen Zeitalter, 1*, 4–11.

Kerres, M., & de Witt, C. (2002). Quo vadis Mediendidaktik? Zur theoretischen Fundierung von Mediendidaktik. *Medienpädagogik: Zeitschrift für Theorie und Praxis der Medienbildung, 6*, 1–22.

Kultusministerkonferenz. (2017). *Qualifikationsrahmen für deutsche Hochschulabschlüsse*. Retrieved from https://www.kmk.org

Vuorikari, R., Kluzer, S., & Punie, Y. (2022). *DigComp 2.2: The digital competence framework for citizens* (EUR 31006 EN). Publications Office of the European Union. https://doi.org/10.2760/115376

Winkler, K., & Niedermeier, S. (2020). Führung in der digitalisierten Arbeitswelt. In S. Wörwag & A. Cloots (Eds.), *Arbeitskulturen im Wandel* (pp. 209–222). Springer Gabler.

Wissenschaftsrat. (2022a). *Empfehlungen für eine zukunftsfähige Ausgestaltung von Studium und Lehre* (Drs. 9470-22). Wissenschaftsrat.

Wissenschaftsrat. (2022b). *Empfehlungen zur Digitalisierung in Lehre und Studium* (Drs. 9848-22). Wissenschaftsrat.

Zeichhardt, R. (2024). How to develop a digital mindset: Insights from executive coaching in Germany. In K. Bodrožić-Brnić, V. Schulte, & T. Thiessen (Eds.), *Leadership for digital transformation—Navigating the journey* (pp. 129–138). Springer Nature.

Markus Langenfurth has been the Rector of BSP Business and Law School since 2023. He studied Economics at the University of Münster (Westfälische Wilhelms-Universität Münster) and later completed his PhD at the Institute for Industrial Economics on the topic The Global Telecommunications Market. From 2000 to 2003, he gained extensive experience in strategy and process consulting for telecommunications and IT companies while working at a management consultancy. His current research focuses on modern forms of teaching and learning and education technology.

Rainer Zeichhardt is a Professor and Prorector for Innovation and Digitalisation at the BSP Business and Law School in Berlin, with a focus on education and digital transformation. Holding a doctoral degree in Business Administration and Management from Free University of Berlin, he works with the Mittelstand-Digital Zentrum Zukunftskultur, funded by the German Federal Ministry for Economic Affairs and Climate Action, helping small and medium-sized businesses with digital shifts. His research interests include leadership adaptation in digital contexts, conflict resolution, and change management.

Digital Literacies: Reflections on Its Challenges and Potentials Through YouTube

Stefania Fachina, Caroindes Julia Corrêa Gomes, Evelyn Araripe, and Vânia Gomes Zuin Zeidler

Abstract This theoretical article aims to reflect on the presence of digital technologies in all spheres of life and their influence on the formation of subjectivities and identities. To this end, we examine the challenges and potentials of digital literacy offered by the YouTube video platform, using the concepts of cultural industry and Halbbildung as categories of analysis. Educators have used this platform to disseminate information and stimulate learning through the virtual environment, but on the other hand, mostly consumerist practices are widely disseminated in this space, mainly aimed at children, mixing entertainment and education to create an unsustainable modus operandi that takes effect with the very development of children and adolescents. Thinking about an education that is coherent with contemporary demands, but that also understands digital technologies as essential for the constitution of citizenship, we propose to broaden the concept of digital literacy by linking it to other literacies, with the aim of promoting more ethical, healthy, and responsible interactions.

Keywords Digital literacy · YouTube · Cultural industry · Halbbildung · Consumerism

S. Fachina
Federal University of São Carlos, São Carlos, Brazil
e-mail: stefania@estudante.ufscar.br

C. J. C. Gomes
Federal University of Bahia, Salvador, Brazil
e-mail: caroindesgomes@ufba.br

E. Araripe
Federal University of São Carlos, São Carlos, Brazil

Leuphana University, Lüneburg, Germany
e-mail: evelyn.araripe@leuphana.de

V. G. Z. Zeidler (✉)
Leuphana University, Lüneburg, Germany
e-mail: vania.zuin@leuphana.de

K. Bodrožić-Brnić et al. (eds.), *Digital Transformation in Knowledge Transfer*, Digital Transformation and Innovation,
https://doi.org/10.1007/978-3-032-07329-7_14

1 Introduction

The increasing and interrelated demands of the planet present a significant challenge that necessitates actions (individual and collective) that ensure the well-being of physical and human environments. These actions must be planned and executed with consideration of not only economic perspectives, as has been the case over the past few decades, but also with a focus on other important factors (Zuin & Kümmerer, 2021).

In this context, the potential of education to develop critical thinking and conscious, responsible decision-making is clear. Education, whether in schools and universities or in lifelong learning, provides opportunities to empower people and train leaders who are committed to the possible and necessary transformations (Araripe & Zeidler, 2024).

Digital technologies also feature prominently in the training context, mainly because they have consolidated new ways of producing and disseminating knowledge and cognitive skills, creating sociability on the (fine) border between online and offline. In 2022, 79% of the world's young people aged between 15 and 29 were connected to the internet, with 98% of this demographic in Europe (International Telecommunication Union, 2022). The proportion of the population with internet access was below 50% in the least developed countries, estimated at 39%. This indicates that the availability of democratic access for the consolidation of rights and citizenship is also a controversial issue in a world that is increasingly developed in cyberspace (International Telecommunication Union, 2022). Furthermore, children are spending more time online. On average, a child in the world goes online for the first time every half a second to learn, socialise, and play. However, this exposure can also lead to the spread of criminal practices and discourse (United Nations, 2024).

Regarding the vulnerability of children and adolescents to the internet, it is important to highlight the forms of advertising made possible by the digital environment. Unlike traditional forms of advertising, these forms are uninterrupted and have characteristics that mask their real intentions. This leads to unthinking and exacerbated consumption, which is inconsistent with perspectives concerned with the present and future of the planet. While television once represented one of the most significant advertising platforms, if not the dominant one, by introducing new marketing techniques, digital technologies have further intensified the discourses of the cultural industry.

In light of these considerations, how might we conceptualise an education that is aligned with contemporary demands, yet also acknowledges the role of digital technologies as an integral aspect of historical and social reality, and thus as a fundamental component of the formation of citizenship?

Given that YouTube receives billions of monthly hits and is the second most accessed website in the world (Hostinger, 2024), a theoretical study was conducted to investigate the challenges and potential of digital literacy provided by the platform. The concepts of cultural industry and semi-formation (*Halbbildung*) were employed as analytical categories considering the universalisation and omnipresence of screens in all spheres of life (Sjöström et al., 2016). This study examines the phenomenon of consumerist marketing actions on YouTube that disguise themselves as entertainment and education. A prime example of this is popular unboxing videos featuring child influencers. However, the study also considers YouTube as a pedagogical tool, exploring the possibilities for teaching and learning through its critical, conscious, and responsible use. In conclusion, we emphasise the significance of critical and dialogical pedagogical approaches that facilitate emancipatory learning, enabling individuals to comprehend digital and media phenomena in the contemporary era.

2 Cultural Industry and *Halbbildung*: Developments in a Society of Universalisation and the Omnipresence of Screens

The term "information society" is particularly apt for characterising the contemporary situation, given the significant role played by digital technologies in the dissemination of content. In a globalised world, information has become a commodity, intensifying existing practices and reconfiguring others. Social media, for instance, can popularise anyone and create engagement, influence, and a way of acting and thinking (Zuin & Zuin, 2019).

If in the past people could distance themselves from screens when the machines were turned off, today this has become nearly impossible primarily due to the use of mobile phones, which represent our own identity and serve functions related to work, leisure, data processing and transmission, concentration and distraction, and even the perception of being ignored or noticed when we use them to access social media (Türcke, 2010; Zuin & Pacca, 2013).

These persistent stimuli transform the act of concentration into a process of dispersion, rendering it challenging to focus on the multitude of information and interconnections between them. The production of forms of forgetfulness is contingent upon the absence of a correlation between transmitted ideas and the lack of elaboration of concepts. According to Türcke (2010), this is a momentary state of attention that is successively interrupted by a multitude of stimuli, resulting in a state of distracted concentration.

> In the context of the current bombardment of audiovisual stimuli, which are consumed primarily using mobile phones, the dispersion of concentration is not merely a consequence but rather an integral and essential aspect of concentration. This is because the historical mediation of such stimuli has led to the formation of an addiction, which in turn has become an inherent and inseparable part of the very concept of concentration. (Zuin & Zuin, 2019, p. 97, translated by the authors)

In his writings, Adorno (2010) presents the logic of production, reproduction, and assimilation of content in a dispersed and unreflective way as a promise of complete and effective (and even more democratic) training. However, this logic reverberates in the opposite direction through the manifestation of superficiality, subordination, and conformism to what is set out. This configuration is characterised as *Halbbildung*, in which there is limited space for reflection and autonomy, because it is based on "a punctual, disconnected, interchangeable, and ephemeral state of information, which one knows will be blurred in the next instant by other information" (Adorno, 2010, p. 33). If the process of *Halbbildung* results in the reification of consciousness and the passivity of subjects, it is because they fail to fully absorb the formative potential of the content. Consequently, their thoughts and actions will be predisposed to the fetishisation provided by the culture industry (Adorno & Horkheimer, 1985; Adorno, 2010).

Although the term "cultural industry" was first used in the book Dialectic of Enlightenment, written by Theodor Adorno (1903–1969) and Max Horkheimer (1895–1973), in the context of North American capitalism during the 1950s, it has become a key concept for understanding the objective and subjective aspects that permeate cultural goods today, in the 2020s (Zuin & Zuin, 2019). This is mainly because, at the time, cinema was characterised by the philosophers as the strongest segment linked to the concept, and screens are now embodied as the very extension of people. Furthermore, exposure to screens occurs across social groups and manifests in all aspects of life at an early age. Children are automatically inserted into this environment by using tablets, mobile phones, and computers as part of their toy repertoire, making it challenging to consider the impact of the current reality on their development and learning (Andrade & Castro, 2020; Brum & Schimidt, 2017; Lira et al., 2019; Zuin et al., 2020).

In contrast with industrial capitalism's emphasis on material goods, post-industrialism emphasises intangible aspects, experiences, and sensations, as well as an educational aspect to consumption that influences styles and ways of being and acting (Lira et al., 2019). The obstacle arises from the immaterial nature of the commodities, which is based on the dynamics of desire and happiness attributed to consumption. The launch of a new product promises a "more efficient" version than the previous one. However, just days after the purchase, the product becomes outdated due to the release of an even "better" option. Furthermore, the functional mechanism of these products is designed to become obsolete, requiring replacement.

The cultural industry presents its products to people with promises of satisfaction and exclusivity, but its real intentions are pre-calculated to turn them into objects and eternal consumers (Adorno & Horkheimer, 1985). According to Zuin and Zuin (2019), consumer perception is more akin to desire than consciousness, creating the illusion that products provide a haven of immediacy and individuality. However, the individual becomes a secondary factor in the process once consciousness becomes irrational and, because of that, a calculated and necessary element in the system's functioning (Adorno & Horkheimer, 1985).

> The identification promoted by the cultural industry gives rise to an unsuccessful relationship between subjects and products (material, artistic, etc.). This is because it conceals taste and encourages conformity, resulting in a semi-formed consciousness that is alienated from its own reality. (Lira et al., 2019, p. 1963, translated by the authors)

The interrelationship between the cultural industry and *Halbbildung* can be understood as a cause-and-effect relationship within an unconscious society driven by excess. The abundance of goods and services, work, experiences, information, stimuli, and distractions hinder the production of meaning and learning due to their speed and frequency. Because digital technologies represent a primary conduit for the dissemination of the cultural industry and that exposure to screens is becoming increasingly prevalent from an early age, it seems reasonable to posit that the ramifications are evident in the trajectory of childhood, conditioning children to associate happiness with excess, particularly in the context of consumption.

Considering the questioning of the social *modus operandi*, which is based on unbridled consumption and devoid of concern for the socio-environmental consequences, it is imperative to reflect on the emergence of these discourses in the digital environment, and, most crucially, on their direction towards children. The following topic will examine the content posted on YouTube aimed at children and teenagers, with a view to analysing the obstacles and formative potential of the platform.

3 YouTube and the Advertising and Consumerist Practices Masked as Entertainment and Education

The advent of the internet and the current generation of children and teenagers, who have grown up surrounded by screens, have led to YouTube being used for a multitude of purposes and comprising a vast array of content that caters to the most diverse tastes and needs of the public. YouTube was created in February 2005 and has since established itself as the most popular video-sharing platform and the second most accessed website in the world, surpassed only by the Google search engine. The platform has over 2.5 billion monthly active users and over 34 billion hits (Alexa, 2023; Forbes, 2023; Hostinger, 2024; Statista, 2024), justifying its selection as the subject of investigation in this research. Its high quantitative indicators and multifaceted presence in digital culture explain this choice.

In the field of education, YouTube has established itself as a pedagogical tool for educators to disseminate educational content (Basgall et al., 2023; Güney, 2023; United Nations Educational, Scientific and Cultural Organisation, 2021; United Nations, 2024), as well as contributing to professional development (Salihoglu & Çetin, 2024). The platform can facilitate learning and serve as a valuable instrument for educational pursuits in early childhood. It has the potential to enhance children's understanding of the world, stimulate emotional growth, and develop skills such as creativity, imagination, and digital literacy. Additionally, it can assist in preparing school projects and tutorials for scientific activities (Neumann & Herodotou, 2020; Salihoglu & Çetin, 2024). The platform can be effective in other educational contexts, such as the implementation of the flipped classroom approach. In this method, students access materials outside the physical classroom as a preliminary preparation for working on them with the teacher's guidance (Junges & Gatti, 2020).

Furthermore, the deliberate and meticulous use of the platform has been shown to foster creativity and student engagement, thereby enhancing the teaching process and significantly improving comprehension of the subject matter (Junges & Gatti, 2020; Mion & Lopes, 2021).

In 2018, Arruda conducted a study analysing the implementation of digital technologies in the school curricula of the Organisation for Economic Co-operation and Development (OECD) member countries. The objective was to propose solutions aligned with each country's specific needs and explore beyond the challenges presented. The study found that digital technologies are a strategic asset for the 35 countries under consideration. It identified a range of opportunities based on the assumption that exercising citizenship, the enjoyment of rights and responsibility is not possible without the requisite skills to live in a digital culture.

Another significant development is the increase in the utilisation of YouTube, particularly following the advent of the Covid-19 pandemic. Integrating digital technologies has become necessary in numerous domains, including education. The sudden transition to remote teaching has compelled educators and students alike to explore and optimise digital platforms. YouTube has emerged as a valuable resource, offering access to a vast array of teaching content and facilitating more dynamic and visual interaction, which in many cases has proven more effective than traditional teaching methods (Ferreira, 2022; Mion & Lopes, 2021; Santana et al., 2023).

We agree with the potential benefits of using YouTube in an educational context. However, we emphasise the necessity for critical and autonomous reflection for these experiences to be fully accomplished. A society characterised by alienated consumption, violent, unequal, and exclusionary practices, and narratives such as "have me", "buy me", and "be me"—which promote an *ethos* of incessant consumption (Padilha et al., 2022; Zuin et al., 2020)—has at its disposal structures that mask its unsustainable essence and help to propagate it.

In this context, there are concerns about the pervasive and unawareness use of these and other platforms, including the risks associated with exposure to commercial advertisements and inappropriate or criminal content. This underscores one of the main dangers faced by children and adolescents in their exposure to the digital environment. Children, being at a peculiar stage of development, are especially vulnerable to the negative effects of commercial exploitation on the internet. Furthermore, the absence of parental supervision and the lack of critical education aimed at digital literacy can exacerbate the situation, exposing children and adolescents to harmful influences that can negatively impact their physical, cognitive, psychological, emotional, social, and environmental development (Güney, 2023; Neumann & Herodotou, 2020; United Nations, 2024; Zuin et al., 2020).

This scenario is corroborated by sample surveys indicating that 80% of children aged 0–7 use YouTube, with 59% using YouTube Kids. Additionally, children aged 3 and older are increasingly engaged on the platform, accessing a wide range of content. For example, the number of downloads of YouTube Kids app has already exceeded 10 million worldwide (Neumann & Herodotou, 2020). A further survey indicated that a significant proportion of young Americans aged 13–17 have regular access to YouTube, with nine out of ten teenagers interviewed reporting that they use it (Pew Research Center, 2023).

An increasingly popular video genre on YouTube is the unboxing of toys, featuring child influencers who employ the act of filming the process of unpacking a product to create a sense of anticipation for what is to come. The unboxing of a toy can be seen to have marketing intentions that stimulate the logic of "having, consuming, accumulating, and discarding" (Bauman, 2001) and "correct and desirable" standards of what to have and how to be. This occurs at an early age and has the effect of moulding subjectivities and identities. It is also pertinent to consider the children's role in the context of peer persuasion, given their demonstrated communicative abilities (Padilha et al., 2022; Zuin et al., 2020).

In their analysis of the objective and subjective aspects of YouTube videos starring children, Bragaglia and Ferreira (2016) observed that advertising content is presented in approximately 96% of the videos. The study's findings indicate that the channels are utilised as a marketing tool and exhibit technical and advertising maturity in their production. This induces consumption in an ostentatious and targeted manner, and through expressions of happiness in the relationship with goods and services.

Despite the illegality and abuse of advertising to children being considered by many countries and legislative efforts being made in this direction, the market continues to find ways of doing it. "New marketing strategies not only circulate in conventional media but also find opportunities in personal relationships to generate the purchase and sale of their products" (Brum & Schimidt, 2017, p. 10).

One example that illustrates this problem is the case study of the doll "L.O.L. Surprise! and its plastic world" (Fachina et al., 2024; Zuin et al., 2020). A critical analysis of an interdisciplinary approach to this toy reveals several concerning issues. These include the early encouragement of unthinking consumption of plastic toys and the potential risks to human health, children's education, and the environment (Fachina et al., 2024; Zuin et al., 2020). Since its market release, the doll has achieved considerable popularity among children, with its success strongly linked to contemporary commercial strategies. These have been promoted by child influencers through the dissemination of unboxing videos on the video-sharing platforms YouTube and TikTok. Nevertheless, the toy and its mode of play provide a transient feeling of happiness and excitement, while simultaneously generating a considerable quantity of plastic waste. This, in turn, results in long-term environmental damage and the questionable teaching of unsustainable values to children (Fachina et al., 2024; Zuin et al., 2020).

Considering the growing prevalence of children's access to the internet, both as consumers and producers of content, new perspectives have emerged that challenge the traditional relationship between children and advertising. These narratives blur the lines between fun and consumption, naturalising the commercial appeal as part of play, and the experience of being a child. In this context, the boundaries between playing, learning, and demonstrating are blurred, with commercial elements becoming integrated into children's daily lives. This has a significant impact on their development and perception of the world. While children have the potential to transcend this logic, this is becoming increasingly difficult, given that the digital environment is also a driver of *Halbbildung*. The very nature of play is based on a stereotyped pattern that acts as a driver of subjectivity and identity formation. This can result in the significant underdevelopment of playful, creative, affective, and symbolic capacities (Lira et al., 2019).

The popularity of unboxing videos and the phenomenon of child influencers reflect a social construction that reconfigures the characteristics of childhood and contributes to the construction of a generation oriented towards consumption and ephemeral, superficial satisfaction. Although YouTube is also used to disseminate educational content, by taking students to the platform, children and teenagers are also invited to interact with abusive information and practices, as evidenced by the examples cited in this article.

Adorno and Horkheimer (1985) argue that the significance of the cultural industry lies in its capacity to shape the consciousness of its consumers. It can be argued that this logic is most effective when it is constructed and perpetuated in conjunction with one's own personal growth and perception of one's place in the world. It is therefore pertinent to consider the long-term effects of this way of thinking and acting from an early age. In this context, it is imperative to interrogate and reflect on the pervasive use of screens, to cultivate technological and social competencies with the objective of comprehending the content presented in the digital domain, to implement educational and regulatory measures to safeguard children and adolescents, and to foster a safer and healthier digital environment (Güney, 2023; United Nations, 2024; Zuin et al., 2020).

4 *Halbbildung* for Digital Literacy: Assumptions and Developments

In 2015, countries across the globe collectively pledged their commitment to the 17 Sustainable Development Goals (SDGs), with the objective of fostering initiatives that promote the well-being of both the physical and human environments, as well as the inherent dignity of all people (United Nations, 2015). One aspect of these endeavours is to ensure that the conditions are in place to guarantee access to the internet and to promote the conscious, ethical, and responsible use of the internet, particularly given that the ability to make decisions and to enjoy rights is increasingly dependent on the digital environment.

This perception is reinforced by the recognition of the crucial role that institutions and governments play in developing digital literacy. This enables people to search for, evaluate, and create content in favour of the common good. It also ensures that they are aware that cyberspace offers countless opportunities and risks, serving as a powerful mechanism for social protection. For instance, the age of Internet of Things has facilitated the dissemination of disinformation, leading to widespread distrust in scientific knowledge and democracy and has the potential to restrict people's freedom of choice (Zuin & Zuin, 2018). Moreover, algorithms can perpetuate prejudice by prioritising specific values and perceptions in search engines, including exacerbated consumption, as discussed in this text.

In light of the aforementioned considerations, it is important to cultivate autonomous thinking and establish interconnections and critical educational practices between education, reality, and digital culture. This facilitates reflection on these phenomena and their controversies within the classroom. Children and teenagers need to be immersed in the digital environment and equipped to navigate, consume, and produce content consciously and responsibly. As we are all immersed in this space daily, whether as spectators or producers, it is demanded to understand the boundaries of what is deemed acceptable and desirable in this context.

A review of the literature on the subject reveals that digital literacy can be effectively developed in school through approaches that integrate digital technologies and platforms, such as YouTube (Lima et al., 2024). Neumann and Herodotou (2020) highlight that the platform, when used with guidance from carers and/or teachers, can facilitate the acquisition of skills in early childhood. Ongoing dialogue and constructive engagement with adults regarding the content accessed provide opportunities for learning and mitigate the potential risks associated with inappropriate material, advertisements and marketing strategies. Furthermore, when selecting videos for children, it is essential to consider their age appropriateness, the quality and message of the content, the design features and their potential to support the intended educational objectives. For example, the authors cite the case of children watching a video on how to bake a cake and subsequently preparing the dessert with adult guidance. This approach fosters collaborative learning, enhances interpersonal relationships, and facilitates the acquisition of scientific knowledge essential for food preparation.

Aranha et al. (2019) emphasise the potential of YouTube as an educational tool for teaching science, particularly when its use is structured with clear objectives and aligned with the activities, enabling reflection on the social, cultural, and technological context of students and teachers. The authors indicate that videos can be located on various channels on the platform, including those designed for scientific experiments and the popularisation of science, as well as those created by students. They are employed in lessons to address specific content, illustrate it, raise awareness, evaluate learning outcomes, and simulate a given learning situation.

Alves Neto and Leite (2023) highlight the necessity of developing new methodologies and pedagogical practices in science education, with a particular focus on chemistry. These new approaches are intended to provide students with alternative avenues for engagement in the teaching and learning process, while simultaneously affording them opportunities to cultivate their autonomy. In this context, YouTube can be employed to elucidate uncertainties regarding content, furnish study materials, and facilitate the visualisation and comprehension of experimental activities.

It can be further observed that the platform offers a plethora of resources that facilitate digital literacy, integrating disparate areas of knowledge. The incorporation of interactive activities, such as online debates and discussions about the videos watched, facilitates the creation of a collaborative learning environment where students engage in the sharing of ideas and insights on the topics covered. The creation of educational videos or the documentation of scientific experiments enables students to develop creativity, communication skills, and critical thinking. Such practices not only enhance the learning experience by exploring diverse methodologies but also foster research competencies, information assessment, and collaboration in the digital domain.

Furthermore, the discussion of ethics, privacy, and online safety is crucial for fostering an awareness of rights and responsibilities within the digital sphere (United Nations Educational, Scientific and Cultural Organisation, 2021; United Nations, 2024), including for children and adolescents (United Nations, 2021). It is similarly important to recognise the value of interdisciplinarity, the diversity of cultures, and the promotion of conscious consumption, particularly in the context of online platforms such as YouTube, which offer an infinite, fast, and often unfiltered variety of information.

Moreover, the incorporation of YouTube into academic contexts has markedly transformed the landscape of teaching and learning in higher education. As a versatile platform for video content, YouTube offers a vast repository of educational resources that cater to a wide range of disciplines. The user-generated content (UGC) functionality enables educators and students to disseminate knowledge beyond the conventional classroom setting, thereby facilitating self-paced and flexible learning. Research indicates that platforms like YouTube are not only popular for entertainment purposes but are increasingly recognised as valuable educational tools that enhance understanding and retention of information (Chintalapati & Daruri, 2017). The Technology Acceptance Model (TAM) has been validated to demonstrate that perceived usefulness and ease of use exert a significant influence on the adoption of YouTube for learning purposes among stakeholders in higher education (Chintalapati & Daruri, 2017). Consequently, YouTube constitutes a key component of the digital literacy framework of contemporary higher education, offering students the opportunity to access and interact with a broad spectrum of learning materials.

Leuphana University in Germany provides an illustrative case study of the strategic integration of digital media in higher education, as exemplified by its Digital Transformation Lab for Teaching and Learning (DigiTaL) project. This initiative, which is supported by the Foundation for Innovation in Higher Education, has the objective of enhancing digital teaching and learning practices across the university's various faculties. The DigiTaL project encompasses a number of sub-projects, the objective of which is to develop innovative digital teaching methods, foster digital literacy, and promote internationalisation through digital platforms (Leuphana University, 2024). By employing digital tools such as YouTube, the project establishes avenues for novel forms of interaction and collaboration among faculty and students, thereby advancing the digital competencies indispensable for contemporary education. This approach is consistent with Leuphana's commitment to rethinking traditional educational models and fostering a learning environment that meets the demands of a digital society (Leuphana University, 2024).

In light of the aforementioned perspectives on digital literacy, it is crucial to underscore that it encompasses the creation, dissemination, and responsible utilisation of information and media, as well as an understanding of the underlying assumptions and implications of the content being conveyed (United Nations Educational, Scientific and Cultural Organisation, 2021). This signifies the use of cognitive abilities that are not only intrinsic to the digital domain but also cultivated in conventional technologies such as textbooks and television. These technologies interrelate and complement one another, mutually shaping the cognitive abilities that are essential for navigating the digital environment.

The act of reading a text on the internet involves the process of indexing, which is the creation of connections between ideas, concepts, and new information. This can be represented by a variety of different media, including words, images, animations, graphics, sounds, and videos. In this sense, it needs specific cognitive abilities that enable users to engage in critical communication within this dynamic and interactive context. Additionally, it requires the prior acquisition of knowledge and skills that predate the advent of the microelectronic revolution. Table 1 provides a summary of the elements of digital literacy, which are based on an interdependent and complementary relationship between information and media literacy (United Nations Educational, Scientific and Cultural Organisation, 2021).

Considering the interconnectivity between the three pillars and their constituent elements, we propose that the term in question be adopted in the plural form, specifically as "digital literacies". This encompasses the domains of information literacy, digital literacy, and media literacy (United Nation Educational Scientific and Cultural Organisation, 2021). This critical and holistic approach not only empowers subjects to consume and produce content ethically and responsibly but also enables

Table 1 A synthesis of the elements that constitute digital literacy, adapted from the United Nations Educational, Scientific and Cultural Organisation (2021, p. 9)

Information literacy	Digital literacy	Media literacy
Define and articulate information needs	Use of digital tools	Understand the role and functions of media, and Internet communications companies in democratic societies
Locate and access information	Understand digital identity	Understand the conditions under which media can fulfil their functions
Assess information	Recognise digital rights	Critically evaluate media content in the light of media functions
Organise information	Assess Artificial Intelligence issues	Engage with media for self-expression and democratic participation
Make ethical use of information	Improve how to communicate digitally	Review skills needed to produce user-generated content
Communicate information	Manage digital health	
Use information and communication technology skills for information processing	Practice digital security and safety	

them to identify and understand the various interfaces of information, media, and digital culture. This requires a new perspective that views digital technologies and their tools as more than just entertainment. Embracing a diverse approach to digital literacies implies a shift in means changing our attitude towards reality, adopting new ways of thinking and acting that prioritise collective well-being as a shared objective. This approach not only provides individuals with the skills to handle today's challenges but also encourages them to help build a more digitally inclusive and secure future (Fig. 1).

This approach, when combined with other technologies, allows for transcending the mechanisms of control and manipulation used by the cultural industry. In a society characterised by the pervasive distraction of digital media (Türcke, 2010), the promotion of traditional educational practices such as reading and baking in early childhood education appears to be at odds with the fluid and volatile habits of contemporary life (Bauman, 2008). This entails comprehending digital literacy not merely in terms of utilising of digital technologies, but rather in the context of autonomous, conscious, and therefore formative processes (Adorno, 2010). It is not the intention to discourage the use of these resources, as it is of paramount importance that students are not merely passive users, but rather that they are able to capitalise on the formative and social potential of these resources in a manner that is autonomous, critical, and responsible. It is therefore recommended that digital literacy be constructed on other forms of literacy and in particular that it be integrated

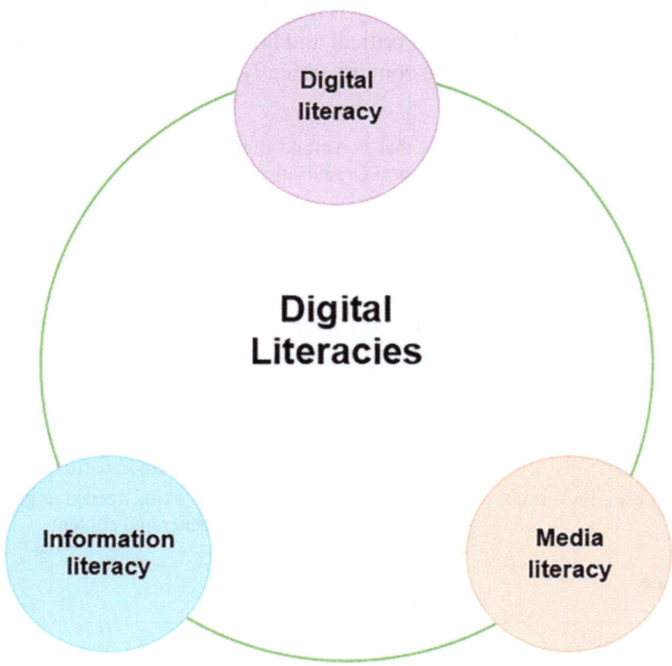

Fig. 1 Digital literacies (elaborated by the authors, 2024)

into the classroom with clearly defined pedagogical objectives that are aligned with the demands of the present era. This will ensure that the resources employed are not merely an end in themselves or are regarded as synonymous with innovative lessons.

The concept of *Bildung* in relation to digital literacies goes beyond the acquisition of knowledge. It also encompasses the technological and media aspects of digital society and their interconnections. This is approached from an emancipatory and transformative perspective, aiming to foster autonomous and reflective thinking. Equally important is the application of this concept to the development of a school that is more participatory, humane, and committed to digital citizenship, especially in terms of understanding and participating in social life. The availability of this *Bildung* provides an opportunity to transform our perceptions and actions concerning technology and its devices, as well as to create positive experiences and learning. This is a significant advantage, as it can serve as a counterpoint it can counteract the influences of *Halbbildung*, objectification, and market fetishisation from an early age. Consequently, it contributes to the development of more ethical, healthy, and responsible modes of interaction.

5 Final Considerations

We are situated in a technological and digital age where human experiences and interactions based on consumerism and superficiality are causing structural changes at all social levels, including education. The process of human development and pedagogical and cultural education is not the same as it was a long time ago. Historically, changes have always occurred; however, with the accelerated prominence of technological and media phenomena, transformations and relationships have become faster, fluid, more liquid, and volatile (Bauman, 2008).

This work has highlighted that digital technologies extend beyond the domain of mass media. The advent of digital era cannot be reduced to a mere marketing strategy for broadcasting advertisements to the public to promote content and sell goods and services. Furthermore, it can be argued that digital technologies can be classified as a form of culture. This is because digital platforms such as YouTube are always present and used in all spheres of life, including entertainment, research, and teaching and learning.

Considering this scenario, it is imperative to comprehend the existence of a historical, social, and cultural configuration that enables the emergence and accelerated advancement of not only digital technologies and the routine use of screens, but also the deeply entrenched phenomena that prescribe "correct and desirable" modes of being and having, thereby shaping our subjectivities and identities. A theoretical study of YouTube reveals how the cultural industry appropriates this space and intensifies the mechanisms of social tutelage through the phenomenon of *Halbbildung*, which is largely established by the excess of information broadcast uninterruptedly, without reflection. That's why a culture of consumerism also promotes a memory deficit, which to a certain extent is relevant to the development of relations between the productive forces and current relations of production, mainly because information can be instrumentally accessed at any time and in any space without being contextualised in relation to the historical mediations that engendered it. These are the rhythms of how the cultural industry renews itself in times of digital culture. So, this context of consumerism practices and perceptions begins as early as childhood, giving rise to an unsustainable *modus operandi* that takes effect alongside the very development of children and adolescents.

Reflecting on the possibility of an education that illuminates these contradictions while simultaneously embracing digital technologies may initially appear paradoxical. However, it tends towards an understanding of the objective and subjective structures that permeate today's cultural goods. This means that those who possess these devices must do so with awareness, responsibility, and ethics. The concept of non-fetishised use implies the existence of specific literacies, which extend beyond mere digital proficiency. These literacies encompass a range of technologies and the associated skills, fostering a dynamic of interdependence and complementarity. This perspective enables the transcendence of concentrated distraction (Türcke, 2010; Zuin & Zuin, 2018) through the consideration of the potential of "ordinary" resources such as books (even digital ones), which are often relegated to dusty shelves. The construction of pedagogical practices in this education should be based on the coherent planning of different technologies in accordance with the intended intentions. This approach should avoid the use of technologies as an end in themselves or as a synonym for innovation, which may not be sustainable.

The cultural industry and *Halbbildung* did not emerge only from digital culture; it is therefore essential to understand how their discourses come into effect, intensify existing mechanisms, and formulate new ones. This encompasses literacies, citizenship, fruition, and the guarantee of rights. Identifying emancipatory possibilities and challenges in the context of digital culture represents a means of acting in accordance with the necessary transformations and challenging the "natural and immutable" realities. The cultural industry, as an integral and fundamental part of this system, cannot be absorbed by people without the spirit of restlessness and discomfort, given the imminence of remaining and agreeing with the social and environmental injustices that have afflicted us for so long.

It should be noted that the subject of this work is of a wide-ranging nature and does not represent a comprehensive account. Rather, it is intended to provide a foundation for further, more in-depth research in this area. In any case, we are seeking to collaborate with this area of research and, in addition to these considerations, specifically related to digital culture, which is still in its inceptive phase and has significant potential for scientific output in the context of systems thinking with a relevant impact on and for a more just, literate, and democratic society.

Acknowledgments This work was supported by the Coordination for the Improvement of Higher Education Personnel (CAPES/Brazil) and National Council for Scientific and Technological Development (CNPq/Brazil).

References

Adorno, T. (2010). Teoria da semiformação. In B. Pucci, A. A. S. Zuin, & L. A. C. N. Lastória (Orgs.), *Teoria crítica e inconformismo: novas perspectivas de pesquisa* (p. 7–40). Autores Associados.

Adorno, T., & Horkheimer, M. (1985). *Dialética do esclarecimento: fragmentos filosóficos*. Jorge Zahar. 254p.

Alexa. (2023). *The top 500 sites on the web.* Retrieved from https://www.alexa.com/topsites

Alves Neto, F. D. A., & Leite, B. S. (2023). Análise dos vídeos produzidos nos canais mais acessados da plataforma YouTube em 2021 para o ensino de Química. *Paradigma, 44*(3), 62–86. https://doi.org/10.37618/PARADIGMA.1011-2251.2023.p62-86.id1322

Andrade, M. P., & Castro, G. G. S. (2020). Youtubers mirins e os vídeos unboxing: uma reflexão sobre a criança conectada nas tramas da publicidade contemporânea. *Revista Mídia e Cotidiano, 14*(1), 96–116. https://www.researchgate.net/publication/339394139_Youtubers_mirins_e_os_videos_unboxing_uma_reflexao_sobre_a_crianca_conectada_nas_tramas_da_publicidade_contemporanea

Aranha, C. P., de Sousa, R. C., Bottentuit Junior, J. B., Rocha, J. R., & Silva, A. F. G. (2019). O YouTube como ferramenta educativa para o ensino de ciências. *Olhares and Trilhas, 21*(1), 10–25. https://doi.org/10.14393/OT2019v21.n.1.46164

Araripe, E., & Zeidler, V. G. Z. (2024). Desafios da educação climática no Brasil: análise crítica à metodologia estrangeira como solução ao país. *Revista Eletrônica de Educação, 18*, e481438. https://doi.org/10.14244/198271994814. https://www.reveduc.ufscar.br/index.php/reveduc/article/view/4814.

Arruda, E. P. (2018). Implementação das tecnologias digitais nos currículos das escolas de Educação Básica dos países membros da OCDE. In I. C. P. Siqueira (Org.), *Subsídios à elaboração da BNCC: estudos sobre temas estratégicos da parceria CNE e Unesco* (pp. 32–78). Moderna.

Basgall, L., Guillén-Gámez, F. D., Colomo-Magaña; E., et al. (2023). Digital competences of teachers in the use of YouTube as an educational resource: Analysis by educational stage and gender. *Discover Education, 2*, 28. https://doi.org/10.1007/s44217-023-00054-x

Bauman, Z. (2001). *Modernidade líquida*. Zahar.

Bauman, Z. (2008). *Vida para consumo: A transformação das pessoas em mercadorias*. Zahar.

Bragaglia, A. P., & Ferreira, A. L. D. N. (2016). Os youtubers mirins e a felicidade através do consumo. *Temática, 12*(12), 57–73. https://periodicos.ufpb.br/ojs2/index.php/tematica/article/view/32058/16605

Brum, A., & Schimidt, S. (2017, June 17). YouTubers mirins: pequenos vendedores e grandes negócios. *XVIII Congresso de Ciências da Comunicação na Região Sul*, Caxias do Sul, RS, Brazil. Retrieved from https://portalintercom.org.br/anais/sul2017/resumos/r55-0872-1.pdf

Chintalapati, N., & Daruri, V. S. K. (2017). Examining the use of YouTube as a Learning Resource in higher education: Scale development and validation of TAM model. *Telematics and Informatics, 34*(6) issn:0736-5853. https://doi.org/10.1016/j.tele.2016.08.008

Fachina, S., Araripe, E., & Zeidler, V. G. Z. (2024). Defining greener, healthier and more sustainable toys: A case study of L.O.L. Surprise! *Sustainable Chemistry and Pharmacy, 41*, 101661, issn:2352-5541. https://doi.org/10.1016/j.scp.2024.101661

Ferreira, K. J. F. (2022). *Canal de YouTube como instrumento para letramento digital e protagonismo de alunos do ensino médio*. VIII CONEDU—GT 19 Tecnologias e Educação. https://doi.org/10.46943/VIII.CONEDU.2022.GT19.038

Forbes, D. (2023, June 28). *The 7 most accessed websites in the world.* Retrieved from https://www.linkedin.com/pulse/os-7-sites-mais-acessados-do-mundo-veja-destaques-desta/

Güney, K. (2023). Considering the advantages and disadvantages of utilising social media to enhance learning and engagement in k-12 education. *Research in Social Sciences and Technology, 8*(2), 83–100. https://doi.org/10.46303/ressat.2023.13

Hostinger, T. (2024, February 7). *Most visited websites globally—Mapping the digital giants [2024 Update]*. Retrieved from https://www.hostinger.com/tutorials/most-visited-websites-in-the-world

International Telecommunication Union. (2022). *Measuring digital development: Facts and figures 2022*. Retrieved from https://www.itu.int/itu-d/reports/statistics/facts-figures-2022/

Junges, D. L., & Gatti, A. (2020). Estado da arte sobre o youtube na educação. *Extensão Tecnológica: Revista de Extensão do Instituto Federal Catarinense, Blumenau, 7*(12), 62–70. https://doi.org/10.21166/rext.v0i12.284

Leuphana University. (2024). *Digital transformation lab for teaching and learning*. Retrieved from https://www.leuphana.de/en/teaching/teaching-development/projects/digital-transformation-lab-for-teaching-and-learning.html

Lima, F. D. D. A., Dias, D., Schütz, J. A., Campos, M., & Nogueira, S. M. (2024). O binômio da educação atual: letramento digital e as tecnologias digitais da comunicação e da informação. *Contribuciones a las ciencias sociales, 17*(1), 6118–6129. https://doi.org/10.55905/revconv.17n.1-368

Lira, A. C. M., Yaegashi, S. F. R., & Dominico, E. (2019). Disguise me that I devour you: Children youtubers, consumption and semi-formation of the child. *Revista Ibero-americana de Estudos em Educação, 14*(esp.4), 1960–1976. https://doi.org/10.21723/riaee.v14iesp.4.12921

Mion, M. R. B., & Lopes, D. D. Q. (2021). Youtube e Educação: uma revisão da pesquisa brasileira no período de 2014 a 2021. *Revista Novas Tecnologias Na Educação, 19*(2), 526–536. https://doi.org/10.22456/1679-1916.121376

Neumann, M. M., & Herodotou, C. (2020). Young children and YouTube: A global phenomenon. *Childhood Education, 96*(4), 72–77. https://doi.org/10.1080/00094056.2020.1796459

Padilha, V., Palos, A. C. P., & da Veiga, C. V. (2022). The importance of digital influencers for consumption desire formation in young Portuguese people. *Acta Scientiarum Human and Social Sciences, 44*(1), e61488. https://doi.org/10.4025/actascihumansoc.v44i1.61488

Pew Research Center. (2023, December 11). *Teens, Social media and technology 2023*. Retrieved from https://www.pewresearch.org/wp-content/uploads/sites/20/2023/12/PI_2023.12.11-Teens-Social-Media-Tech_FINAL.pdf

Salihoglu, N. C., & Çetin, A. (2024). Examining preschool teacher's use of social media in terms of their professional development. *Journal of Educational Technology and Online Learning, 7*(1), 132–148. https://doi.org/10.31681/jetol.1307348

Santana, C., Amaral Corrêa Ughini Villarroel, M., & de Castro Bertagnolli, S. (2023). As práticas de letramento digital para estudantes e docentes do ensino médio e/ou técnico: uma revisão sistemática de literatura. *#Tear: Revista De Educação, Ciência E Tecnologia, 12*(1). https://doi.org/10.35819/tear.v12.n1.a6425

Sjöström, J., Eilks, I., & Zuin, V. G. (2016). Towards eco-reflexive science education. *Science and Education, 25*, 321–341. https://doi.org/10.1007/s11191-016-9818-6

Statista. (2024, May 22). *Most popular social networks worldwide as of April 2024, ranked by number of monthly active users*. Retrieved from https://www.statista.com/statistics/272014/global-social-networks-ranked-by-number-of-users/

Türcke, C. (2010). *Sociedade excitada: filosofia da sensação*. Editora da Unicamp.

United Nations. (2015). *The 17 goals*. Retrieved from https://sdgs.un.org/goals

United Nations. (2021). *General comment no. 25 on children's rights in relation to the digital environment*. Retrieved from https://criancaeconsumo.org.br/wp-content/uploads/2021/04/general-comment-n-25-2021.pdf

United Nations. (2024). *Child and youth safety online*. Retrieved from https://www.un.org/en/global-issues/child-and-youth-safety-online

United Nations Educational, Scientific and Cultural Organisation. (2021). *Media and information literate citizens: Think critically, click wisely!* UNESCO. isbn:978-92-3-100448-3. https://unesdoc.unesco.org/ark:/48223/pf0000377068

Zuin, V. G., & Kümmerer, K. (2021). Towards more sustainable curricula. *Nature Reviews Chemistry, 5*, 76–77. https://doi.org/10.1038/s41570-021-00253-w

Zuin, V. G., & Pacca, J. L. D. A. (2013). Formación docente en química y ambientación curricular: estudio de caso en una institución de enseñanza superior brasileña, Enseñan. *Ciencias: Revista de Investigación y Experiencias Didácticas, 2013*(31), 79–93. Retrieved from https://raco.cat/index.php/Ensenanza/article/view/285705/373677

Zuin, V. G., & Zuin, A. Á. S. (2018). A indústria cultural algorítmica na era da Internet das Coisas. *Educação e Filosofia, 32*(66), 1131–1156. https://doi.org/10.14393/REVEDFIL.issn.0102-6801.v32n66a2018-07

Zuin, A., & Zuin, V. G. (2019). A indústria cultural na era da tela onipresente. *Cadernos de Pesquisa: Pensamento Educacional, 14*(36), 89–104. https://doi.org/10.35168/2175-2613.UTP.pens_ed.2019.Vol14.N36.pp89-104

Zuin, V. G., Araripe, E., & Fachina, S. (2020). *Plasticized childhood: The impact of plastic toy advertising to children on their health and the environment* (p. 107). Alana Institute. https://www.oneplanetnetwork.org/knowledge-centre/resources/plasticized-childhood-impact-plastic-toy-advertising-children-their

Stefania Fachina A teacher at SENAC (São Paulo, Brazil) with a MSc and a PhD in Education from the Federal University of São Carlos (UFSCar, Brazil) (2019; 2025). Her expertise lies in education for sustainability, focusing on Environmental Education, the Consumer Society, and Child Consumerism.

Caroindes Julia Corrêa Gomes A Professor at the Chemistry Institute of the Federal University of Bahia (UFBA, Brazil), with a PhD in Education from the Federal University of São Carlos (UFSCar, Brazil), as well as an MSc and a Degree in Chemistry, both obtained from UFSCar. Her expertise lies in green and sustainable chemistry education, specifically working with social and scientific issues in chemistry teacher training.

Evelyn Araripe An interdisciplinary scholar working in the fields of science education and sustainability science. With a BA in Social Communication—Journalism (Unimep, Brazil, 2008), a specialisation in Environmental Education (Senac, Brazil, 2011) and MSc and PhD in Education from UFSCar (2020; 2025), her expertise lies in creating case studies that weave sustainability and climate change issues into education.

Vânia Gomes Zuin Zeidler Full Professor at the Institute of Sustainable Chemistry, Leuphana University, Germany, where she is also Pro-Dean for Gender and Diversity and Coordinator of the master's Programme Sustainability Science. Her expertise lies in green and sustainable analytical chemistry, particularly in developing methods for analysing renewable bioactive compounds from agro-industrial wastes and new green and sustainable curricula for universities. She founded the Green Chemistry Section of the Brazilian Society of Chemistry and her contributions to the field have been recognised with numerous awards, including the National Literary Jabuti Awards.

A Contemporary Business Model for Integrating Company Needs Through Education–Company Collaboration

Miia-Maija Vakkuri

Abstract In today's fast-changing business environment, it is essential to examine future competence requirements for managers, as a gap remains between current educational frameworks and the realities of service business management. This paper presents a contemporary collaboration between business and higher education, aiming to develop a model that narrows the skills gap between managerial needs and academic training.

The model is introduced through a case company project and outlines the main steps of a practical business collaboration. To address the identified gap, the study presents a platform-based concept focused on digital transformation in knowledge transfer. It highlights how business and education can align through emerging technologies and flexible business models.

This collaborative approach emphasises digital co-creation and the use of virtual tools. The chapter introduces the *Right Away Ready Deal* project, developed by Laurea University of Applied Sciences (Laurea UAS). The initiative supports digital knowledge transfer within a platform model that integrates virtual learning and real-world collaboration.

The project is implemented using *Canvas* as the learning environment, *Zoom* for communication, and *Trello* as a project management tool. This model exemplifies how digital tools can strengthen the connection between education and business, fostering future-ready managerial competencies.

Keywords Business–education collaboration · Digital knowledge transfer · Managerial skills gap · Virtual learning environments · Platform-based business model

M.-M. Vakkuri (✉)
Laurea University of Applied Sciences, Espoo, Finland

Estonian Business School, Tallinn, Estonia
e-mail: miia.vakkuri@laurea.fi

K. Bodrožić-Brnić et al. (eds.), *Digital Transformation in Knowledge Transfer*, Digital Transformation and Innovation,
https://doi.org/10.1007/978-3-032-07329-7_15

1 Introduction

With *Laurea's Right Away Ready Deal* for students and key partners, in a changing operating environment, it is possible to respond nimbly to the needs of Laurea's key partners, while also giving students even more opportunities to influence what kind of projects they want to implement. Flexibility, genuine continuity in key partner cooperation collaboration, and the extent of utilising expert networks are especially emphasised in the cooperation model. In this concept the idea is to implement the process of creating a collaboration, aiming for a co-creation between actors of UAS, students, and companies.

The evolving business environment calls for a thorough evaluation of future management competence requirements. Management education must adapt accordingly by developing new, functional learning models. Current research suggests a gap between the theoretical frameworks of business management and the practical needs outlined in educational business studies (Huang & Lin, 2010). Increasing competition in the business world demands the continuous development of innovative strategies. Therefore, business management programmes should place greater emphasis on key competencies such as knowledge application, communication, customer service, problem-solving, and leadership (Cheung et al., 2010).

2 Background

Universities of Applied Sciences (UAS) in Finland must actively maintain and strengthen the connection between education and working life. Study activities are designed to link students with real-world projects, enabling them to contribute to business development within companies. According to a survey (Arene, 2024) by the chambers of commerce, universities of applied sciences are the most interesting partners for companies in research, development, and innovation work. Universities of applied sciences are particularly interesting in Research and Development (R&D) partners for small and medium-sized companies. It is now possible to influence the conditions for the growth of companies and increase the Research, Development, and Innovation (RDI) activities of Small and Medium-sized Enterprises (SMEs). About 25% of the companies that employ 50–250 people named universities of applied sciences as their most potential partners.

To steer the Finnish economy back towards growth, it is essential to encourage stronger investment in research, development, and innovation (RDI) by the SME sector. As small and medium-sized enterprises view universities of applied sciences as their most promising RDI partners, public RDI funding should be increasingly allocated to ecosystems that promote collaboration between SMEs and universities of applied sciences in applied research and development efforts. The university of applied sciences network covers the entire country and operates closely with businesses. Universities of applied sciences are best suited as partners of SMEs in research and development activities due to their expertise, priorities, and operating models. According to Tikkanen and Vakkuri (2013), due to heavy competition within the service sector and owing to changing customer needs, the business services require to be continuously developed and innovated based on recent research results. Subsequently, development and innovations demand advanced knowledge and research skills.

2.1 *Laurea UAS*

One key element of the Laurea strategy 2030 (Laurea UAS, 2019) is 'expanding and deepening the strategic regional, national, and international partner network'. Laurea's strategic choice is to integrate three tasks: education, R&D, and regional development.

Laurea UAS has selected a pragmatic philosophy of education as the basis of its pedagogic strategy (Raij, 2013). All teaching in Laurea UAS follows the Learning by Developing (LbD) action model which was created at Laurea at the beginning of the year 2000. The pragmatic philosophy of education is based on the thesis by John Dewey. According to Dewey (1984; see Learning by Doing) pragmatic learning is a collaboration with actors in a project. Learning is active process and experience of developing new ways of doing. This pedagogical model allows teaching in innovative ways in close cooperation with companies.

The LbD development-based learning model includes authenticity, partnership, experience, and research. By using the LbD model, a new approach to learning has been invented. The foundation for development-based learning is a real life's development project redesigning practice, and the implementation of it requires cooperation between teachers, students, and work–life companies, where ideally new knowledge and competencies are presented (Kallioinen, 2008). According to Raij (2007) the characteristics of Learning by Developing have elements that make the model unique. LbD development projects derived from working life and the implemented case can be problem-based or innovation based. The actors in a development case are based on authentic partnerships between lecturers, students, and experts from the work–life sector. The development project functions as a learning platform that integrates workplace knowledge, research-based insights, and newly generated knowledge.

The LbD process requires each student to join a development team. Students work collaboratively to solve real-world problems by applying the phases of Design Thinking, aiming to create the most effective service solution. The outcome should be a practical implementation that can be applied within a company (Taatila, 2014). Company collaboration projects often begin with an identified development need, leading to target-oriented discussions and agreements between the higher education institution and the company.

The LbD process is not only a one-way route towards students. LbD projects can lead to different outcomes—new product or service developments and improvement on customer experience, or even developing company strategy (Taatila, 2014).

Laurea's key partnership programme is a paid partnership that engages the partner in extensive and systematic cooperation with Laurea's various degree programmes. It can involve cooperation with students, research, development, and innovation activities as well as business activities. The key partnership concept encompasses project and recruitment cooperation and a visibility package. The aim is to expand and deepen Laurea's partnership network to support the development of our competence areas and further enhance their effectiveness. At the same time, the aim is to activate the network more systematically, for example, regarding RDI activities (Key Partnership, 2004).

3 Knowledge Transfer in Project Work

Knowledge-Based Theory of the Firm (KBV) emphasises resources and organisational capabilities as the primary sources of competitive advantages and the foundation for strategy conceptualisation. Theories of the firm are models of business enterprises that explain their structure and behaviours. The theory is interesting when the topic is to evaluate and develop management competences and service economy education. The research aims to bring together the working life organisations and educational institutions, and to form a model of a learning ecosystem in which future competences and knowledge are co-created through interaction between the various participants. In today's rapidly evolving business environment, it is essential to examine the future competence requirements of managers and the role of the learning ecosystem. Current educational business studies indicate a gap in the understanding of service business management frameworks.

The knowledge-based view of the firm differs from other theories that emphasize organisational factors in generating competitive advantage. KBV focuses on the internal structure of the firm, viewing it as a complex organisation composed of multiple individuals. The central role of management is to establish the coordination mechanisms necessary for effective knowledge integration. Coordination is the main implication, especially when tacit knowledge is involved. An interesting feature of the knowledge-based approach is that it offers a theoretical basis for understanding several recent organisational innovations and trends. These include empowerment and the development of new organisational forms of the firm (Grant, 1996).

3.1 Action Model of the Project Work

These project conditions can be analysed through the lens of Ostrom's (1990) concept of the *tragedy of the commons*. In classical commons dilemmas, individuals tend to act in their own self-interest, extracting benefits for themselves. As a result, common resources are treated as belonging to no one, and shared responsibility is largely absent. In project management we think that the benefits are common, and the idea is that everyone gets the same. Sometimes, team members are not actively engaged in the project and are on holiday rather than contributing. These individuals are known as free riders—those who benefit from the efforts of others without contributing themselves. This situation reflects the classic challenges of governing the commons, which was the focus of Ostrom's (1990) research. She notices that the tragedy of commons can be prevented with different kinds of regulations, norms, contracts, and shared values. The idea was to prevent free riding by agreeing to the sanctions that were so powerful that an employee was kicked out of the community. Sometimes the problem in a project is that it is hard to agree in advance on what the solution or the output will be. Ostrom (1990) prefers that the project team works closely together to draw the rules. That way the project is able to be common action or collective action to reach the mutual goals.

Four basic principles for governing the tragedy of commons in a project:

1. Define the actors in a project and their responsibilities.
2. Plan the project organisations rules and the boundaries.
3. Involve the project groups to determine the rules.
4. Build up a system, where the actors' action can be openly monitored—in this case, it is easier to solve problems right away.

4 Description of the Working Life Project Concept

Nowadays quick experiments and research are desired in business life. Laurea UAS Right Away Ready Deal working life project concept is a solution to create company projects on a flexible schedule. The design of the study unit found in the curriculum under the name work life project has been carried out in close cooperation with various stakeholders. The project-based operating model is used daily at Laurea according to LbD—the new features in this 'turnkey' course offered to partners are: (1) flexibility, (2) genuine continuity in key partner collaboration, and (3) leveraging expert networks. The implementation can be organised online as well as live, or with the recently popular hybrid model.

The implementation of the course is started based on needs and its progress is agreed with the key partner. The plan is to shape the implementation over time into a whole that would truly integrate into a meeting platform for multidisciplinary teams, bringing Laurea's different education programmes to work together, e.g., in addition to sprint implementations. The first study course prototype has been started together with the student team and Laurea's key partner in the Spring of 2021, researching the future of the bar industry.

The goal is to promote the continuum through the modelled process, project formalisation, so that resources both on the part of Laurea and the key partners can be allocated genuinely to development while the time taken for preparation and deliberation is reduced. At the beginning of the study period, the key partners will present the projects for the coming semester to the students. Projects may include development assignments, planning tasks, or everyday office activities such as market research, competitor analysis, trend forecasting, trade fair representation, pricing studies, customer event planning, digital development, mystery shopping, or customer satisfaction surveys. There are no limitations on the project topics. Students participating in the course can select projects that align with their personal development and learning goals. Each student team is introduced to the company's operations and needs through a structured control plan that guides the collaboration process. Thus, a joint cooperation reflected through a mutual effort model can be built in genuine teamwork. The course proceeds with weekly meetings between the company and the student team, where the project's progress is to be monitored.

The actors of the study course naturally include representatives of the key partner company, Laurea's study course coordinator, and university students—in addition, depending on the topic of the project, experts selected from Laurea's staff and their networks are also invited. In this way, the partnership ecosystem expands—supporting the goal of simultaneously growing the networks of all participating stakeholders.

4.1 Quality of Learning Experience

A good and high-quality, and at the same time, suitably challenging learning experience increases the students' expertise and simultaneously brings the identified working life skills, which have also appeared in the working life guidance group of the restonomy training, into a meaningful way as part of the learning path. Restonomy training refers to an educational programme that prepares students for a career as a hospitality field. A restonomist is a specialist in the hospitality, tourism, and service industries, with expertise in various areas of service business management. The training focuses on customer service, leadership, business development, and the design and marketing of experience and service products. The programme often includes work-based projects, internships, and practical learning experiences that equip students with the skills needed for the demands of working life.

During the project course, the student implements a project applying the latest existing research information and working as a member of the project team in projects together with working life. With the project accomplishment, the student develops creativity, problem-solving skills, and the confidence to take initiative. Students participate in the development task according to the project assignment, from planning to implementation and evaluation. The team prepares a project plan and implements the project together with various national and, if necessary, also international joint partners and networks. As a continuation of the course, the aim is to elaborate possible thesis topics for the students with key partners and to receive an opportunity for employment in the company. The student also has the option to complete an internship during the study course.

4.2 *The Novelty Value of an Idea*

In this implementation, the existing base, a piece of coal, has been polished into a diamond. The goal in planning the work–life project course has been to coordinate and systematically structure the development tasks provided by companies into a cohesive and manageable framework. With the help of the study course, we can connect students and companies to the edge of doing things together, also considering the feedback from students received earlier which is that they would like to be able to choose more actively what kind of projects they are involved in implementing. The basic idea is that Laurea as a 'by-product' strengthens its attractiveness as a preferred partner, offering key partners a new service concept, which can also be used to conduct quick investigations.

LbD is naturally integrated as part of the implementation. In accordance with its goals, new expertise is created in this entity, connecting students, partners, and lecturers. Students play an active role in searching for information, finding solutions, and enabling successful implementation. The project receives support for network cooperation and, e.g., from the responsible lecturer/lecturers. The evaluation is carried out under the leadership of pedagogy professionals in cooperation with partners. The key partners' role is to act as support in the development process, enabling students to access the necessary resources.

Student feedback collected from the pilot phase has been positive—students feel that doing business projects has strengthened their learning. According to the students, the cooperation with the company's representative has been flexible and useful. The students gained a deeper understanding of the field and the expertise it demands. They reported having sufficient freedom within the project and emphasized that the learning-by-doing approach significantly enhanced their overall learning experience. The company representative considered the study course to be an innovative and good solution for their needs. Doing projects together with students was efficient and brought new ideas. As the project progressed, regular meetings made it possible to monitor the team's work and discuss and brainstorm more with the students.

4.3 Project Work Process Model

The goal has been to restructure the students' project work to make it more effective and professional. Additionally, the project should include better-defined rules and planning stages. The new approach begins with pre-planning the project in collaboration with companies. Currently, the process of planning projects with companies involves teachers creating agreements to initiate a development project with the firms. This also includes defining the scope of the project, which will become the final development case.

At Laurea UAS Finland the future task is to increase the connection between education and industry. Studies aim to bridge the gap between work life and students, fostering the development of business practices within companies. An ideal learning process model should equip students with managerial-level competencies and hands-on experience, as illustrated in Fig. 1.

The cooperation project model gives students the opportunity to negotiate the project instructions, rules, goals, and contracts before even the project starts. In the future, we can give the students more power and responsibility to co-operate with companies. In that case, they learn a wide range of work life practices in project decisions. Figure 1 illustrates the process between companies and education institutions.

The process (Fig. 1) visualises the pre-project plan template. The idea of the process is to start with gathering data from the cooperative company. After that, students will meet the representative of the company for the first time. The idea is to get to know the actors in the project. Then there will be a data gathering from the customers about their opinions of the company's service and products. The goal of this research is to find out the developing issues that will be the actual project in the

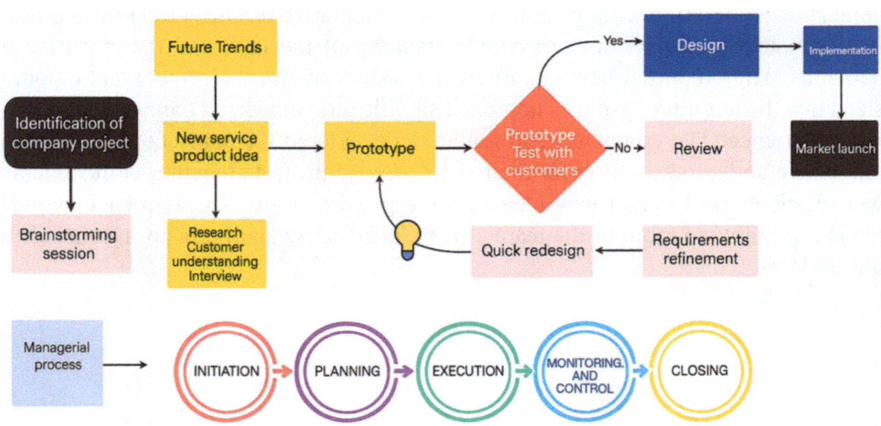

Fig. 1 Model of managerial learning process in university-industry project created by the author for the purpose of this article)

end. After that, the project actors will meet again to set the rules and the final goals. Next, there are specific stages to determine whether or not to initiate the project.

1. Survey (net scouting and other observation data gathering methods).
2. Company meeting, introduction, and presentation.
3. Developing customer understanding and insights (interviews).
4. Creating the developing questions and the goals for the project. Making decisions related to project management issues.
5. Prepare the final applications.
6. Actual project starts (or not).

In project coating, the scalability of the 'wire model' is everything. The prototype implementations naturally take time, but the investment's benefit enables future resource-efficient operations. However, as in all high-quality teaching, it is important to note that sufficient resources must be allocated to project management. Based on previous experiences, serving key partners should be seen as an essential part of business, and this helpful teaching and guidance activity should be supported.

4.4 Importance of Customer Understanding in the Firm

The success of this new project planning process lies in identifying development challenges before the actual project begins. It involves engaging students in researching customer needs early on, defining key perspectives, and formulating a clear problem statement. Collaborative creation and proactive development, where customers, companies, and competitors co-participate, represent the modern approach to innovation. Anticipating the future and seeking new service innovations are the essential requirements in the business world. For that reason, business management must create new ways to research the markets (Osterwalder et al., 2014).

The approach in this research of gathering data from companies' customers will be qualitative research, where the research strategy is to use action research method. Action research is essentially based on problems, problem-solving abilities. Action research enables one to influence the environment of the researched phenomenon in a community by developing the community's problem-solving intelligence. To do action research, someone must participate in the practices of the community in the context of the research phenomenon (Lähdesmäki et al., 2010).

Action research is an interactive process that balances problem-solving actions implemented in a collaborative context with data-driven collaborative analysis to understand underlying causes, enabling future predictions about human and organisational change (Reason & Bradbury, 2008). Action research can be used in action, rather than research about action. Action research is participative, concurrent with action and an approach to problem-solving. Action research methods consist of six steps: data gathering, data feedback, data analysis, action planning, implementation, and evaluation. According to Coughlan and Coghlan (2002), monitoring is a continuous step throughout the process. They explain that action research is a scientific model that differs from experimental physics but still is a legitimate scientific study of the effects of human behaviours. Their paper offers an in-depth review of action research as a valid method for research in operations management.

4.5 *Virtual Learning Environment*

In collaboration with companies and education, virtual tools such as *Canvas* (a learning management system) and *Trello* (a communication system that also helps in project management) have been used to create teaching and learning activities based on digital knowledge transfer. These tools are used by both, companies and students. They provide a way to develop learning methods that increase student engagement and enhance their ability to use technology to support their learning. The virtual environment built with *Canvas* and *Trello* allows the integration of various aspects of creative media, improving the learning experience for both students and company members.

The tools and equipment used to implement the solution include Canvas and Zoom, which serve as the primary teaching and communication platforms for the course. Additionally, key partner resources—such as facilities, specialised equipment, and digital platforms—are utilised throughout the process. Canvas functions as a hub for reports, course materials, discussions, announcements, and information sharing (Canvas, 2023). Trello (see Fig. 2) is used as a project management tool to support planning and coordination.

Trello is used in company projects to make visible for all parties what is happening in the team. Users can create task boards with different columns and move tasks to other users of the same group. Columns include task statuses like 'To Do', 'In Progress', and 'Done'. The tool can be used for personal and business purposes including project management, school assignment boards, and planning.

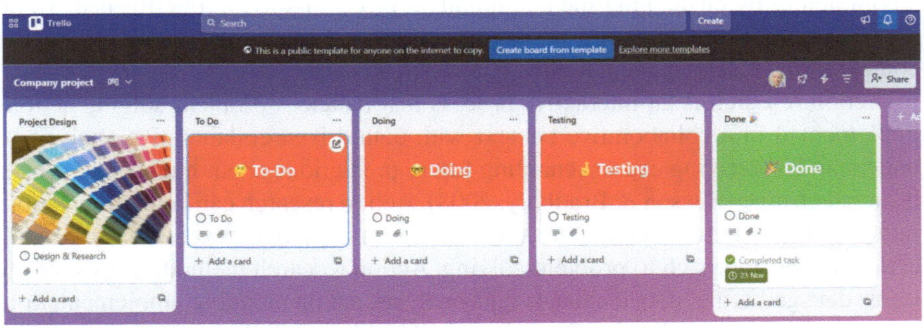

Fig. 2 Project management tool by Trello Online planner (Trello, 2023)

4.6 *Result of Project Work Process*

The introduction of a new approach to student projects is expected to generate numerous success stories. Cooperation between all actors becomes increasingly important throughout the entire process, with students taking on more active roles. This model allows for more thorough planning before action is taken. Clear rules and structures are co-created by students and companies, encouraging responsibility and initiative. Overall, the model supports professional growth and enhances students' project management skills. Students will plan the procedures of their own teams and set the team's regulations. The actions of 'free riding' and the tragedy of commons have to be sanctioned. The most effective penalty would be to force the team member to leave the group or something of the kind.

The empirical result illustrates that a new model can be developed from the viewpoints of the theoretical framework of collective action and the template idea of Ostrom commons (1990). However, the challenge in the project was efficient work skills and timelines. The important measure of productivity improvement can be difficult to achieve. The importance of cooperation between actors is critical. Furthermore, the model supports professional growth and learning, offering the opportunity to develop the skills of cooperation and interaction, and a greater sense of personal responsibility.

5 Conclusion

In collaboration with companies and education, projects successfully develop a collaborative model that integrates procedures, ground rules, and roles based on partnership and risk analysis. It emphasises collective action, aiming to create an operational framework between businesses and students. The model offers businesses a platform to experiment with their ideas and prototypes, while students gain hands-on experience solving tangible business challenges with real-world projects. Furthermore, the project highlights the importance of flexible communication, industry-specific skills, and company culture, all of which contribute to a mutually beneficial partnership.

As a developmental research project, this initiative fosters the creation of innovative work methods through collaboration, attentive listening to students' experiences, and the practical implementation of their ideas. This research provides an opportunity to explore the effectiveness and management of various models. Through project innovation, students are inspired and motivated to generate new solutions that directly enhance customer service experiences. The project model serves as a practical development platform, rooted in everyday scenarios, revealing opportunities to innovate better products and address service-related challenges within the company.

Future research should focus on investigating the long-term effects on student learning and professional growth, as well as business benefits from knowledge-sharing partnerships. Also, the communication channels and collaboration tools must be updated. Evaluating the impact of company culture, skills requirements, and industry competencies on the project's success must be measurable. These steps will strengthen the connection between education and business, providing practical solutions to improve customer service and create better products.

References

Cheung, C., Law, R., & He, K. (2010). Essential hotel managerial competencies for graduate students. *Journal of Hospitality and Tourism Education, 22*(4), 25–32.

Coughlan, P., & Coghlan, D. (2002). Action research for operations management. *International Journal of Operations and Production Management, 22*(2), 220–240.

Dewey, J. (1984). In J. McDermott (Ed.), *The philosophy of John Dewey*. The University of Chicago Press.

Grant, R. (1996). Toward a knowledge-based theory of the firm. *Strategic Management Journal, 17*, 109–122.

Huang, Y.-L., & Lin, C.-T. (2010). Management trainee core competencies in the hospitality industry: Differences between managers and scholars. *Journal of Human Resources in Hospitality and Tourism, 10*(1), 1–13.

Canvas. (2023). *Instructure overview*. https://www.instructure.com/canvas

Kallioinen, O. (2008). Näkökulmia oppimiseen ja osaamisen kehittymiseen LbD-toimintamallissa. In O. Kallioinen (Ed.), *Oppiminen learning by developing—Toimintamallissa* (pp. 112–133). Laurea Publications A-61, Edita Prima Oy.

Key Partnership. (2004). *Laurea.fi*. Retrieved from https://www.laurea.fi/en/key-partners/

Lähdesmäki, T., Hurme, P., Koskimaa, R., Mikkola, L., & Himberg, T. (2010). *Mapping research methods: Methods paths for humanists*. Retrieved from https://koppa.jyu.fi/avoimet/hum/menetelmapolkuja/en

Laurea UAS. (2019). *Laurea strategy 2030*. Laurea UAS Publication.

Arene (2024). *Yrityskysely osoittaa: Ammattikorkeakoulut kiinnostavimpia TKI-yhteistyökumppaneita yrityksille—Arene*. Retrieved from https://arene.fi/ajankohtaista/yritykysely-osoittaa-ammattikorkeakoulut-kiinnostavimpia-tki-yhteistyokumppaneita-yrityksille/

Osterwalder, A., Pigneur, Y., Bernarda, G., Smith, A., & Papadakos, T. (2014). *Value proposition design: How to create products and services customers want*. Wiley.

Ostrom, E. (1990). *Governing the commons: The evolution of institutions for collective action*. Cambridge University Press.

Raij, K. (2007). *Learning by developing*. Laurea Publications A58.

Raij, K. (2013). Learning by developing in higher education. *Education Sciences, II*, 6–21.

Reason, P., & Bradbury, H. (2008). *The Sage handbook of action research: Participative inquiry and practice* (2nd ed.). Sage.

Taatila, V. (2014). Some experience-based considerations on the LbD action model. In K. Raij (Ed.), *Learning by developing action model. Laurea Publications 36* (pp. 60–68). Laurea University of Applied Sciences.

Tikkanen, I., & Vakkuri, M. (2013). Developing a teaching restaurant as an R&D&I environment. *Higher Education, Skills and Work-Based Learning, 3*(3), 207–218. https://doi.org/10.1108/heswbl-01-2012-0002

Trello. (2023). *Trello*. Retrieved from https://trello.com/

Miia-Maija Vakkuri is a senior lecturer in Hospitality Management and Service Design at Laurea University of Applied Sciences. Her research interests include service design, the experience economy, multi-scale services, business model development, and innovative, sustainable service solutions. She is a member of a project group dedicated to developing models for university–industry R&D collaboration and enhancing cooperation between universities of applied sciences (UAS), students, and companies in the hospitality field. Her PhD research focuses on creating a model for a learning ecosystem by applying principles of management and leadership design.

Towards a Software Platform Supporting Qualification-Based Learning

Simon Wetzel and Matthias Hemmje

Abstract Convenient and seamless access to information and education is crucial for professional and personal development. Today, learners can consume content via various advanced devices. Consequently, the foundational IT infrastructure must establish a digital ecosystem capable of delivering the necessary services to meet learners' needs. A reliable and scalable solution is necessary to operate in environments with rapidly changing and ambiguous requirements. Simultaneously, a learning management framework needs to be established. Qualifications-Based Learning (QBL) serves as a learning management framework. To facilitate QBL, the Qualifications-Based Learning Model (QBLM) introduces an underlying conceptual reference architecture. The QBLM proposes a service-oriented architecture and data models. However, the suggested QBLM lacks horizontal scalability and flexibility in adapting to the rapidly changing and ambiguous demands of different digital ecosystems. Furthermore, the prototypical implementations of software implementing QBLM functionalities are tightly coupled. A software platform called the 'QBLM Platform' is proposed to address these challenges, which utilises a modular software architecture concept. The QBLM Platform provides a foundation for QBLM and capabilities to integrate on-demand extensions, such as games or customised solutions. It includes a standardised communication pattern to facilitate internal communication and interactions with remote digital ecosystems.

Keywords Qualifications-based learning · Modular software architecture · Digital ecosystems · Learning management framework · Service-oriented architecture

---

S. Wetzel (✉) · M. Hemmje
University of Hagen, Hagen, Germany
e-mail: simon-alexander.wetzel@fernuni-hagen.de; matthias.hemmje@fernuni-hagen.de

K. Bodrožić-Brnić et al. (eds.), *Digital Transformation in Knowledge Transfer*, Digital Transformation and Innovation,
https://doi.org/10.1007/978-3-032-07329-7_16

1 Introduction, Motivation, and Approach

Advice to the reader: See 'Appendix' for abbreviations used throughout the text.

With the *Bologna Process*, the need for comparability and standardisation of learning arose (European Ministers of Education, 1999). The members of the *European Union* decided to harmonise study programs of *Higher Educational Institutes* (HEI) (European Ministers of Education, 1999). Therefore, the so-called *formal learning* (O'Neill, 2019), which is the structured education following a curriculum, gets aligned between the different HEIs and countries (O'Neill, 2019) (European Ministers of Education, 1999). However, for enterprises, structured formal learning is also highly valued (Bundesministerium für Wirtschaft und Energie—BMWi, 2019). *Competence-Based Learning* (CBL) by Koper et al. (2008) provides a learning management approach to tackle these challenges and enable the comparability of learning efforts. CBL is based on *competencies* describing factual knowledge (Koper et al., 2008). These competencies are achieved by the learners through the completion of *Learning Objects* (LO), e.g., web pages, quizzes, educational games, or videos (1EdTech Consortium, Inc., 2003).

Then et al. (2016) introduced an advancement known as Competence-Based Learning (CBL). Later, the term *Qualification-Based Learning* (QBL) was introduced to better reflect the scope of the approach (Then et al., 2019). QBL is based on *Competency Qualifications* (CQ), which represent the assessed and approved achievement of competencies in professional or interdisciplinary subjects such as methodological skills, social skills, and personal skills (Wallenborn, 2018). The CQs can be achieved via the completion of LOs. It is also possible to define the ownership of CQs as a prerequisite to start an LO. In addition, CQs can be preconditions for modules, courses, or activities.

To facilitate QBL Then (2019) introduced the *Qualifications-Based Learning Model* (QBLM). QBLM postulates data models for the exchanged data objects between software components and within the software components as well as a *Service-Oriented Architecture* (SOA) to orchestrate the software components (Then, 2019). The prototypical implementation of the QBLM within the *Knowledge Management Ecosystem Portal* (KM-EP) (Vu, 2019) hosts several services, i.e. *QBLM Software*, to provide the required functionalities. These functionalities are the management and authoring of courses, management of learners' and LO corresponding CQs sets, i.e. *Competence Profiles* (CP) and the management of CQ master data, i.e. *Competence Frameworks* (CF) (Then, 2019). The related QBLM Software implementations are, among others, the *Course Authoring Tool* (CAT), the *Competence Profile Manager* (CPM), and the *Competence Manager* (CM) (Wallenborn, 2018).

1.1 Problem Statement

However, the prototypical implementation of QBLM within the KM-EP has some remaining challenges. Like its biological counterpart, a *Digital Ecosystem* (Briscoe et al., 2011) defines the available resources and provides an environment for individuals suited to their specific needs. Within a Digital Ecosystem, multiple *Application Habitats* (Briscoe, 2009) are present, which provide explicit functionalities to serve a specific purpose to satisfy a group of users (Briscoe et al., 2011). The prototypical QBLM implementation and its QBLM Software are explicitly implemented for the KM-EP as their Digital Ecosystem. Within the KM-EP are also other Application Habitats that provide non-QBL-related functionalities. As the KM-EP is, from IT infrastructure perspective, a single-server instance, any change in its configuration or hosted applications could potentially have an impact on other hosted applications or its functionality (Wallenborn, 2018). Therefore, it is necessary to remove the coupling between the QBLM implementation and its surrounding Digital Ecosystem to allow the usage of QBLM in any Digital Ecosystem. In addition, the QBLM Software itself has to be interchangeable with interoperable, alternative implementations, i.e., an implementation of the same functional domain, e.g., using another implementation of a CM. Another aspect of the KM-EP is the missing scalability. The single-server approach cannot flexibly add more resources or provide redundant instances of services to enable high availability.

In consequence, a novel approach is required to allow the utilisation of QBLM in any Digital Ecosystem and enable flexible usage of QBLM software. A Software Platform can encapsulate various software components, such as applications, databases, or networks, while abstracting the underlying IT infrastructure (Wangen, 2021). The software platform has to be deployable within any Digital Ecosystem of a HEI or enterprise and contains a composition of software components. A software platform providing all functionalities to facilitating QBL using QBLM is called a *QBLM Platform* and transforms any Digital Ecosystem into a *Digital QBLM Ecosystem*. The QBLM Platform has to provide QBLM Software and the required resources to facilitate them, such as databases, network gateways, and others. The QBLM Software can be clustered into two groups: the *QBLM Base Software* and the *QBLM Extension Software*. The QBLM Base Software provides the essential functionalities to perform QBLM, while the QBLM Extension Software enlarges the system with additional features. The catalogue of the QBLM Software implementation, including their categorisation and setup, is summarised in the *QBLM Ecosystem's Service Component Framework* (QBLM-ESCF).

A conceptual software architecture is required to orchestrate the QBLM Software of the QBLM-ESCF and the related resources within the QBLM Platform. However, the QBLM Platform has to provide the ability to add or remove on-demand QBLM Extension Software to allow customisation based on user requirements. Additionally, the QBLM Software has to be interchangeable on demand and replaced with another implementation of the same functional domain. The QBLM Platform must ensure the interoperability of all the QBLM Software via a communication pattern facilitating standardised and proprietary interfaces, including protocols. The communication pattern has to provide the ability to transform proprietary protocols, respectively, their data structure, into standardised ones to ensure the interoperability of custom implementations. The QBLM Platform must publish the interfaces for the internal QBLM Software. It also has to publish the interfaces for external applications in the surrounding Digital QBLM Ecosystems. QBLM Platform instances in other Digital QBLM Ecosystems, i.e., *Remote QBLM Platforms*, may also need to consume the interfaces. Therefore, any QBLM Platform must be able to provide its interfaces to optional Remote QBLM Platforms.

However, such a QBLM Platform does not exist yet, nor is there another approach to satisfy the described demands. The targeted solution has to tackle the following three problems to build up a QBLM Platform with the characteristics mentioned.

Firstly, a conceptual software architecture reference model for the QBLM Platform has not yet been developed. This includes the ability to host QBLM Software on demand within the QBLM Platform and its Application Habitat, i.e., *QBLM Application Habitat*. The demands are based on the various kinds of *user stereotypes*, e.g., learners, authors, managers, and others, which describe the role and interests of the Digital Ecosystems' *stakeholders*. Stakeholders are groups or individuals affecting or affected by an enterprise, venture, or project (Freeman, 2010). In consequence, the first problem is that a conceptual software architecture reference model for a QBLM Platform within a Digital QBLM Ecosystem and its QBLM Application Habitat considering its corresponding stakeholders in a QBLM Formal Learning context does not exist.

Secondly, the interfaces, including the related protocols, have to be supported. Therefore, the second problem is the lack of support for existing user interfaces, application programming interfaces, service interfaces, and other interfaces by the QBLM Platform. That includes their protocols for the internal communication flow between QBLM Platform components as well as for the external communication flow between QBLM Platform components and third-party software in a surrounding Digital QBLM Ecosystem.

Lastly, the prototypical implementation of a QBLM Platform, including interchangeable and interoperable software, is still undeveloped. It is also required that Remote QBLM Platforms can be connected, and data exchange is possible. This sums up into the third problem, which is the absence of an exemplar, modular, extensible, interoperable, and arbitrarily distributable proof-of-concept reference implementation of a QBLM Platform incorporating QBLM Application Habitats and Remote QBLM Platforms.

1.2 Research Questions, Scientific Approach, and Outline of Work

The problems mentioned above result in *Research Questions* (RQ). These RQs are to be answered to solve the described challenges.

RQ 1: How can a conceptual software architecture reference model for QBLM Platforms in any Digital QBLM Ecosystem be designed to fulfil the QBL-related demands of stakeholders?

RQ 2: How can relevant existing standardised and custom interfaces and corresponding protocols be found to enable and distribute their utilisation for the internal communication between components within a QBLM Platform, the communication with Software in Application Habitats of the surrounding Digital QBLM Ecosystem and other Remote QBLM Platforms?

RQ 3: How can an exemplar minimal, modular, extensible, interoperable, and arbitrarily distributable proof-of-concept implementation of a QBLM Platform be established?

The methodology of Nunamaker et al., from 1991, is chosen to address the RQs. In this methodology, the four phases of *observation*, *theory building*, *system development*, and *experimentation* can be executed (Nunamaker et al., 1990). The remaining structure of this paper follows the methodology of Nunamaker et al. by presenting the observation and theory-building phases. In the second section, the initial results of the observation phase related to the state of the art are addressed. The third section addresses the initial conceptual design of the theory-building phase. As this paper serves as a declaration of intent towards a QBLM Platform, it does not cover the system development and experimentation phases. In consequence, the system development phase, which addresses the prototypical implementation, and the experimentation phase, which evaluates the prototypical implementation, remain future challenges. This paper closes with the conclusion and outlook.

2 State of the Art in Science and Technologies

This section handles the observation phase. The structure follows the order of the RQ to give an overview of the related technologies and the state of the art. An observation of stakeholders, including their interactions with a Digital QBLM Ecosystem, functional requirements on a QBLM Platform, and potential architecture patterns to model the QBLM Platform, is required to answer RQ 1. The observation phase of RQ 1 is reflected in Sect. 2.1. To answer RQ 2, the observation of relevant interfaces, including their protocols, principles for the usage of custom interfaces including their protocols, and communication patterns, is necessary. RQ 2 observation phase is in Sect. 2.2. The observation of RQ 3 addresses the literature research on available QBLM software, their migration and distribution into a QBLM Platform, and cloud technologies. The RQ 3 observation phase is in Sect. 2.3 described. Section 2.4 closes the state of the art with a summary.

2.1 Stakeholder Identification and Research on Potential Architectural Patterns for the QBLM Platform

Before identifying stakeholders, it is essential to clarify the term. Stakeholders are all direct or indirect parties affected by a business and are both internal and external groups or individuals that have an impact on the business (Freeman, 2010). Examples of stakeholders are the government, suppliers, employees, media, competitors, customers, owners, and others (Freeman, 2010). In a project context, the stakeholders have an impact on the scope, time, and budget of the product (Vogwell, 2003). Therefore, it is necessary to identify, classify, and understand the stakeholders' interests and power regarding the project (Vogwell, 2003).

The following section identifies stakeholders within the context of QBLM by considering the groups and individuals outlined by Then (2019) and Wallenborn (2018), as well as stakeholders commonly involved in software projects. These are:

- students
- academic staff
- directors
- software providers
- IT and technical support staff
- administrative staff
- external content providers
- developers
- software engineers
- policymakers
- educational authorities

Students, as one type of stakeholder, participate in assessments and utilise educational resources (Then, 2019; Wallenborn, 2018). Academic staff, e.g., tutors and professors, are responsible for creating and designing courses, provide assessments, and use QBLM Software to facilitate QBL (Then, 2019; Wallenborn, 2018). The HEI, respectively, enterprise directors manage the integration of QBLM Software into their Digital Ecosystem (Kaya-Kasikci et al., 2023). Software Providers offer applications for usage within the Digital QBLM Ecosystem (Wallenborn, 2018). IT and Technical Support Staff are responsible for the operation of the technical infrastructure of HEIs or enterprises, which also includes the integration of QBL systems and ensuring their interoperability (Then, 2019). Administrative staff manages the organisational aspects of QBL, such as course registration, student records, and qualification tracking (Wallenborn, 2018). External content providers, developers, and software engineers provide additional educational resources or software components, such as assessments, educational games, software extensions, or new QBLM Software systems (Then, 2019). Policymakers and educational authorities create policies and standards for educational institutions (Then, 2019).

The investigation of stakeholders is considered complete, though further revisions may be made. Eleven stakeholders have been identified, and their anticipated interactions with the QBLM Platform have been described. This information is used as input in the theory building to identify user stereotypes and functional requirements of the QBLM Platform. Additionally, they are used to identify constraints on the system architecture of the QBLM Platform. However, for the implementation of the QBLM Platform, a conceptual software architecture reference model is required.

Therefore, based on Ford et al. (2017), various *architectural styles* and their corresponding *architectural patterns* are investigated, evaluated, and selected as the foundation for the conceptual software architecture reference model. The first architectural style is the *Big Ball of Mud*. The Big Ball of Mud may use frameworks and libraries, but the structure and concepts arise without purpose which leads to tight coupling and high efforts for any change.

Secondly, *Monoliths*, respectively, monolithic architectural patterns consist of multiple classes interacting with each other while using shared common functionalities. In case there is no structuring within the Monolith, the structure is imperceptibly better than the Big Ball of Mud. However, there are multiple approaches to structure Monoliths like *Layered Architecture*, *Modular Monoliths*, and *Microkernel*. The layered architecture intends to separate the technical capabilities into layers. These layers are building up on each other, e.g., on the bottom is the persistence layer, the business rules are in the middle, and at the top is the presentation layer. Next, Modular Monoliths postulate a logical grouping of functionality into modules. The various modules have to be designed and implemented in a way that ensures a loose coupling between the modules to gain the benefits of this approach. Lastly, Microkernels place a core into the middle of the architecture while plug-in components connect with the core and provide functionalities. If the plug-in components do not have to interact with each other, the coupling is limited between the core and the respective plug-in components.

Another architecture style is the *Event-Driven Architecture* (EDA). Mainly, EDA is used to integrate multiple systems using message queues. Two common patterns to implement EDA are *Broker* and *Mediator*. In the Broker pattern, an incoming event is pushed to a message queue, where it is picked up by an event processor. These event processors execute the business logic and—if required—pass a new event to another message queue to trigger the next event processor. Mediators introduce another component appearing as a coordinator into the system. Incoming events are pushed to the mediator component, which distributes the event to various message queues, where it can be picked up to process the business logic.

The SOA style is implemented by plenty of patterns. Some common ones are the *Enterprise Service Bus (ESB)-driven SOA*, *Microservices*, and *Service-based architecture*. The ESB-driven SOA places a service bus, i.e. ESB, into the centre of the system. It acts as a mediator but also provides the ability for message transformation. Business services interact with the ESB and execute the business logic. The Microservices pattern intends to define independent services, i.e. Microservices responsible for a single business domain and encapsulate all their required software components. Therefore, each Microservice is independent and provides its own technical architecture. The interaction and communication are handled via messaging between the Microservices and are organised by an *Application Programming Interface Layer* (API layer). The Service-based architecture pattern is similar to Microservices but differs in three aspects. Service-based architecture intends to have a larger service granularity, no strictly separated database scopes between services, and the usage of middleware to integrate legacy systems.

Lastly, *Serverless Architectures* focus on the abstraction of infrastructure and use of shared services of cloud providers. There are two different patterns to mention here: *Backend as a Service* (BaaS) and *Function as a Service* (FaaS). BaaS utilises third-party applications and cloud services to provide functionalities to the users. The system depends on the consumed services and no or less code is written. FaaS avoids infrastructure entirely. Services and computing power are provided on demand and scale accordingly in a cloud infrastructure.

Concluding, the previous section observed several architectural patterns. These architectural patterns are to be considered as input for the conceptual software architecture reference model of the QBLM Platform. In the theory-building phase, the presented architectural patterns must be assessed and selected according to the identified functional requirements. Besides the identified functional requirements, the communication approaches, including interfaces and protocols of software components of a QBLM Platform must be considered for the design of the conceptual software architecture reference model.

2.2 Research on Communication Requirements for Performing QBLM

The communication between the components of a QBLM-implementing system is to be observed, too. The defined interfaces, including protocols, of Then (2019) and further developments are investigated.

Then (2019) outlines the fundamental elements of the QBLM, which are detailed in the following section. Central to the QBLM is the *QBLM Domain Model* (QDM). The QDM provides concepts, data structures, and a common notation for the representation and the exchange of elements and information in a QBL context. A central element of the QDM is the *Qualifications Relevant Learning Elements* (QRLE), which include *Study Programs*, *Modules*, *Courses*, *Learning Activities*, *Knowledge Resources*, and *Competence/Qualification Assessments*. These elements collectively represent the educational content and activities essential for achieving specified learning goals. Besides the QDM-defined interfaces, some common interfaces are utilised. One is the *Learning Tools Interoperability* (LTI), which enables the integration of externally hosted learning tools. The mentioned interfaces have to be considered for the QBLM Base Software and provide some fundamental data structures.

Examples of QBLM Extension Software and their interfaces, including protocols, can be identified in Srbecky et al. (2022). One example is a Learning Record Store (LRS), which saves the user interactions for a later analysis. To track learners' progress and activities, the *experience Application Programming Interface* (xAPI) (Rustici Software LLC, n.d.) is used (Srbecky et al., 2022). Another data structure used in the QBLM context is the *Didactical Structural Template* (DST) (Winterhagen et al., 2021), which provides the ability to arrange LOs as courses or modules (Srbecky et al., 2022). To manage DSTs the *Didactical Structural Template Manager* (DSTM) is used (Winterhagen et al., 2021). In consequence, the DSTM is also identified as an example of QBLM Extension Software.

In the QBLM Platform, the specified protocols must be employed using an appropriate communication pattern. Additionally, the potential for utilising proprietary interfaces, including protocols, has to be explored.

Enyinna (2023) defines the following communication patterns:

- Request-Response
- Publish/Subscribe
- Short Polling
- Long Polling
- Push

Based on Enyinna (2023), the patterns are described in the following section. The Request-Response pattern describes synchronous exchanges between clients and servers. The pattern is simple and reliable but lacks in a manner of latency and inefficiency in real-time scenarios. The Publish/Subscribe pattern enables asynchronous communication through message brokers, facilitating loose coupling and scalability. However, the pattern is suitable for real-time applications, but its complexity increases on scale. Short Polling involves clients periodically requesting updates from the server. It is simple to implement but introduces latency and inefficiency. Long Polling is a variation of Short Polling and holds the client's request until the server has new data, providing near real-time updates. However, it requires more resources to maintain open connections. The Push pattern allows the server to push updates to clients as they become available, ensuring real-time communication. This model is highly efficient but can be challenging to scale due to the required open connections.

For the utilisation of proprietary protocols and to address inconsistent communication patterns, the related data structures and communication processes have to be transformed (Mandalaparty, 2014). These transformations are necessary to ensure that the proprietary protocols, and respectively, data structures, can be exchanged between systems using different proprietary or standardised interfaces (Mandalaparty, 2014). In consequence, the approach facilitates communication and functionality across heterogeneous systems by abstracting the complexities involved in handling multiple proprietary protocols and data structures into a middleware (Mandalaparty, 2014).

Summarising the observations of communication within the context of a QBLM Platform, various potential interfaces, including protocols, are identified. Subsequently, the potentially used communication patterns are examined to describe the underlying message transfer. Given that the QBLM Software implementations may not follow a common approach for interfaces, including protocols nor communication patterns, the need for a middleware is identified. In consequence, the modelling of the QBLM Platform in the theory-building phase must consider a potential need of transformation during the communication between QBLM Software.

2.3 Research on Available QBLM Software Solutions

As a next step of observation, prototypical implementations of previous research and development approaches implementing the mentioned functionalities and interfaces are investigated. Some are already mentioned like the CAT, CM, CPM, and DSTM. Another element of a Digital QBLM Ecosystem is a *Learning Management System* (LMS) (Wallenborn, 2018). LMSs are web-based applications designed to manage, deliver, and track educational courses and training programs (Khan et al., 2019). Then (2019) extended the LMS Moodle with the plug-in *QBL4Moodle* to support the necessary interfaces to perform QBL as mentioned in the QDM. All the mentioned examples of prototypical QBLM Software implementations are currently hosted within the KM-EP. However, the KM-EP serves further functionalities like the management of learners and authorisation (Vu, 2019).

As an alternative for the hosting within the KM-EP, *Cloud Computing* (CC) (Bundesministerium für Wirtschaft und Energie (BMWi), 2019) can be investigated. According to Mell and Grance (2011), CC provides:

- on-demand self-service
- broad network access
- Resource Pooling
- rapid elasticity
- measured services

Cloud-native features, such as container orchestration, enable faster application development and deployment (GitLab B.V., n.d.). On-Demand Self-Service allows users to independently create and assign cloud-native features. Broad Network Access ensures services are accessible via standardised networks. Resource Pooling allocates physical and virtual resources to multiple tenants simultaneously. Rapid Elasticity enables the cloud to scale resources dynamically as needed. Measured Service optimises and monitors resources based on performance metrics. Cloud services are delivered through three models: Software as a Service (SaaS), offering ready-to-use applications; Platform as a Service (PaaS), providing IT infrastructure without the need of maintaining it; and Infrastructure as a Service (IaaS), delivering virtual resources on demand (Mell & Grance, 2011).

The preceding section observed existing QBLM Software and approaches to host them. Initially, the CAT, the CM, the CPM, Moodle extended by QBL4Moodle, and the DSTM are identified as QBLM Software. Given that the QBLM Software must be facilitated by CC, the related concepts are observed. Within the theory-building phase both results have to be utilised to create a concept for the hosting of QBLM Software in a cloud.

2.4 *Summary of the State of the Art*

In the state-of-the-art section, multiple observations have been conducted to establish a foundation for addressing the RQs. After the identification of user stereotypes and their functional requirements, various architecture patterns to serve their demands are investigated. As remaining challenges, the definition of the use context and the modelling of a suitable conceptual software architecture reference model are pending. Furthermore, the interfaces and corresponding protocols in the context of QBLM are observed. As a remaining challenge, the modelling of a concept for the utilisation of standardised and proprietary interfaces in the QBLM Platform is pending. Subsequently, QBLM Software is identified. A remaining challenge is the creation of a concept for facilitating QBLM Software using CC. After discussing the state of the art, the next section utilises the observations to model the QBLM Platform. This involves the modelling of the conceptual software architecture reference model, defining communication patterns, and transitioning QBLM Software towards CC.

3 Towards Initial Design

In this section, the theory-building phase and, thus, the initial concept of the QBLM Platform is prepared. As an underlying design methodology, the *User Centred System Design* (UCSD) is used to address the theory building of the RQs. The methodology focuses on the needs, preferences, and limitations of users during the design process (Norman & Draper, 1986). Therefore, in Sect. 3.1, the use context of the QBLM Platform is defined. Based on the previously identified stakeholders and their interactions, user stereotypes and their functional requirements are identified. Afterwards, Sect. 3.2 places the user stereotypes within the context of the proposed QBLM Platform design. Potential conceptual software architecture reference proposals are presented based on the investigated architectural patterns. Therefore, potential architectural patterns for use in the QBLM Platform are selected based on the identified functional requirements. Thereafter, in Sect. 3.3, the content and visual design are addressed. This includes the initial conceptual design of the interactions between QBLM Software components within the QBLM Platform and the approach to providing the QBLM Software.

Within the theory building, formal modelling is not yet attempted and remains a challenge. Therefore, the figures given are for clarification purposes and are informal.

3.1 Use Context of the QBLM Platform

Based on the identified stakeholders in the observation, user stereotypes can be defined. In consequence, the user stereotypes are:

- learners
- authors
- system owners
- technology professionals
- editorial staff

The learners, derived from the stakeholder group students, consume the educational resources by executing LOs and achieve CQs based on their progress. Authors are based on multiple stakeholders, which are academic staff, policymakers and educational authorities, external content providers, developers, and software engineers. The authors provide LOs and organisational content. The user stereotype system owner is derived from the stakeholders' group directors and administrative staff. System owners care about the financial and strategic aspects of the Digital Ecosystem. Technical professionals as a user stereotype are derived from the stakeholders: developers, software engineers, software providers, IT and Technical Support Staff. They implement new or maintain existing QBLM Software or applications in the Digital Ecosystem. Lastly, the user stereotype editorial staff is derived from policymakers and educational authorities. These take care or give guidance in regard to legal aspects such as data protection, organisational issues, and documentation.

However, by utilising the defined user stereotypes and their specific demands, the functional requirements for the QBLM Platform can be derived. The learners and authors have requirements based on the concept of QBL, such as access, creation, utilisation, and management of LOs, including related CQs. Besides the functional requirements derived directly from the learning management approach, the learners require progress tracking, insights into personal CP and master data, the ability to personalise the study program, and a possibility to communicate with each other and authors. The authors require the ability to collaborate, check their created content against compliance, use standards for their implementation, and use data analytics to get feedback about their content. In regard to system owners, the Digital

QBLM Ecosystem has to provide expense tracking, user management, system performance monitoring, and integration with other Application Habitats. The technical professionals require tooling, including documentation for the development and operation of QBLM Software. Therefore, the Digital QBLM Ecosystem must provide technical documentation, the ability for interoperation and integration of QBLM Software, and reusable, respectively shared software components such as databases. Derived from the editorial staff user stereotype, the Digital QBLM Ecosystem has to provide audit and compliance monitoring, training resources, documentation, and data protection. Lastly, some general functional requirements are to be named. Therefore, the Digital QBLM Ecosystem must provide an intuitive user interface with real-time responses. Additionally, the system has to provide high availability, backup, and recovery options.

In Fig. 1 the previously identified user stereotypes are placed into the context of the QBLM Platform. The user stereotypes have various interactions with the QBLM Platform according to their profession and role. The learners can consume LOs and achieve CQs on successfully completed LOs. Authors provide the LOs and organisational content and gain user feedback. System owners expect to generate revenue by operating the QBLM Platform while managing the financials and directing the strategy. Technology professionals implement or maintain QBLM Software, expecting proper tooling to support their development efforts. Regulatory provides legal content and documentation to achieve a compliant QBLM Platform.

However, the use context is an abstracted view on the QBLM Platform, and a definition of use cases remains as a challenge. Therefore, a formal user modelling based on the identified user stereotypes and the use context is pending.

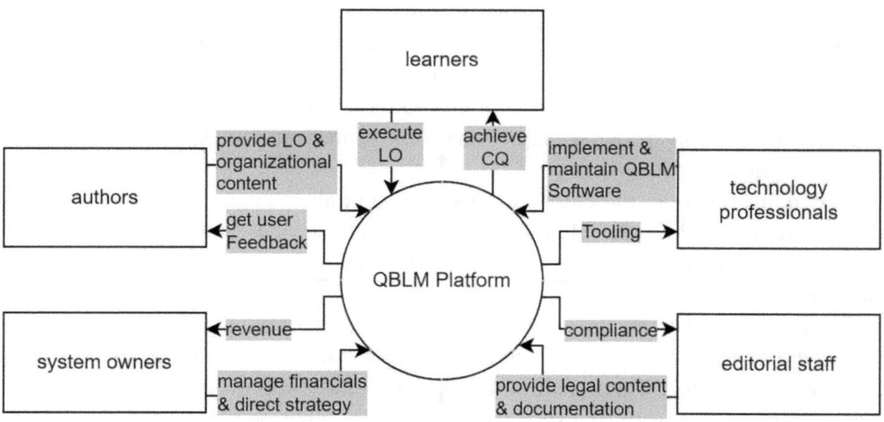

Fig. 1 Preliminary design of the proposed QBLM platform's use context

3.2 Integrating User Stereotypes into the QBLM Platform Design

By utilising the use context, the functional requirements derived from observations, and the investigated architecture patterns, potential conceptual software architecture reference models can be proposed. Therefore, the investigated architecture patterns have to be prefiltered first. As the Big Ball of Mud is an antipattern, it is not used as an approach. The monolithic architectural patterns propagate communication on a class level within a single runtime. A reason not to consider Monoliths is that QBLM Software implementations like the LMS have their own runtime with specific requirements. An implementation as a Monolith would lead to version conflicts between QBLM Software with different system requirements. An EDA requires communication to be handled through events. However, some QBLM Software requires synchronous communication (Wallenborn, 2018) (Then, 2019). Additionally, QBLM does not describe sequential business processes with event processors building up on each other (Then, 2019). Therefore, the broker pattern is not considered. The Mediator pattern is considered as there is the need of event distribution in the context of QBLM, as stated in Then (2019). Next, the SOAs are considered. ESB-driven SOAs are used for complex event interactions (Ford et al., 2017). These are not present in the QBLM (Then, 2019). Therefore, ESB-driven SOAs are not considered. Microservices would encapsulate the QBLM Software and allow synchronous and asynchronous communication. Therefore, Microservices are considered as patterns. The Service-based architecture is another potential pattern. The pattern has similarities to the SOA proposed by Then (2019). The Serverless Architectures are also to be considered. BaaS utilises cloud services. However, it is a remaining challenge to investigate available third-party applications, and respectively, services available in the cloud that provide QBL functionalities. Assuming suitable cloud services are accessible, BaaS can be considered. Lastly, FaaS is considered a pattern. In this pattern, cloud-native features are used to utilise QBLM and provide, e.g., serverless functions to serve the required functionalities.

In conclusion, as architecture patterns for potential conceptual software architecture reference models, the Mediator pattern, Microservices pattern, Service-based pattern, BaaS, and FaaS are to be considered. Therefore, preliminary sketches for each architectural pattern are proposed.

Firstly, the *QBLM Mediator Design Proposal* is conceptually designed based on the Mediator pattern. Actions of the users trigger events, which are pushed towards the *QBLM Mediator*, which distributes receiver related sub-events via queues to the various QBLM Software. If a sequence of event distribution is required, the QBLM Mediator follows a business workflow and sends it to the QBLM Software one after another. Figure 2 visualises the proposal.

Next, the Microservice pattern is utilised to propose an architectural approach. Therefore, the *QBLM Microservice Design Proposal* is outlined and visualised in Fig. 3. Each QBLM software has its own infrastructure, including a runtime and its

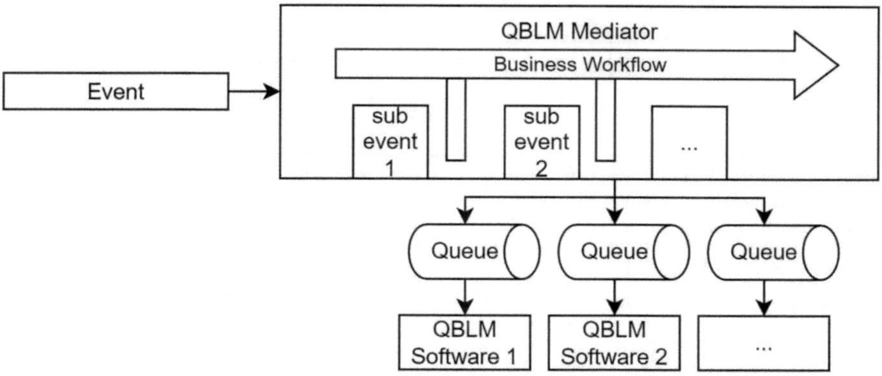

Fig. 2 QBLM mediator design proposal

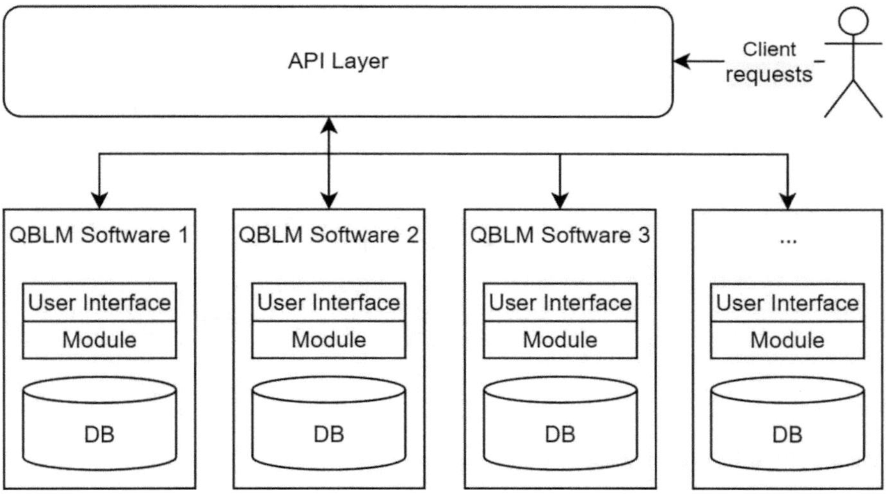

Fig. 3 QBLM microservice design proposal

required resources, such as a database. The microservices communicate via an API layer. Also, external, respectively, client requests are handled by the API layer and distributed to the respective QBLM Software.

Another SOA to be considered is the service-based architecture pattern. The resulting proposal is the *QBLM Service-based Architecture Design Proposal* visualised in Fig. 4. The design proposal introduces the possibility of shared database usage of middleware and has a larger service granularity, which could lead to consolidation of responsibility. Communication between QBLM Software components is facilitated via an API layer. The middleware can perform transformations if required.

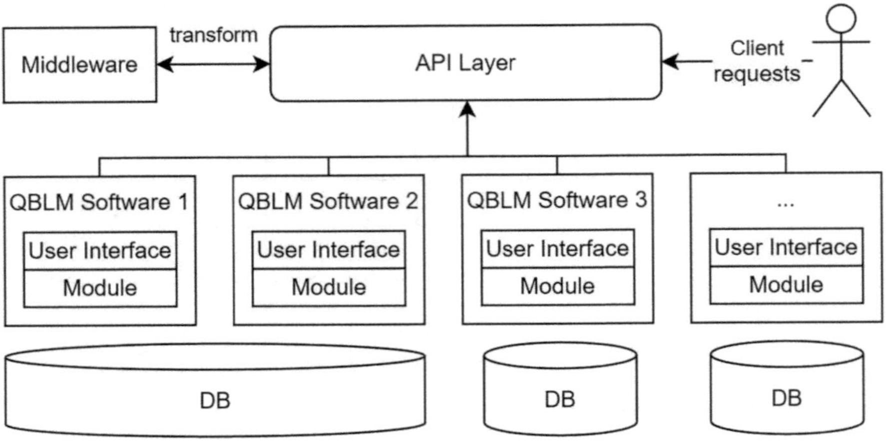

Fig. 4 QBLM service-based architecture design proposal

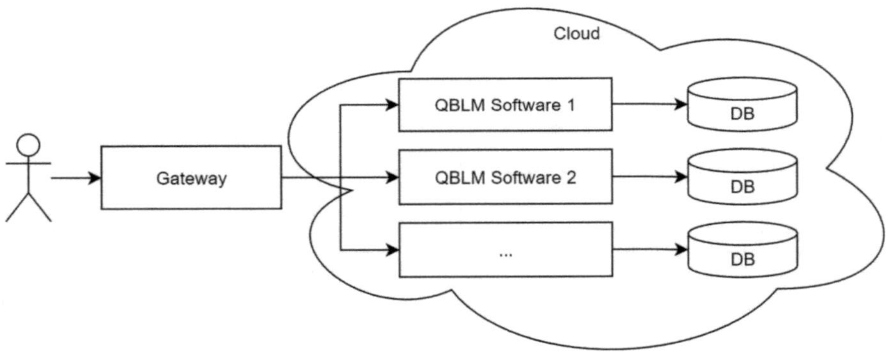

Fig. 5 QBLM BaaS design proposal

Based on BaaS, the *QBLM BaaS Design Proposal* is shown in Fig. 5. QBLM Software provided by third parties is provided to the users via a gateway. While the gateway is part of the QBLM Platform, the QBLM Software implementations are provided as cloud services.

Lastly, the FaaS pattern is utilised in the context of the QBLM Platform. The *QBLM FaaS Design Proposal*, shown in Fig. 6, suggests transforming QBLM Software to compute required functionalities serverless. *QBLM Functions* serve functionalities to perform QBLM without providing them within QBLM Software. The infrastructure is provided by a cloud provider, while the system owner provides the application code. The requests are forwarded via a gateway to serverless computing, where the QBLM Functions are executed.

In summary, suitable architecture patterns are utilised in the context of the QBLM Platform to propose potential conceptual software architecture reference models. A remaining challenge is verifying and selecting a design proposal or a

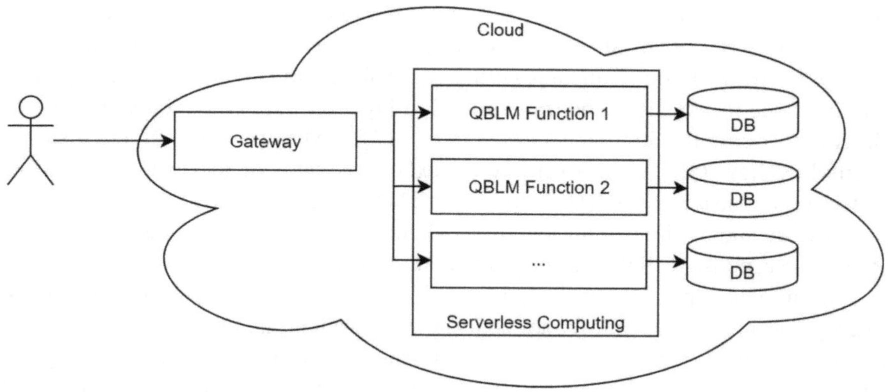

Fig. 6 QBLM FaaS design proposal

combination of proposed designs to create the specific conceptual software architecture reference model. A formal modelling of the conceptual software architecture reference model remains a challenge.

3.3 Conceptual Content and Visual Design for the QBLM Platform

Next, the content and visual design are performed. Therefore, the conceptual design of content exchange, i.e., communication between the QBLM Software, is shown. The concept is based on the observation of the used interfaces in the context of QBLM and potential communication patterns. As a preliminary result, conceptual data flow approaches are sketched. Additionally, the concept for providing QBLM Software on demand is designed. The concept utilises the observed prototypical implementations of previous research and development approaches and other QBLM Software implementations. Furthermore, CC is considered for the hosting and supplying of the QBLM Software.

The protocols of the identified interfaces are already specified or proprietary. However, the communication concept has to target interoperability on an abstracted layer. Instead of ensuring the interoperability of the QBLM Software implementations, the QBLM Platform must provide the ability for interoperation. Therefore, the QBLM Platform ensures that QBLM implementations can communicate between each other directly or via a transformation layer, respectively, middleware. Consequently, *QBLM Platform Communication Pattern Approaches* are required, which define the data flow for data exchange between QBLM Software of the QBLM Platform. The requesting QBLM Software (QBLM Software 1) could already implement the interface of the offering QBLM Software (QBLM Software 2). In that case, no data transformation is required, and direct interoperation is possible. In case QBLM Software 1 does not implement the interface or communication pattern of QBLM Software 2, indirect interoperation is necessary. Therefore, QBLM Software 1 communicates with the transformation layer using the approach and interface it demands. The transformation layer forwards the request to QBLM Software 2 using the approach and interface of QBLM Software 2. Figure 7 shows exemplary how QBLM Software could exchange data. In the example, QBLM Software 1 consumes QBLM Software 2. The figure visualises the data flow for both direct and indirect interoperation when QBLM Software 2 uses either the Request-Response or Publish/Subscribe communication pattern.

Summarising the content design for the data flow, a generic approach for the interoperation of QBLM Software is designed. A remaining challenge is the merging of the QBLM Platform Communication Pattern Approaches with the conceptual software architecture reference model. Another remaining challenge is the pending modelling of the remaining QBLM Platform Communication Pattern Approaches including approaches for the communication with Software in Application Habitats of the surrounding Digital QBLM Ecosystem and other Remote QBLM Platforms.

To continue the content design, the provision of QBLM Software must be considered. Therefore, the conceptual design of the QBLM-ESCF using the observed QBLM Software and CC concepts must be done. As a result, the concept of the

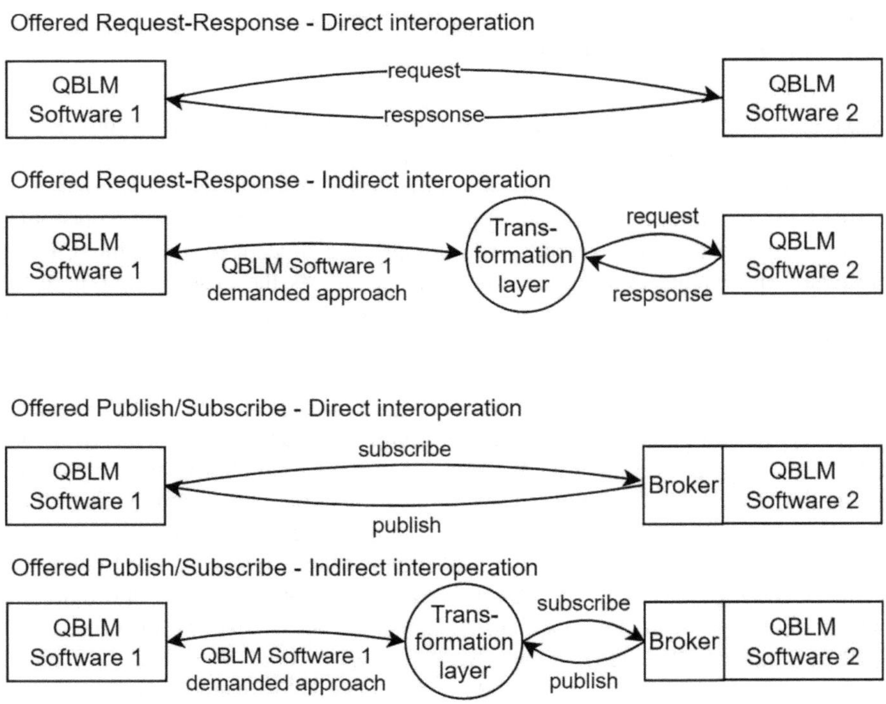

Fig. 7 Informal design of data flows for QBLM platform communication pattern approaches

QBLM-ESCF, including the preliminary list of QBLM Software and a CC-based distribution approach, has to be designed.

To proceed with content design, it is essential to address the provisioning of QBLM Software. Therefore, a conceptual design of the QBLM-ESCF is necessary. The conceptual design of the QBLM-ESCF utilises the observed QBLM Software and CC concepts. Consequently, the QBLM-ESCF concept has to include a preliminary list of QBLM Software, and a distribution approach based on CC.

Based on the observation of available QBLM Software, Table 1 shows the list of the QBLM Software, categorising them as QBLM Base Software or QBLM Extension Software. The QBLM Software is also assigned to a functional domain it serves. Currently, no alternatives of QBLM Software serving the same functional domain are investigated. However, QBLM Software is defined as QBLM Base Software if at least one implementation serving the functional domain is required to support QBLM. For example, at least one LMS is required in the QBLM Platform to serve QBLM.

Therefore, the QBLM-ESCF has to contain the listed and additional QBLM Software. It has to hold the information about the setup and provisioning of the QBLM Software. In consequence, the QBLM-ESCF provides a catalogue of QBLM Software, which can be used to set up or adapt the QBLM Platform. The catalogue can be utilised via the *QBLM Platform Assistant*. Through the QBLM Platform Assistant, the QBLM Software demanded out of the QBLM-ESCF, i.e., the *QBLM Platform Configuration* can be chosen. Subsequently, the QBLM Platform Configuration can be applied to the QBLM Platform. The QBLM Platform uses CC abilities, respectively cloud-native features, to implement the QBLM Platform Configuration and provide QBLM Software, including their resources. The specific implementation of the QBLM Software within the QBLM Platform is described via the setup information provided by the QBLM-ESCF. Figure 8 visualises the described flow as the initial design of the *QBLM-ESCF-based QBLM Software Providing Approach*. It describes the process of QBLM Software deployment into the QBLM Platform from the QBLM-ESCF, based on QBLM Platform Configuration managed in the QBLM Platform Assistant.

The QBLM Platform Assistant includes a user interface designed for managing the QBLM Platform Configuration. An initial visual design of the QBLM Platform Assistant could be as follows: On the left side, the user can configure the

Table 1 Preliminary QBLM software categorisation into the QBLM-ESCF

QBLM software	QBLM software category	Functional domain
CAT	QBLM Extension Software	Management and authoring of courses
CM	QBLM Base Software	Manage CQ
CPM	QBLM Base Software	Manage competence profiles
Moodle	QBLM Base Software	LMS
DSTM	QBLM Extension Software	Manage DSTs
KM-EP	QBLM Base Software	Management of learners
KM-EP	QBLM Base Software	Authorisation

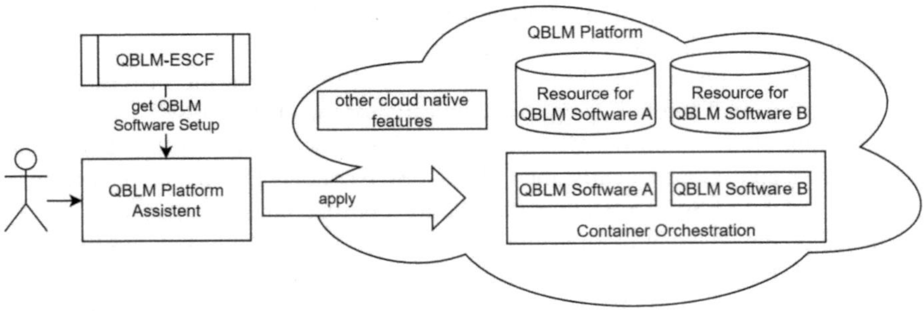

Fig. 8 QBLM-ESCF-based QBLM software providing approach

constellation of QBLM Base Software. Each row displays all QBLM Base Software available in the QBLM-ESCF for a specific functional domain. The user has to select at least one QBLM Base Software of each functional domain. On the right side, users can search for and add QBLM Extension Software, which is optional. Users have the flexibility to add none or multiple QBLM Extension Software.

In summary of the content and visual design of QBLM Software deployment, the QBLM-ESCF concept and its utilisation through the QBLM Platform Assistant are described. As a remaining challenge, further investigation on additional QBLM Software for the QBLM-ESCF is pending. Additionally, a modelling of the QBLM-ESCF data models and interfaces is a remaining challenge. An approach to providing QBLM Software, including setup information, remains a challenge, too. Furthermore, the QBLM Platform Assistant, including the interfaces to manipulate the QBLM Platform, is not yet designed.

Concluding, the initial Design settled a preliminary theory building. It included the definition of a use context, the identification and design of potential conceptual software architecture reference models, the design of QBLM Platform Communication Pattern Approaches, the conceptual design of the QBLM-ESCF, and the design of the QBLM Platform Assistant. However, multiple remaining challenges are identified. First, the detailed design of use cases is pending. Next, the definition of a specific conceptual software architecture reference model considering the potential conceptual software architecture reference models, the QBLM Platform Communication Pattern Approaches, and the QBLM-ECSF, remains a challenge. Furthermore, additional Data Flow of QBLM Platform Communication Pattern Approaches are to be modelled. Lastly, the design of the QBLM-ESCF, in combination with the QBLM Platform Assistant managing the QBLM Platform, has to be detailed.

4 Conclusion and Outlook

This section concludes the paper by summarising the initial efforts towards a software platform supporting QBL, i.e. the QBLM Platform. The motivation and approach behind developing a QBLM Platform are presented. Following the methodology of Nunamaker et al. (1990), preliminarily observation and theory-building phases are executed. The system development and experimentation have not yet started.

During the Introduction, Motivation, and Approach, it was possible to elucidate the demand to utilise QBL in any Digital Ecosystem. Previous research and development approaches introduced various applications in the context of QBL (QBLM Software) and the QBLM to facilitate QBL. The remaining challenges are identified, such as missing scalability and tight coupling. Therefore, the QBLM Platform and the QBLM-ESCF are proposed. The QBLM Platform offers the pending functionalities and flexibility. The QBLM-ESCF provides a catalogue of QBLM Software, including related setup information.

Through the State of the Art in Science and Technologies, the foundation for designing the QBLM Platform is established. Firstly, the stakeholders of a QBLM Platform within the various Digital Ecosystems are elaborated. Secondly, architectural styles and architectural patterns are investigated. Communication patterns for internal and external communication of QBLM Software are discussed. The available QBLM Software is identified, and possibilities for operation using CC are observed.

The third section, 'Towards Initial Design', addresses the initial conceptual design of the QBLM Platform utilising the UCSD. First, the user stereotypes and their functional requirements are defined based on the previously identified stakeholders. These user stereotypes are placed into the use context of the QBLM Platform. The functional requirements are used to define constraints for the conceptual software architecture reference model, allowing for the elimination of multiple inappropriate architectural patterns. Utilising the remaining potential architectural patterns, design proposals are suggested. Next, communication pattern approaches for the QBLM Platform are conceptually designed. The approach includes direct and indirect interoperation, which is facilitated by a transformation layer. Lastly, the QBLM-ESCF is designed, which includes a preliminary categorisation of QBLM Software and a concept for a QBLM Software providing approach. Through the QBLM Platform Assistant, the QBLM-ESCF can be used to adjust the QBLM Platform Configuration. Consequently, the QBLM Platform Configuration is applied on the QBLM Platform to deploy the demanded QBLM Software.

As this paper does not address the system development and experimentation, they remain challenges. However, some challenges remain pending within the observation and theory-building phases. The preliminary observation of stakeholders is closed, but further observation is pending. The detailed verification of user stereotypes, including a completeness check, has not yet been performed. Observing QDM protocols and data structures in the context of the QBLM Platform remains a challenge. Consequently, identifying the interfaces that need to be natively supported by the QBLM Platform has not yet been completed. The observation of methods for API management, including offering APIs to third parties, is pending.

Furthermore, an investigation into commonly available QBLM Software, such as other LMS, has not been considered. CC technologies for deploying QBLM Software out of the QBLM-ESCF have not been observed. A formal user modelling and detailed use case definition is a remaining challenge. A design and modelling of a specific conceptual software architecture based on an evaluation of Design Proposals is not performed. A formal design of the communication approaches, and the transformation layer has to be considered. The modelling of the QBLM-ESCF, including data structures and approaches for QBLM Software management, is pending. Another remaining challenge is conceptualising the QBLM Platform Assistant including the definition of use cases, the formal modelling, and further visual designs. Lastly, a modelling of the QBLM Platform Configuration, including its utilisation in the QBLM Platform has not been considered.

In conclusion, this paper has laid the foundation for the conceptual design of the QBLM Platform. While considerable progress has been made, further work is required to realise the QBLM Platform. Future research should address the mentioned remaining challenges to advance towards the implementation of the QBLM Platform.

Appendix

Abbreviation 1	Full form 1	Abbreviation 2	Full form 2
API	Application Programming Interface	API layer	Application Programming Interface Layer
BaaS	Backend as a Service	BMWi	Bundesministerium für Wirtschaft und Energie
CAT	Course Authoring Tool	CBL	Competence-Based Learning
CC	Cloud Computing	CF	Competence Framework
CM	Competence Manager	CP	Competence Profile
CPM	Competence Profile Manager	CQ	Competence/Qualifications
DST	Didactical Structural Template	DSTM	Didactical Structural Template Manager
EDA	Event-Driven Architecture	ESB	Enterprise Service Bus
FaaS	Function as a Service	HEI	Higher Educational Institutes
IaaS	Infrastructure as a Service	KM-EP	Knowledge Management Ecosystem Portal
LMS	Learning Management System	LO	Learning Object
LRS	Learning Record Store	PaaS	Platform as a Service
LTI	Learning Tools Interoperability	QBLM	Qualifications-Based Learning Model

Abbreviation 1	Full form 1	Abbreviation 2	Full form 2
QBL	Qualifications-Based Learning	QDM	QBLM Domain Model
QBLM-ESCF	QBLM Ecosystem's Service Component Framework	RQ	Research Question
QRLE	Qualifications Relevant Learning Element	SOA	Service-Oriented Architecture
SaaS	Software as a Service	xAPI	experience Application Programming Interface
UCSD	User-Centred System Design		

References

1EdTech Consortium, Inc. (2003, January 20). *1EdTech learning design information model*. Retrieved July 17, 2024, from https://www.imsglobal.org/learningdesign/ldv1p0/imsld_infov1p0.html

Briscoe, G. (2009). *Digital ecosystems*. Imperial College.

Briscoe, G., Sadedin, S., & Wilde, P. D. (2011, August 10). Digital ecosystems: Ecosystem-oriented architectures. *Natural Computing, 10*(3). https://doi.org/10.1007/s11047-011-9254-0

Bundesministerium für Wirtschaft und Energie (BMWi). (2019). *Für eine zukunftsfähige Lernkultur im Unternehmen*. BMWi.

Enyinna, C. (2023, September 12). *Communication design patterns for backend development*. Retrieved June 30, 2024, from https://www.freecodecamp.org/news/communication-design-patterns-for-backend-development/

European Ministers of Education. (1999, June 19). *The bologna declaration of 19 June 1999*. Retrieved January 22, 2023, from http://www.ehea.info/Upload/document/ministerial_declarations/1999_Bologna_Declaration_English_553028.pdf

Ford, N., Parsons, R., & Kua, P. (2017). *Building evolutionary architecture—Support constant change*. O'Reilly.

Freeman, R. E. (2010). *Strategic management: A stakeholder approach*. Cambridge University Press.

GitLab B.V. (n.d.). *What is Cloud native?* Retrieved July 12, 2024, from https://about.gitlab.com/topics/cloud-native/

Kaya-Kasikci, S., Zayim-Kurtay, M., & Kondakci, Y. (2023). The role of leadership in developing a climate of technology integration in public schools. *Teaching and Teacher Education, 132*, 104234.

Khan, M., Naz, T., & Medani, M. A. (2019). A multi-layered security model for learning management system. *International Journal of Advanced Computer Science and Applications, 10*(12). https://doi.org/10.14569/IJACSA.2019.0101229

Koper, R., Schoonenboom, J., Manderveld, J., Kluijfhout, E., Arjona, M., Griffiths, D., Angehrn, A., & Van Rosmalen, P. (2008). Updated use case models and underlying vision documents and pedagogical model definitions. *TENCompetence*. Retrieved from https://www.narcis.nl/publication/RecordID/oai%3Adare.uva.nl%3Apublications%2Feeac99e5-58b2-4af9-966b-503fba26232e

Mandalaparty, S. P. (2014). *A domain-protocol mapping based middleware for distributed application development*. Colorado State University.

Mell, P., & Grance, T. (2011). *The NIST definition of cloud computing*. NIST.

Norman, D. A., & Draper, S. W. (1986). *User centered system design—New perspectives on human-computer interaction*. Lawrence Erlbaum Associates.

Nunamaker, J. F., Chen, M., & Purdin, T. D. (1990). Systems development in information systems research. *Journal of Management Information Systems, 7*(3), 89–106. https://doi.org/10.1080/07421222.1990.11517898

O'Neill, E. (2019, July 25). *Formal and informal learning*. Retrieved June 25, 2022, from https://www.learnupon.com/blog/formal-and-informal-learning/

Rustici Software LLC. (n.d.). *xAPI (experience API) overview*. Retrieved June 29, 2024, from https://xapi.com/overview/

Srbecky, R., Winterhagen, M., Wetzel, S.-A., Ochsendorf, I., Hedderoth, A., Then, M., et al. (2022). Dynamic and adaptive playout of competency-based learning games based on data in learners' competency profile considering didactical structural templates. In *Gamification—Analysis, Design and Development*. IntechOpen.

Then, M. (2019). *Supporting Qualifications-Based Learning (QBL) in a higher education institution's IT-infrastructure*. FernUniversität in Hagen.

Then, M., Wallenborn, B., Fuchs, M., & Hemmje, M. (2016). Towards a domain model for integrating competence frameworks into learning platforms. *Formamente—International Research Journal on Digital Future, 3-4, p.15-49.*

Then, M., Hoang, M. D., & Hemmje, M. (2019). *A Moodle-based software solution for Qualifications-Based Learning (QBL)*. FernUniversität in Hagen.

Vogwell, D. (2003). *Stakeholder management*. Project Management Institute.

Vu, B. (2019). *A taxonomy management system supporting crowd-based taxonomy generation, evolution, and management*. FernUniversität in Hagen.

Wallenborn, B. (2018). *Entwicklung einer innovativen Autorenumgebung*. FernUniversität in Hagen.

Wangen, E. N. (2021, January 26). *What is a software platform & how is it different from a product?* Retrieved October 30, 2023, from https://blog.hubspot.com/marketing/software-platform

Winterhagen, M., Hoang, M. D., Wallenborn, B., Heutelbeck, D., & Hemmje, M. (2021). Supporting qualification based didactical structural templates for multiple learning platforms. In *Advances in software engineering, education, and e-learning*. Springer.

Simon Wetzel started his career as a software and framework developer at Roche Diabetes Care after completing a bachelor's degree in information technology at the Cooperative State University in 2015. Simultaneously, he started his master's degree at the FernUniversität in Hagen. In 2018, he transitioned to Mercedes-Benz Mobility, initially serving as a system developer in the insurance sector before transitioning to the enterprise architecture team in 2023. Meanwhile, Simon finished his master's degree and, in 2022, became an external PhD candidate at FernUniversität in Hagen.

Matthias Hemmje is a full professor at FernUniversität in Hagen. His research focuses on virtual information environments, digital libraries, information retrieval, and visualisation. He has led numerous national and European R&D projects and advises on IT strategy, roadmapping, and emerging technologies. He also works in knowledge technologies, e-learning, and mobile services. Prof. Hemmje is a board member of NESTOR (Germany's Network of Excellence for Digital Preservation) and part of the CCSDS MOIMS-DAI working group on space data systems.

MIX
Papier aus verantwortungsvollen Quellen
Paper from responsible sources
FSC® C105338

If you have any concerns about our products,
you can contact us on
ProductSafety@springernature.com

In case Publisher is established outside the EU,
the EU authorized representative is:
Springer Nature Customer Service Center GmbH
Europaplatz 3, 69115 Heidelberg, Germany

Printed by Libri Plureos GmbH
in Hamburg, Germany